REALIZING the AMERICA of OUR HEARTS

Also by Eleazar S. Fernandez
from Chalice Press:

*Reimagining the Human: Theological Anthropology
in Response to Systemic Evil*

REALIZING THE AMERICA OF OUR HEARTS

Theological Voices of Asian Americans

Fumitaka Matsuoka and
Eleazar S. Fernandez, eds.

CHALICE
PRESS
ST. LOUIS, MISSOURI

Biblical quotations, unless otherwise noted, are from the *New Revised Standard Version Bible,* copyright 1989, Division of Christian Education of the National Council of the Churches of Christ in the United States of America. Used by permission. All rights reserved.

Cover and interior design: Elizabeth Wright

This book is printed on acid-free, recycled paper.

Visit Chalice Press on the World Wide Web at
www.chalicepress.com

10 9 8 7 6 5 4 3 2 1   03 04 05 06 07 08

Library of Congress Cataloging–in–Publication Data

Realizing the America of our hearts : theological voices of Asian Americans / Fumitaka Matsuoka and Eleazar S. Fernandez, editors.– 1st ed.
  p. cm.
Includes bibliographical references and index.
  ISBN 0-8272-3251-9 (alk. paper)
  1. Asian Americans–Religious life. 2. Theology, Doctrinal. I. Matsuoka, Fumitaka. II. Fernandez, Eleazar S. III. Title.
  BR563.A82R43 2003
  230'.089'95073–dc21
                                        2003012839

Printed in the United States of America

Contents

PART 3
Visions of Hope
Realizing the America of Our Hearts

PART 4
Asian Americans and Global Connections
Challenges and Prospects

List of Contributors

Eleazar S. Fernandez is associate professor of constructive theology at United Theological Seminary of the Twin Cities, New Brighton, Minnesota.

Young Lee Hertig is a lecturer in global studies and sociology at Azusa Pacific University.

Deborah Lee is program director for the PANA Institute, Berkeley, California.

Sang Hyun Lee is K. C. Han Professor of Systematic Theology at Princeton Theological Seminary, Princeton, New Jersey.

Fumitaka Matsuoka is professor of theology at Pacific School of Religion, Berkeley, California, and Director of the PANA Institute.

Greer Anne Wenh-In Ng is professor emerita of Christian education at Emmanuel College, Toronto School of Theology, Toronto, Ontario, Canada.

Andrew Sung Park is professor of theology at United Theological Seminary, Dayton, Ohio.

Peter C. Phan is the Warren-Blanding Professor of Religion and Culture at the Catholic University of America, Washington, D.C.

Lester Edwin J. Ruiz is professor of theology and culture at New York Theological Seminary, New York, New York.

Roy I. Sano is professor of United Methodist studies at Pacific School of Religion, Berkeley, California.

M. Thomas Thangaraj is D. W. and Ruth Brooks Associate Professor of World Christianity at Candler School of Theology, Emory University, Atlanta, Georgia.

Sharon G. Thornton is associate professor of pastoral theology and pastoral care at Andover Newton Theological Seminary, Newton Centre, Massachusetts.

Timothy Tseng is associate professor of American religious history at American Baptist Seminary of the West, Berkeley, California.

Randi Jones Walker is associate professor of church history at Pacific School of Religion, Berkeley, California.

Introduction

FUMITAKA MATSUOKA

Realizing the America of Our Hearts is a poignant matter for North Americans of Asian descent. Ever since the first arrival of the early settlers from Asia to the North American continent in the late 1800s, countless numbers of people have dreamed of an America that made good on the promise of "life, liberty, and the pursuit of happiness." But such an America has been elusive for many Asian North Americans. Those who have been fortunate enough to catch a glimpse of their dreams have often paid an enormous price, sometimes sacrificing their own souls. This partial realization of dreams is fleeting and does not ensure any stability.

This anthology is written from a variety of ethnic, national, and cultural perspectives of those who claim themselves to be Americans of Asian ancestry who reside in Canada and the United States. Their depictions of "America" are necessarily theological in nature, if "theology" is understood as a depth reading of reality through a particular lens that has been nurtured and reshaped within the communities of faith called Asian North American churches. Some of these voices are of the "post '65" arrivals, when the discrimination against Asians was removed from the U.S. immigration policies. Others are of those who were born and had their lives nurtured on this continent only to have their sense of belonging betrayed by the very governments that were entrusted to protect them and their well-being. Their stories are often filled with tears and silent pain. A few voices in this anthology are of those who belong to the "dominant" cultural and racial/ethnic groups, but who, nevertheless, have had their sense of identity profoundly affected by their association with Americans of Asian origin. No matter which group these voices belong to, the "Americas" that they describe are not the familiar "America" of mainstream literature. Their

1

"Americas" are ignored "Americas," depictions that have seldom surfaced in print, let alone in theological literature.

Ever since Carlos Bulosan shouted in an unheated barrio in the ghetto of Los Angeles, "I will use the power of words to tell Americans what I know about America," faint but persistent voices have spoken up about their experiences of "the America of [their] hearts." In this volume, this tradition of the power of words continues through the voices of Asian North American theological educators. Their voices are varied: Some speak of the hermeneutical distinctness of Asian North American theology. Sang Hyun Lee, for one, speaks of the idea of marginality as coerced liminality providing a lens through which one can analyze the Asian American experience. Lee shows how this way of reading the Asian American experience can be a useful key to a reappropriation of the biblical message in the Asian American context. Lee describes some of the ways in which marginality has been used in Asian American theology and argues that the notion of "coerced liminality" is a more adequate conceptualization than other ideas of marginality. It is so because it can refer to the in-between or potentially creative liminal condition of marginality as well as to the dehumanizing results of racism in that particular marginalization.

Lee describes the twin experiences of Asian Americans: in-between-ness, or liminality, on the one hand, and racism on the other. He talks about the debilitating consequences of this predicament as well as the creative potential of liminality that is suppressed and frustrated in the lives of Asian Americans. He argues that one of the advantages of this interpretive key is that, correctly used, it has the potential of speaking not only to Asian Americans but also, at least to some limited extent, to all groups. He proposes a correlation between the marginality of Asian American lives and biblical messages. Lee argues that the biblical message has the priority over experience. It helps enlarge and broaden the interpretive key of marginality; but at the same time, the interpretive key contributes to the reappropriation of the biblical message.

Fumitaka Matsuoka's chapter focuses on the impact of historical injuries, particularly of the internment experience, suffered by Japanese Americans. This is an exploration of Christian faith embodied in Japanese American faith communities as these communities struggle with affirming human dignity amidst their communal memories of historical injuries, and as they strive toward the creation of a just and compassionate society. The central issue is how Japanese Americans participate in the society that has denied their membership and human dignity and yet still does necessarily exist in an increasingly close interwoven web of relationships across racial and ethnic lines.

Matsuoka employs the experiences of Japanese Americans, their internment experiences in particular, as a hermeneutical lens in exploring their quest for identity and their understanding of the society in which they live. A disturbing issue he presents to the society is that the experiences of historical injuries suffered by Japanese Americans point to their willingness to go beyond their inclination to dwell in the pain of the past and to reach out for strengthening a web of all people in the U.S. society. However, this society has not been able to value their generosity. Matsuoka contends that this is the challenge that awaits America in truly becoming the America of all our hearts.

Andrew Park treats the historical and cultural hermeneutical origin of Korean American experiences. Due to the long suffering of their ancestors, Korean Americans have been sensitive to human suffering. Wounded by a variety of oppression in this country, they have developed the deep collective pain of victims, which can be called *han* in Korean and Vietnamese languages. Although Asian Americans, particularly Korean Americans, might discover common denominators in their backgrounds in Asian religions and cultures, the experience of *han* in this country can offer new ground of shared identity and spiritual underpinning to suffering Asian Americans. While Western minds are attentive to the burdens of sin and guilt, Asian American hearts are keen to *han* and its shame. Sin causes *han*, and *han* can create sin or *han*. The vicious cycle of sin and *han* produces evil. Set against this backdrop, Park follows the plight of Asian Americans who journey in the hope of finding spiritual and theological underpinning for their lives.

Historian Timothy Tseng attempts to claim the "historical subject" of Asian Americans beyond the perception of Orientalism and assimilation. American historiography and sociology (religious or otherwise) have filtered the Asian Pacific American experience through Orientalist and/or assimilationist lenses. Consequently, Asians in North America have been viewed as either "forever foreigners" or "honorary whites" (to cite the title of a recent study by Mia Tuan). This hermeneutical lens has legitimized social and religious denominational policies that impact Asian Americans negatively. It also reproduces persistent stereotypical images that objectify Asian Americans. Tseng suggests a new hermeneutical lens that begins with Asian Americans as subjects of their own history. Through this lens, historical, sociological, and theological studies based in Asian American religious communities can utilize a theoretical framework that frees Asian Americans from the Orientalist/assimilationist paradigms. Tseng claims that the history of downtrodden and oppressed Asian American faith communities is vital for an accurate historiographic representation of Asian Americans, not simply to critique the elitist paradigms but also to discover when, where, and how the U.S. society failed to pay attention to the oppressed. Tseng argues that church history at its best must become concerned and interested in the oppressed.

There are Asian American theologians who treat cultural distinctness as the primary context of their theological readings of America. Eleazar

Fernandez talks about the distinct Filipino cultural and sociological context in America. Fernandez proposes an interpretive framework as well as a rereading of the Filipino American journey from the "unfinished country" (Philippines) to the land of "unfinished dreams." Multiple sources, analytical tools, and literary genre are employed to take account of the Filipino American experience. Fernandez identifies and develops theologically several motifs that best capture the Filipino American, such as multiple identities, plight, dreams, and vision–all different angles of reading the sociobiology of Filipino Americans in a globalized context.

Chinese Canadian Wenh-In Ng also talks about the perspective of her multifaceted identity shaped by a complexity of contexts, sharing in particular struggles and insights stemming from such factors as the minority status of her Canadian location, of her field within the theological disciplines (pastoral theology and religious education), of being a woman, and of her ethno-cultural heritage (Chinese/Asian) in a still predominantly white Anglo-European environment in church, academy, and society.

Ng maintains that the biblical images of a journey involve juxtapositions of Abraham/Sarah vs. Hagar-Ishmael, Orpah vs. Ruth, Jeremiah's exhortation to "build houses and live in them" vs. Psalm 137. The theology that emerges out of these contexts is a "bamboo theology" that is "on the way," and that moves toward a theology of solidarity.

Writing in a feminist-liberative mode, Ng not only provides cases and data but identifies issues and then raises concerns. She invites readers to consider possibilities for pastoral/ministerial action for the nurturing of Asian North Americans in ways that honor their complex identities, locations, and contexts–spiritually/liturgically as well as societally.

Retired United Methodist Bishop Roy Sano depicts the contextualizing of faith and practice. He argues that depending on the agenda, the spiral of contextualizing can expand or contract its scope as it follows a variety of trajectories. Eventually, however, the spiral seeks to clarify who God is and what God is saying and doing in a particular setting so that we may join this God in the larger mission.

The spiral shapes models of "action-reflection" associated with Latin American and other liberation theologians. Sano begins by naming the experiences, actions, and praxis of a people at a given period of time in a particular geographic setting. This provides raw material for critical reflection and the constructive task of contextualizing. Resources from various sciences, or fields of study and knowledge (e.g., political economy, cultural anthropology, and historiography in various fields, including history of religions), uncover the deeper or "thick" dimensions of the raw material. In turn, the witnesses of biblical and theological forebears offer resources to recast the religious dimensions of the raw material and thus construct a faith and calling, a theology and ethics, and a spirituality and esthetics for faithful participation in the mission of the triune God.

The escalating presence of Asian and Pacific peoples in the U.S. and Canada has resulted in a wider variety of peoples, and in the same way, the variety among their pilgrimages from their homelands and their sojourns to North America has increased. Their contextualizing will, therefore, produce different results. Family resemblances in their stories, however, invite collaborative efforts. Furthermore, while various groups live and work in their distinct contexts, the biblical stories and diverse strands in the theological traditions offer these groups images to contextualize or to reformulate their faith and calling within the wider-ranging divine mission. Sano maintains that seeing one another at distinct points within the broader mission of the triune God can nurture mutual appreciation and support across our differences and thus lay foundations for unity among diverse groups.

Then there are contributors in this volume who talk about the visions of what "America" can be, not only for those who claim themselves as Asians in North America but also for the entire society with people from other ethnic, cultural, and racial heritages. Young Lee Hertig views the social, cultural, and psychological struggles surrounding the Los Angeles riots of April 1992 through a theological lens. After the riots, Korean immigrant Christians were confronted with the challenge of reinterpreting their identity and who they set out to become.

Hertig cautions that a fixated self-understanding only aggravates the problems, exhausting rather than revitalizing the body of Christ. Only when the Korean immigrant church balances its inward and outward journey can a healthier connection with the transforming power of the gospel become represented. For this endeavor, an ongoing theological reflection of the riots is needed in order to fill the void in the public arenas as the body of Christ. She uses the theological and epistemological lens of *yinism.* It reconciles the pitfall of the dualistic and dichotomous paradigm that divides rather than connects the diverse parts. *Yinism* bridges both *usness* and *otherness* to become whole.

Deborah Lee's depiction of a drama that unfolded in Little Saigon in southern California displays the level of distrust, to the brink of violence, that exists within one mono-ethnic community sharing linguistic, cultural, and historic ties. She points to the fact that the challenge of reconciliation in our society is to address not only the painful wounds of racism embedded in our domestic contest but also the pains and scars that people bring with them. The task of reconciliation and healing is not only between whites and groups of color but also between and within groups of color. The complex racial context in which we live challenges us with the task of theologically addressing the "messy" state in which we find ourselves. What implication does this have for civil rights and racial justice movements today? What implications does this have for faith communities, ethnic congregations and caucuses, and the development of pertinent theologies that respond to this? She proposes the renewed significance of kinship that binds people "if not by blood, then by some other value or experience...[allowing people to] share in rituals and practices of giving, sharing, eating, praying and singing." Family and kinship, particularly in a multiracial and ethnic configuration, provide a context and opportunity to confront racism and move past the culture of distrust, the climate of alienation—toward a new dynamic human interaction, a new vision of human relatedness. Through these practices and theological stances, faith offers hope and healing toward the wounds of race relations in our society.

Vietnamese American Peter Phan's chapter is titled "The Dragon and the Eagle: Toward A Vietnamese American Theology." Phan addresses the theme of what Vietnamese Christians can contribute to the development of a truly religious plural America. The focus is on Vietnamese culture and religious traditions in dialogue with American Christianity and society. The dragon is the sacred animal whose descendants Vietnamese are said to be. The eagle is the sacred totem of the United States. Phan's chapter examines the possibility of constructing a theology of "home" for Vietnamese immigrants who live in the U.S. The chapter discusses the cultural and religious conflicts that Vietnamese Americans have experienced in the U.S. and explores the theological categories with which these conflicts may be resolved so that Vietnamese people may find a new "home/habitat" in the New World.

Randi Walker's own ancestors were Anglo European immigrants to North America. Her people, who experienced both welcome and rejection as newcomers in this land, have learned little about hospitality, Walker says. She is also aware of the tensions in Anglo American Protestant churches about the influx of Protestant Christians from Asia (particularly from Korea and the Philippines). A vision of what it means to be an American Protestant is circumscribed by language, a traditional role in society, shared theological themes from the Reformation and the American Revolution, as well as by the traditional animosities toward each other. Both vision and reality of what it means to be American become changed and contested in unpredictable ways as both Asian and Anglo American Protestants settle in with each other in what is relatively new terrain for both.

As she reflects on what it means to be American in this setting, and as she develops a theological framework for understanding the meeting places of Anglo American and Asian American Christians, her own vision of America changes. Walker traces the history of interaction and influence between Korean American and Anglo American Protestants on the West Coast. On the Pacific Coast of North America, Anglo American and Asian American Christians over the next few generations have the opportunity to help forge a new America born, not from the West, but from the heart.

"America of the Broken Heart" is Sharon Thornton's reflection on what it means to be an Anglo American whose life has been profoundly touched by her experience of living among an Asian American community. As an Anglo American Protestant Christian woman living in the culturally diverse and basically secularized social environment of the North American West Coast, specifically in the San Francisco Bay area, with its history as a cultural meeting place, Thornton enters this conversation with her Asian American counterparts holding a sense of anticipation, but also a sense of trouble and anxiety.

Her poignant conclusion is that "'My Country, 'Tis of Thee' is...a hymn of the brokenhearted. To sing 'My Country, 'Tis of Thee' means to cry, so we might learn to laugh together, a laughter filled with longing, compassion, and 'getting to know you.'" Thornton then reflects that "getting to know you" is more than rational knowing, "for it has to do with compassion, endurance, practicing forgiveness, and relinquishing worn-out ways of getting on with life." It is a hymn that embraces a worthy vision and "enfolds" completely all of America, even in her brokenness. For Thornton, the song expresses a hope that this society, broken and yet beloved, might one day know its true identity and become the home for all her people.

Finally, a few voices expand their context to a global scene. Their voices are prophetic voices that see "America" from a wider ecological perspective. Lester Edwin Ruiz is interested in exploring the connections between "The Global, the Local, and the Political" as they are articulated in the context of religious and cultural movements. The way we phrase this matter poses the problem in a much broader framework. In some respect, the phrase "global civil society" has come to be used as a plausible way of describing, labeling, and/or explaining a broad range of contemporary political practices, not least in relation to social movements, NGOs, human rights, cultural and communications circuits, and so on.

They especially make sense in relation to claims about the emergence of some sort of "global" society, governance, and so on. In other respects, however, the very term "civil society" itself seems to be radically at odds with its deployment in this context, not least because it is a term that historically referred to a counterpoint/resistance to state institutions by social forces within, and subservient to, the territorial jurisdictions of these state institutions. The very possibility of a society in general, and a civil society in particular, was given only by the prior existence of statist authority. Whether framed in the primary traditions of liberal political theory or in relation to the primary force of "democratization" in relation to "state socialism" or "globalization from above," the concept of civil society retains its "essentially domestic" reference.

So, what are we to make of contemporary usages in some kind of "global context"? Ruiz explores the significance of a "Filipino Diaspora" in the U.S., with Filipinos understood not as "immigrants" to the U.S., but rather as "colonials" moving from the periphery to the core country. By focusing on this problematic, Ruiz attempts to identify some of the challenges and prospects for Asian Americans in this globalizing and urbanizing "America."

Thomas Thangaraj, an American of Indian origin, deals with the way in which the people from India who have migrated to this country have dealt with globalization. The group includes both Hindus and Christians. Thangaraj is aware that *globalization* is a heavily loaded word with both positive and negative connotations. He puts forward a descriptive definition that describes the process of globalization, then makes judgments on it. Thangaraj's main arguments are that the process of globalization has enabled Hindus and Christians from India to be in touch with their homeland in a new and fuller way than before. This has led to a few consequences. Christians keep in touch with their home churches and Christian communities back home and engage in missionary activity much more than before. Hindus have maintained their contacts through some of the contemporary Hindu organizations such as Vishwa Hindu Parishad and charitable organizations. There has been considerable involvement by the Non-Resident Indians in both the political and the economic life of India.

Changes are brought about by the processes of globalization in the ways Hindus and Christians from India shape their religious life in this country. Thangaraj explores such questions as, What are the theological metaphors/images that make sense of the experience of Christians from India in the United States? What other images may one create and suggest as ways to help better self-understanding? His findings are that Hindus whose religious tradition is rooted in "geo-piety" and "bio-piety" are compelled to redefine their religion in much more "catholic" terms. There are sources within the Hindu tradition itself for such a reconstruction of Hindu faith, theology, and practice.

This anthology is, in a sense, a collection of small pieces of the emerging mosaic called America. When theology moves into the public arena of discourse out of the womb of the faith community, it challenges both the public itself and theology's own credibility. Realizing the America of Asian North Americans' hearts is such a double-edged task. This project is just as multifaceted as our own racial, ethnic, cultural, gender, and generational makeup. Our task is a quilt of many colors and many patterns. At least this much can be said: In the midst of what seems to be a bewildering array of colors and patterns, there seems to be a yearning on the part of all the contributors of this volume both to value the distinctness of each identity and, at the same time, to "get along" with one another, not just as Asian North Americans, and to create a different and more caring way of relating with one another as a whole society. Such a yearning has to do with faith convictions that begin from, yet go beyond, their own readings of reality into the realm that is more than their own making. The theological perspectives of the contributors to this volume are grounded in the piety of their faith and the passion of their yearnings.

PART 1

Hermeneutical Lenses
in Reading Asian American
Experience

Marginality as Coerced Liminality

Toward an Understanding of the Context of Asian American Theology

SANG HYUN LEE

The aim of this chapter is to propose a working definition of *marginality* as the context of Asian American theology. *Marginality,* I am suggesting, can be used as a hermeneutical principle in understanding the nature of Asian American experience. Such a proposal consists primarily in becoming as precise as possible about *marginality* as a concept per se and as a concept that represents as faithfully as possible at least some important aspects of the actual Asian American experience itself.

The Two Faces of Asian American Experience

Let me first speak autobiographically and experientially about what I am calling the "Asian American experience."[1] My existence in this country as an Asian American always seemed to have two fundamental dimensions. The first is the experience of being in between two worlds, the Korean world and the American, belonging to both in some ways, but not wholly belonging to either. I am placed at the edge of both worlds and thus not at the center of either–a situation that puts me betwixt and between those two worlds. Ronald Takaki, in his landmark history of Asian Americans, *Strangers from a Different Shore,* says that Asians' immigration to the United States placed them within a new dynamic and transitional context, an ambiguous situation "betwixt and between" all fixed points of cultural classification.[2] They reached a kind of geographical and cultural margin where old norms became detached, and they found themselves free to new associations and new enterprises.

The other dimension in the Asian American experience of marginality is that as nonwhite persons we may never be fully accepted by the majority of the dominant group in this country.

However long I remain here, there seems to be the unsurmountable barrier between me and the white America. Belonging to the center does not seem to happen. I have been in this country now more than forty-five years. Yet white people still ask me, "Where are you from?"–a question to which "Princeton, New Jersey" is hardly ever a sufficient answer. Countless day-to-day experiences confirm that I am still a guest or a stranger–at best– in this nation.

It is instructive to note that the development of the marginality concept in sociological literature confirms the two dimensions in marginality that I have just discussed on the basis of experience. So we now turn to the sociological understanding of the Asian American experience as marginality. The classic discussion of marginality by sociologists Robert E. Park and Everett Stonequist in the 1940s already recognized the existence of the two elements I just mentioned. A marginal person, according to Stonequist, "is poised in psychological uncertainty between two (or more) social worlds; reflecting in his soul the discords and harmonies, repulsions and attractions of these worlds, one of which is often 'dominant' over the other." Such a person "emulates and strives to be accepted by a group of which he is not yet, or is only peripherally a member."[3]

The above quotation indicates that Stonequist at least implicitly recognized the two dimensions of the experience of marginality–namely, the "psychological uncertainty between two (or more) social worlds," on the one hand, and the implied role of "the dominant" group in making the minority group's belonging to that group only "peripheral," on the other. But still, one of the criticisms of Stonequist's work by subsequent researchers has been that he did not emphasize sufficiently the factor of exclusion by the dominant group in the marginalization of minority people.

And it is to this factor of exclusion in the marginality experience that the work of H. F. Dickie-Clark, for example, paid particular attention. According to Dickie-Clark, marginality results from a hierarchical relationship of groups in which "a resistance is offered by members of the non-marginal and dominant group, to his [the marginal person's] entry into the group and the enjoyment of its privileges." It is due to the dominant group's resistance, and due to a "barrier set up by that group, that an individual in a marginal position who possesses characteristics (those gained through acculturation) which would 'ordinarily' give him [*sic*] a higher status, is not granted that status. What makes a situation marginal, in other words, "lies in inconsistencies between rankings." And such inconsistencies brought about by a higher and more powerful group deny "the enjoyment by an inferior one, of their powers, privileges and opportunities."[4] In this way, Dickie-Clark's discussion helps to bring out clearly the fact that marginality is a condition affected by both status and power issues. What I referred to as the second face of marginality—namely, the effect of the nonacceptance by the dominant group—means both an inconsistency of status and also a deprivation of power. Thus, Asian Americans are not just in an "in-between" or peripheral predicament but are pushed to be there and to remain there by the barriers set up by the dominant center.

The two dimensions in a marginal situation—in-between-ness and nonacceptance by the dominant group—are not discrete but interrelated. The in-between-ness of the Asian Americans' marginality is neither a temporary nor an entirely voluntary situation. Asian Americans are forced to remain in between, pushed to stay there. The spatial image of in-between-ness has to be combined with the power phenomenon of being pushed to remain in between. The Asian American in-between-ness is a forced in-between-ness. Thus, as we relate the two dimensions in the marginal predicament of Asian Americans, we come to the realization that the marginality of Asian Americans is a *coerced in-between-ness,* or an in-between-ness that is made seemingly permanent by the dominant group.

The Creative Powers of the In-Between Liminality

Now that we have noted the two elements in the experience of marginality and their interaction with each other, we must look a bit deeper into the nature of each of those two dimensions. First, we should note the potential creativity of the first element of the first aspect, namely, in-between-ness. Stonequist already in 1937 noted the inherent creativity of a marginal person. He wrote:

> The marginal man is the key-personality in the contacts of cultures. It is in his mind that the cultures come together, conflict, and eventually work out some kind of mutual adjustment and inter-penetration. He is the crucible of cultural fusion…Thus the practical efforts of the marginal person to solve his own problem lead him consciously or unconsciously to change the situation itself. His interest may shift from himself to the objective social conditions and launch him upon the career of a nationalist, conciliator, interpreter, reformer, or teacher.[5]

However, neither Stonequist nor other sociologists, as far as I am aware, have articulated systematically a concept of the potentially creative nature of the in-between aspect of the marginality experience.

I shall outline at this point three salient aspects of the inherent creative powers of the in-between situation, utilizing mainly the insights of anthropologist Victor Turner and other thinkers. Borrowing from Turner, I use the term *liminality* to name what I have been referring to as the in-between dimension of the marginality experience. Empirically, these potentials do not exist or function in their pure form, but are suppressed and distorted by the second aspect of the marginal situation, namely, the racist barriers. We must know what the potentials of in-between liminality are, however, if we are to recognize the creative activities that the marginalized persons are capable of in their struggle against marginalization if they could somehow be freed from what suppresses their liminal, or in-between, creativity.

1. *Openness to the new.* It was Dutch anthropologist Arnold van Gennep who first spoke about the transitional period in a *rite de passage* as marked by "margin" or "limen" (meaning "threshold" in Latin) —that is, a period of liminality.[6] Turner developed further the idea of liminality in his many influential studies of the change processes in traditional societies. The revitalization of a society, according to Turner, involves a dialectic movement between structure and antistructure. And the antistructure is experienced as a transitional condition wherein certain individuals have left behind them the structure (such as social roles, statuses, etc.)—a condition from which those individuals can return to structure revitalized. That revitalizing condition of being freed from social structure, according to Turner, is the liminal situation of being in a "temporary antinomic liberation from behavioral norms and cognitive rules." It is a kind of "social limbo" or the predicament of not being at a fixed place but rather "betwixt and between." And, for Turner, it is in this liminal experience that something new in a society can emerge. Liminality is society's "subjunctive mood, where suppositions, desires, hypotheses, possibilities, and so forth all become legitimate." Liminality is "a realm of pure possibility whence novel configurations of ideas and relations may arise."[7] Liminality, in short, is an openness and potentiality for what is new and different.

Theorists of change process also talk about the discomforting but necessary and creative stage of the transitional in-between period. All changes have an ending, the "in-between place of neutrality," and the reaggregation or new beginning. The neutral period of transition from the old to the new is a frightening period because the guidance and validation by the old situation has been left behind and the future is yet indeterminate. It is a chaotic period. But as William Bridges points out, this "chaos is not a mess, but rather it is the primal state of pure energy to which the person returns for every true new beginning."[8]

Recent literature on hermeneutics also points to the liminal condition of in-between-ness as the necessary component in the human activity of reinterpreting the tradition to make it work in a new way in the present context. Hermeneutics, which originally meant the art and science of interpreting texts, is seen now as an essential activity of human beings who can carve out a new future only by reinterpreting the tradition. According to Terry A. Veling, "Marginal space is the gap in which hermeneutics begins and ends—forms and re-forms." Veling continues to point out that hermeneutical process begins when human beings recognize "a gap"—"a blank space, a space like that of the margin"—between the tradition and our lives. This in-between space between tradition and the present is the place of interpretation. Veling then points out that this liminal "blank space" or "gap" is "as much about what is missing and excluded as it is about the hope or vision for what could be, for new possibility."[9] Hans-Georg Gadamer is one of the seminal thinkers who have mapped out in his influential writings the contours of the hermeneutical process. For Gadamer, it is only from the predicament of our radical belonging to tradition that our projections of future possibilities can be carved out. Gadamer also points to the liminal space in this process: the space between tradition, to which we ineluctably belong, and the interpreter's own historical situation with its questions and possibilities. "This between," according to Gadamer, "is the true locus of hermeneutics."[10] In this in-between space, in David Tracy's words, "a mutually critical appropriation between the horizons of the tradition and the present encounter" is worked out.[11]

Jurgen Habermas adds a crucially important factor to Gadamer's understanding of hermeneutical process. Habermas's work emphasizes the need to avoid an overly confident appeal to tradition. Tradition, for Habermas, can be deeply dominating and oppressive, particularly over the weak and the powerless in the world and, therefore, needs to be approached and interpreted with a critical and even suspicious stance. If Gadamer's approach is a "hermeneutics of retrieval" or a "hermeneutics of trust," Habermas calls for a "hermeneutics of suspicion." Veling comments, "There are times when we need to let our prior constructions fall apart—yet this breakage can be seen not only as the shattering of the past artifacts but also the breaking open of new, imaginative futures." So an interpreter, according to Veling, is located not only in the in-between space between tradition and the present but also in the in-between space between the hermeneutics of trust and the hermeneutics of suspicion. We can work with the tradition even while being critical of it. Veling, therefore, calls for a "hermeneutics of creative reconstruction" that is shaped in the interplay between retrieval and suspicion. In short, "we need to learn how to retrieve traditions appreciatively as well as critique them." And such an appropriation of the past and a moving toward a new future cannot occur unless one embraces the ambiguous space of liminality in the interpretive process. This liminal space is "the interpretative space [which] merges the language of trust with the language of suspicion and leans transformatively into the language of possibility."[12]

If the liminal condition has the inherent power of being "open to the new," and if Asian Americans can be somehow appropriately empowered, could they not use their liminal situation to mold a new identity and selfhood that is neither just Asian nor just Western but "Asian American"? If the liminal openness is necessary for all changes, could not Asian Americans and all other marginalized persons function as the critical change-agents in the American society?

2. *The emergence of communitas.* According to Turner, liminality is not only an openness for society's new possibilities but is also conducive to genuine human community. Turner uses the Latin term *communitas* to distinguish the spontaneous, egalitarian, and direct modality of human relationship from "an area of common living."[13] It is when individuals have set aside social roles and status that they can experience a mode of relationship in which people "confront one another not as role players but as 'human totals,' integral beings who recognizably share the same humanity." Communitas is "a generic bond underlying or transcending all particular cultural definitions and normative ordering of social ties." Communitas is "men [*sic*] in their wholeness wholly attending."[14] Such a genuine human communion, in other words, cannot be programmed or manufactured through structure, but spontaneously emerges precisely when programs and structure are left behind and when individuals are freed to relate to one another completely on an egalitarian ground. So for Turner, "communitas breaks in through the interstices of structure, in liminality; and at the edges of structure, in marginality; and from beneath structure, in inferiority."[15]

Communitas, according to Turner, cannot stand alone, however. "The immediacy of communitas gives way to the mediacy of structure" because structure is necessary "if the material and organizational needs of human beings are to be adequately met."[16] But at the same time, structure without egalitarian values of communitas becomes inhospitable to human beings. Turner assumes here that communitas as a communion of human beings as equals is an essential human need, an "indispensable human social requirement." For a society to function properly, according to Turner, the experience of communitas must infuse structure with antistructural values and, in so doing, transform everyday social structure.[17]

If liminality is conducive to communitas, would not the self-consciously liminal Asian Americans be more able to experience solidarity among themselves as well as with other self-consciously liminal people of other ethnic groups and races? Would it not be requisite for marginalized Asian Americans to become painfully aware of their marginality if they are to experience a genuine community among themselves and with others? What would empower them to face up to their liminal predicament instead of running away from it into oblivion?

3. *The creative space for the prophetic, knowledge, and action.* As we saw earlier, liminality is conducive to an openness to the new and also to communitas. Now we turn to what liminality is capable of vis-à-vis the structure and the center. To be in between and at the edge is to attain a distance from structure and the center. In liminality, there is not only a kind of freedom to be, think, and act in a way not quite "allowed" in the

structure or the center but also a freedom to be critical of structure and the center both negatively and constructively. Liminality is the creative space where one has the freedom to break down the status quo and also the freedom to rebuild it in a different way.

On the "negative" side, liminality is the space where a *critical knowledge* of structure and the center is possible. We turn to Turner again. For him, the openness for the new that is possible in liminality is inherently an openness to the problems of the old—that is, an openness to be critical of the way things are in the structure and at the center. Liminality as a disruption of the norm can give greater insight into the norm than direct perception. Thus, "liminality…raises basic problems for social structural man [*sic*]"[18] because it "invites him [*sic*] to speculation and criticism."[19] In short, from the point of view of social structure, liminality is "essentially ambiguous, unsettled…unsettling," and, consequently, "subversive."[20]

Sociologist Alfred Schultz, in an essay called "The Stranger," is in agreement with Turner. For Schultz, the stranger, who I take to be a liminal person, is capable of an "objective" perspective on the society in which he or she is a stranger. The stranger "is not radically committed to the unique ingredients and peculiar tendencies of the group, and therefore approaches them with the specific attitude of 'objectivity.'" Further, the stranger is "freer, practically and theoretically; he surveys conditions with less prejudices; his criteria for them are more general and more objective ideals; he is not tied down in his action by habit, piety, and precedent."[21]

I must note immediately here that in real life the stranger may not actually be functioning with as much "objectivity" as he thinks. The stranger is not just an alienated person but also an oppressed and dominated one who may have deeply internalized the center's perspective, thus being rendered incapable of any "objectivity." We shall return to this matter at a later point. I should add, however, that Schultz is correct at least to the extent that the stranger inherently has the *potential* to be objective about the status quo—a potential that in real life may be frustrated and made ineffective.

It is important to stress that for Turner liminality not only provides the "negative" capacity to be critical and subversive about what is wrong with the structure and the center but also generates a "positive" and even transformative capacity.[22] To be open to the new and to possess a critical knowledge about what is wrong with structure and the center is also a capacity to generate an alternative structure or way of life. "When I speak of anti-structure," writes Turner, "I really mean something positive, a generative center…from which forms may be 'unpacked.'" The liminal space allows old forms to be "unpacked" and also allows "new models" of structure to be "generated" that "may have sufficient power and plausibility to replace eventually the force-backed political models that control the centers of a society's ongoing life."[23] So the first positive and transformative capacity of liminality lies in its being a free space in which new ideas and models can be generated.

Second, liminality is positive and transformative in that it provides a space where an alternative reality (vis-à-vis the existing society) can actually be enacted—namely, in the form of communitas. The "very existence" of communitas, for Turner, challenges the society to rethink and to reform its way of doing things by "proposing in however extravagant a form new paradigms and models which invert or subvert the old."[24] Here, Turner seems to be arguing for the transformative capacity of powerful "examples."

Third, liminality functions in a positive and transformative way when the new and subversive models that emerged in liminality are somehow brought into and incorporated in the existing structure and center. Bobby C. Alexander interprets Turner as maintaining that "liminality is most subversive when it provides the impetus to carry over its inventive arrangements into everyday life, especially when these involve communitarian relations that challenge social hierarchy." The new model's emerging liminality, as we saw above, may also have "sufficient power and plausibility to replace eventually" the existing structure.[25]

In summary, liminality's creative potential consists in its capacity (1) to bring about an openness to the new and the possible, (2) to generate communitas as the alternative human relatedness, and (3) to challenge and transform the existing society by prophetic and subversive knowledge and criticism, envisioning and enacting new ideas and models.

Before leaving my discussion of the creative potentials of liminality primarily based on Turner's thought, I need to make two comments. First, I need to point out Turner's insufficient attention to the role of ideology in motivating a group of people to utilize the liminal situation for a creative and prophetic activity often vis-à-vis an oppressive structure or center. Alexander studied a Pentecostal congregation's experience of liminality during its ritual possession. Alexander found that this congregation's possession ritual characterized by liminality was not a safety-valve through which their pent-up feelings about their own oppression were apolitically sublimated, but rather it led to concrete political activism. Liminality, in other words, is conducive to a creative ("subversive") political activity. But Alexander also found that working in the congregation's experience of liminality was a strong theologically articulated ideology of opposition to racism.

Without this theological grounding, the congregation would not have been motivated to action.[26] If Alexander is right in this assessment of Turner, we can still accept Turner's concept of the creative potentials of liminality but would also have to acknowledge people's inherent yearning for some motivating factor—a factor that is required for the fulfillment of the liminality's creative potentials.

The second comment has to do with Turner's insufficient attention to the fact that in the cases of minority groups the liminal experience is not just an in-between experience but also an experience of being dominated and dehumanized by, for example, the racist hegemony of a society's controlling center. Liminality's creative potential in such cases would not be able to be played out without some prior freeing of liminality from its suppressed and frustrated condition. So in the case of Asian Americans, their liminal creativity does not exist in abstraction but rather in their particular historical context of being dehumanized by racism. This racist context is what we have referred to as the second aspect of the Asian American experience. The first aspect of the Asian American experience–namely, their liminal in-between experience, with all of its creative potentials–has to be viewed in its interaction with the second aspect. I now turn to a discussion of this second aspect.

The Invisibility of Anti–Asian American Racism

People are dehumanized and oppressed in many different ways, and the determinative factors vary: for example, race, ethnicity, culture, gender, age, education, economic class, job, and so forth. White American people with low income would be dehumanized economically with consequences in some other areas of their life. White American women are dehumanized due to sexism. But neither the low-income white Americans nor white American women would be alienated on the basis of their race.

For Asian Americans, race appears to be the all-important factor for their dehumanization. Before going into this matter, however, I need to note the fact that the general impression in the American public at large and even in some quarters of Asian American communities is that the white racism against Asian Americans is minimal at most and is quickly decreasing.

One reason for this is the myth of Asian Americans as the so-called model minority, disseminated widely by the mass media, according to which the economic and educational successes of many Asian immigrants prove that they are not really discriminated against and that America is still a land of opportunity. The "model minority" idea has many problems. It draws people's attention to those Asian American young people who have gone to Ivy League schools and to the success of some Asian immigrant small business establishments. The concept of "model minority" ignores, however, many realities, such as the heavy involvement of Asian immigrant family members in their small businesses (for the punishing fourteen to sixteen hours a day of labor), which makes their per capita income much lower than that of the white laborers. The concept also ignores many Asian immigrant youth who are having severe psychological problems in coping with their deeply alienated predicament. It has been further pointed out that the concept of "model minority" only serves a racist political function. Sociologists Won Moo Hurh and Kwang Chung Kim list the following practical functions of the "model minority" idea:

> (1) exclusion of Asian Americans from social programs supported by public and private agencies (benefit-denying/fund-saving function); (2) disguise of Asian Americans' underemployment (institutional racism promoting function); (3) justification of the American open social system (system preserving function); (4) displacement of the system's fault to less-achieving minorities (victim blaming function); and (5) anti-Asian sentiment and activities (*resentment* reinforcing function).[27]

In short, the myth of "model minority" only serves, as Wesley Woo has pointed out, to maintain the racist status quo and "masks the real issue—that Asians, like other people of color, are victims of institutional racism."[28]

Another reason it is sometimes hard to talk about racism against Asian Americans is the present-day American situation of the white-black paradigm in the common discourse—a discourse in which the experiences of Asian Americans as a "middle minority," a buffer people between the whites and the blacks, are often trivialized and dismissed. In this situation, you are either black or white. Asian Americans are often perceived, especially by blacks, as a people who want to be white. If Asian Americans cry racism, they are considered hypersensitive. This predicament has led Elaine H. Kim of the University of California, Berkeley, to call for the creation of "a third space"—the space where Asian Americans can be themselves and have their experiences recognized for what they are without being dismissed via the white/black dichotomy.[29] In any case, Asian Americans' assertion of the validity of their own experiences as Asian Americans and also their sense of a solidarity with the blacks and other minority groups are both called for.

The third reason for the invisibility of anti–Asian American racism stems from some Asian Americans themselves. For one thing, the awareness of white racism requires that nonwhite people, at least to some degree, adopt the white American society as their reference group—that is, the group of which they would like to, at least to some degree, join. For Asian Americans who do not consider white America their world (as is the case for many recent arrivals) or who for whatever reason choose to confine their lives mostly to their ethnic enclaves, white people's attitudes are not significant at all. These Asian Americans are still objectively marginal in American society, but they would not have the subjective or personal awareness of their marginality. They may be aware of racism in this country, but it is not much of a personal problem.[30]

There are also Asian Americans who take up an extreme assimilationist perspective and try to ignore the white racism they encounter. Some may even accept racism as a price they are willing to pay for access to the American Dream. For these and possibly other reasons, the anti–Asian American white racism is often dismissed as the result of hypersensitivity or even as something of amusement.

The Not-So-Subtle Consequences of Subtle/Isolated Racism

There are times, however, that white racism against Asian Americans is not so invisible. But even then its significance tends to get undermined or brushed aside. The so-called "isolated discrimination" is distinguished by some scholars from "institutional racism." Isolated discrimination is defined as "harmful action taken intentionally by a member of a dominant group against members of a subordinate racial or ethnic group, without being socially embedded in the larger organizational or community context."[31] In spite of the careful definition of the term by sociologists, "isolation discrimination" can easily be dismissed by the larger public as insignificant "isolated incidents" when it is compared to such large-scale acts of "institutional discrimination" as the Chinese Exclusion Act of 1882, the Asian Exclusion Act of 1924, and the internment of Japanese and Japanese American citizens in 1942. Are the acts of "isolated discrimination," I wonder, really so "isolated" both in their origin and in their consequences?

As I was thinking about these questions, I was handed a copy of an article in the December 9, 1995, issue of *The New York Times* that reported a story about the increasing incidents of anti-Asian racist crimes–the so-called acts of "isolated discrimination." The article was prompted by an incident in which Eddy Wu, twenty-three, who was coming out of a supermarket, was allegedly attacked by a white man, Robert Page of Novato, California, leaving Mr. Wu with stab wounds to his back and shoulder and a punctured lung. The police report contains the attacker's confession that a few hours before the incident he had told himself, "I'm going to kill me a Chinaman."[32]

The same article also mentions another incident in May of 1995 involving John Lee, twenty-eight, an American citizen of Korean ancestry. Mr. Lee stopped at a gas station where a white man approached him and began taunting him by putting his hands together and bowing "Buddha-like," squinting his eyes, and mimicking an Asian accent. When Mr. Lee confronted the attacker by saying that the latter's antics were not amusing, he was punched several times by the original attacker and two other whites. One of them then kicked Mr. Lee to the ground, while the others followed by kicking and punching him in the head as he lay on the pavement.

The same article cites a study done in July of 1995 by the National Asian Pacific–American Legal Consortium, according to which there was a 35 percent increase in anti-Asian crimes nationwide to 452 incidents in 1994, up from 335 incidents in 1993. The article carefully noted that those who commit these crimes "seem to hate Asians without drawing distinctions between newly arrived immigrants and native-born Americans, or between Chinese, Japanese, Cambodians and other Asian nationalities and ethnic groups." When Mr. Page said to himself, "I'm going to kill me a Chinaman," in other words, he meant any Asian American person and not necessarily a Chinese American.[33] No person of Asian ancestry can read reports like this and not have a chilling sensation down his or her spine. These acts of "isolated discrimination" do not seem so "isolated" from the victims' points of view.

In my forty-plus years in this country, I myself have run into numerous incidents where racist insults and gestures were thrown at me, usually by white males. But just about every time it happened I tried to ignore it and just walked away. As I read *The New York Times* article, I found myself shudder somewhere deep inside, thinking about what might have happened to me, or to any other Asian American, if we had confronted the abusers as Mr. Lee did.

In addition to the distinction between "isolated discrimination" and "institutional discrimination," there is also the distinction between "subtle discrimination" and "blatant discrimination." "Subtle discrimination," writes sociologist Joe Feagin, "can be defined as unequal and harmful treatment of members of subordinate racial and ethnic groups that is obvious to the victim but not as overt as traditional, 'door-slamming' varieties of discrimination."[34] It is said that the white racist acts against Asian Americans today are more of the "subtle" variety than the "blatant" variety. Because they are "subtle," it is usually very difficult to talk about them. You just appear as though you are making a big deal about nothing. But are these incidents really nothing?

The maddening thing, for an Asian American person, is that those subtle racist messages and acts occur every day. Here are some samples. I go to a shopping center to pick up a perfume for my wife for Christmas. I patiently stand at the counter and wait for one of the salespersons to become available. Then a white woman walks up to the counter. The salesperson, who knew very well how long I had been standing there, ignores me and waits on the white lady first.

Two white persons and I (all of similar social and educational status) are in a conversation. At one point, I make a remark or raise a question. One of the two white persons responds to me, not looking toward me, but rather looking at the other white person. (Invariably, I would say to myself, "I should never, just never, get myself in this kind of situation again!")

One or two white friends and I walk into a store because I need to purchase something. I ask the person at the counter if the store has the item. The salesperson will usually look to my two white friends to give the answer and never look at me.

I (a fifty-nine-year-old) walk into a flower shop. Two white men sitting on the front steps greet me, "Hey, Boy!" At the airport, I stand in line to check in at the "Premier Members" counter. (For some years I used to fly a lot and had a "Premier Executive" membership with one of the airlines.) A white lady also in line behind me taps on my shoulder and says, "Are you sure you are in the right line? This is for Premier Members only!"

I had better stop here. I am beginning to feel "cheap" writing down these stories. My feeling cheap, however, is a symptom of the fact that I have for so long repressed and internalized these insults, telling myself that a "big person" (a minister and a professor) like me should not make a big deal out of these little things and instead take the "high road." But those "little" incidents of insults occur sometimes more than once a day, day after day, week after week, month after month, year after year, decade after decade.

I used to wonder why those "little" and "subtle" incidents upset me so much. One reason is that they have cumulative effects. Again, Feagin is helpful here. Writing about the acts of "subtle discrimination" against black persons, Feagin points out that when those acts "accumulate over months, years, and lifetimes, the impact on a black person is far more than the sum of the individual instances." They add up, in other words, in terms of the amount of humiliation and anger. History cannot be dismissed. Feagin writes:

> Particular acts, even anti-locution that might seem minor to white observers, are freighted not only with one's past experience of discrimination but also with centuries of racial discrimination directed at the entire group, vicarious oppression that still includes racially translated violence and denial of access to the American Dream.[35]

"The Strangers from a Different Shore"

So, white racism functions as the barrier that pushes Asian Americans out of the center of the American society and keeps them at the edges of that society. Other factors also marginalize Asian Americans. For some, economic or educational factors may also make them marginal. Asian American women suffer from a double marginalization because of the sexism that exists both in the white American society and also within their own Asian American communities.[36] Without diminishing the significance of these other determinants of Asian Americans' marginalization, it is still true, I believe, to say that white racism is the most universal determinant— a factor that applies to all Asian Americans' marginalization.

The racism barrier keeps Asian Americans from achieving what sociologists call "structural assimilation." Most Asian immigrants have no problem in the area of "cultural assimilation"—the adoption of many of white America's cultural values and mores, and the attainment of sufficient linguistic and social skills to function in white American society. Those

Asian Americans who are born here, of course, have all the cultural traits of their white American peers.

But "structural assimilation" is quite another matter. This kind of assimilation means Asian Americans' becoming truly "one of us" in white American society and having the same privileges and "life-chances" as white people. But this does not happen to Asian Americans who, in the eyes of the dominant group, are never "one of us." Recent studies of Korean immigrants in the Chicago and Los Angeles areas show that regardless of the length of their stay in this country, their educational levels, or their professional and economic attainments, "structural assimilation" does not really happen to them, and they tend to gravitate around their ethnic enclaves.[37] Some first-generation Korean immigrants' continuing problems with English and also their inevitable human tendency to cling to the comforts of their ethnic communities may also function to prevent "structural assimilation." But the primary factor for Asian Americans' exclusion from the center of white society is the barriers set up by the white dominant group. I have heard so many stories of American-born second- or third-generation Korean American students on college and university campuses running into white students and sometimes faculty who ask them with surprise, "How come you speak English so well?" In other words, race "sticks" for us Asian Americans. Korean American sociologist Won Moo Hurh concludes:

> Non-white immigrants may attain a high degree of cultural assimilation (adoption of American life-style), but structural assimilation (equal life-chances) is virtually impossible unless the immutable independent variable, "race," becomes mutable through miscegenation or cognitive mutation of the WASP. Koreans are no exception to this *Lebensschilsal.*[38]

As the title of Ronald Takaki's landmark history of Asian Americans has it, they are indeed "strangers from a different shore."[39] The white racist barriers that prevent "structural assimilation" for Asian Americans are precisely the reason why the straight-line theory of assimilation does not apply to Asian immigrants.[40] According to that theory, an immigrant would arrive in this country and go through a period of cultural adaptation—a period that would automatically be followed by "structural assimilation"— that is, a total acceptance by the white group as "one of us." In fact, even if a white European immigrant does not totally adapt to the American style of life and maintains an attachment to his or her ethnic heritage, such an immigrant, however, would still be accepted by the white population in this country as "one of us" almost immediately. Think of an immigrant from Germany, who hardly speaks English. When that person walks down the main street in practically any town or city in this country, he or she will be seen as "an American."

But straight-line assimilation does not happen to non-white immigrants such as Asian immigrants.[41] An Asian American person may speak English very well, adopt a name like Nancy, John, or Peter, and may have even been born in this country; but when this Asian American walks down that main street, she or he is an alien, a stranger. Let me point out here that I am not implying that total cultural assimilation by an Asian immigrant to the white American culture is even desirable. The idea of America as a "melting pot" in practice has always been a demand by the white dominant group for a "transmuting pot"–namely, the non-white person's rejection of (or at least not asserting) his or her own cultural heritage. The message of the white dominant culture to non-white persons has always been, "Why can't you be like us?" No person can remain whole when his or her cultural persona is fundamentally disrespected. My point here simply is that for non-white persons in this country, cultural adaptation does not lead to social acceptance by the dominant group.

Marginality as Coerced Liminality

Now that we have looked at each of the two dimensions of the particular marginality experience of Asian Americans, we need to see how those two dimensions are mutually related. We can put the matter in this way: Asian Americans' liminality (the first aspect of their marginality) exists in a particular context–namely, in the context of the exclusion by the dominant group in America (the second aspect of Asian Americans' marginality). Asian Americans do not experience liminal in-between-ness as a temporary condition or as a creative opportunity; they are pushed to liminality and are coercively made to stay there by the barriers set up by the racist center. Their liminality does not naturally lead to reaggregation or entrance or re-entrance into structure, as would be the case in a normal change process.

I wrote earlier about the creative potentials of the liminal condition. Such potentials would still be in Asian Americans' marginality; but those creative potentials are repressed, thwarted, and frustrated by the second aspect of their marginality experience. The dehumanizing effect of the second aspect of marginality often debilitates the first aspect of Asian Americans' liminal creativity by taking away from them the courage and self-respect needed to face up to the creative challenge of the liminal experience.

I noted above that the liminal condition can be an openness to the new. But when the new identity of Asian Americans as a synthesis of the Asian and American worlds is not celebrated but considered often as inferior by the larger American society, how can these Asian Americans feel encouraged to welcome their new identity? Self-hatred will often be the result.

I also noted that liminality is conducive to community. But the dominant group would not leave their structure and join the Asian American strangers in the wilderness of liminal in-between-ness. White racism makes Asian American strangers even more reluctant to venture out of their ethnic enclaves. Liminality is certainly promoted when self-consciously liminal Asian Americans gather together. But realities of American society today certainly do not encourage Asian Americans to embrace their liminal wilderness experience. They are more often tempted either to unrealistically cling to their ethnic roots or to be oblivious to their ethnic past and live in the illusion that they are "Americans." The possibility of using their liminality as an opportunity to venture outside of Asian American ethnic enclaves and of trying to forge communitas with people across racial and ethnic lines certainly does not receive much encouragement and usually remains unfulfilled.

The third creative potential of liminality is its conducive nature to the attainment of a critical and prophetic insight about the center. But white racist hegemony sometimes leads Asian Americans and others at the edge to internalize the racist views of themselves and thus remain incapable of seeing the problems at the center. Even when some brave ones at the edge gain critical and prophetic insights, they are often not welcomed by either the American center, which only wants to protect the status quo, or the Asian center, which does not want anybody to rock the boat. In short, my proposal for an understanding of Asian American theology's context is that Asian Americans are in the predicament of "marginality" defined as "coerced liminality"–an in-between-ness that is suppressed, frustrated, and unfulfilled by barriers that are not in one's own control. Liminality as such is a potentially creative condition. But a coerced liminality that is made permanent is "marginalization" with all of its dehumanizing consequences. This definition of marginality, I believe, enables us to recognize a potential creativity of liminality in the Asian American experience without ignoring the negative effects of racism in American society. The Asian American minority in America, in other words, are a liminal people who can use their in-between liminality precisely to struggle against marginalization. But their liminality is forcibly suppressed by racist hostilities, and it has been crying out to be freed from suppression.

In any Christian theology, the human context must be reinterpreted in the larger theological context of what God is doing in the world. But Christian theology surely cannot ignore the particular context in which such theology is being done. Asian American theology, in other words, has to be faithful to the historic Christian tradition and also meaningful to the Asian Americans' situation of "marginality" as "coerced liminality." Such a task is indeed a challenging one. But having a working conception of the context is at least one important step in undertaking the task of a constructive Asian American theology.

Notes
[1]By using the shorthand term *Asian American* I do not mean to exclude the Pacific Islanders, nor do I mean to ignore the experiences of Asian Canadians. The most inclusive term would be *Asian Pacific North American.* One of the recent publications on the Los Angeles riots of 1992 emphasizes the diversity of Korean Americans. See Nancy Abelmann and John Lie, *Blue Dreams: Korean Americans and the Los Angeles Riots* (Cambridge, Mass.: Harvard University Press, 1995).

[2]Ronald Takaki, *Strangers from a Different Shore: A History of Asian Americans* (New York: Penguin Books, 1989), 18.

[3]Everett V. Stonequist, *The Marginal Man: A Study in Personality and Culture Conflict* (New York: Russell & Russell, 1937), 8. See also Robert E. Park, "Migration and the Marginal Man," *The American Journal of Sociology* (May, 1928).

[4]H. F Dickie-Clark, *The Marginal Situation: A Sociological Study of a Colored Group* (London: Routledge & Kegan Paul, 1966), 24, 31.

[5]Stonequist, *Marginal Man*, 221.

[6]Arnold van Gennep, *The Rites of Passage* (London: Routledge and Kegan Paul, 1960).

[7]Victor W. Turner, *Dramas, Fields, and Metaphors: Symbolic Action in Human Society* (Ithaca, N.Y.: Cornell University Press, 1974), 273–74; *From Ritual to Theatre: The Seriousness of Human Play* (New York: Performance Art Journal Publications, 1982), 24; *The Ritual Process: Structure and Anti-Structure* (Ithaca, N.Y.: Cornell University Press, 1969), vii; *The Forest of Symbols: Aspects of Ndembu Ritual* (Ithaca, N.Y.: Cornell University Press, 1967), 97.

[8]William Bridges, *Transitions: Making Sense of Life's Changes* (Reading, Mass.: Addison-Wesley Publishing Co., 1980), 119.

[9]Terry A. Veling, *Living in the Margins: Intentional Communities and the Art of Interpretation* (New York: Crossroad, 1996), 18.

[10]Hans-Georg Gadamer, *Truth and Method,* trans. Joel Weinsheimer and Donald Marshall (New York: Crossroad, 1989), 295.

[11]David Tracy, *Analogical Imagination: Christian Theology and the Culture of Pluralism* (New York: Crossroad, 1981), 136.

[12]Veling, *Living in the Margins,* 20, 118, 136, 145.

[13]Turner, *Dramas, Fields, and Metaphors,* 269.

[14]Ibid., 68.

[15]Turner, *Ritual Process,* 128.

[16]Turner, *Dramas, Fields, and Metaphors,* 243.

[17]Turner, *Ritual Process,* vii.

[18]Turner, *From Ritual to Theatre,* 27.

[19]Ibid., 47.

[20]Turner, *Fields, Drama, and Metaphors,* 274.

[21]See the discussion in Georg Simmel, *The Sociology of Georg Simmel,* trans. Kurt H. Wolf (Glencoe, Ill.: The Free Press, 1950), 404–5.

[22]Turner, *Dramas, Fields, and Metaphors,* 51.

[23]Turner, *Ritual Process,* vii.

[24]Turner, *From Ritual to Theatre,* 51; "Frame, Flow and Reflection: Ritual and Drama as Public Liminality," in *Performance in Postmodern Culture,* ed. Michel Benamou and Charles Caramello (Madison, Wisc.: The Center for Twentieth Century Studies, University of Wisconsin-Milwaukee, 1977), 39.

[25]Bobby C. Alexander, *Victor Turner Revisited: Ritual as Social Change* (Atlanta: Scholars Press, 1991), 18 (I have relied considerably on Alexander's excellent discussion of Turner's ideas of liminality and *communitas* for references to many of Turner's works); Turner, *Ritual Process,* vii.

[26]Alexander, *Victor Turner Revisited,* 95–104.

[27]Won Moo Hurh and Kwang Chung Kim, "The 'Success Image' of Asian Americans: Its Validity, and Its Practical and Theoretical Implications," *Ethnic and Racial Studies* 12 (October 1989): 531.

[28]Wesley Woo, "Asians in America: Challenges for the Presbyterian Church (USA)," an unpublished study paper, May 1987, 13.

[29]Elaine H. Kim, "Creating a Third Space," *San Francisco Bay Guardian,* 10 March 1993.

[30]Won Moo Hurh and Kwang Chung Kim, *Korean Immigrants in America: A Structural Analysis of Ethnic Confinement and Adhesive Assimilation* (Rutherford, N.J.: Fairleigh Dickinson University Press, 1984), 146–49.

[31]Joe R. Feagin, *Racial and Ethnic Relations* (Englewood, N.J.: Prentice-Hall, 1989), 15.

[32]"Attacks Against Asian-Americans On the Rise, Especially in California," *The New York Times,* 9 December 1995.

[33]Ibid.

[34]Feagin, *Racial and Ethnic Relations,* 16.

[35]Joe R. Feagin, "The Continuing Significance of Race: Antiblack Discrimination in Public Places," *American Sociological Review* 56 (February 1991): 115.

[36]See, for example, Elaine H. Kim, *With Silk Wings: Asian American Women at Work* (San Francisco: Asian Women United of California, 1983); Inn Sook Lee, ed., *Korean American Women: Toward Self-Realization* (Mansfield, Ohio: The Association of Korean Christian Scholars in North America, 1985).

[37]Hurh and Kim, *Korean Immigrants in America,* 73–86.

[38]Won Moo Hurh, "Comparative Study of Korean Immigrants in the United States: A Typology," in *Koreans in America,* ed. Byong-Suh Kin, et al. (Memphis, Tenn.: The Association of Korean Christian Scholars in North America, 1977), 95.

[39]Takaki, *Strangers from a Different Shore,* 18.

[40]Ibid., 73–75.

[41]Harry H. L. Kitano and Roger Daniels, *Asian Americans: Emerging Minorities* (Englewood Cliffs, N.J.: Prentice-Hall, 1988), 2.

2

Creating Community Amidst the Memories of Historic Injuries

FUMITAKA MATSUOKA

This chapter is an exploration of Christian faith as it is embodied in Japanese American faith communities as these communities struggle with their affirmation of human dignity amidst their experiences and memories of historic injuries inflicted on them, yet strive toward their participation in the creation of a just and compassionate society. The central issue to be explored is how Japanese Americans participate in the society that has denied their membership and human dignity and yet in which they still need to exist in an increasingly interwoven web of relationships amidst racial and ethnic divides. The experiences and memories of historic injuries suffered by Japanese Americans, their internment experiences in particular, serve as a hermeneutical len, in exploring their quest for identity and their understanding of the society they live in.

Introduction

The impact of race and ethnic pluralism on societal coherence has not been sufficiently acknowledged even in our continuing national conversations about race and ethnicity. Racial and ethnic diversity has profound implications for every aspect of American public life as we begin to renegotiate the "we" of "We the People." A striking visible landscape of race and ethnic pluralism and the resultant alienation among different groups that have emerged in recent decades present us with a significant challenge of a national and societal coherence. The challenge is due primarily to the deep divisions in race/ethnicity relations that exist only beneath the surface of our public life. The divisions are caused in a large part by the *Rashomon* effect.

The term refers to divergent interpretations and understandings given to a single event depending on the particular vantage point of an interpreter. It was named after Japanese movie director Akira Kurosawa's classic work *Rashomon.* The story focuses on the reasons why people could have such differing recollections of the same event, the murder of a man, in the movie. It explores the motives for telling the truth, telling a story, telling lies: The desire for revenge, honor, notoriety, jealousy, hatred, contempt, fame, greed, shame, sexual gratification–they all alter or influence memory. The ability of a third party (the court or the commoner under the gate) to distinguish between truth and falsehood and mixtures of the two (stories, history, legal evidence, memory) is also an important factor in the *Rashomon* effect. The different types of evidence presented–eyewitness accounts, reporting what transpired at the court, the evidence presented by the camera, too–impact the various readings of the event.

The celebrated O. J. Simpson trial exemplifies the *Rashomon* effect. The trial was interpreted through radically different perspectives across mostly racial lines. Race relations are one arena in which the *Rashomon* effect often gets played out today. *The New York Times* recently carried a series of articles on the state of race relations in the United States today. These articles, exploring various aspects of life, church, military, media, and so forth, once again pointed out the *Rashomon* perspectives that play deeply in today's race relations. Race issues are today being defined less by political action than by daily experience in schools, in sports arenas, in pop culture, at worship, and especially in the workplace. In many cases, there is evidence of progress, moments of growth and reconciliation, small epiphanies when one side comes to understand the motivations of the other and both come to understand that they need each other. In others, however, the divisions are too great to bridge due in large part to the different interpretations of a common life by those who see race issues out of their own vantage points.

Building a pluralist society from such diversity with the impact of *Rashomon* effects is no easy task, especially when the divergent perspectives and interpretations have to do with the historical injuries suffered and long remembered by racially and ethnically underrepresented groups of people, such as those injuries caused by slavery and the internment of American citizens of an Asian ancestry. American public debate is charged with the power of these issues. Some say a multiracial and multiethnic society is impossible. Their voices have been raised at each and every stage of American immigration, and they are present today. What does it mean to speak of "our own" culture? What do "we" mean when we say "we"? How are "difference" and "otherness" defined, and by whom? These are increasingly key questions facing our society. These are significant theological questions as well because they have to do with our deeply-held convictions, values, life formations, and the ways we relate with one another. These questions ultimately have to do with the reality of alienation and the possibility of forgiveness and reconciliation. Thus, our public life intersects with our faith convictions in our racial and ethnic diversity fraught with the weight of historical injuries. In this chapter, I will address the ways Americans of Japanese ancestry cope with the idea of societal coherence–"We, the People"–amidst the experiences and memories of the historic injuries they suffered, particularly during World War II through their camp incarceration.

A Common Culture?

Sociologist Robert Bellah claims that there is an enormously powerful common culture in America that attracts diverse groups of people. It is "carried predominantly by the market and the state and by their agencies of socialization: television and education."[1] A common culture does not mean that people are the same. It is driven with argument, controversy, and conflict. A family, for example, is a common culture. It is sometimes understood as "the place we go to fight."[2] However, a common culture needs "sacred conventions" to survive. For Bellah, the American "sacred convention" is "utilitarian individualism," which manifests itself in our popular culture:

> Our Anglo students do not come to college with a deep knowledge of Jane Austen or Nathaniel Hawthorne any more than our Japanese-American students bring a knowledge of Lady Murasaki or Natsume Soseki. What they bring, they bring in common: Oprah Winfrey, ER, Seinfeld, Nike, Microsoft, the NBA and the NFL. If the common culture is predominantly Euro-American, or, more accurately, Anglo-American, in its roots, the enormous pressure of the market economy, and the mass media and mass education oriented to it, obliterate the genuine heritage of Anglo-American, European, African, and Asian culture with equal thoroughness.[3]

The core of the "utilitarian individualism," according to Bellah, is religious and was probably expressed not by John Winthrop but rather by de Tocqueville (*Democracy in America*) or Roger Williams. There is a real link between the "sectarian notion of the sacredness of conscience and what we mean by multiculturalism today."[4] An inherent significant problem of this brand of American common culture, Bellah warns, is that "just when we are moving to an ever greater validation of the sacredness of the individual person, our capacity to imagine a social fabric that would hold individuals together is vanishing."[5] This is in part because of the fact that religious individualism is linked to an economic individualism that, ironically, knows nothing of the sacredness of the individual. Fortunately, argues Bellah, hopes still exist, however. In spite of the fact that people of whatever race or gender are tempted to exalt our own individual selves, there are still social contexts and traditions of interpretations that can moderate our individual egoism and offer a different understanding of personal fulfillment. "Every church and synagogue that reminds us that it is through love of God and neighbor that we will find ourselves helps to mitigate our isolation. Every time we engage in activities that help to feed the hungry, cloth the naked, give shelter to the homeless, we are becoming more connected to the world."[6] These safeguarding social contexts and traditions serve as what Jurgen Habermas calls "lifeword" and prevent the market from destroying the moral foundations of our society. Bellah thus calls for reclaiming our "sacred conventions" in the way that will hold our common culture, radical individualism.

Bellah challenges us to cope with our rampant market "common culture," which does not seem to know any moral restraint. He calls us to recover the "sacred conventions" even in our temptations to acquiesce to the rampant economic individualism. However, Bellah falls short on his analysis of the ways the "sacred conventions" can be redeemed and recovered. What I have witnessed in Japanese Americans and particularly in their Christian churches is that the motivation for the recovery of "sacred conventions" is rooted deeply and foundationally in their experiences of the historical injuries caused by the incarceration into concentration camps during World War II. The motivations for Japanese Americans do not merely derive from their desire to overcome the destructive power of radical individualism. The necessity for sacred conventions does not become real in a mere desire or awareness of importance to recover the "sacred conventions" in any given institution. Instead, it derives mainly from painful experiences that remind them what it means to have an alternative vision of society, an alternative value, a "second language." In the individual and communal awareness that God wills good in evil (Romans 5:20) an awareness that emerged from experiences of injustice and its pain, the commitment to the recovery and preservation of the conventions that cohere a people was born.

Historic Injuries for Japanese Americans

In recent years a growing number of people have become aware of the injustice of incarcerating 120,000 Americans of Japanese ancestry, 77,000 of whom were U.S. citizens, during World War II. While it was ostensibly for the purposes of "national security," their imprisonment in ten camps within the interior of the United States was motivated by mounting antagonism toward Japanese Americans. They were the most accessible targets for the hysteria and hatred against Japanese abroad in the midst of the war. The painful experience of incarceration and its lasting memories are deeply implanted in the lives not only of those who underwent it firsthand but also of the subsequent generations of Japanese Americans. The interned were both those who held Japanese citizenship and also American-born citizens. In spite of the fact that many of the Japanese citizens wished to become U.S. citizens, they were denied U.S. citizenship because of the racist immigration restrictions of the time. The American citizens of Japanese descent were also denied their basic constitutional rights in their incarceration. Their faith in the inviolability of the rights of citizenship was shattered.

> With no one to turn to, with their structures and institutions dismantled, with little political or economic power, with cultural norms and values emphasizing conformity and non-conflictual behavior, with a lack of feasible alternatives and facing the awesome power of the United States Government, the Japanese marched into camp. Could they have really done otherwise?[7]

Their internment experiences and legacy remain part and parcel of what it means to be Japanese Americans today. Anthropologist Yasuko Takezawa believes that two events were crucial to the transformation of Japanese American ethnic identity, one being the internment and the other, the redress movement.[8] Ethnicity is expressed differently over time. It is continually being constructed and reconstructed by interpretation of the past, particularly of injuries that were unjustly imposed on a people, as related to the present. For Japanese Americans, the internment experiences they suffered during World War II and the subsequent redress movement play a decisive role in forming their identity.

The impact of historical injuries on the identity formation of a community and its members is yet to be appreciated. The multicultural reality of today's society signals the fact that every dimension of American culture has become more complex. Racial and ethnic issues became multisided. Religious diversity shattered the paradigm of an America as a "three religion country." Ethnic identity, however, unlike race, is less a matter of a common gene pool than of shared history, perceptions, and group identity. Some of the strongest ethnic divides run between people of the same stock, whether in Bosnia or Northern Ireland, where there are telling differences in history on the two sides. The alienation of people one from another is sometimes a by-product of investment in one's own ethnic identity. When the difference between groups are small, greater importance is placed on minor distinguishing features, a phenomenon Freud called the "narcissism of minor differences." The closer the resemblance between neighboring groups, the greater the emotion they invest in maintaining small differences.

However, a potent source of people's ethnic identity is a collective memory of their past glories and traumas. Passing on these memories to the next generation feeds ethnic animosity but also helps keep the group's identity alive. Past oppression by another ethnic group is remembered mythically, as though the past were the present. For the Serbs, for example, one historical trauma that has persisted with freshness in the collective memory is the 1389 defeat of the Serbs and their Christian allies at the hands of the Muslim Turks in the Battle of Kosovo. It was the beginning of five hundred years of Turkish occupation, which the Serbs remember as oppression. Likewise, the Muslims of Bosnia remember the massacres of Muslims by Serbs in World War II.

For Japanese Americans, their incarceration during World War II can be said to play the decisive role in their collective memory, which contributes to their present identity. Robert Jay Lifton points out that, in addition to collective memory, what also comes into play is a current political force that fans antagonisms between people who may have lived together without violence. In the case of Japanese Americans, they became victims of the United States, which had become very susceptible to the worldwide political and military forces of World War II after the country experienced a major dislocation, a loss of its bearings, with traditional verities, meanings, and values threatened by outside forces. Japanese Americans became an easy target for the nation. The ideology of the national political leaders who inflamed antagonism against Japanese Americans was a vision of revitalizing the whole nation, which was undergoing a grave trauma of war. The political leaders' jingoistic promise of the defense of the nation was carried out at the expense of Japanese Americans, who were painted as a threat to the national security.

Fanned by the perception of nationwide prejudice against Japanese Americans, this prejudice was exaggerated by the war. Nevertheless, the net effect of this misperception was to suggest a stronger consensus than truly existed for actions against the ethnic group. The reticence of the majority of people who did not hold the biased view against Japanese Americans to speak up against those who wanted a public discrimination of the group played a major role in the escalation of bias to outright violence that occurred at times. Their silence encouraged those who spoke for an ideology that promised a secure future for the nation.

Given the far-reaching implications and impact of the internment of Japanese Americans, particularly on their perspectives on the coherence of the nation (the notion of "We, the People"), the correlation between their ethnic identity and their experience of the historic injury plays a significant role in the discussion of "a common American culture." Historic injuries stay with us. Time does not heal all wounds. If a common American culture is to be understood as the dignity of individuals in the sense of Roger Williams, as Bellah claims, then its recovery through the practice of "sacred conventions" for Americans needs to take into account the often alienated state of interracial and ethnic relations among us. Ethnically and racially underrepresented groups of people all have experienced some form of historically imposed injury one way or another. A national coherence in the form of reconciled diversity cannot take place without acknowledging this fact.

Creating Community Amidst the Memories of Historic Injuries

Albert Einstein spoke to the core of our discussion when he insisted that we must learn to understand the motives, illusions, and sorrows of other human beings in order to obtain a reliable attitude towards single persons as well as towards the community. How do Japanese Americans participate in the society that once denied their membership and human dignity? Are there any insights within their faith communities? Something about an act of attentive listening to "the motives, illusions, and sorrows of other human beings" is related to the promise of community-building across the dividing walls of hostility.

The internment of Japanese Americans had a profound effect on their place in society. Intended or unintended, Japanese Americans at the outbreak of the war were perceived as most susceptible to assimilation among ethnically underrepresented groups of people by society, even in their isolation. Richard Drinnon, in *Keeper of Concentration Camps: Dillon S. Myer and American Racism,* points out that the War Relocation Authority isolated Japanese Americans into concentration camps in order to prepare them for their eventual assimilation into a wider society and the dominant Anglo-European culture.[9]

> Do you remember the directives we were given when we left camp? We were not to congregate among our kind; we were not to speak Japanese nor be conspicuous; we were not to talk about camp. In other words, we were not to be Japanese in any way. But to the dominant society we were not only Japanese, we were "Japs." Certainly not American. So where the hell did that leave us?[10]

The tenacious power of assimilation by the act of internment during World War II was equally met by tenacious efforts of the Japanese American community to protect and assert its own ethnic coherence, identity, and integrity. The preservation and legitimization of their own community and ethnicity were paramount in the minds of those who were incarcerated. The Japanese American ethnic identity was expressed in two distinct ways. The "No, No Boys," those who refused to pledge an allegiance either to the U.S. because of the unjust denial of their basic rights as citizens or to Japan for which they had no citizenry relationship, insisted on their own unique place in society. They considered themselves American, but without all the rights and privileges. Their ethnicity was expressed in this fashion. There were also those Japanese Americans whose ethnic identity was expressed through their service to the U.S. military. Their identity was symbolized by those servicemen who served in the famous all-Nisei 100th

Infantry Battalion and the 42 Regimental Combat Team in the European theater, which won the largest number of distinguished medals in the history of the U.S. military. Nisei in the Military Intelligence Service served no less importantly in the Pacific theater. Those solders, with the support of their families, wanted to prove their loyalty to the nation through their own sacrifices. In either case—those who refused the loyalty allegiance and those who participated in the U.S. military with unspeakable sacrifices—Japanese Americans were determined to prove to society their own ethnic identity and pride even in the midst of the tide that tried to sweep them into the dominant culture.

The internment experience is a reminder that Japanese Americans are viewed as ethnically "different" from the rest of the society. "Difference is interpreted by those in power as less than," says Katie Cannon. "Conformity is the norm, and anyone who cannot be bleached out and neutered has to be isolated, alienated, and eventually exterminated."[11] The isolation of Japanese Americans into camps, in terms of both the containment of their influences and the attempt to eradicate their distinctness through assimilation, presented them with an awareness that their very existence could be threatened anytime and their rights taken away by the very government and society that were created to protect them in the name of "life, liberty, and the pursuit of happiness."

Their deep sense of betrayal by the nation runs deep in their psyches, even beyond those who experienced internment firsthand. The subsequent generations of Japanese Americans—the Sansei folks, the third-generation Japanese Americans—still carry the legacy of the internment experiences of their parents and grandparents. Although most Sansei were not alive during World War II, a growing number of them are discovering that their experiences of emotional, psychological, and spiritual conflict or cultural discomfort seem to have significant roots in the internment camps or in the ways their Nisei parents reacted to the camps.

A potent source of Japanese American group identity is indeed their collective memory of the internment experiences. Passing on the memories to the next generation helps keep the group's identity alive. In this respect, the redress movement and the eventual passage of the Civil Liberties Act of 1988 that authorized the payment of $20,000 to eligible Japanese Americans interned during World War II were powerful means to reassert the Japanese American identity that was in a large part shaped by the historic injury they suffered. "For the first time in the history of mass exclusion and detention of Japanese-Americans and their aftermath, the defendant is identified and the plaintiffs defined. For the first time in this history, we, the plaintiffs, spell out our injuries from our perspective, as the injured parties," says William Hohri, the chairperson of the National Council for Japanese American Redress (NCJAR).[12]

Indeed, past oppression and injustice inflicted by the nation are also remembered mythically and in narrative form. It is no wonder that there is a recent surge of publications by Japanese American writers on the internment experience. Japanese American children learn about Poston, Manzanar, Jerome, and other internment camps in the story books written, for example, by Yoshiko Uchida and other writers.[13] The infamous Executive Order 9066 decreed by President Franklin Roosevelt on February 19, 1942, to incarcerate Americans of Japanese ancestry is still regularly remembered today in Japanese American communities throughout the nation as "the Day of Remembrance." The memories persist with such power because it is a sign of allegiance to share these painful memories among the members of the particular ethnic group.

The story of the historic injuries experienced by Japanese Americans illustrates the depth of the ethnic diversity present in society today. The ethnic groups are separated as much by their particular cultural distinctness as by their collective memories and experiences of injustice, betrayal, and pain imposed on them by another group or by a society itself. These shared experiences and memories help groups form their own identities and shape their own perspectives for the understanding and interpretation of our society. The *Rashomon* effect has its origin in historically imposed injuries suffered by ethnic groups. The real issue of ethnic diversity, then, is the deep sense of alienation between and among ethnic groups caused by historic injuries that are acted out over and over in both public and private arenas of life. A societal coherence, a common bond that brings diverse people together, must take into consideration the deep gulfs that exist among us in order to be aware of the need for its recovery through whatever "sacred conventions" that make the recovery possible. The acknowledgment of the pain of alienation is a necessary step toward the recovery of the common culture based on the sacredness of the individual envisioned by de Tocqueville and Roger Williams.

The Pain and Promise of Ethnic Diversity

Bellah reminds us that "just when we are moving to an ever greater validation of the sacredness of the individual person, our capacity to imagine a social fabric that would hold individuals together is vanishing."[14] The reason he gives for this societal trend is the emergence of consumer and economic individualism. A capacity for social coherence and compassion toward neighbors is fostered through an empathetic imagination on the part of those who are willing to acknowledge the pain of alienation among different groups of people that comprise this society. The real threat of the commodified notion of life embedded in the current economic individualism is its tendency to minimize the alienated state of people one from another. To be sure, America is not experiencing the racial and ethnic

divide so sharply forewarned by the Kerner Commission in 1966. There is
much fluidity in interracial and interethnic relationships. However, the
deep gulf remains across racial and ethnic lines today evidenced by such
celebrated cases as police department incidents in Los Angeles, Cincinnati,
and New York and other quarters.

The historic injuries suffered by Japanese Americans and their legacy
passed down to the subsequent generations attest to the magnitude of the
alienating state of race and ethnic relationships in America today. The
same can be said of the experiences of African Americans, native Americans,
and Hispanic Americans. At the same time, no one is on the verge of
providing a single, convincing, institution-revolutionizing idea of
comprehensive human community. All our definitional and institutional
ploys fall short of their bright promises in our vision, in historical effects,
or in inherent logic. Sacred conventions based on empathetic compassion
for others are still yet to merge in our society. This is the deepest pain of
racial and ethnic pluralism today.

Promise in Pain: Insights into Reconciled Community

"One of the saddest moments of my life occurred while we were driving
over the Terminal Island draw-bridge the next day. Being evicted from our
business place meant a great financial loss, but to be torn asunder from our
homes, our church, and our community was worse, a cataclysmic
experience...our crucifixion experience."[15] Rev. Sadaichi Asai's words
speak of the betrayal of trust Japanese Americans experienced at the hands
of the United States and its government. In the midst of such a traumatic,
crucifixion experience, however, unexpected responses sprouted from
incarcerated Japanese Americans toward the nation and its government.
While decrying the injustices done to them, there are those who chose not
to become vindictive toward the very society that imposed unjust sufferings
on them. Instead, they chose to work toward a just and compassionate
society.

In the sacrifices of the Japanese American soldiers as well as of the
"No, No Boys," and in the countless other sacrificial acts of folks during
and after the war, lie the cosmology, worldviews, and value orientations
that are deeply embedded in the lives of Japanese Americans. The first
and foremost for the interned Japanese Americans is the unnegotiable state
of human life. In Japanese language, humanity, *ningen,* is defined in terms
of relationships, intimacy as well as tension, harmony as well as distance,
and individuation amidst relatedness. There is no clear-cut dichotomy
between these opposites. Even in the midst of betrayal and the resulting
alienation experienced in the internment, there exists the unnegotiable
state of human bonds and possibility for reconciliation. This cultural
cosmology—whose origin perhaps goes back to an amalgamation of Taoism,
Confucianism, and other Eastern faiths—continues to incarnate in the lives

and worldviews of Japanese Americans. What has emerged is a distinct cosmology that is a mixture of the religious and cultural heritages originated in Asia, and the harsh experiences of immigrant lives and the stigma of racist treatment suffered by their offspring. The historic injuries suffered during World War II deeply impacted the formation of such a cosmology. Christian faith lived and articulated by Japanese American Christians cannot be understood without this newly formed cosmology. Christian faith is expressed through it.

In the church life of Japanese Americans, such a cosmology manifests itself in their understandings of Christianity as reflected, for example, in the Pauline passages of Galatians 3:28–29 or Ephesians 2:13–14: "But now in Christ Jesus you who once were far off have been brought near by the blood of Christ…" These passages point to the reality of the basic relatedness of all beings and the whole creation even in spite of tremendous sufferings imposed on them. Sacred conventions begin with an affirmation and confession of the givenness of human bond as affirmed in faith: the reality that our very being hinges on our relatedness to the rest of humanity.

The Tie that Binds Us Together

The "second language" that binds our society together in the midst of an increasingly plural makeup of our racial and ethnic compositions in the U.S. needs to be more than an ideal. The language of Roger Williams, the sacredness of conscience, needs to be incarnated in the actual state of life for Americans with an increasing effect of *Rashomon* syndrome. The "second language" of the sacred conventions properly belongs to the realm of religion as defined by Robert Bellah: religion in its original notion of *religio*, to bind people together. For Christians, our faith needs an intersection with the public life. The incarnation of Christian faith is both deeply personal and deeply public at the same time. Japanese American Christians remind us of a key that does bind the people of the *Rashomon* effect together. What manner of people are these? Refusing to flinch in the face of the painful and unjust experiences of incarceration, attacking the unjust system that had bound them, they reach out to those who betrayed their trust and inflicted injustice to them, offering to build together a new society. Who were these prophets who came out of the camps in work-tattered clothes and the military uniforms of the country that betrayed them and who made the ten camps in desolate deserts into precincts of sanctified hope? If the experiences of historical injuries suffered by Japanese Americans point to their willingness to go beyond their inclination to dwell in the pain of the past and to reach out for strengthening a web of all people in the U.S. society, this society has not been able to value their generosity. This is the challenge that awaits America in truly becoming the America of all our hearts.

40 *Fumitaka Matsuoka*

Notes

[1]Robert N. Bellah, "Is There a Common American Culture?" *Journal of American Academy of Religion* 66/3 (1998): 616.

[2]Ibid.

[3]Ibid., 616–17.

[4]Ibid., 608.

[5]Ibid., 622.

[6]Ibid., 623–24.

[7]Comments at a UCLA symposium, printed in the *Pacific Citizen,* 9 June 1967.

[8]Yasuko I. Takezawa, *Breaking the Silence: Redress and Japanese American Ethnicity* (Ithaca, N.Y., and London: Cornell University Press, 1995).

[9]Richard Drinnon, *Keeper of Concentration Camps: Dillon S. Myer and American Racism* (Berkeley and Los Angeles: University of California Press, 1987).

[10]Mei Nakano, *Japanese American Women: Three Generations 1890–1990* (Berkeley & Sebastopol: Mina Press Publishing; San Francisco: National Japanese American Historical Society, 1990), 159.

[11]Katie Cannon, *God's Fierce Whimsy: Christian Feminism and Theological Education* (New York: Pilgrim Press, 1985), 37.

[12]William Minoru Hohri, *Repairing America* (Pullman: Washington State University Press, 1984), 192.

[13]*The Birthday Visitor, Invisible Thread, Journey to Topaz,* and *Samurai of Cold Hill* are some of the thirty-some works, intended both for children and adults, written by Yoshiko Uchida.

[14]Bellah, "Common American Culture," 622.

[15]Rev. Sadaichi Asai in *Triumphs of Faith: Stories of Japanese-American Christians During World War II,* ed. Victor N. Okada (Los Angeles: Japanese-American Internment Project, 1998), 6.

3

A Theology of *Tao* (Way)

Han, *Sin, and Evil*

ANDREW SUNG PARK

Asian Americans have faced the issues of prejudice, discrimination, alienation, exclusion, and shame in this society. Their experiences can be called *han,* the deep pain of a victim. Sin and guilt are less pressing issues than *han* and shame.[1] To Asian Americans who are facing a variety of oppressions, a Western theology that has been concerned about sin may not be good enough for resolving their problems. The term *theology* consists of *theos* plus *logos,* and its primary focus is *logos,* "reason" and "word." For Asian Americans, the rational aspect of religion has its place but does not help much in their own struggle. To deal with their *han,* a more intuitive term is needed: *Tao.* The word *Tao* literally means "way," "road," or "path," but symbolically denotes a way of living and truth. In lieu of the theology of the *Logos,* Asian American Christians need to develop the theology of the *Tao.*[2] The term *logos* is not a Hebrew, but a Greek, word. Under the Hellenistic civilization, the New Testament writers deliberately chose the word *logos* to explain the activity of God in Jesus Christ. It was a remarkable apologetic move to explain the Way of Jesus Christ. The fact that the Johannine writer adopted the term *logos* from his or her historical and cultural background provides a great foundation for Asian and Asian American biblical hermeneutics and for Asian and Asian American apologetic theologies. The notion of *Tao* helps Asian Americans interpret and understand the Jesus event cross-culturally in connection with the issue of *han.*

Han and Sin

The incident of Wen Ho Lee may help explain the term *han.* Dr. Lee, a Los Alamos computer expert, was charged with fifty-nine counts of criminal activity and was held in solitary confinement for nine months. He was born in Taiwan and is a naturalized U.S. citizen. Because of his ethnicity, he was targeted in an investigation of Chinese espionage at the lab. After his guilty plea in September 2000 to one count of improperly transferring nuclear secrets to portable computer tapes, the remaining fifty-eight charges against him were dropped.

Lee, 60, who had worked at Los Alamos since the 1970s, was the target of an FBI espionage investigation for three years before he was fired. He later was accused of mishandling nuclear secrets—but not espionage—and jailed for nine months before being released in September as part of a plea bargain. The government dropped all but one of its fifty-nine charges against him. Lee's lawyers had argued in court that Lee, an American citizen who was born in Taiwan, became the target of the FBI investigation because of his Chinese heritage. Former Attorney General Janet Reno has denied that Lee was singled out because of his race.[3] This case prompted some ethnic Asian scientists to leave the national laboratories, and the number of Asian postdoctoral fellows at Los Alamos dropped from about seventy in June 1999 to fewer than fifty in 2000.[4]

Until proven guilty, he should not have been treated as a criminal. He had lived in this country more than thirty years as a citizen, yet he was considered a stranger, a foreigner, and a spy prior to trial. His handcuffed and humiliated image, which was transmitted all over the world, represents the plight of Asian Americans in this society. Although being naturalized or born here, Asian Americans remain outsiders, people to be suspected. In this so-called melting-pot society, Asian Americans have been unwelcome and "unmeltable." This enduring rejection by society is *han* for Asian Americans.

Han is a critical wound generated by unjust psychosomatic, social, political, economic, and cultural repression and oppression.[5] It entrenches itself in the souls of the victims of sin and crime, demonstrated by diverse reactions such as those of the survivors of the Nazi Holocaust, the Palestinians in the occupied land, the discriminated-against, the battered, the molested, the abused, and the exploited. It is a festering wound in the broken soul.

Han is a frustrated hope. Hope undergirds our existence: *ex* (out) and *stentia* (standing). We exist because we stand out. This means that we live in hope. Only when we look out, look forward, and look up can we *be*. When hope is frustrated, thwarted, and blocked, it turns into *han,* producing sadness, bitterness, helplessness, and resentment.

Han can arise from either internal repression or external oppression. The *han* of internal repression arises when one earnestly aims at attaining something and is unable to achieve it. It is a self-imposing *han*. The *han* of external oppression emerges when one is sinned against, oppressed, injured, or violated. In this essay we will focus on the *han* of external oppression.

Han has three levels: individual, collective, and structural. At its individual level, it is a reaction to individualistic oppression, which is often connected to collective and structural oppression. At its collective level, *han* is the collective consciousness and unconsciousness of victims, such as the ethos of a cultural inferiority complex, racial lamentation, racial resentment, the sense of physical inadequacy, and national shame. At its structural level, it is a chronic sense of helplessness and resignation before powerful monopolistic capitalism, tenacious racism, pervasive sexism, and repressive classism.

Han is dormant energy. *Han* can be resolved either negatively or positively. When it explodes negatively, the person of *han* seeks revenge and destroys others. When resolved positively, *han* can be the energy to change sinful situations and *han*-causing elements, cutting off the chain of the vicious cycle of sin and *han*.

In general, sin causes *han*, and *han* produces sin. Sin is of oppressors; *han* is of the oppressed. The sin of oppressors may cause a chain reaction via the *han* of the oppressed. Although for convenience we have divided the sin of oppressors and the *han* of the oppressed, most people experience both sin and *han*. Many people who are oppressed in one aspect of life are oppressors in another. The notion of *han* may help us transcend the one-dimensional approach to the problem of the world from the doctrine of sin, liberating Western theology from its own premises. With the rational *(logos)* doctrine of sin alone, Christian theology would be helplessly trapped treating deep issues superficially.

Han *and* Logos

To resolve the *han* in our society, particularly Asian Americans' *han*, it would be good for Western theologies to tap into Eastern insight. The idea of the *logos* may be good for a theology of sin, but is not sufficient to undertake the issue of *han* because *han* has emotive and transrational aspects. For dealing with *han* in Asian American communities, the idea of *Tao* is much more effective. From a Taoist perspective, any forced energy can generate *han*, while natural energy releases people from their *han*. *Tao* is harmonious living with the balance of yin and yang.

Although the synoptic gospel authors did not employ the term *Logos* in describing Jesus' incarnation or mission, the Johannine author adopted this Greek term to help the people of the Hellenistic civilization understand the nature of Jesus' coming. The gospel of John turned the Jewish concept of wisdom into the Greek notion of *logos*. Had the Johannine author lived in Asia, he or she would have used the term *Tao* instead of *Logos* for his or her apologetic work.

In the writing of Heraclitus (c. 490 B.C.E.) we first find the idea of the immanent *Logos*. Heraclitus, a pantheist, speaks of the One as God and God as the universal *Logos* (Reason or Law) pervasive in all things, uniting all things, and determining relentless changes in the world. For him, the One is the primal Fire on the material plane, regulating the Principle of all things.[6] The *Logos* neither transcends the world nor exists before the world, but exists in the world.

Later, Stoicism, founded by Zeno of Citium (c. 300 B.C.E.), developed this idea of the Logos as the primal Fire.[7] It was one of the most prominent traditions in the philosophy of the Hellenistic world. For Stoics, the *Logos* is more than the primal Fire; it is the intelligent, self-conscious world-soul, whose part is our reason. This all-pervading Fire is a single living whole that connects the total universe and determines all particulars. This eternal activity of the primal Fire is called *Logos* or God. More specifically, this productive power is named *logos spermaticos,* the Seminal *Logos* or life-giving Word. We are the offspring of the *Logos,* which resides in us.[8]

In Jewish-Hellenistic philosophy, Philo of Alexandria (c. 25 B.C.E.–40 C.E.) made use of the notion of *Logos* to describe its relation to God. For him, the *Logos* is inferior to God, being the firstborn of God. The *Logos* is placed in the rank of *hosa gegone,* which includes many other agents besides the *Logos,* which is the highest.[9]

The Johannine author (90–100 C.E.) introduces the notion of *Logos* in the beginning of the book to describe the preexistence of Jesus Christ and his full participation in creation. Justin the Martyr (d. c. 165 C.E.) adapted the notion of *Logos* in his apologetic efforts. Following the fashion of Stoicism, the divine *Logos* is omnipresent and is always operative to teach the Greeks, the Jews, and the Barbarians. To him, this all-enlightening divine *Logos* became incarnate in Christ so that the fullness of God is seen.[10]

As seen above, the early Christians freely used the Greek notion of *Logos* to articulate the event of Jesus Christ in the Greco-Roman world.

Tao

A pervasive notion in Far East philosophy is *Tao,* meaning "way" or "path." More precisely, there are two basic types of *Tao.* One is "the eternal *Tao,*" the Ultimate Way or Endless Dynamic Principle of the universe. The other is *"tao,"* a common way or road, implying the ordinary way of life. The former is philosophical; the latter, mundane. In fact, they are inseparable in daily life. In this chapter, although drawing from both, I particularly underscore the *Tao* that Lao tzu delineated in *Tao Te Ching.* Besides Lao tzu, Confucius, Chuang tzu, Buddhists, and others talked about the *Tao.* Confucius had a deep desire to understand *Tao:* "In the morning, hear the Way; in the evening, die content" (Analects 4:8). Since Lao tzu is the founder of Taoism, we will see several traits of *Tao* in *Tao Te Ching.*[11]

Oneness

The *Tao* creates the One, the Great Ultimate or the original material force. The One generates yin and yang. With the One, yin and yang produce the ten thousand things (*Tao Te Ching:* Ch. 42). Whatever obtains the One comes to maximize its potential. Heaven with the One becomes transparent. Earth with the One becomes serene. The valley with the One becomes full. The innumerable things with the One live and grow (*Tao Te Ching:* Ch. 39). The One generates, nurtures, and preserves all things. The universe is an expression of the One in the *Tao*. It does not mean that there is no distinction under the One. Beings and things are distinguished in one form or another. However, a distinction doesn't mean the separation of things and beings, for the One is present.

Reversal

There are priorities in chains of opposites: doing something vs. doing nothing, active vs. passive, male vs. female, full vs. empty, moving vs. still, hard vs. soft, and yang vs. yin. The former categories are preferred in general. Lao tzu reverses the order by preferring the latter categories. He favors yin over yang, female over male, passive over active, and doing nothing over doing something. This inversion is hardly found in Chuang tzu, but is found in Lao tzu from the beginning. Although there is a preference, they are not in conflict, but are complementary.[12] The idea that the softest things rise above the hardest things and that femininity overwhelms masculinity is revolutionary.

No Active Action

Lao tzu taught that all effort and energy to control things are not only useless but destructive. We should simply do nothing *(wu-wei)*. The term *wei* indicates deliberate human action, while *wu* means nothing. Thus, *wu-wei* is the spontaneous process of nature that does not "interfere when things are already running well by themselves."[13] People of *Tao* perceive and go along with the course of nature.

Logos *and* Tao

Tao means more than the Way; it also means the Direction, Process, Purpose, Source, and Destiny. In the Far East, *Tao* needs little explanation. People understand it, just as the common people understood the *Logos* in the world of the Greco-Romans. The *Tao* in the Asian context is as significant to people as the *Logos* was in Hellenism.

Influenced by the thought of Heraclitus, the Stoics held that all reality is material, including God (materialism), but is shaped by a universal working reason (God) that permeates everything (pantheism). God is tied to the world just as the soul is to the body.

The ethical teaching of the Stoics may be summed up in two principles: First, the universe is ruled by absolute law, which knows no exception; second, the indispensable nature of humans is reason. Both recapitulate the famous Stoic maxim, "Live according to nature." In their ethics, the prime virtue is wisdom. The wise are synonymous with the good. From the root-virtue, wisdom, derive the four cardinal virtues: intelligence, bravery, justice, and self-control. Like the *Logos* in Stoicism, the *Tao* is an impersonal supreme Perfection. *Tao* is firmly impartial and uncompassionate.

> Nature is not kind;
> It treats all things impartially.
> The Sage is not kind,
> And treats all people impartially (*Tao Te Ching:* Ch. 5).

Unlike the *Logos* of Stoicism, the *Tao* is the source of all being and nonbeing, producing the universe. The *Logos* in Stoicism is absolute reason. It did not create the world, but permeates all matter as the primal Fire. This *Logos* is God, the principle of order regulating the universe. But the Johannine author used a concept of the *Logos* that differs from that of Stoicism. The *Logos* of the Johannine author is ultimate, yet participates in creation. Like the *Logos* of the Johannine author, the *Tao* is ultimate, yet participates in creation: "Tao produces the One. The One produced the two. The two produced the three. And the three produced the ten thousand things. The ten thousand things carry the yin and embrace the yang, and through the blending of the material force *(chi)* they achieve harmony" (*Tao Te Ching:* Ch. 42).

The reality of *Tao* affirms the goodness of creation, and the way of Nature is *Tao*. In this sense, it casts out the view of dualism. It celebrates creation and life.

The Fourth Gospel heavily uses the notion of *Logos:*

> In the beginning was the *[Logos],* and the *[Logos]* was with God, and the *[Logos]* was God. He was in the beginning with God. All things came into being through him, and without him not one thing came into being. What has come into being in him was life, and the life was the light of all people. (Jn. 1:1–4)

If the Johannine writer were a Far East Asian, the Fourth Gospel would begin with the term *Tao*. It fits the description of the introduction of the Fourth Gospel:

> In the beginning was the [*Tao*], and the [*Tao*] was with God, and the [*Tao*] was God. [*Tao*] was in the beginning with God. All things came into being through the [*Tao*], and without [*Tao*] not one thing came into being. What has come into being in [*Tao*] was life, and the life was the light of all people.

In fact, some Chinese Bible translations use the term *Tao* instead of *Logos*. Furthermore, as the *Logos* becomes flesh, the *Tao* comes to be flesh.

The *Tao* created the universe. Can the *Tao* be a person? Of course the *Tao* is not a personal God, but is an impersonal Being. This can be astounding news to Asians: "How can the *Tao* become a human being?" That was the shock the Johannine writer created in the Hellenistic world when he or she declared that the *Logos* became flesh. Far East Asians will not feel much when they hear that the *Logos* became flesh, but when they hear that the *Tao* became flesh, they will be amazed.

To Asians and Asian Americans, it is more challenging to accept Jesus Christ as the *Tao* than as the *Logos.* The concept of *Jesus' Tao* immediately calls Far East Asians and Asian Americans to engage in dialogue with Christian truth. Therefore, we should use and develop the term *Tao* to make the Christ event alive in the inner hearts of Asian Americans and Asians.

Tao *as the Way of the Cross*

According to Lao tzu, "the pursuit of Tao is to decrease day after day" (*Tao Te Ching:* Ch. 48).Why do we have to decrease everyday in order to follow *Tao?* This saying is related to Jesus' "self-denial": "If any want to become my followers, let them deny themselves and take up their cross daily and follow me" (Lk. 9:23). To follow Jesus, we need to walk in his Way *(Tao).* Taking up the cross of Jesus is pursuing *Tao* with him. It means to transcend self-centeredness:

> Therefore the sage
> Puts himself last,
> Finds himself first;
> Abandons his self,
> Preserves his self.
> Is it not because he has no self
> That he is able to realize his self?[14]

To be selfless is not to cut off our limbs from ourselves, but to choose our great self by decreasing our small self. To pursue our great self, we should go after Jesus' *Tao,* not our own. Jesus' *Tao* is the way of the cross.

Far East Asians call Christianity "the *Tao* of the cross." To take up our daily cross denotes having no self. It is the act of emptying what we have and what we are. Emptying can be interpreted from two perspectives. One is from the perspective of the oppressors; the other from the perspective of the oppressed. For the oppressors, *Tao* means to empty their avarice and their power-worship so that they may fill the resulting emptiness with *Tao:*

> Therefore in the government of the sage,
> He keeps their hearts vacuous *(hsü),*
> Fills their bellies,
> Weakens their ambitions,
> And strengthens their bones. (*Tao Te Ching:* 3).

The oppressors should relinquish the monopoly of their power–political, economic, social, moral, and spiritual. To empty themselves signifies the letting go of their power and influence.

For the oppressed, *Tao* signifies the emptying of their denied selves. Because they are already denied or rejected by the oppressors and internalize the rejected images, they do not need to deny themselves. They need to uphold their worth by affirming themselves. For them, self-denial does not mean to reject themselves again, but to deny their denied selves or to refuse to accept the internalized self-images projected by the oppressors, so that their genuine selves may emerge. Lao tzu says, "Therefore the sage knows himself but does not show himself. He loves himself but does not exalt himself. Therefore he rejects the one but accepts the other" (*Tao Te Ching:* Ch. 72). The oppressed should negate the negated self and accept the genuine self.

Among the oppressed, many endure the agony of *han*. For the *han*-full, the *Tao* of the cross denotes the emptying of their *han*. Everyday they eviscerate their *han*. How do they do that? They can do that paradoxically. If they want to draw on their *han* only, they may not achieve their goal. Alleviating their own *han* begins only when they serve the needs of other wounded people and try to help and heal them. In the process, the *han*-laden experience their own wounds well. For the oppressed, healing others' *han* starts the process of emptying themselves. It involves acknowledging their own *han* and finding, accepting, and loving themselves by unraveling others' and their own *han*-laden selves. This takes place while the *han*-laden begin to embrace the *Tao* of the cross–filling their own emptiness with *Tao*'s emptiness. Emptying their own emptiness is filling their hearts with God.

Furthermore, to implement the *Tao* of the cross, the *han*-laden need to move beyond self. They need to work on social transformation in *Tao*.

The people of *Tao*, however, do not force anything, including social transformation. They know that any forced action will generate a vicious cycle of coercion. Any violent action produces a violent reaction, resulting in *han*. They know how to wait for bringing forth change in the course of nature. They aim at a fundamental change, not a superficial one. The fundamental change starts with self-transformation and spreads to social reformation. It is not their own work that makes transformation possible, but the *Tao* or the power of the Holy Spirit. Through the *Tao* of the cross, people of *Tao* are crucified with Christ so that the power of the Holy Spirit may use them as channels to elicit necessary fundamental changes. The *Tao* seeks a silent revolution–a holistic one.

For instance, racism is a sin and a *han*-causing reality in our society. How does *Tao* help to reduce racial prejudice and discrimination? It can be achieved through a yin and yang balance. The yin and yang balance may be achieved as the structural change of a racist society (yang) and the internal change of the heart of racial prejudice (yin) concur. No social change should be unilaterally imposed on others without first starting to convert racist hearts. If forced, change turns into repression, continuing the vicious cycle of sin and *han*. No internal change is effectively viable without structural change. If it happens unilaterally, the change grows into frustration and despair. If there is to be a long-term change, it should take place in a natural way (Tao), balancing personal and social changes:

> Tao invariably takes no action, and yet there is nothing left undone. If kings and barons can keep it, all things will transform spontaneously. If, after transformation, they should desire to be active, I would restrain them with simplicity, which has no name. Simplicity, which has no name, is free of desires. (*Tao Te Ching:* Ch. 37)

The *Tao* seeks no active transformation, but lets natural transformation come about. We can work for changing racist laws and discrimination, but cannot force the altering of racist prejudice. The change of racist laws and structure must coincide with the change of racists' hearts. No one can legislate the change of people's hearts, which only happens naturally and spontaneously. This explains why *Tao* takes no action.

Moreover, to melt the *han* of racism permanently, we need to be reunited with the One. When we are in union with *Tao,* no evil can harm us. Uniting with the One signifies death to ourselves on the cross. When dead in *Tao,* we can live with *Tao.* As the *Tao* of Jesus lives in us, it is no longer we who live in us but Jesus who died for us (Gal. 2:20). By dying with the *Tao* of Jesus, we can transcend all evil power:

> Close the mouth.
> Shut the doors (of cunning and desires),
> Blunt the sharpness.
> Untie the tangles.
> Soften the light.
> Become one with the dusty world.
>
> This is called profound identification (or "the original oneness")
>
> Therefore it is impossible either to be intimate and close to him or to be distant and indifferent to him.
> It is impossible either to benefit him or to harm him,
> It is impossible either to honor him or to disgrace him.
> For this reason he is honored by the world. (*Tao Te Ching:* Ch. 56)

Lao tzu maintains that if our understanding of the world is based primarily on the union with the One, nothing can disturb our peace of mind. The ultimate way to resolve *han* is to be in union with the One–the *Tao.* In the act of union with the *Tao,* the *han*-laden will experience transcendence of their *han* and release themselves from *han*. To cultivate this oneness, people need to empty themselves and dance with the *Tao*. Dancing calls for attuning to the voice of the *Tao*.

Tao *as Water*

Attuning with the *Tao* is following its nature. The *Tao* is the Cosmic Way, reflecting the unending dynamics of the universe. To understand the *Tao* is to live in perfect accord with Heaven and Earth that is, the cosmic order. Water explains the way of the *Tao*.

> The best (man) is like water.
> Water is good; it benefits all things and does not compete with them.
> It dwells in (lowly) places that all disdain.
> This is why it is so near to Tao.
> [The best man] in his dwelling loves the earth.
> In his heart, he loves what is profound.
> In his associations, he loves humanity.
> In his words, he loves faithfulness.
> In government, he loves order.
> In handling affairs, he loves competence.
> In his activities, he loves timeliness.
> It is because he does not compete that he is without reproach.
> (*Tao Te Ching:* Ch. 8)

Water epitomizes the nature of the *Tao*. The persons of *Tao* conduct themselves as water, bringing forth benefit and goodness to others. They would rather choose a lower place, yet they are highly esteemed; compete against none yet win for all; achieve nothing yet fulfill dreams for all. The persons of *Tao* love people, goodness, profundity, integrity, truthfulness, and propriety because these are natural ways. The action of *Tao* causes no jealousy, resistance, or resentment.

The *Tao* as water assuages the wound of *han*. Its natural action prevents any *han*-causing and calms simmering *han*. It helps a victim of sin not return evil with evil but with good: "Act without action. Do without ado. Taste without tasting. Whether it is big or small, many or few, repay hatred with virtue" (*Tao Te Ching:* Ch. 63). Hatred is not a natural way and will pass away. Virtue is the way of the *Tao* for us to follow. So we need to leave it behind: "To patch up great hatred is surely to leave some hatred behind" (*Tao Te Ching:* Ch. 79). Like water under the bridge, we let hatred go. We do not cling to it. This act of nonaction does not mean "let injustice run." It indicates its quiet opposite: "transform injustice from its foundation, let injustice go, and usher justice in."

Like water, the *Tao* gently flows around a rock, yet overcomes its roughness and toughness. It is fluid and soft, but overcomes the strong and the hard. "There is nothing softer and weaker than water, and yet there is

nothing better for attacking hard and strong things" (*Tao Tè Ching:* Ch. 78).
The *Tao's* weakness is stronger than human strength (cf. 1 Cor. 1:25). While
passing a hard rock (racism, sexism, and authoritarianism), it reshapes its
form slowly and surely. The person of *Tao* exercises true strength, not violent
power, to change evil at the personal and social levels (*Tao Tè Ching:* Ch. 8).
While letting go their pain of *han,* the wounded challenge the wrongs of
offenders through integrity, softness, persistence, mercy, and order. Water
is the symbol of healing, changing sin and evil into the energy of construction
for a community.

Jesus as the Way (*Tao*)

Tao in a common usage is the way that connects us with other ways.
There is no island in the *tao*. Everything is related to everything else. No
way exists in disconnection or isolation. If a road is isolated, by definition
that is not a way but a dead end. The *tao* connects people, ideas, and visions.
The *tao* interweaves cultures, races, values, hopes, and beliefs. It does not
promote a religion, but a way of living together. Religious beliefs may
divide people, but the *tao* connects people. It excludes no one but includes
all races, ethnicities, genders, sexual orientations, beliefs, statuses, and ages.
The *tao* is connected to the eternal *Tao,* pointing to a direction of truth. The
eternal *Tao* is the direction itself. The *tao* leads us home. While the *tao* is the
way home, the eternal *Tao* is the home itself.

As Christians, we believe that the eternal *Tao* became flesh in Jesus
Christ. Jesus is the Way. Here, Jesus meets our *tao*, our way. Walking along
with us, Jesus beckons us to follow his Way. As soon as we respond to his
beckoning, we walk on the *Tao* of Christ. Jesus does not belong to any
religion, including Christianity. Jesus was never a Christian. He came to
show us the Way of living according to God's purpose of creation. Had all
human beings lived in God's will, Christ would not have become flesh. In
a similar vein, *Tao Tè Ching* says, "When the great Tao declined, the doctrines
of humanity *(jen)* and righteousness *(i)* arose" (*Tao Tè Ching:* Ch. 18). Because
the *Tao* degenerates in the world, it was necessary for the *Tao* of God to
become incarnate. If people followed God's will, there would be no need
for the coming of Jesus or the rise of the *Tao* in the form of humanity and
righteousness. Jesus Christ was interested not in establishing an institutional
religion, but in spreading the Way of God's will. If the way of nature is in
the divine will, it signifies the way of nature as God's will. Thus, the *Tao* can
be interpreted as divine will or the mandate of heaven itself.

If we use the term *Tao* for Asian American and Asian believers, we can
transcend the acrimonious relationship between Christianity and other
religions. In an Asian context, the concept of *Logos* (Word) is very foreign
to everyone, but the term *Tao* is intuitively understood. Before the existence
of Christianity, the Jesus movement was called the Way *(hodos)*: "If [Saul]
found any who belonged to the Way, men or women, he might bring them

bound to Jerusalem" (Acts 9:2b). The early followers of Jesus Christ devoted their time to spreading the Way: "[Apollos] began to speak boldly in the synagogue; but when Priscilla and Aquila heard him, they took him aside and explained the Way of God to him more accurately" (Acts 18:26). If the church had not propagated Christianity but the *Tao* (the Way of God), it could have cooperated with other major religions in spreading the *Tao* of Jesus. In the first century, the mission of Jesus' followers was to share the Way of God, not a set of dogmas. The *Tao* does not stress a belief system, but the Way of God or the Way of Life. When we focus on how to live together according to divine will or *Tao,* religious strife subsides while religious cooperation thrives.

Whereas the *Logos* is the Word or Reason, the *Tao* is the Way. Jesus is the Way, Truth, and Life (Jn. 14:6); the *Tao* is the Way, Truth, and Natural Living itself. In contrast with Jesus as the *Logos,* Jesus as the *Tao* naturally affects Asians and Asian Americans. Thus, emphasizing Jesus' Way will open a new and exciting door to Christian mission.

In addition, the *Tao* underlines love. One of its three treasures is deep love *(Ts'e),* which connotes a motherly quality. Jesus taught us love. He stressed the divine love that is symbolically fatherly. Jesus is the love of God. In Taoism the love of heaven is the *Tao.*

I have three treasures. Guard and keep them:

The first is deep love,
The second is frugality,
And the third is not to dare to be ahead of the world.
Because of deep love, one is courageous.
Because of frugality, one is generous.
Because of not daring to be ahead of the world, one becomes
the leader of the world...

For deep love helps one to win in the case of attack,
And to be firm in the case of defense.
When Heaven is to save a person,
Heaven will protect him through deep love. (*Tao Te Ching:* Ch. 67)

The way of Jesus and the *Tao* concurs in love. For Jesus, loving God and loving neighbors sums up the essence of the scriptures. For the tradition of *Tao,* heavenly love and human love are interconnected in courage and generosity. Without love, human courage and virtuous frugality can be blind, scratching only the surface of our problems, bearing little fruit. Deep love is the most fundamental nature of the *Tao.* Based on this love, our courage and virtues can be useful in partaking of the Heaven that saves people. These two Ways of Jesus and *Tao* lead us to deep love, which liberates human beings from forcedness and artificiality.

Conclusion

In closing, the sins and crimes of diverse oppressions are rampant in our society. Asian Americans have experienced *han* as a major issue. To these *han*-laden people, it is more vital and significant to develop a theology of *Tao* than a theology of the *Logos*.

If the vicious cycle of *han* and sin are unresolved for a long time, evil arises as its consequence. The *Tao* can resolve *han* and sin in their entanglement. It defeats sin at its root not by violent reaction or oppression but by a natural process. The strength of the *Tao* is to persuade people rather than to force them not to do a wrong or commit a crime. The *Tao* depends on inspiring people to do what is right. It also supports a structural effort to change the world only if it is based on natural order, not on unnatural chaos. The action of nonaction is the key to attuning with the nature of the *Tao*. No coerced system can peacefully lead the world, for violent actions are bound to generate violent reactions. The ultimate strength is gentle persuasion, soft defiance, and deep love.

The *Tao* heals the wound of *han* at its depth. *Han* is rooted not only in consciousness (mind), but also in unconsciousness (spirit). Through "doing nothing," the *Tao* makes people's *han* whole. The natural course of life takes good care of *han*'s wounds. The cross and water symbolize the process to heal *han,* and they signify the gentle challenge to change sin and evil at personal and structural levels. The ultimate way to resolve *han* is, however, to be in union with the One–the *Tao.* The *Tao* makes the negative energy of *han* transform into the energy of creativity and construction. This personification of the *Tao* in Jesus Christ, one that embodies love, gentleness, and true human-heartedness in the universe, is the way we should take in our journey to healing *han*.

Notes

[1] Generally, sinners undergo guilt, while the *han*-laden experience shame.

[2] Since the term *theology* itself consists of *theos* and *logos,* technically speaking it is more accurate to describe the theology of the *Tao* as *TheoTao.* But for the sake of familiarity, we will use the expression, "theology of the *Tao*." Some Asian scholars have worked on this issue of *Tao* and *Logos:* Tong Sik Ryu, *Tao and Logos* (Seoul: The Christian Literature Society, 1978); Kay-Keng Khoo, "Logos, Tao and Wisdom," *Ching Feng* (June 1997); Heup Young Kim, "Toward a Christotao: Jesus as the Theanthropocosmic Tao," paper presented at the annual meeting of the American Academy of Religion, Boston, November 1999.

[3] CNN, "U.S. Energy Secretary Seeks Racial Profiling Investigation," 9 October 2000. http://www.cnn.com/2000/US/10/09/racial.profiling.ap.

[4] CNN, "Morale at Los Alamos Improves as Lee Case Fades," 19 October 2000. http://www.cnn.com/2000/US/10/19/los.alamos.morale.ap.

[5] *Han* is a term that Korean *minjung* (downtrodden) theologians began to employ in the 1970s. See Yong Bock Kim, ed., *Minjung Theology* (Singapore: The Christian Conference of Asia, 1981).

[6]Frederick Copleston, *A History of Philosophy,* vol. 1 (New York: Image Books, 1946), 43.

[7]Ibid., 502.

[8]Williston Walker, *A History of the Christian Church* (New York: Charles Scribner's Sons, 1959), 7.

[9]Copleston, *History of Philosophy,* 458–59.

[10]Walker, *History of Christian Church,* 46–47.

[11]I am using the translation by Wing-Tsit Chan, "*Tao-te ching,*" in *A Source Book in Chinese Philosophy* (Princeton: Princeton University Press, 1969).

[12]A. C. Graham, *Disputers of the Tao: Philosophical Argument in Ancient China* (La Salle, Ill.: Open Court, 1989), 223–31.

[13]Ibid., 232.

[14]Herrymon Mauer, trans., *The Way of the Ways* (New York: Schocken Books, 1985), chap. 7.

4

Beyond Orientalism and Assimilation

The Asian American as Historical Subject

TIMOTHY TSENG

The Color-line in American Religious Historiography

*On the contrary, I am not asking for trouble. I am troubled. I am
disturbed about the slow response of the guild of religious historians to
the intellectual and moral implications of not having far more religious
historians who are deeply conscious and knowledgeable about the history
of pseudospeciation.*

–James M. Washington[1]

Historian David Wills has observed that American religious
historiography has centered on two themes: (1) pluralism and toleration,
and (2) Puritanism and collective purpose. Many historical narratives
accentuate the "triumph of democratic pluralism" in American religion
and claim that "the problem of religious diversity" has been successfully
solved. The U.S. Constitution and the First Amendment is viewed as the
"crucial landmark in the emergence of a normative religious pluralism in
America." The separation of church and state was an initial step on the
way to the age of religious pluralism that was somewhat realized in the
middle of the twentieth century. These narratives have located the origins
of American religious liberty in the stories of Roger Williams and Anne
Hutchinson and the histories of Rhode Island and the mid-Atlantic colonies.

Other narratives have bemoaned the loss of the Puritan sense of
collective purpose. However oppressive they may have been toward
religious dissenters, Puritans are to be admired for their sense of a common
purpose that stood apart from "the prevailing privatism and individualism

of much of our subsequent history–including our religious history." These narratives have focused on New England Puritanism as the primary site for the origin of American religion.

Wills then suggests that a missing theme in American religious historiography is the Southern experience. Advocates of the aforementioned themes have attempted to assimilate the Southern story but may have missed the latter's central defining focus, namely, "the problematic encounter of black and white." This theme "tests the limits of all our views of pluralism and undermines every attempt to formulate a sense of collective purpose." Wills then shows how the gap between black and white shrank and expanded throughout periods of evangelical and ecumenical preeminence in the United States. He concludes:

> Since the late 1960s, there has been a clear retreat from a direct facing of the gap between black and white as it was then so strikingly revealed. Laments for the loss of community in America and calls for a renewal of collective purpose are once more issued and debated with little or no mention of the realities of race. Religious pluralism in the United States is analyzed and celebrated with little acknowledgment that the polarities of race in our history are not quite the same thing as the varieties of our religion. Acknowledged or not, however, the gap between the races–a gap involving both the interpretation of American experience and the degree of empowerment within it–remains one of the foundational realities of our national life. And however much members of both races might sometimes wish it were otherwise, the painful encounter of black and white is likely to remain in the future what it has been in the past–one of the crucial, central themes in the religious history of the United States.[2]

Wills' analysis goes beyond simply adding the history of African American religion to the existing American religious historiography. He is suggesting that W. E. B. DuBois's idea of the "color-line" is central to understanding how the story of American religion is told. With this important statement about how historians interpret the past, he affirms the late James M. Washington's observation that "the intellectual challenge posed by the problem of expanding the historian's field of vision is more than a methodological difficulty for church historians. It is an epistemological and cosmological problem as well." Washington calls for a "new aesthetics" that would allow church historians to "value and see more of the grand panorama they are so privileged to survey."[3]

Developing a "new aesthetics" is critical for historians of American religion because it has implications for how the stories of various communities, especially those marginalized from the grand narratives, are interpreted. Both Wills and Washington call for greater attention to race and racial encounter in the interpretation of American religious history, and not only for more research of racialized religious communities. Indeed, like other scholars, historians of racialized communities enter the "field" with preconceived interpretive theories that often determine how the histories of these communities are told. These preconceived and often not clearly developed theories are invariably linked to a historiography shaped and developed largely from the perspectives of white American historians.

Wills' analysis of the themes of American religious historiography, however, is limited to a "black-white" paradigm. Without denying the significance of the encounter between black and white, biracialism runs the risk of either excluding other racialized communities or assimilating their distinct encounters with whites into the "black-white" paradigm. While there are great similarities between Asian and black encounters with whites, the Asian-white encounter has a distinct history and character. The same can be said about European and white American perceptions of Asians.

"Color-Blinded by the Light: Asian Americans and American Religious History"

Among America's half-million Japanese as among its quarter-million Chinese, the tendency to Christian affiliation has been very strong. Especially since 1945 ethnic religious commitments have not figured prominently in their self-consciousness as peoples. White anti-Oriental hostility has also markedly waned.

–Sydney Ahlstrom[4]

The interpretation of Asian Americans by historians of American religion has been dominated by a particular view that, for our purposes, can be labeled "Orientalist." Since Edward Said's groundbreaking study of European social scientific and other literature pertaining to the Islamic world in the nineteenth and twentieth centuries, Asian American scholars have applied his central ideas to analyze the encounters between Asians and white Americans.[5] Said asserts that the "Orient" is a Western construct and "a system of ideological fictions." The purpose of this representation is to justify Western colonial domination over the "Orient" and to establish Western supremacy.[6] While Said's very somber view focuses on the Middle East and Islam, other scholars have somewhat more positive perspectives with regard to European and American perceptions of South and East Asian societies. J. J. Clarke, for instance, argues that the Asian Orient was often romanticized and constructed as a means of critiquing the foibles of Western culture. Nevertheless, even in its critique of the West, this gentler form of Orientalism continues to serve the purposes of "the West" and reveals more about the West than about the so-called Orient.[7] Americans in the mid-nineteenth century, for instance, held a sympathetic view of Asians that coexisted with absolute confidence in Western supremacy. T. Christopher Jespersen notes how missionaries, Henry R. Luce's *Time* magazine, United China Relief, and other China lobbyists projected a favorable image of

China that also reflected a glowing American self-image in the early twentieth century. Luce believed that under the guidance of well-intentioned Americans, China would develop into a Christian democracy.[8] Though sympathetic, this type of Orientalist representation of Asia does not reflect the views of Asians themselves. Thus, Said's central point linking American Orientalism with racialized power and privilege remains a crucial thesis.[9]

To assert that American religious historiography has viewed Asian Americans through Orientalist lenses is to suggest that Asian Americans have been perceived as innately foreign or completely assimilated. This is no less true for American historiography in general and popular perceptions as well. Historian Gary Okihiro contends that the images of the "yellow peril" and the "model minority" are "flip sides of the same coin" of the American racial construction of Asian Americans.[10] In other words, whatever it is that makes Asians different from what is considered American is construed as something that is permanent or something to be erased. The few contemporary American religious historians who give attention to Asian Americans gravitate toward either an assimilationist reading of the Asian American Christianity or a sentimentalized and disembodied Orientalist reading of non-Christian Asian religious communities. Asian cultural difference is either erased beneath the canopy of white Christianity or constructed as the "other" (especially for the sake of religious toleration). Furthermore, both the traditional study of Christian history and the comparative religious studies approach to American religious history have been "color-blind" to the racialized aspects of the Asian American experience. In part, this "color-blindness" has been created by and continues to perpetuate Orientalism in American religious historiography.

Influenced by the social history and comparative religious studies, some recent American religious histories have given greater attention to the growing presence of Eastern religious beliefs and practices in the United States. One particular text broke new ground on the traditional Protestant-centered and intellectual history–oriented study of American religious history. In 1981, Catherine L. Albanese's *America: Religions and Religion* opened the doors to viewing American religious history from the perspective of a religious pluralism that went beyond (while acknowledging) Protestantism's centrality in shaping American religion. Now in its third edition, *America: Religions and Religion* devotes an entire chapter to Eastern religions in the United States.[11] However, the book reproduces an Orientalist framework by lumping Eastern Orthodox Christianity, Islam, Hinduism, and Buddhism together into one chapter.

As significant as Albanese's text has been in the study of American religious history, the tendency of this approach has been to utilize a comparative religious studies approach in their narratives about Asian Americans. This has often led to the exclusive identification of Asian Americans with Eastern religions. For instance, in Amanda Porterfield's recent study of late-twentieth-century America, she asserts:

> After severe restrictions on Asian Immigration were lifted in 1965, Asians became the largest immigrant group in the United States. Buddhists from Korea, Vietnam, Japan, Tibet, Sri Lanka, Burma, Cambodia, Laos, and Thailand established new temples and religious centers in the United States making this country home to more cradle Buddhists than ever before, as well as to more different forms of Buddhism than any other country in the world.[12]

Latino and Hispanic people might dispute the claim that Asians are the largest immigrant group in the United States, but it is clear that Porterfield strongly identifies Asian Americans with Buddhism. She also connects Asian Indians with Hinduism and discusses Islam; and there is virtually no reference to Asian Christianity or popular religion.

Another example can be found in Jacob Neusner's textbook for introductory courses on American religion, *World Religions in America*. This textbook recognizes the significance of racialized religious communities and gender by devoting chapters to African Americans, Hispanic Americans, and women. But the chapters about Asian religions do not address the history and experiences of Asian Americans themselves.[13] Thomas Tweed and Stephen Prothero's *Asian Religions in America: A Documentary History* does a more satisfactory job of including texts written by Asian Americans who practice East Asian religions. Unlike the aforementioned texts, *Asian Religions in America* is able to bring together race and East Asian Religions. It includes bell hooks's reflections on the racial divide within American Buddhism and is periodized around the history of Asian immigration.[14]

These studies are important because they broaden our understanding of the growing religious diversity in the United States. They are calls to respect difference and embrace inclusivity. As such, they can be said to reflect David Will's "pluralist" narrative typology. There is an implicit vision of the United States as a cosmopolitan "city on a hill" from which the light of liberty emanates to the world. In their descriptions of non-Christian religions in America, these texts can be seen as efforts to critique the hegemony of European religion, society, and culture.[15] Their tendency to exclude Asian American Christian narratives, however, reveals an excessive dependency on phenomenology or comparative studies of religion to interpret "Eastern" religions. Consequently, even though they question the dominance of Christianity in "Western" societies, they reproduce the Orientalist tendency to reify the difference between East and West. Narratives of white American appropriation of "Eastern" religions may challenge the assumption of Christian hegemony in Europe and the Americas, but they do not critique Orientalist interpretations of Asians. Religious Asians, therefore, are required to be viewed through the lenses of "Eastern" religions.

At the heart of the matter are the problematic assumptions of religious studies itself. According to Timothy Fitzgerald, the discourses of liberal ecumenical theology, comparative religion, and the phenomenology of religion are all framed within a Western understanding of "religion." These assumed universal categories are then imposed on non-Western cultures and do not adequately represent Asians within their own historical and social contexts.[16] Whether or not one agrees with Fitzgerald's scathing critique of religious studies, by describing Asian culture and religions ahistorically, much of European American–based religious studies have interpreted Asians and Asian Americans through the lens of Orientalism.

It is important to note that that the comparativist religious and phenomenological approaches have not been the only challenges to "traditional" (i.e., Protestant-centered) American religious historiography. In recent years, the introduction of social scientific disciplines such as anthropology and postmodern sociology have greatly broadened the historical field. David Lotz notes that since 1965 the "new social histories" have dramatically transformed American *church* history into American *religious* history. The change in location of religious historians from the seminary to university settings, the "decline of Protestant Christendom" in the United States and Canada, and the "growth of a radical religious pluralism" have all contributed to this shift from a theologically oriented intellectual history to a secularized social historical approach. The impact of the new social history on American religious history became the subject of a historians' conference at Racine, Wisconsin, in 1993. Participants were asked to bring the "old 'Church History'–Protestant centered and intellectually based–into dialogue with the new, nonmainline-centered and socially based 'religious history.'" Out of this conference came a significant text named after the conference itself, *New Directions in American Religious History.* Most of the essays reflected substantial re-thinking of the more traditional Protestant-oriented historiography, and a few addressed the impact of studies of gender, ethnicity, and race on the field.[17] In the same year that *New Directions* appeared, another edited reassessment of American religious history, *Retelling U.S. Religious History,* was published. This text, more explicitly than *New Directions,* suggested new approaches to interpreting American religious history. It even included essays that sought to view American religious history from the perspectives of the Pacific Rim and Native American communities.[18]

Despite these changes, Asian Americans have still not received much attention from American religious historians. As early as 1993, in an essay reviewing the scholarship in American religious history in the 1980s, Martin E. Marty bemoaned the absence of research in Asian American religious history.[19] In his own recent project on modern American religion, Marty gives significant attention to the history of Asians in the United States as victims of discrimination, conveyors of Eastern Religion. He also briefly discusses Asian American Christianity. Overall, though, his treatment of the Asian American religious experience is still limited to secondary sources.[20] This is understandable because so few scholars are examining Asian American religious history. Less clear is why ten years after Marty's *Church History* article first appeared, there is still only a handful of scholars examining Asian American religious history.

There is another reason for Asian American invisibility in recent American religious historiography. Though the "traditional" Protestant-centered narratives have broadened in recent years, its disciplinary assumptions remain rooted in an assimilationist or "color-blind" framework. This framework prevents American historians of religion from seeing Asian American religious people as historical subjects.[21]

Unlike the pluralist histories that interpret Asian Americans through the lens of religious difference, these historians view the Asian American experience as one of inevitable cultural assimilation. Thus, Sidney Ahlstrom was able to claim in 1972–without citation of sources–that among Chinese and Japanese Americans "ethnic religious commitments have not figured prominently in their self-consciousness as peoples."[22]

I argue that the religious historian's journey to an assimilationist interpretation of the Asian American experience begins with discomfort with racial or ethnic difference. There is more comfort with religious diversity, though ecumenical unity is often favored over schism and separatism. Edwin Gaustad, one of the most respected "traditional" American religious historians, illustrates this point of view in his popular survey textbook. He associates Asian immigrants with Asian religions:

> Similarly (as in the case of Chinese immigrants), the influx of Japanese along the West Coast, even more in Hawaii, led to sharp restrictions of those who would introduce Buddhism and Shinto, even as the Chinese had brought with them Confucianism and Taoism. Nonetheless, despite unmistakable anti-Oriental prejudices and actions, Asian religions established their beach heads all along the Pacific shores, never to be successfully dislodged therefrom.[23]

Gaustad values the religious diversity created by Asian immigrants, but is less sanguine about racial diversity. Racial segregation is considered a failure on the part of American religion. "The nation's religious forces were no more effective in promoting a blindness to race with respect to the Oriental than they had been with respect to the black," he acknowledges. The inability of early missionaries and schools to Christianize and Americanize "these distinctive immigrants" created "ethnically restricted churches" such as "the Korean Baptist Church, the Chinese Methodist Church, [and] the Japanese Presbyterian Church." For Gaustad, ethnic-specific congregations do not have innate value because their existence is primarily a reflection of white American racial consciousness. The Japanese American internment camp experience during World War II occurred because Americans "continued to see so much through race-colored glasses."

But the physical presence of Asians on American soil also fueled racist policies. "The large Oriental presence," Gaustad asserts, "was a major factor in making the nation's immigration policy far more restrictive in the early decades of the twentieth century." He concludes that though ethnicity could be "sometimes seen as enriching and brightening the whole fabric of American society, it could also be regarded as detrimental to social cohesion and religious destiny."[24] When Asian presence and white prejudice are paired in this manner, the implicit resolution is the erasure of Asian difference in the American mind.

There is no doubt that the recognition of racial differences has led to racism and social strife. But nonrecognition or erasure of racial difference has not proven to be a solution either. Racial tensions that develop in contexts of both enforced assimilation and segregation suggest social dynamics that are much more complex than the mere presence of racial difference. Indeed, power dynamics, patterns of privilege, and the ideology of race that lie beneath the surface of racial difference need to be examined more carefully by American religious historians. Until that day arrives, the current default historical interpretation of Asian Americans by American religious historians remains, viewing Asian Americans as the religious "other" or the racially assimilated.

The Historical Construction of Assimilation

From a more sober standpoint, church historians must not only come to grips with the exclusion of minority people from their histories of the church, but they must also try to determine why they overlooked them in the first place.

–James M. Washington[25]

What accounts for an "assimilationist" reading of Asian American religious history (and of Asian American Protestantism in particular)? American religious historians have depended greatly on the influential sociological theories that emerged from the University of Chicago between the two World Wars. Such theories assumed a unidirectional embrace of modern, democratic, and cosmopolitan values on the part of the descendents of immigrants. The research from which these theories were derived mostly centered on experiences of European immigrants. Yet sociologists such as Robert Park were confident that they could be applied to blacks and Asians as well. The assimilation of difference, as evidenced by fully acculturated (so it seemed) Asian Americans such as Flora Belle Jan, a flapper in the 1920s, would undermine the credibility of linking perceived intellectual capability and cultural value to biological definitions of race.

The Chicago sociologists were instrumental in tearing down the intellectual foundations of segregationist public policies. But as historian

Henry Yu has noted, these sociologists, who valued detached objectivity, were unable to see the racial undertones of assimilation. Their vision of a modern, democratic, and cosmopolitan society that embraces all peoples was itself rooted in the racialized perspectives of particular white sociologists. Consequently, though they contributed to mid-century movements toward racial integration, they could not value racial diversity or cultural preservation.[26]

One of the consequences of over-dependency on these social theories was mainline Protestant retreat from missionary work among Asian Americans after World War II. Mainline Protestants assumed that Asian Americans (as well as all immigrants) would inevitably assimilate into the mainstream and therefore did not require any special attention. Though many Asian Americans in these denominations have worked tirelessly to rectify this benign neglect through the caucus movements in the 1970s, mainline Protestants have not had a good record of incorporating the large numbers of Asian American immigrants since 1965.

A consequence of historians' dependency on sociological theories of assimilation has been a tendency to subsume Asian Americans within the narrative of immigration historiography. Singled out as an undesirable and unassimilable race, Asian Americans experienced greater discrimination than most European immigrants between the Civil War and the Second World War. But historians and social scientists after World War II have usually assumed that Asian Americans overcame these initial antagonisms by integrating into the American mainstream. The negative images of the "Oriental heathen" in the latter half of the nineteenth century appeared to have vanished by the middle of the twentieth century. But on closer inspection, the journey from the "exotic Oriental" to the racially inferior "Asiatic" and, finally, to the nicely assimilated "model minority" was neither historically plausible nor sociologically demonstrable. The transition to "model minority" was especially problematic, for it assumed that assimilation was a natural process for Asian Americans. Ignoring their struggles to overcome anti-Asian racism, many historians have implied that Asian Americans, like European immigrants, have moved beyond the "race relations" problems. This is true despite the recent modification and/ or repudiation of Robert E. Park's theories of assimilation.[27]

It would be far too simplistic to conclude that the inability of mainline Protestant denominational leaders and American religious historians to understand Asian Americans was a result of their dependency on sociology. To a very large extent, these social theories themselves reflected the hopes and aspirations of American Protestants at the turn of the twentieth century. I suggest that an assimilationist discourse was largely an American Protestant construct that emerged out of their missionary encounters with Asian Americans in the late nineteenth and early twentieth centuries. It is true that most historical studies acknowledge the presence of Protestants in the history or sociology of Asian Americans. For instance, Henry Yu begins his study with American missionaries who helped underwrite Robert Park's study of Asian Americans in the 1920s. Izumi Hirobe's study of efforts to modify the anti-Asian exclusion clause in the 1924 Immigration Act demonstrates how significant American Protestant missionaries were in seeking to give Japanese Americans a more equitable immigration quota.[28] With the exception of Hirobe's work, most of these studies offer rather shallow readings of the history of American Protestantism and its influence on the development of sociology. In the following I hope to show how white American Protestants constructed the idea of Asian assimilability in the face of strong anti-Asian sentiment.

In the second half of the nineteenth century, most white Americans believed that the waves of immigrants from both shores had furnished the "brawn" for Anglo-Saxon "brains" to modernize the United States. "It is remarkable," Jay Backus declared before the 1869 annual meeting of the American Baptist Home Mission Society in reference to the transcontinental railroad, "that American brains planned it, but American muscle did not build it. God sent to us men from Asia—the Chinese—to build the embankments of its western division, and men from Europe—the Irish—to build the embankments of the eastern."[29] This division of labor reflected an emerging confidence in American exceptionalism and Anglo-Saxon superiority.[30] Ironically, the changes caused by modern industrialization only aggravated the social dislocation experienced by many Americans at the time. By the turn of the century, the United States had become what the late Robert Wiebe called a "distended society" in a "search for order" in the midst of glowing confidence in American destiny.[31]

The economic disparity engendered by industrialization and the religious, ethnic, and racial pluralism created by the influx of immigrants eventually challenged faith in Anglo-Saxon exceptionalism. As self-appointed guardians of the national covenant, Anglo-Saxon Americans watched with alarm as boatload after boatload of European immigrants landed on American shores, bringing with them diverse customs, religious traditions, and most significantly, the "old world." The idea of an Anglo-Saxon exceptionalist national covenant, derived from the Puritan vision of community and renewed in nineteenth-century evangelical convictions of America as the redeemer nation with a manifest destiny and a millennial role for the world, sought to stem the tide of history. The United States was the land of "new creations." The decay of historic Europe would vanish as immigrants were "born again" into a new American humanity. The autocracies of the "old world" were to yield to the republican institutions and democratic heritage of the "new world."[32]

But the crisis that became apparent during the Gilded Age issued forth divergent responses. For some, the loss of the Anglo-Saxon Protestant definitions of exceptionalism did not mean the loss of faith in that ideology. Dorothy Ross has noted that American exceptionalism was transformed into liberalism in the hands of Progressives. They tenaciously adhered to a faith in America as the natural "melting pot" of all European nationalities. Nativists, however, sought to rein in laissez-faire immigration policies. Some abandoned the belief in America as the asylum for the world's outcasts and "the melting pot." Inspired by the success of anti-Chinese exclusionary policies since 1882, many nativists now attempted to exclude Eastern and Southern European immigration by portraying them as inferior races. By 1924, the National Origins Act imposed strict quotas on immigration from Eastern and Southern Europe, which has usually been interpreted as a nativist victory.[33]

Within the context of American exceptionalism and its fate in the course of immigration history, Chinese and Japanese were the most visible non-European immigrants to arrive and settle in the United States. Nativist hostility toward European immigrants assumed even greater racial undertones when directed toward Chinese and Japanese immigrants. European immigrants and their descendents could pass as white Americans, but Asian Americans could not do so easily. Hence, while it appeared that European immigrants had a chance of assimilating into American life, Asians were considered unassimilable and rendered ineligible for citizenship and excluded from immigration.

There was a distinct "Orientalist color-line" through which Americans represented Asians in the nineteenth century. According to John Tchen,

> the representation of Chinese things, ideas, and people shifted dramatically from 1776 to 1882, in a manner that coincided with shifts in the political, economic, and social institutions of the United States. Moreover, both representations–the positive and the negative–played a role in the formation of a modern "white" identity…Orientalism, therefore, became a cultural phenomenon intrinsic to American social, economic, and political life.[34]

Tchen identifies three distinct and overlapping types of American Orientalism:

> Each form of Orientalism operated according to its own internal logic and sense of time. These patterns were animated by the faith in civilization, progress, and destiny that prevailed during this era of U.S. social, economic, and political development. Each formation of Orientalism began with some admiration or fascination for the actual Chinese thing, idea, or person, then went through a phase of emulation and mimesis, and ended with European American mastery and dominance.[35]

Although Chinese immigration started on the Pacific Coast, American Orientalist perceptions originated among wealthy mercantile families in New York City. In the early decades of the nineteenth century there appeared a form of what Tchen calls "patrician orientalism" that was largely derived from British and continental sources in China and primarily of interest to New York City elites who craved for expensive goods from China and exotic Chinese ideas. By mid-century, Tchen identifies the emergence of a "commercial orientalism," a response to a rapidly expanding populist marketplace economics in the middle of the nineteenth century. Representations of Chinese people, things, and ideas were now being generated for popular consumption even as real Chinese people became a presence in New York City. "This pastiche of commercial orientalism was subject to a marketplace that catered to consumers who would buy only certain products and representations about Chinese things, people and ideas," Tchen asserts. "Actual Chinese and European Americans in yellowface performing on New York stages and in museums were presented in ways that further elaborated and reinforced attitudes transplanted from England, among other European influences, but also invoked new competing views in response to reading and viewing publics."[36]

By the 1880s, a new Orientalist formation emerged. "This political orientalism recast desire-imbued and ambiguous representations into an exclusionary and segregationist discourse."[37] Consequently, anti-Chinese sentiment became engrained in American politics and resulted in immigration exclusion. It was "political orientalism" that aroused the American Protestant missionary quest for an alternative discourse with regard to Asian Americans. Though missionaries also relished opportunities to exoticize Chinese and Japanese people, things, and ideas, thereby contributing to the "commercial orientalism," they rejected the "political orientalism."

Essentially, white Protestants attempted to construct an ideological alternative to the exclusivist and nativist anti-Asian discourse that dominated American public opinion at the end of the nineteenth century. Protestant faith in Asian assimilation was both a humanitarian response to the victims of American racism and a hope that the failure to fully "Christianize" the "Oriental in America" would find eventual success in their gradual and natural assimilation into American society.

During the early Protestant encounters with the Chinese in the 1850s, missions and evangelism were promoted as the primary vehicles for the incorporation of the Asian into American society. It is important to note that prior to Protestant cognizance of the tremendous industrial-labor problems emerging in American society, much of the mission efforts were enmeshed in a milieu of smoldering anti-slavery and revivalist sentiment. Soul winning was often accompanied by an abolitionist desire to "uplift" racialized peoples and incorporate them into American society. Shortly after the Civil War, Presbyterians, Baptists, Congregationalists, and Methodists leapt into the fray of Chinese mission work in San Francisco. As the Chinese (and later Japanese) population grew and shifted into urban centers, several mission centers were established in these locations.

Protestant hope for the Chinese and Japanese to assimilate into American life through Christian conversion was severely tested. Anti-Chinese and anti-Japanese discrimination on the Pacific slope and in national politics were severe obstacles. Though Protestants were among the very few who advocated on behalf of Asians and protested the discriminatory treatment of Chinese and Japanese and lobbied against immigration legislature that excluded Asians, their efforts ultimately failed in the face of an American society that had become increasingly hostile toward Asian immigrants. Furthermore, Chinese and Japanese transience and reluctance to embrace Christianity discouraged Protestants and contributed to the loss of confidence in Christian conversion as a means of assimilation. By the end of World War I, many Protestant mission boards felt that they had overcommitted their ministry resources among Asian Americans.

But the failure to Christianize the Asian American and the Asian American Christian failure to assimilate into or be accepted by American society during the Progressive years left Protestants to ponder the future of the Asian in America. Efforts to consolidate and make more efficient the social impact of Asian American missions yielded ambivalent results, at best. Nevertheless, the rhetoric of assimilation was renewed in the early decades of the twentieth century. As the presence of women missionaries became more pronounced at the turn of the century, greater attention was given to the wives and children of Chinese and Japanese immigrant men. Many women missionaries began to articulate the hope that Christianized Asian wives and children would uplift their people and thus qualify them for either mission work in Asia or citizenship in the United States. Furthermore, the national awakening and modernization of China and Japan during this time gave the impression (both admired and feared) that these Asian nations had the potential to join the family of civilized and modern nation states. This was accompanied by signs of Chinese and Japanese Protestant growth in Asia and in the United States. There appeared to be evidence that the "heathen" Asian might be assimilable after all.

Throughout this period, Protestants publicly protested the discriminatory treatment of Asian Americans in exclusion and naturalization legislation. Whether their protests were motivated by a concern for the civil rights of Asian Americans or a desire to secure international peace and goodwill (or both), Protestants continued to refute anti-Oriental advocates who claimed that Asian Americans were unassimilable. While exclusionists were often vague in their definitions of assimilation, Protestants consistently made a distinction between biological amalgamation and cultural-social assimilation. The former was unnecessary for the latter to occur, Protestants argued, as they held tenaciously to the view that Americanization was a "spiritual" process.

Consequently, Protestant advocates of "Oriental" missions turned to sociological analysis in the 1920s in hope of securing their faith in the assimilability of Asian Americans. Employing Robert Park and his race relations cycle, American Protestants entrusted their mission work to an ideology of "natural" assimilationism for Asian Americans. Asian Americans, like other immigrants, would undergo a natural, inevitable, and progressive process of assimilation into modern America. This ideology justified the Protestant transference of the Asian American missions to local religious jurisdiction and "secular agencies" in the 1930s. It became the intellectual foundation in opposition to policies of segregation and exclusion that assumed that Asian Americans were innately and obstinately foreign.

The search for the assimilation of Asian Americans was one aspect of the Protestant effort to secure their vision for a Christian American commonwealth in the face of dramatic social changes in the United States between the Civil War and World War II. Toward the end of this period, most leaders in the mainline American Protestant denominations became more tolerant of racial and religious pluralism, but maintained their faith in a "secularized" liberal national covenant. Thus, assimilation and its younger cousin "integration" remained the Protestant watchwords throughout the 1950s and 1960s. By this time, Asian Americans had been subsumed under the assimilationist narrative of European immigration history. Historians and church leaders in the mid-twentieth century erased this "color-line" by dissolving Asian Americans into the European immigrant narrative and reducing Asian American difference to ethnicity.

Asian Americans, at it turned out, represented one of the great challenges to nineteenth- and early twentieth-century Protestants in their efforts to impose their Anglo-Saxon Christian vision on American society. Some Protestants, through their encounters with other races and nationalities, learned that their claims to a universal religion could be legitimated only as long as their faith was not too closely associated with European American racialist culture. But for the most part, Protestants retreated to a more comfortable view that the assimilation (and eventual Christianization) of Asian Americans was a natural and gradual process. By helping to shape the ideology of assimilation, Protestants inadvertently contributed to the merging of the Asian American experience with the European immigration narrative and the development of the Asian American "model minority" thesis. Hence, insofar as the American religious historiography remains influenced by its Protestant roots, it continues to interpret the Asian American experience through the lens of assimilation.

Retrieving the Asian American Subject

I believe the history of the victims of Christian history, as well as the history of downtrodden Christians, is so vital. We need their views not simply to critique our own elitist views but because we need to discover when, where, and how we failed to love them as the Lord commanded us to do. Church history at its best must become concerned and interested in the oppressed. Otherwise it runs the risk of betraying the Gospel's allegiance to the downtrodden. It would remain, as it often is, the history of pious elites written by sometimes pious, sometimes irreverent elites.

–JAMES M. WASHINGTON[38]

This chapter attempted to explicate how Orientalism has limited the interpretive options of religious historians who seek to study Asian American religion. In particular, it centered on how white Protestant roots of the assimilationist paradigm became so pervasive in the interpretation of Asian Americans today. The interpretive lenses that represent Asian Americans as exotic religious other or as "model minority" Christians have given little room for alternative perspectives. By not giving enough attention to the social and historical experiences of religious Asian Americans, they risk essentializing Asian American subjects or rendering them invisible. In this conclusion, I will suggest three possible directions that historians may wish to go in order to interpret the Asian American religious experience beyond Orientalism and assimilation. Hopefully, these approaches will more effectively retrieve the Asian American subject in American religious history.

First, the retrieval of religious Asian American subjects will require engagement with current Asian American and racialization theorists. Researchers need to bring these perspectives with them as they engage Asian American communities. Mia Tuan's study of second- to fifth-generation middle-class Asian Americans in California is a good example of a sociologist's effort to get past the "foreigner–model minority" paradigm. Her study does not entirely reject the sociological categories of assimilation, but also includes racialization as part of the Asian American experience. Historians and theologians need to do likewise and also engage recent studies of American Orientalism.[39]

A second approach views Asian American religious communities and individuals as creative sites and agents of cultural synthesis. The debate over African retentions and black assimilation in African American religious communities can provide some conceptual help. In discussing the phenomena of African American Christianity, for instance, Charles Joyner notes, "The slaves did not simply adopt the God and the faith of the white missionaries. In establishing a spiritual life for themselves, they reinterpreted the elements of Christianity in terms of deep-rooted African religious concerns." Thus, he concludes, "The originality of African-American Christianity, then, lies neither in its African elements nor in its Christian elements, but in its unique and creative synthesis of both."[40] So rather than interpreting them as bearers of Asian religion or assimilated Christians, religious Asian Americans (including Asian American Christians) can be viewed as agents who construct and express their religion in unique and creative ways.

Finally, American religious historians need to incorporate themes of transnationalism and diaspora in their study of Asian American religious communities.[41] Even in the case of Chinese American Protestantism, historical developments in China and the Chinese Diaspora have had significant impact on the shape and character of Chinese Protestants in North America.[42] This approach reveals the impact of Asian nationalisms on Asian American religions (including Christianity) and can provide a rich repository for an interpretation of the Asian American religious experience that is not so United States–centered.

The hermeneutical labor of the historian of Asian American religion is a daunting challenge because of the pervasive presence of Orientalist and assimilationist assumptions in American society today and the paucity of Asian American religious historians. Yet Asian American theologians and religious leaders require a historical framework that more accurately reflects the Asian American experience. Furthermore, American religious historiography can benefit not only from the history of religious Asians in America but also from the history of Orientalism among historians. The latter not only interprets the Asian American experience but also sets forth a new center for viewing American religious history. David Wills rightly argued for a Southern hermeneutical starting point. I argue for a Trans-Pacific starting point.

Though the challenge is great, the prospects are also very exciting because the field of American religious history (despite this chapter's critique) is gradually opening its doors to alternative perspectives. Perhaps this chapter will help widen the hermeneutical options for the study of Asian American religious history.

Notes

[1]James Melvin Washington, "Craven Images: The Eiconics of Race in the Crisis of American Church Historiography," in *The Agitated Mind of God: The Theology of Kosuke Koyama,* ed. Dale T. Irvin and Akintunde E. Akinade (Maryknoll, N.Y.: Orbis Books, 1996), 131.

[2]David W. Wills, "The Central Themes of American Religious History: Pluralism, Puritanism, and the Encounter of Black and White," in *African-American Religion: Interpretive Essays in History and Culture,* ed. Timothy E. Fulop and Albert J. Rabateau (New York: Routledge Press, 1997), 9–20.

[3]Washington, "Craven Images," 136.

[4]Sydney E. Ahlstrom, *A Religious History of the American People* (New Haven, Conn.: Yale University Press, 1972), 1051.

[5]Henry Yu, *Thinking Orientals: Migration, Contact, and Exoticism in Modern America* (New York: Oxford University Press, 2001); Robert Lee, *Orientals: Asian Americans in Popular Culture* (Philadelphia: Temple University Press, 1999); Lisa Lowe, *Immigrant Acts: On Asian American Cultural Politics* (Durham, N.C.: Duke University Press, 1996).

[6]Edward A. Said, *Orientalism* (New York: Vintage Books, 1978).

[7]J. J. Clarke, *Oriental Enlightenment: The Encounter Between Asian and Western Thought* (New York: Routledge, 1997), 8–11; Jonathan D. Spence, *The Chan's Great Continent: China in Western Minds* (New York: W. W. Norton, 1998).

⁸T. Christopher Jespersen, *American Images of China: 1931–1949* (Stanford, Calif.: Stanford University Press, 1999). In the case of Japan, Francis Hall's journals and the YMCA in Japan are good examples of this form of Orientalism. Francis Hall, *Japan Through American Eyes: The Journal of Francis Hall, 1859–1866,* ed. and abridged Francis G. Notehelfer (Boulder and Oxford: Westview Press, 2001).

⁹See, for instance, Michael H. Hunt, *Ideology and U.S. Foreign Policy* (New Haven, Conn.: Yale University Press, 1987); Alexander Deconde, *Ethnicity, Race and American Foreign Policy: A History* (Boston: Northeastern University Press, 1992); Victor Kierman, *The Lords of Human Kind: European Attitudes to Other Cultures in the Imperial Age* (London: Serif, 1995).

¹⁰Gary Y. Okihiro, *Margins and Mainstreams: Asians in American History and Culture* (Seattle: University of Washington Press, 1994).

¹¹Catherine L. Albanese, *America: Religions and Religion,* 3d ed. (Belmont, Calif.: Wadsworth, 1998). Another significant work has been Peter W. Williams, *Popular Religion in America: Symbolic Change and the Modernization Process in Historical Perspective* (Urbana and Chicago: University of Illinois Press, 1989). Williams examines religious practices outside institutionalized religions.

¹²Amanda Porterfield, *The Transformation of American Religion: The Story of a Late-Twentieth Century Awakening* (New York: Oxford University Press, 2001), 134.

¹³Jacob Neusner, ed., *World Religions in America: An Introduction,* 2d ed. (Louisville, Ky.: Westminster John Knox Press, 1999).

¹⁴Thomas A. Tweed and Stephen R. Prothero, eds., *Asian Religions in America: A Documentary History* (New York: Oxford University Press, 1999). bell hooks' article, "Waking Up to Racism," was originally published in *Tricyle* (Fall 1994): 42–45.

¹⁵For example, see Diana L. Eck, *A New Religious America: How a "Christian Country" Has Now Become the World's Most Religiously Diverse Nation* (San Francisco: HarperSanFrancisco, 2001).

¹⁶Timothy Fitzgerald, *The Ideology of Religious Studies* (New York: Oxford University Press, 2000).

¹⁷David W. Lotz, "A Changing Historiography: From Church History to Religious History," in *Altered Landscapes: Christianity in America, 1935–1985,* ed. David W. Lotz (Grand Rapids, Mich.: Eerdmans, 1989), 312–39; Harry S. Stout and D. G. Hart, eds., *New Directions in American Religious History* (New York: Oxford University Press, 1997).

¹⁸Thomas A. Tweed, ed., *Retelling U.S. Religious History* (Berkeley: University of California Press, 1997). See essays by Laurie F. Maffly-Kipp ("Eastward Ho! American Religion from the Perspective of the Pacific Rim") and Joel W. Martin ("Indians, Contact, and Colonialism in the Deep South: Themes for a Postcolonial History of American Religion").

¹⁹Martin E. Marty, "American Religious History in the Eighties: A Decade of Achievement," *Church History* 62, no. 3 (Sept. 1993): 335–77.

²⁰Martin E. Marty, *Modern American Religion,* vol. 1, *The Irony of It All, 1893–1919* (Chicago: University of Chicago Press, 1986); *Modern American Religion,* vol. 2, *The Noise of Conflict, 1919–1941* (Chicago: University of Chicago Press, 1991).

²¹The exception may be the study of African American religious history in the aftermath of the civil rights and black power movements. American religious histories now recognize race as a strictly black and white affair. For example, Jon Butler and Harry S. Stout's 1998 collection of essays limits discussion about race to black and white relations. Jon Butler and Harry S. Stout, eds., *Religion in American History: A Reader* (New York: Oxford University Press, 1998).

²²Ahlstrom, *Religious History,* 1051.

²³Edwin Gaustad, *A Religious History of America,* rev. ed. (San Francisco: Harper & Row, 1990), 162–63.

²⁴Ibid., 187–88, 285. Mark Noll follows a similar pattern of thinking: "Most believers in the United States and Canada maintained a shameful silence when ethnic Japanese, many of

them Christian, were interned for much of the war," Mark A. Noll, *A History of Christianity in the United States and Canada* (Grand Rapids, Mich.: Eerdmans, 1992), 437.

[25]Washington, "Craven Images," 144.

[26]Yu, *Thinking Orientals.*

[27]Recent ethnic studies have qualified this approach to immigration history. The flurry of Asian American research in recent years is an instance of the challenge to the assimilationist paradigm. Ewa Morawska, "The Sociology and Historiography of Immigration," in *Immigration Reconsidered: History: Sociology, and Politics,* ed. Virginia Yans-McLaughlin (New York: Oxford, 1990), 187–238.

[28]Izumi Hirobe, *Japanese Pride, American Prejudice: Modifying the Exclusion Clause of the 1924 Immigration Act* (Stanford, Calif.: Stanford University Press, 2001).

[29]*Annual Report of the American Baptist Home Mission Society 1869* (Philadelphia: American Baptist Publications Society, 1869), 20.

[30]Reginald Horsman, *Race and Manifest Destiny: The Origins of American Racial Anglo-Saxonism* (Cambridge, Mass.: Harvard University Press, 1981); Alexander Saxton, *The Indispensable Enemy: Labor and the Anti-Chinese Movement in California* (Berkeley: University of California Press, 1971); David R. Roediger, *The Wages of Whiteness: Race and the Making of the American Working Class* (London & New York: Verso, 1991).

[31]Robert H. Wiebe, *The Search for Order, 1877–1920* (New York: Hill and Wang, 1967).

[32]Michael Adas recently called on American historians to broaden their "exceptionalist" motif. See "From Settler Colony to Global Hegemon: Integrating the Exceptionalist Narrative of the American Experience into the World History," *American Historical Review* 106, no. 5 (Dec. 2001): 1692–1720.

[33]Dorothy Ross, *The Origins of American Social Science* (Cambridge: Cambridge University Press, 1991); Ernest Lee Tuveson, *Redeemer Nation: The Idea of America's Millennial Role* (Chicago: University of Chicago Press, 1968); Barbara Miller Solomon, *Ancestors and Immigrants: A Changing New England Tradition* (New York: John Wiley & Sons, 1956); John Higham, *Strangers in the Land: Patterns of American Nativism, 1860–1925,* 2d ed. (New Brunswick, N.J.: Rutgers University Press, 1988).

[34]John Kuo Wei Tchen, *New York before Chinatown: Orientalism and the Shaping of American Culture, 1776–1882* (Baltimore: Johns Hopkins Press, 1999), xv, xvi; see also Robert Lee, *Orientals: Asian Americans in Popular Culture* (Philadelphia: Temple University Press, 1999).

[35]Tchen, *New York before Chinatown,* xx.

[36]Ibid., xxii.

[37]Ibid., xxiii.

[38]Washington, "Craven Images," 136.

[39]Mia Tuan, *Forever Foreigners or Honorary Whites? The Asian Ethnic Experience Today* (New Brunswick, N.J.: Rutgers University Press, 1998).

[40]Charles Joyner, "'Believer I Know': The Emergence of African-American Christianity," in *African American Christianity: Essays in History,* ed. Paul E. Johnson (Berkeley and Los Angeles: University of California Press, 1994), 37. Like Albert Raboteau, Joyner attempts to get past the classic Frazier-Herskovits impasse by stressing the creative agency of African American Christians. Ref. J. Herskovits, *The Myth of the Negro Past* (Boston: Beacon Press, 1958), and E. Franklin Frazier, *The Negro Church in America* (New York: Schocken Books, 1964).

[41]A good recent study that does not analyze religion very closely but utilizes a transnational theme is Madeline Y. Hsu, *Dreaming of Gold, Dreaming of Home: Transnationalism and Migration Between the United States and South China, 1882–1943* (Stanford, Calif.: Stanford University Press, 2000).

[42]Timothy Tseng, "Trans-Pacific Transpositions: Continuities and Discontinuities in Chinese North American Protestantism," in *Revealing the Sacred in Asian and Pacific America,* ed. Jane Naomi Iwamura and Paul Spickard (New York: Routledge, 2002).

PART 2

From Context to Context

Theological Readings of Asian American Journey

5

Postcolonial Exorcism and Reconstruction

Filipino Americans' Search for Postcolonial Subjecthood

ELEAZAR S. FERNANDEZ

Until the lions have their historians, tales of hunting will always glorify the hunter.

–African Proverb

"They can't silence me anymore! I'll tell the world what they have done to me!"[1] These were the passionate words of Carlos Bulosan in a letter to his brother Macario after realizing, "like a revelation," that he could "actually write understandable English." It is not, however, only the simple self-discovery that he could write or articulate "understandable English" that made this occasion momentous, but also because Bulosan had discovered a medium to give voice to his pain, rage, and dreams. The young Bulosan eventually found a voice that could not be silenced anymore. Writing, Bulosan soon found out, is a political act.

Since the day of his arrival on the shores of the "land of the free and the home of the brave," Bulosan witnessed and personally experienced the suffering of his "kababayans" (countryfolks) and of other racial minorities. Of his many painful experiences, he shared a particular moment in his life when he felt extremely "violated and outraged." This was on an occasion when two policemen invaded a party at a Filipino restaurant, waving their pistols and physically abusing Bulosan and a guest from the Philippines. Hurt and humiliated, he thought of getting his gun. "I wanted my gun," Bulosan wrote. "With it I could challenge our common enemy bullet for bullet. It seemed my only friend and comfort in this alien country—this smooth little bit of metal."[2] Bulosan went to his hotel room to get the "smooth little bit of metal," but his brother Macario grabbed the gun away from him. Outraged and enraged, Bulosan vowed to fight back!

Indeed, Bulosan fought back. He fought back not with bullets, but with his writings. He fought back with his words that no tyrant could silence. Bulosan proclaimed to the world the suffering of the laborers in the fields and fish canneries of America. Through his writings, Bulosan decided to offer his talent in order to give voice to the voiceless. Once feeling powerless, Bulosan experienced empowerment through his writings. He wrote and wrote even as he was struggling for his own life. "That's it, Carl," Pascal (an editor of a workers' newspaper) would shout with resounding approval to Bulosan. "Write your guts out! Write with thunder and blood!"[3]

It took the right confluence of events and circumstances, though painful, for Bulosan to understand what his brother Luciano had told him way back during his boyhood years in the Philippines. Luciano had encouraged the young Carlos "never to stop reading good books...Maybe someday you will become a journalist." At that time Bulosan did not know exactly what it meant to be a journalist. As his life in America unfolded, Bulosan came to know what being a journalist meant. Remembering his parents' hardships and those of the peasants in the Philippines, he sobbed, "Yes, I will be a writer and make all of you live again in my words."[4]

Bulosan's writings are an inspiration. He experienced the pain that led to rage. But the rage found direction through his weapon—writing. Through his words Bulosan made those who were in the margins or whose experiences did not count based on the norms of the dominant social order sprout and live again. Even as he was enraged, Bulosan was not willing to give up the America of his dreams and the America of his heart. He saw the other side of America that has yet to be fulfilled. America, for Bulosan, is still in the making. Understanding America is not enough, says Bulosan. Something must be done to make it a just society. This is the America of his heart.[5]

With the spirit of Bulosan I attempt in this chapter to make the pains, longings, and dreams of those in the margin, especially Filipino Americans, live again. In my own way I carry forward his weapon of words through minority Christian studies and discourse. More particularly, I speak of this minority discourse as postcolonial exorcism and imaginative reconstruction.

Discourse from the Margins

In introducing our jointly-edited volume *(A Dream Unfinished: Theological Reflections on America from the Margins)*, Fernando Segovia laid out the task of minority Christian studies and discourse in a three-pronged fashion: "pursuing archival work in marginalized religious practices and values; undertaking a critical analysis of Western Christianity and its missionary project of universal church and theology; drawing upon the marginalized religious practices and beliefs retrieved for alternative visions of church and theology."[6] Segovia speaks in particular of minority Christian studies and minority discourse, so his three-pronged thrust is directed at the church and theology. Yet even as the thrust is directed at the church and theology, Segovia is emphatically clear that "[w]e must pursue this task by looking at the realm of religion and its study not in isolation from other realms but rather as deeply imbricated in all other realms, such as the cultural and the social, the economic and the political."[7]

The three-pronged thrust that Segovia identified–archival work, critical analysis of hegemonic practices, and exploration of alternative visions–is shared by minority scholars and other scholars who theologize/interpret text/context from the margins or from the underside. Archival work or hermeneutics of retrieval is not a simple uncovering of the past but, from the perspective of the marginalized, a retrieval of painful memories. It is not a retrieval of the "good old days" to reassure those who are enjoying the present; rather, it is a reading of the past against the grain. While hegemonic scholarship seeks to cover up the subversive memories, minority scholarship struggles to exhume the memories. Archival work cannot be dissociated from the second task: critical analysis of Western hegemony in the church and in theological discourse. Critical analysis of hegemonic practices supports archival work just as archival work supports critical analysis. Western hegemony in the church and in theological discourse has been challenged by minority scholars, yet it has prevailed even in the face of rigorous criticism. It is the continuing task of minority discourse to expose existing hegemonies.

Critical analysis and archival work must lead to reconstruction of alternative ways of thinking, dwelling, and acting. As minorities name their pain and engage in critical analysis of the structures of oppression, they also have to explore alternative ways to do theology and find what it means to dwell together. By no means should this be equated with providing a blueprint for the future, but it involves funding imagination and articulating visions that have been spawned by minorities' experience of in-between-ness and liminality. Generating and articulating alternative visions is an enormous undertaking, but minority scholars have refused to be intimidated by the task.

I take the task–archival work, critical analysis, and exploration of alternative visions–that Segovia has laid out for minority Christian studies very seriously for my own work as a minority theological scholar. These three dimensions will be given attention in this chapter as I attempt to do postcolonial exorcism and imaginative reconstruction.

Exorcising Colonialism: Engaging in Postcolonial Discourse

What easily comes to popular mind when we speak of exorcism are the horror movies, such as *The Exorcist*. There is a time for Hollywood flash, but my interest in dealing with exorcism is to link it with colonialism–a concern that is generally foreign to Hollywood celebrities. Colonialism is an expression of idolatry: It is the raising of the self-interest, security, and worldview of a particular race or people to a position of ultimate concern, and the relegating of others as sacrificial offerings. Colonialism's power for destruction is far greater than what we can imagine with individual demon possessions. Its expressions are visible from the outside, but its control is lodged deep in the individual and collective psyche. As an idol that feeds on the blood of the conquered, colonized, and exploited, colonialism must be exorcised.

Walter Wink in *Unmasking the Powers* provides an extensive account of exorcism and its relevance to contemporary issues from a theological angle.[8] "Exorcism in its New Testament context," notes Wink, "is the act of deliverance of a person or institution or society from its bondage to evil, and its restoration to the wholeness intrinsic to its creation."[9] The evil condition is not only purged, but it is going to be replaced with a new way of life. In other words, it means liberation of those who have been possessed by the powers of death and their restoration to a liberated life. Wink points to Jesus' act of cleansing the temple (Mk. 11:11, 15–19) as the paradigmatic act of collective exorcism in the New Testament. What made Jesus' acts of exorcism powerful and also frightening, especially for the guardians of the reigning order, Wink argues, is the integration of his acts of exorcism into his proclamation of the inbreaking of the new order–the kingdom of God.[10]

In relating exorcism to colonialism, I say that postcolonial discourse is an attempt at exorcising colonialism. Postcolonial discourse presents to us a variety of methodological approaches and agenda, such as critique of hegemonic discourse, images, and representations, as well as the raising of issues regarding identity, race and ethnicity, diaspora, and so forth. But in spite of being a salmagundi of hermeneutical concerns, there is a common thread. Postcolonial discourse, according to R. S. Sugirtharajah, "signifies three things–representation, identity, and a reading posture emerging among the former victims of colonialism."[11]

Postcolonialism is not so much about a period after the colonial era when colonized countries gained their independence from Western colonial powers, though that is a significant expression, as it is a "methodological revisionism that enables a wholesale critique of Western structures of knowledge and power since the Enlightenment."[12] Sugirtharajah puts it well:

Postcoloniality is a critical enterprise aimed at unmasking the link between ideas and power which lies behind Western texts, theories, and learning…[I]t is an active interrogation of the hegemonic systems of thought, textual codes, and symbolic practices which the West constructed in its domination of colonial subjects…It is a discursive resistance to imperialism, imperial ideologies, and imperial attitudes and to their continual reincarnations in such wide fields as politics, economics, history, and theological and biblical studies.[13]

I would, however, make a qualification of Sugirtharajah's articulation about postcolonial hermeneutics. While he speaks of the link of "ideas and power which lies behind the Western texts, theories, and learning," I make the claim that ideas and power do not simply "lie behind" but are also expressed in texts, theories, and learning. "Ideas" and "power" are not simply "behind" the texts but are expressed through the texts and in front of the texts. Texts are productions or creations of power and vice versa: Texts create and perpetuate power.

Postcolonial hermeneutics offers an approach to reading texts/contexts that resonates with the pathos and dreams of people who have experienced colonization and who are struggling to unshackle the vestiges of colonialism even in the territorial heartland of the empire. It is a hermeneutical tool, according to Homi Bhabha, that functions to "bear witness" to inequities in modes of representation between the West and the non-West.[14]

In what follows, I am going to employ postcolonial hermeneutics in reading the Filipino American experience. The Filipino American experience is an excellent case of putting postcolonial discourse into practice, for this experience is right at the heart of the thrust of postcolonial discourse. I will take account of the Filipino American past, following Ella Shobat's advice, "not as a static fetishized phase to be literally reproduced, but as fragmented sets of narrated memories and experiences on the basis of which to mobilize contemporary communities."[15] Whether it be a focus on the past or a critical engagement with more recent events, the intention is to "mobilize contemporary [Filipino-American] communities" to become postcolonial subjects in the heart of America and as inhabitants of our highly globalized world.

I Discovered You, Therefore I Am: I Discovered You, Therefore You Exist

Against the background of the dark ages of human history, modernity presents itself as a welcome relief from the shackles of the past, especially from heteronomous religious powers that controlled both heaven and earth. Modernity is a revolt against heteronomous religious powers and everything that represents the incarceration of reason and free spirit. Theologically, the rise of the modern period also has been interpreted as freedom from the "house of authority," in which the form of theologizing is basically citation and translation of unchangeable deposits of faith under the guardianship of the church hierarchy.[16]

There is much to celebrate of the age of modernity, but there is another side to it. This is not an occasion to provide a laundry list, but simply to say that the much celebrated age of reason, enlightenment, and progress is also the age of "discovery" and the resultant conquest, colonization, and exploitation of other races by peoples of European descent. The age of reason has been barbaric and violent. True to its spirit as the age of reason, the barbarism of the modern period has been couched with reasonably noble intentions: civilizing and Christianizing the pagans, spreading democracy and prosperity.

In this history of "discovery," conquest, colonization, and exploitation, the church, unfortunately, has been complicit. The age of modernity and Western expansion is also the age of Christianity's expansion throughout the world. Wherever there was colonization, there was Christian mission. Alongside the sword of the conqueror was the Christian crucifix or the Bible. Any account of the history of Christianity must deal with this shameful side. "Today, I cannot speak of the history of the sixteenth century," Justo González puts it, "without taking into account that on May 26, 1521, the same day that the imperial Diet of Worms issued its edict against Luther, Hernán Cortés was laying siege to the imperial city of Tenochtitlán."[17]

Synonymous with the birth of modernity, which Enrique Dussel locates as early as 1492, is the birth of the European "I."[18] Outside of this European "I" is the faceless other that has to be conquered and civilized. Rene Descartes' "I think, therefore I am" is also the "I conquer/discover, therefore I am." This "*ego cogito* of Descartes," I argued elsewhere, "is the theoretical foundation of the *ego conquiro,* and the *ego conquiro* is the practical expression of the *ego cogito.* In actual history, the *ego cogito* is not simply the *homo sapiens* or the *homo faber* (human being as worker), but the conqueror."[19]

When we pursue the metamorphosis of the European "I" in the current era of transnational capitalist globalization, the "I think, therefore I am" and the "I conquer, therefore I am" is also the "I purchase, therefore I am" or "I consume, therefore I am." Possession and consumption define one's subjectivity and identity. And what is possessed and consumed is not simply the use value of something but the exchange value or, more specifically, the image value. The "endless acts of consumption provoked by the *danse macabre* of capitalism," says Peter McLaren, "organizes subjectivity in specific ways around the general maxim: I purchase, therefore I am."[20] In his trenchant critique, McLaren speaks of the hybrid and splayed identity of the postmodern self as being patterned on the cathedral of capitalism and the shopping mall. The "shopping mall self (the self as the rhetorical effect of image value)," as McLaren calls it, "has become the quintessential model of panic identity in the contemporary United States."[21]

Attractive as it is, Third World people have bought into this consumeristic project. While one often hears the lament that people are in economic crisis, malls are always crowded and many malls are still being constructed. Of course, there are other reasons why malls in the Third World are crowded: They serve as air-conditioned hang-out places.[22] From the First World to the Third World, from the North to the South, globalization is creating a "global culture" typified, writes Robert Schreiter, "by American cola drinks, athletic and casual clothing, and American movie and television entertainment."[23]

Discovering, conquering, and consuming are expressions of the European "I" and its extension–the European American "I." Discovering and conquering others, for the colonial masters, are an adjunct and a proof of their existence. The act of "discovering" assures the colonial masters that they, indeed, are "thinking" and "existing" subjects. While it is the selfhood of the "discoverer" that is parasitic to the "discovered," by curious alchemy it is now the parasite that grants selfhood to the "discovered." The "discoverer" becomes the guarantor as well as the mirror of the existence and selfhood of the "discovered." The existence and identity of the "discovered" is established as derivative of the "discoverer." In effect, the "discoverer" says to the "discovered" and the conquered: "I discovered you, therefore you exist." Or, "I discovered you, therefore you are." It is only at the point of "discovery" that the history of the "discovered" begins to unfold. Before the "discovery," the life of the discovered is prehistory.

Yet even as history begins to unfold in the lives of those "discovered," their history continues to be viewed from the perspective of the "discoverer" and colonizer. History has begun for the "discovered," but only insofar as it is beneficial to the "discoverer" and colonizer. In effect, what is considered history is not the history of the "discovered" and conquered, but the history of the triumphant. Only the history of the triumphant counts as history, and the "regime of truth," following Michel Foucault, has established it to be so.[24]

Even after the colonizer is long gone physically, the stamp of the colonizer remains. The day-to-day discourse of the once-colonized inhabitants continues to mirror that of the colonizer's discourse. The colonizer's classification and "order of things" continue to reign, even as voices of protest are present.[25] People call themselves according to the name given or conferred to them by their conqueror and colonizer. In spite of their resistance, they continue to use the language of the colonizer to refer to themselves and to challenge its hegemony.

The history of the Filipino people mirrors the concerns that I have lifted up. In the history of the Filipino people, the European American ego became real with the "discovery" of the Philippines on March 16, 1521, by the Portuguese navigator Fernando Magallanes and the arrival of the first Spanish occupation force led by Miguel López de Legaspi, and the subsequent colonization by agents of the United States of America. The "discovery" of the Philippines proved fatal to the Filipinos from many angles (economics, politics, and culture).

One angle that I would highlight at this point is the Filipinos' perception of their identity as a people. From that fateful day of "discovery" and onward they were made to believe that they owe their existence to their "discoverer." Centuries of this kind of education also made them believe that, indeed, they derive their existence from their colonial "discoverer." In gratitude for attesting to their existence, Filipinos have constantly mirrored and sought approval from their "discoverer." In a kind of love-hate relationship, they love being admired by the colonial/neocolonial masters and hate it when they are not given attention by the same masters.

The Making of a Colonial Soul

The Filipino people, according to nationalist historian Renato Constantino, had experienced being "liberated" four times in their history.

> First came the Spaniards who "liberated" them from the "enslavement of the devil," next came the Americans who "liberated" them from Spanish oppression, then the Japanese who "liberated" them from American imperialism, then the Americans again who "liberated" them from the Japanese fascists. After every "liberation" they found their country occupied by foreign "benefactors."[26]

After centuries of being "liberated" by their foreign benefactors, the Filipino people are among the most conquered and colonized people on the face of the earth. To be sure, the colonial masters are gone, but the demon of colonization is far from dead, not to mention its current transmutation in the guise of globalization. The colonial masters are no longer in direct control of the country, but they are no less present, for their control already has claimed the Filipino psyche. The late Paulo Freire put it this way:

> Every act of conquest implies a conqueror and someone or something which is conquered. The conqueror imposes his objectives on the vanquished, and makes them his possession. He imposes his own contours on the vanquished, who internalize this shape and become ambiguous beings "housing" another.[27]

In the long history of colonization, the Filipino people have become "houses" of the colonizers. This phenomenon is what Filipinos call "colonial mentality," which punsters have turned into the more derogatory "mental colony." They may be brown in skin complexion (though many have light skin—*mestizo* and *mestiza*), but their souls and imaginations have been whitened. Brown skin, but white souls. This resonates with the "black white men" of Africa or what Franz Fanon calls "black skin, white masks."[28] A poem helps articulate this Filipino malady:

> We are a brown race
> with white gods
> and whitened soul.
> We are aliens
> in our land,
> hostage by our past.[29]

Years of tutelage under foreign powers have made Filipinos hostages of their colonial past. This colonial past is not simply the dead past but a living one, for it has continued to shape the Filipinos of the present. Filipinos need to deal with this past if they are to free themselves from its grip and if they are to deal with the new expressions of colonizing forces in this era of globalization. There is no way to become postcolonial subjects unless they exorcise the colonial demon that is lodging in their souls.

Through a long process of colonization, both in the Philippines and now in the U.S., Filipino Americans have, indeed, become "housings" of the colonial master. Mary Ballou and Nancy Gabalac's account of the process of the internalization of patriarchal identity among women can be applied to the colonization of Filipino Americans.[30] Through a long process of humiliation and inculcation they have learned to despise themselves and to identify with their colonizers. This colonization is so deep that it cannot be undone by a few seminars on decolonization. A continuing praxis of decolonization must happen: The colonial demon must be exorcised.

America Is a Presence as Huge as God

The colonial masters have all left their marks in the Filipino psyche, but the influence of the United States is, I believe, the most pervasive. Unlike Spain, which took the posture of not educating the Filipinos in order to maintain control, the United States did the opposite. The United States embarked on a massive educational program to transform the Filipinos into its own image. When the U.S. granted the Philippines its independence on July 1946, the Americanization or "whitening" of the Filipinos was already in place.

Even before coming to the land of the free and the home of the brave, Filipino Americans know, following Eric Gamalinda's words, that "America is a presence as huge as God."[31] During my boyhood years on the island of Leyte (the landing site of General Douglas MacArthur's "liberation" forces during World War II), I encountered the association of hugeness with Americanness in the literal physical sense through objects, plants, and animals. The largest frog that I came to know was what the barrio inhabitants called "the American frog," and the largest bread that I dreamed of eating someday *hanggang sawa* (eat until I drop) was the "American bread" (rectangular loaf bread). I learned that when something is huge, it must be American. But the hugeness of America, I later realized, was more than what was incarnated in that huge American frog. "America is a presence as huge as God" because every Filipino is expected to acquire an exhaustive understanding of America the beautiful and is expected to love America with all his heart and to denounce those that smell Filipino with all her might.

Early in their education, Filipinos are trained to think and see things from the perspective of our colonial and neocolonial masters. In my elementary education I had to memorize the names of U.S. presidents and the various states that comprise the U.S. Abraham Lincoln often was cited by my teachers as a person to be emulated, and students were told that in America even a poor boy has a chance to become president. The recipe is hard work and determination. The colonial education that I learned at school also was reinforced at home. I remember, for example, those Christmas holidays when my mother had to make white Christmas trees by painting them white or using white soap. Soon I was dreaming of a white Christmas, even in the tropical Philippines.

In the Belly of America: Trying Hard to Be American

"I want to go to America," echoes a line from one of the songs that Union Theological Seminary (Philippines) choir was practicing for a choir tour to the U.S., although the trip did not materialize. I did not sing that line out loud because I was not a member of the choir, but I, too, without knowing it, sang silently deep down in my colonized heart of going to America. After serving some years in the pastoral ministry on the island of Leyte, by some turn of events the day came when the torrential current of societal push and pull drifted me onto the shore of the "land of the free and the home of the brave"–America!

Colonized before coming to America, when Filipino Americans immigrated to America they thought that they would blend in with the mainstream society. "In our desire to assimilate into the mainstream of society," notes Reuben Seguritan, "we isolated ourselves from one another. Lack of unity, the lack of interest and concern for each other's welfare, lack of compassion for the other's needs are just some of the pernicious effects bred by our colonial culture which have stalled our progress."[32]

Our isolation from one another and our efforts to assimilate as quickly as possible have contributed to our disempowerment and invisibility. This is in spite of the fact that Filipino Americans rank as the second largest Asian American ethnic group. If the current growth rate of Filipino Americans continues, it is estimated that in the next ten years the Filipino American population will reach more than 2 million, becoming the largest Asian immigrant group.[33]

"Trying hard to be an American," but still "falling short" from the normative American (the European American), is the plight of people of color in the U.S. "I have been four years in America," a Filipino immigrant in California said sadly, "and I am a stranger. It is not because I want to be. I have tried to be as 'American' as possible. I live like an American, eat like American, and dress the same, and yet everywhere I find Americans who remind me of the fact that I am a stranger."[34] Many young Filipino Americans, in an effort to be as American as possible and be cool, even deny their cultural and ethnic identity and, at times, even blame their parents for their physical features. They want to be just like any white youth because that is the basis of getting out of the hell of nonacceptance. Whites, often with the intention of being nice, say: "We consider you to be just like us. You don't seem [Filipino]."[35]

"Missing the Mark": Another View of Sin

No matter how hard people of color try to be Americans, they cannot be Americans if the normative American is the European American; they will forever fall short of the norm; they will remain aberrations from the norm, forever "missing the mark" (*hamartia* in Greek); they will forever remain sinners. Falling from this norm is like falling from grace; outside of this norm is hell, a place where an encounter with God is seen as impossible. This is the predicament of people of color in a white racist society, and it provides a different angle in looking at what theologians call sin.

The establishment by whites of the normative "whiteness" by which all are judged is a prime instance of idolatry. It is an expression of what Eugene Victor Wolfenstein terms "epidermal fetishism."[36] The sin of white people in the U.S., asserts James Cone, "is the definition of their existence in terms of whiteness."[37] White people's sin is the elevation of whiteness to the status of normativity and the relegation of other colors to deviancy.

How is the sin of racism experienced by people of color? Or, how do we interpret the victimization of people of color in theological terms? Speaking in particular about the experience of African Americans, Cone is emphatic in saying that the sin of blacks is the "desire to be white." It is the refusal of blacks to accept who they are. "It is," Cone continues, "saying yes to the white absurdity—accepting the world as it is by letting whites define black existence."[38]

"Desiring to be white" is an experience of alienation; it is a manifestation of internalized racism. It not only is a loss of identity or an expression of confused identity but it also leads people of color to accept mistreatment. Internalized racism, says Gloria Yamato, "leads me to believe that being treated with less than absolute respect, at least this once, is to be expected because I am Black, because I am not white."[39]

Cone's theological discourse and Yamato's confession have something to say to Filipino Americans and to all people of color in a white-dominated society. In our efforts to be accepted and to become "just like them," we betray who we are, participate in our own marginalization, and perpetuate the idolatrous reign of whiteness with all its expressions. Within the regime set by whiteness, Filipino Americans will forever "miss the mark." If they do not question the normative whiteness, Filipino Americans will be condemned to perpetual marginalization.

Out of this experience of white racism has emerged a new self, a new subject. It is a subject that has struggled to liberate itself from being a mere reflection of the white image. This, for people of color in general and for Filipino Americans in particular, is an expression of a decolonized self that has gained the courage to say, "I beseech you, color-loving God; do not make me white on the day of resurrection." If this de-colonized subject expects transformation to happen on the day of resurrection, it is not that it wants to become white or colorless, but that each color finds a distinct place among others in a colorful world.

We cannot continue talking of an emerging decolonized person of color apart from the selfhood of the white person. In a colorful world in which each color has a distinct place, the white person also assumes a new identity that is not a function of white privilege. I know that it is painful for whites to lose this white privilege, but it is the only way for whites to be truly human. When a white person can stand with others not on the basis of his or her race but on mutual respect and recognition, he or she is on the road to being a liberated white person. This metamorphosis into a new person may mean the acceptance by white-skinned people that whiteness is not an absence of color, but one among the many colors. White is a color, and white people are as colorful as the so-called people of color.

Created in the Image of God: Exorcising the White God

In the story of the garden of Eden, the serpent tempted the first couple with these words: "You will be like God" (Gen. 3:5c). The first couple succumbed to the temptation because they wanted to be "like God." Filipinos and Filipino Americans, like the first couple in the primeval garden, have succumbed to the temptation. They, too, desire to be "like God," but this time, more specifically, to be like the "white gods," their colonial and neocolonial masters. The "fall" of Filipino Americans is their desire to be "white," to be an image of the white gods. "Dealing with Filipino-ness," says writer Luis Francia, "is to deal with this condition, with a fall from grace, when the twin-headed snake of Spain and America seduced us with the promise of boundless knowledge—we too could be white gods!—even as we reposed in an unimaginably beautiful garden."[40]

Francia's lines point to various dimensions in critiquing God-talk. One dimension that I would like to highlight is that it shows us, although indirectly, the connection between our construal of God and our self-image. So, following this statement, the first order related to the task of restoring

Filipino American self-image, from a theological point of view, is not in affirming that we are created in the image of God, as the whites are, but to ask the question, Who is this God in whose image we want to be created? My purpose in raising these questions is not to posit a being, no matter how big, who is "out there" who can help us. My intention is to point out that the white God is a mirror of our alienation. It is an expression of our alienated self-identity. As God-talk is reflective of our alienation, we need to engage in the iconoclastic work against the hegemony of the European American God in order to construct a God-talk that gives way to a positive self-imaging of Filipino Americans.[41]

"I encountered God in my ethnicity" is a succinct but deep statement that comes from the mouth of Elizabeth Tay.[42] How else could it be? It cannot be otherwise, especially if one's race has been a factor that has brought so much suffering. In a society in which people of color have suffered because of their racial identity, the way to their liberation requires an encounter with a God who affirms their race and with the message that points to self-identification as a precondition for experiencing the gospel. This point is well articulated by Fumitaka Matsuoka: "Self-identification of each racial and ethnic group is necessary, for the task of self-identification is the precondition to acknowledge the very nature of the gospel."[43]

Tay, who said that she encounters God in her ethnicity, also helps us see the other side of her statement: "My identity as an Asian American woman who has been marginalized in American culture shapes, propels and is analogous to my understanding of God."[44] When God encounters us in our ethnicities or race, we are also led to see who God is for us. This shows us the theological character of our own search for identity and the anthropological character of our understanding of God.

"In a racist society," Cone strongly asserts, "God is never color-blind."[45] If God would be "pissed-off" when we pass by the color purple somewhere in a field without noticing it, to paraphrase Alice Walker's line, likewise I would say that God would be pissed-off at the idea of a "color-blind" God.[46] God would just go berserk with such an attribution, which so many whites are fond of using. A "color-blind" God (white God) has no place for people who suffer because of their color. People of color do not need a "color-blind" God.

"In the eyes of God color does not matter" are words often heard from our pulpits. "Don't worry brother, don't worry sister; after all, we are equal in the sight of God" is commonplace pulpit rhetoric. No matter how good our intention is, I believe that it is counterproductive to preach as if color does not matter to God. The idea that color does not matter to God does not deal with the unchangeable reality that we have different colors. This approach continues to devalue the people of color's color and fails to criticize our ideological distortion: that the problem is not that we are different but how we interpret our differences.

Instead of saying that color does not matter in the eyes of God, I would say that color matters in the eyes of God because God loves color. To say that color does not matter in the eyes of God, rather than showing impartiality to all colors, obliterates other colors in favor of whiteness (colorlessness). Yes, God transcends colors not by becoming colorless and "color-blind," but by becoming colorful and color-loving. God transcends colors by loving colors–not by ignoring colors–and by becoming thoroughly immersed in the various colors of the universe.

De-centering and Re-centering Notions of "Model" and "Success"

It has been pointed out, I think rightly, that Filipino Americans, especially the younger generations, need Filipino American role models. Filipino Americans need role models with whom they can readily identify. No one could serve that role better than a Filipino American. In response to this need, *Filipinas,* a Filipino American monthly magazine, published in 1997 a series of articles about Filipino Americans who have "broken the glass ceiling" in various fields: corporate America, politics, show business, the health care industry, journalism, and so forth. From ethnic marginalization, some Filipino Americans have made breakthroughs into the mainstream of American society; to name a few: military (Major General Edward Soriano and Brigadier General Antonio Taguba of the Army), entrepreneurship (Diosdado Banatao and other Silicon Valley success stories), medicine (Jorge Garcia, Jorge Camara), sports (Tiffany Roberts, Benny Agbayani, Dorothy Delasin, Akiko Thomson, Elizabeth Punsalan), journalism (Carlos Bulosan, Jessica Hagedorn, Byron Acohido, Alex Tizon), show business/entertainment (Paulo Montalban, Tia Carrere, Jocelyn Enriquez, Enrico Labayen), and the political arena (Gov. Benjamin Cayetano of Hawaii, Mayor Pete Fajardo of Carson City, California).[47]

"One Filipino American's accomplishment," says Seguritan, "is an achievement for all of us."[48] Indeed, the accomplishment of one Filipino American is an accomplishment of all, and we need to be proud of any one's achievement. Moreover, we need to rally our support around Filipino Americans who have achieved excellence in a particular endeavor, especially in light of the homogenizing proclivity of white America to lump together people of color in general and Filipino Americans in particular.

While we need to be proud of Filipino Americans who have "made it" or who have broken the glass ceiling, we also need to examine seriously our notions of "model" and "success." We need to ask, Against what criteria of "success" are we measuring Filipino Americans? There should not be an unquestioning allegiance to the American Dream. "Success" should not be measured solely in terms of having "made it" to the top of the social ladder, but more fundamentally also in terms of living with integrity.

Our role models may even include those Filipino Americans–and there are many of them–who have not "made it" by the standard of material gains, fame, or political power. Many humble Filipino Americans who are not materially wealthy can serve as our models. Our model can be the World War II veteran Macario Nicdao, who died of tuberculosis in San Francisco with an "unfinished mission"–to claim veteran's benefits.[49] It can be a lowly domestic helper, a nursing aid, a factory worker who has not given up and who has continued to hope amidst adversity. These Filipino Americans can serve as our models as well as those who have broken the glass ceiling.

Moreover, even as we are proud of the accomplishments of Filipino Americans, let us not be fooled into thinking that because a few have made breakthroughs into the mainstream that the system is, indeed, open to those who attempt to pull themselves up by their own bootstraps. Let us not be too quick to say without qualification that the accomplishments of some Filipino Americans "show us that it is possible for anyone, regardless of ethnic origin or color, to succeed in the mainstream."[50] Perhaps it is more accurate to say that the accomplishments of some Filipino Americans show that, if opportunities open up, Filipino Americans can excel in any field of endeavor. Putting it this way does not make us oblivious of the discriminatory practices that people of color in white America have to undergo. The "success" of a few minorities is not a direct proof that the system is truly open; rather, I argue that the system can be so sinister as to allow a few to break the glass ceiling, while the systemic odds are still stacked against the people of color.

The sinister machination of the system can even make use of what seems to be a neutral idea–"model minority." This notion has often functioned to hide the discriminatory practices of the system. If a few minorities have "made it," as the argument goes, then there is nothing wrong with the system, but the fault lies with complacent individuals. In this case not only has the "model minority" functioned to show that the system works, it also has functioned to condemn those who have "failed."

Studies indicate that Asian American males in general and Filipino American males in particular earn less than white males with the same level of education. When we look at the income of Filipino American women in relation to white males, the disparity of income is even more alarming. Even if Filipino American women represent a higher percentage of college graduates than white males, their income represents only a little more than one-half of the income of white males.[51] I could go on with additional statistics, but my point is to make us realize that the model stories of those who have "made it" should not make us oblivious to the systemic obstacles that people of color have experienced and continue to experience in the U.S.

Reclaiming Our Great Heritage and Proud Tradition

We are hostages of our colonial past; that is the impact of our long history of colonization. But running away from this past is not the way to get out of this captivity. Besides, we cannot really run away from our past.

We continue to be its hostage if we do not face our colonial past, exorcise it, and strive to forge a postcolonial identity. Reclaiming our proud tradition will provide us with roots and propel our imagination. Our colonial education has muted our tradition, so we need to reclaim and reinterpret it for our times.

In thinking about tradition, I am reminded of the metaphor of a footpath. Stephen Bachelor speaks of a path as a "witness to the presence of creatures like ourselves...Even if the path is deserted, even if no one has passed by in days, we are reconnected to the human (and animal) community."[52] A footpath points to those who have already walked on it. It means that there were those who have gone before us. We are not alone in our journey: We belong to a cloud of witnesses long before we took the first steps of our journey. And to continue the metaphor of a path, "simply by walking along it, we too maintain it for those who will come later. Being on a path implies both indebtedness to those who have preceded us and responsibility for those who will follow."[53]

How do we stand in relation to the tradition of which we are a part? "To stand in the living tradition," says Douglas Ottati, "is to participate in a community that is consciously informed by its common memory, actively engaged in the realities of the present, vitally concerned about its future direction, and genuinely responsive to personally creative acts of appropriation."[54] To put it differently, to stand in a living tradition is to participate in the dynamic process of interpretation *(actus tradendi)* of the received tradition *(traditum)* in light of the realities and challenges of the present.[55]

We need to retrieve and share our proud tradition *(traditum)* with the new generations and to generate the process of interpretation to make it relevant to our present struggles and our hopes for the future. Tradition gives us both roots and wings: roots that draw nourishment from the history of our community, and wings to soar and imagine new possibilities.[56] Only those who are rooted can truly reach out and imagine new possibilities. Without being deeply rooted in our tradition, our imaginations cannot soar to new heights.

Reclaiming and reinterpreting our tradition to the younger generations is significant in forging a Filipino American postcolonial subjecthood. Filipino American parents must work hard in making sure that the younger generations know about the Philippines, its people and history, and the history of Filipino Americans. Rootless assimilation to the dominant culture will not shield them from racism. As much as we value formal education, we must provide our children a good grounding in Filipino heritage. We need to organize informal classes and work for the formation of Philippine studies in the academy.

We have a rich cultural and religious heritage. Before we "encountered" our European conquerors–which is really more of an *encontronazo* (clash), according to Segovia,[57] the richness of our culture was reflected in our form of government, religiosity, festivals, writings, music and dance, and cuisine. With the European American "encounter," new forms of cultural expressions have evolved. Whatever our political affiliation, our cultural heritage unites us, and it is something of which all Filipino Americans should be proud.

However, if we are seeking empowerment, we need to combine *tinikling* (bamboo dance) and *sosyalan* parties (social parties) with political solidarity. It is premature, hollow, rootless, and deceptive to talk about some Filipino Americans breaking the glass ceiling without knowing about the Filipino American tradition of breaking silence. Starting with the coming of the Spaniards, the Filipino people broke their silence and engaged in a revolution against the colonizers. When the United States came to conquer us, we fought for our freedom. Likewise, when the Japanese landed on our shores, we engaged in guerilla warfare to resist the invaders. Whether parliamentary struggle or armed revolution, we did not just keep quiet. We broke our silence.

We brought with us this proud tradition starting with the "old timers" who landed on the shores of America. Filipino Americans have realized that it does not pay to remain silent, and silence, to paraphrase José Comblin's lines, is a lie when truth needs to be spoken.[58] The Filipino workers in Hawaii, for example, formed a union and broke their silence against unfair treatment. At first they raised their voices as an ethnic group, but later on Filipino Americans realized that they must establish a common cause with other minorities and form an interracial union.[59] Between 1920 and 1940, the Filipino workers organized twelve strikes, the most dramatic and bloodiest of which occurred in 1920, 1924, and 1937.[60]

The 1920 strike took place in the sugarcane plantations of Ewa, Waipahu, Kahuku, and Waimanalo. It was the first interracial strike organized by Filipino Pablo Manlapit and Japanese leaders. Among the strikers' demands were better wages, improved working conditions, and equal pay without regard to one's race and sex. This strike lasted for three months before it was crushed.

Also known as the Hanapepe Massacre, the Hanapepe strike happened on the island of Kauai in 1924. About twelve thousand Filipino laborers from twenty-three of the forty-five plantations went on a long strike that lasted for eight months. On September 9, 1924, a violent confrontation erupted between the strikers from the Makaweli plantation and the planters' forces. When the smoke cleared, sixteen Filipinos and four policemen were found dead and scores were wounded. Seventy-six Filipino strikers were brought to trial, of whom sixty were given four-year prison sentences.

In 1937 the Filipino workers launched another strike, which is also known as the Maui strike of 1937. Leaders took the union underground to avoid early preemptive moves by the planters and their cohorts. When the union openly launched the strike, three thousand Filipinos joined. After three months, a settlement was negotiated, the first in Hawaii's history. The strikers were awarded a fifteen percent wage increase. The Maui strike also marked the first time that *haole* (white) labor leaders extended support to the strikers.

As the largest ethnic group in the sugarcane and pineapple plantations, the Filipino workers played a significant role in the outcome of the strikes. Victory or defeat hinged on their unity and determination to go on with the struggle. There were setbacks, but the rewards of the struggle came in the form of improved working conditions and privileges for the workers.

Significant battles between Hawaii's workers and the known Big Five corporations continued after the wake of World War II, such as the 1946 Sugar Strike that lasted for three months, the Pineapple Strike of 1947, the four-month-long Sugar Strike of 1948, and the bitter six-month-long Long-Shore Strike of 1949. The International Longshore and Warehouse Union (ILWU) won in each of these strikes.

Like their countryfolks in the sugarcane and pineapple plantations of Hawaii, Filipinos also broke their silence and launched strikes in the fields of California. By 1933 agricultural workers' strikes were taking place in the fields of California. Reminiscing about a Salinas valley lettuce strike, the elderly Manuel Luz, who was wounded at that time, proudly said, "I was ready to die for what I believed in." On September 21, 1934 (which reminds me of September 21, 1972, when the dictator Ferdinand Marcos proclaimed the infamous Martial Law Decree), anti-union vigilantes torched to the ground a Filipino union's camp. Even in the face of reprisals, the Filipino workers continued to organize and press for their demands.[61]

If we fast-forward history to more recent events, we see contemporary Filipino Americans continuing this tradition of breaking silence and fighting for what they believe. In 1996, for example, Filipino American nurses protested against Mayor Rudolph Guiliani's order to lay off more than one thousand nurses from New York City–owned hospitals.[62] Also, Filipino veterans of World War II have raised their voices in the major centers of the U.S., pressing for veterans benefits. These are just a few examples of our proud tradition of breaking silence.

Turning Monuments into Movements

We should be proud of and grateful for the past monuments of our struggles. Genuine expression of our debt of gratitude *(utang na loob)* to the past and to our present companions demands that we turn their pain into a transforming anger and hope: anger directed against the oppressive situation, and courage to transform the situation. Concretely, this means that true expression of our gratitude comes when we turn the monuments of the past into movements of continuing transformation.

Turning past monuments into people's movements is our way of making the victims and the "dis-appeared" into martyrs or witnesses.[63] We proclaim liturgically the turning of the tortured bodies and the "dis-appeared" into martyrs in the eucharistic meal, but it is in the concreteness of people's movements that carry forward the memory of the "dis-appeared" that they are made bodily present. Like Bulosan, who took the task of making the poor peasants of the Philippines "live in [his] words," it is also our task to make the monuments of the past live in our contemporary movements.

The story of Ligaya Domingo and her father Silme Domingo–both labor organizers–illustrates true gratitude to the labors of the past, the shift from anguish into anger, and the turning of monuments into movements.[64] Ligaya Domingo was only five years old when her father (Silme), along with a fellow activist, was shot to death by Ferdinand Marcos' henchmen in Seattle on June 21, 1981. Silme became the target of the Marcos regime's ire for his responsibility in making the International Longshoremen and Warehousemen's Union (ILWU) take an unprecedented international focus on the Philippines.

Twenty years after the incident, Ligaya is following in the steps of her father. In an interview, Ligaya says that her father is still a persistent presence in her life: "Sometimes I think about what he would want me to do, and how he would see me in what I'm doing…Sometimes I really get sad about it." Silme's memory is very much alive in Ligaya's life.

In speaking about her labor involvement, Ligaya said that her father taught her an important lesson: "It's that you cannot simply give up the fight." But there were moments when her tone, as organizers can easily understand, revealed weariness and fatigue. "One thing that's frustrating for me," she said, "is that even when we see victories, they're small, they're really small." As an example: "We had a strike at West Seattle Psychiatric Hospital last year, and after 138 days we got the contract that we wanted. But you know, that's just one victory in a cloud of a million other things to fight for."[65]

As Ligaya was speaking about the enormity of the things to fight for and how small a single victory is, her words came out "between laugh and sigh." "Between laugh and sigh" is an expression of a Filipina upbringing, perhaps part of the survival mechanisms of people who have to surmount hardships of various sorts. "Between laugh and sigh" also captures a deep moment in the life of a person who is committed to a better tomorrow, but who also experiences the stubborn forces of closure. What Ligaya has done is small when we think of the millions of issues to fight for, but she has done something significant. She has turned the monuments of her father's labor and sacrifice into a movement.

There are other Filipino Americans who have risen from their anguish, turning it into rage and further into movements of transformation. We can use as an example the events that transpired in the wake of Joseph Ileto's murder, a post office worker in California who was gunned down by white supremacist Buford Furrow on August 10, 1999, while delivering mail.[66] In memory of Joseph Ileto, his sisters created an acronym that represents a movement. Joseph stands for "Join Our Support: Educate, Prevent Hate." And Ileto: "Instill Love, Equality, and Tolerance to Others." What happened to Ileto is a wake-up call not only to Filipino Americans but also to the wider society. Our silence will not protect us from hate crimes. In solidarity with the previous generations of Filipino Americans who have broken their silence, we need to turn the past monuments into movements of today.

Filipino American Subjecthood in a Globalized World

Filipino Americans need to realize that their presence and plight in the U.S. is a microcosm of the plight of Third World people all over the world. I agree with Robert Blauner that "the economic, social, and political subordination of third world groups in America is a microcosm of the position of all peoples of color in the world order of stratification." This is not an accident, Blauner continues, but "is part of a world historical drama in which the culture, economic system, and political power of the white West has spread throughout virtually the entire globe."[67]

It is out of this global drama that Filipino Americans must take account of their presence in the U.S. Why are they in the United States? Their presence in the U.S. is an outcome of the globalization phenomenon. Globalization, both in its earliest and latest expressions, has led to the marginalization of the Philippines–economically, politically, and culturally– in relation to the affluent countries of the world. With this peripheralization, it is not surprising that Filipinos often make their way into the socioeconomic centers of the world. Globalization has created a diaspora people with multiple identities and belongings who are shaped by the interweaving of the global and the local.[68] Filipino Americans, especially the first generation, exhibit these characteristics of a diaspora people: multiple identities and "belongings." They know that they belong to the United States, but they also maintain a sense of belonging to the country of their origin, which is commonly expressed by sending the almighty dollar back home to family members and in *balikbayan* (literally, "visit to one's hometown") trips. Filipino Americans embody in their very selves the interweaving of the global and the local, between a home here and a home back there.

My coming to the U.S. has given me a new lens with which to see and understand in a much deeper way the question of identity in a global context. In the Philippines, though I was doggedly committed to issues of social justice, I was not concerned about the connection between social justice and the politics of identity in a globalized setting. In fact, I basically understood identity through an essentialist and monochromatic lens. My experience in the U.S. has informed my perception of my complex identity and belonging as one of being forged in the nexus of the global and the local.

When Filipino Americans see themselves in the interweaving of the global and the local, they also will see their ethnic identity in a broader light. Their struggle to understand their identity and plight will propel them to see matters that transcend specific ethnic concerns. Beyond sending the almighty dollar to the folks back home, Filipino Americans need to understand that the global and the local are interwoven. If Filipino Americans understand this interweaving, they will not be unequivocally happy when the U.S. dollar is up and the Philippine peso is devalued, for their economic advantage is predicated on their fellow Filipinos being disadvantaged along with other people, as well. Knowing that their existence lies at the nexus of the global and the local, Filipino Americans can affirm with R. B. J. Walker that "behind the insistence on acting locally is a challenge to rework the meaning of human community in an age in which our vulnerabilities are indeed global in scale while our capacity to act is circumscribed by who and where we are."[69]

As people who have embodied marginalization and who have experienced what it means to cross geographical and cultural divides, Filipino Americans can help build bridges of connections. As people who have known what it means to suffer as a result of one's color, they also can help project a vision of a just, colorful, and sustainable tomorrow. But they must learn to articulate what they have embodied and experienced if they are to help in making the larger U.S. society realize the interconnecting dynamics of the plight of Third World people and the plight of marginalized groups in the U.S. They must publicly express their protest against globalization's "downward harmonization where [they] are and help others resist it where they are."[70]

A realistic hope for our globalized world today does not lie in some miraculous intervention, whether supernatural or techno-capitalist, but in the groaning and greening socially conscious and active people who have resolved to make a difference in various locations and stations in life. No critical realism, business-as-usual realism, piecemeal pragmatism, hyperactive cynicism, post-utopian cynicism, pessimistic determinism, and couch-potato optimism can take us out of sick bay. No group of "think tanks"–the so-called paragons of knowledge–can provide us with easy solutions, nor can the fresh concoctions from intellectual mandarins and adroit gurus of the cathedrals of capitalism. No bumper sticker or sound bite solutions can suffice, nor can a single voice. The notion that without a single light to guide us we are lost is passé, and this fallacious claim needs to be exposed to blistering criticism.

We are in this journey for postcolonial subjecthood for the long haul, always aching and aiming for the promise while gathering nourishing provisions along the way, and celebrating moments of life-giving openings whenever and wherever we can. Filipino Americans' quest for postcolonial subjecthood can only be forged in the wakefulness of transformative praxis. This involves the long and arduous task of exorcising colonial selfhood and the visionary praxis of articulating a new social self. I hesitate to say that our time is the most challenging time, but this is *our* time and *our* challenge. Filipino Americans must dare to be postcolonial subjects!

Notes

[1]Carlos Bulosan, cited in Ronald Takaki, *In the Heart of Filipino America: Immigrants from the Pacific Isles* (New York and Philadelphia: Chelsea House Publishers, 1995), 90.

[2]Ibid., 88.

[3]Ibid., 91.

[4]Ibid., 90.

[5]Carlos Bulosan, *America Is in the Heart: A Personal History* (1946; reprint, Seattle: University of Washington Press, 1973).

[6]Fernando Segovia, "Introduction: Minority Studies and Christian Studies," in *A Dream Unfinished: Theological Reflections on America from the Margins,* ed. Eleazar S. Fernandez and Fernando Segovia (Maryknoll, N.Y.: Orbis Books, 2001), 25.

[7]Ibid.

[8]Walter Wink, *Unmasking the Powers: The Invisible Forces that Determine Human Existence* (Philadelphia: Fortress Press, 1986).

[9]Ibid., 59.

[10]Ibid., 58.

[11]R. S. Sugirtharajah, *Asian Biblical Hermeneutics and Postcolonialism: Contesting the Interpretations* (Maryknoll, N.Y.: Orbis Books, 1998), 16.

[12]Wong Wai Ching, "Postcolonialism," in *Dictionary of Third World Theologies,* ed. Virginia Fabella and R. S. Sugirtharajah (Maryknoll, N.Y.: Orbis Books, 2000), 169.

[13]Sugirtharajah, *Asian Biblical Hermeneutics and Postcolonialism,* 17.

[14]Homi Bhabha, cited by Wong Wai Ching, in *Dictionary of Third World Theologies,* 169.

[15]Ella Shobat, "Notes on the 'Post-colonial,'" *Social Text* 31, 32 (1992): 99–113, cited in Sugirtharajah, *Asian Biblical Hermeneutics and Postcolonialism,* 18.

[16]See Edward Farley, *Ecclesial Reflection: An Anatomy of Theological Method* (Philadelphia: Fortress Press, 1982).

[17]Justo González, "The Changing Geography of Church History," in *Theology and the New Histories,* College Theology Society Annual, ed. Gary Macy, no. 44 (Maryknoll, N.Y.: Orbis Books, 1999), 25.

[18]Enrique Dussel, "1492: The Apparition of the Other–Conquest and Prophetical Criticism in the Origin of Modernity," (Cole Lectures, Vanderbilt University, February 5, 1992).

[19]Eleazar S. Fernandez, *Toward a Theology of Struggle* (Maryknoll, N.Y.: Orbis Books, 1994), 69–70.

[20]Peter McLaren, *Revolutionary Multiculturalism: Pedagogies of Dissent for the New Millennium* (Boulder, Colo.: Westview Press, 1997), 197.

[21]Ibid., 198.

[22]A similar phenomenon is happening in the U.S. as teenagers, dubbed "mall rats," use malls as hang-outs. See Thomas H. Naylor and William H. Willimon, *Downsizing the U.S.A.* (Grand Rapids, Mich.: Eerdmans, 1997), 59.

[23]Robert Schreiter, "Contextualization from a World Perspective," *ATS Theological Education* 30 (Autumn 1993): 82; Schreiter, *The New Catholicity: Theology Between the Global and the Local,* Faith and Culture Series (Maryknoll, N.Y.: Orbis Books, 1997).

[24]The notion of "regime of truth" helps us to understand that the relationship between truth and power is not simply a relationship of cause and effect respectively. It is not simply that truth is power or that might is right, but that truth and power co-produce each other. See Michel Foucault, *The Foucault Reader,* ed. Paul Rabinow (New York: Pantheon Books, 1984), 51–75.

[25]Refer to Michel Foucault's *The Order of Things: An Archeology of the Human Sciences* (New York: Vintage Books, 1973).

[26]Renato Constantino and Letizia Constantino, *The Philippines: A Past Revisited,* vol. 1 (Quezon City, Philippines: Renato Constantino, 1975), 12.

[27]Paulo Freire, *Pedagogy of the Oppressed,* trans. Myra Bergman Ramos (New York: Herder and Herder, 1972), 134.

[28]Franz Fanon, *Black Skin, White Masks,* trans. Charles Lam Markmann (New York: Grove Press, 1967).

[29]"Aliens in Our Land," *Philippine Resource Center Monitor* 9 (November 1990): 2.

[30]Mary Ballou and Nancy Gabalac, *A Feminist Position on Mental Health* (Springfield, Ill.: Charles C. Thomas, 1985).

[31]Eric Gamalinda, "Myth, Memory, Myopia: Or, I May Be Brown But I Hear America Singin'," in *Flippin': Filipinos on America,* ed. Eric Gamalinda and Luis H. Francia (New York: The American Writers' Workshop, 1996), 3.

[32]Reuben Seguritan, *We Didn't Pass Through the Golden Door: The Filipino American Experience* (Institute of Filipino American Research, 1997), 117–18.

[33]Aurora Tompar-Tiu and Juliana Sustento-Seneriches, *Depression and Other Mental Health Issues: The Filipino American Experience* (San Francisco: Jossey-Bass, 1995), 8. Since the last major wave of Filipino newcomers, the Filipino American population has increased tremendously. The 1990 census counted 1.4 million Filipino Americans. Most of these Filipino Americans belong to the first generation of immigrants.

[34]Ronald Takaki, *Strangers from a Different Shore: A History of Asian Americans* (New York: Penguin Books, 1998), 316.

[35]Grace Sangkok Kim, "Asian North American Youth: A Ministry of Self-Identity and Pastoral Care," in *People on the Way: Asian North Americans Discovering Christ, Culture, and Community,* ed. David Ng (Valley Forge, Pa.: Judson Press, 1996), 203.

[36]Eugene Victor Wolfenstein, cited in McLaren, *Revolutionary Multiculturalism,* 270.

[37]James Cone, *A Black Theology of Liberation,* twentieth anniversary ed. (Maryknoll, N.Y.: Orbis Books, 1986), 107.

[38]Ibid., 108.

[39]Gloria Yamato, "Something About the Subject Makes It Hard to Name," in *Race, Class, and Gender: An Anthology,* ed. Margaret Andersen and Patricia Hill Collins (Belmont, Calif.: Wadsworth, 1992), 67.

[40]Luis Francia, "The Other Side of the American Coin," in *Flippin': Filipinos on America,* 6.

[41]See Christie Neuger, "Feminist Pastoral Theology and Pastoral Counseling: A Work in Progress," *Journal of Pastoral Theology* 2 (Summer 1992): 53, for the relationship between image of God and self-understanding and its application for pastoral counseling.

[42]Elizabeth Tay, quoted in Fumitaka Matsuoka, *Out of Silence: Emerging Themes in Asian American Churches* (Cleveland, Ohio: United Church Press, 1995), 134.

[43]Matsuoka, *Out of Silence,* 134.

[44]Tay in Matsuoka, *Out of Silence,* 134.

[45]Cone, *A Black Theology of Liberation,* 6.

[46]Alice Walker, *The Color Purple* (New York: Washington Square Press, 1978), 178.

[47]See Ely Barros, "The U.S. Army's First Filipino Generals," *Filipinas* (October 1997): 27–28; Emil Guillermo, "Tiffany Roberts: Gold Mettle," *Filipinas* (March 1997): 38–39, 41; *Filipinas* (June 1998): 40; Laura Schiff, "She's Just Drawn That Way," *Filipinas* (August 1997): 38–42. See also Veltisezar Bautista for a longer list of Filipino American success stories: *The Filipino Americans: From 1763 to the Present* (Farmington Hills, Mich.: Bookhaus Publishers, 1998).

[48]Seguritan, *We Didn't Pass Through the Golden Door,* 144.

[49]Rick Rocamora, "Unfinished Mission: The American Journey of Filipino World War II Veterans," *Filipinas* (June 1998): 25.

[50]Seguritan, *We Didn't Pass Through the Golden Door,* 144.

[51]Dean Alegado, "The Growth of Filipino America," *Filipinas* (December 1999): 45.

[52]Stephen Bachelor, "The Other Enlightenment Project: Buddhism, Agnosticism, and Postmodernity," in *Faith and Praxis in a Postmodern Age,* ed. Ursula King (London: Cassell, 1998), 115.

[53]Ibid.

[54]Douglas Ottati, "What It Means to Stand in a Living Tradition," in *From Christ to the World: Introductory Readings in Christian Ethics,* ed. Wayne Boulton, Thomas Kennedy, and Allen Verhey (Grand Rapids, Mich.: Eerdmans, 1984), 86.

[55]Peter Hodgson, *Winds of the Spirit: A Constructive Christian Theology* (Louisville, Ky.: Westminster John Knox Press, 1994), 22.

[56]See Jay B. McDaniel, *With Roots and Wings: Christianity in an Age of Ecology and Dialogue* (Maryknoll, N.Y.: Orbis Books, 1995), 23.

[57]See Fernando Segovia, "Aliens in the Promised Land: The Manifest Destiny of U.S. Hispanic American Theology," in *Hispanic/Latino Theology: Challenges and Promise,* ed. Ada María Isasi-Díaz and Fernando Segovia (Minneapolis: Fortress Press, 1996), 16.

[58]José Comblin, *The Church and National Security State* (Maryknoll, N.Y.: Orbis Books), 15.

[59]Dean Alegado, "Blood in the Fields," *Filipinas* (October 1997): 63–64, 76, 90.

[60]Ibid., 63–64.

[61]Brandy Tuzon, "The War in Salinas," *Filipinas* (October 1996): 66–67, 74.

[62]Seguritan, *We Didn't Pass Through the Golden Door,* picture page.

[63]See William Cavanaugh, *Torture and Eucharist* (Oxford, England: Blackwell Publishers, 1998).

[64]Jennifer Soriano, "Organizer's Daughter: Labor Organizer Ligaya Domingo," *Filipinas* (March 2000): 28–29, 31–32.

[65]Ibid., 32.

[66]Emil Guillermo, "What Joseph Ileto Stands For," *Filipinas* (October 1999): 32.

[67]Robert Blauner, "Colonized and Immigrant Minorities," in *From Different Shores: Perspectives on Race and Ethnicity in America,* ed. Ronald Takaki (New York and Oxford: Oxford University Press, 1987), 159.

[68]See Fernando Segovia for the connection between postcolonial studies and diasporic studies as they relate to the field of theology. Segovia, "Interpreting Beyond Borders: Postcolonial Studies and Diasporic Studies in Biblical Criticism," in *Interpreting Beyond Borders,* ed. Fernando Segovia (Sheffield, England: Sheffield Academic Press, 2000).

[69]R. B. J. Walker, *One World, Many Worlds: Struggles for a Just World Peace* (Boulder, Colo.: Lynne Rienner Publishers, 1988), 102.

[70]Jeremy Brecher and Tim Costello, *Global Village or Global Pillage: Economic Reconstruction from the Bottom Up,* 2d ed. (Cambridge, Mass.: South End Press, 1998), 108.

6

Land of Maple and Lands of Bamboo

GREER ANNE WENH-IN NG

I think I've got it
I know I've got it
I'm sure I've got it—
the theology of Asian women in North America,
the theology I'm developing, nay growing,
the faith we've been practicing,
is none other than—bamboo theology!
For that's the way I, and others like me,
have survived—by being bamboo...
Like bamboo, we've had to be
tall and hollow, so as to be able to
withstand wind and storm, yet
reaching high into the sky.
And, like bamboo, we've had to exist
in clusters—not singly, not alone,
each caring only for its own...
As a rule, the bamboo is alien
to North American soil, except in mild climes
like B.C. or L.A.
How can we Asian women claim a space
in which to grow, nay, to flourish
in this adopted or native land?
How can we, as bamboo, stand up
and be counted among mighty oaks,
syrup-producing maples, towering cedars?... [1]

What happens when someone moves from lands lush with bamboo, surrounded by the ocean, to lands covered with cedar, oak, and maple, fed by lakes great and small? How does one reorient oneself not only in lifestyle, study expectations, and work demands but also in faith convictions, liturgical expression, and spiritual practice? What has to change? What remains? What is gained? What is lost? What is different about an emerging "bamboo theology" that can contribute to the theological discourse of the whole?

Whose Journey: How Much Does It Matter?

At the outset, I must "come out" with the particularities of my identity and social location, because my theological understanding and perspective, like those of anyone else, are grounded in my particular heritage, generation, and context. I am a first-generation, middle-class, female heterosexual Chinese immigrant of the "second wave" (post-1965). That is, my "Asian Americanness" is more in the sense of being an "Asian in North America" rather than that of an "Asian American" born and raised on this continent, as ABCs and CBCs are.[2] In other words, my North American experience may differ in significant ways from that of descendents of an earlier imported Chinese labor-force "sojourner" group lured by dreams of a "gold mountain," and again from that of more recent "1.5"-generation Chinese or Korean children and young teens who emigrated to this continent as part of their immediate families. At the same time, this "Asian Americanness" comes chiefly by way of Canada, rather than through residing and belonging in the United States itself—though there were six years in New York as a graduate student. In a volume dedicated to the theological struggles, learning, and discoveries of Asian Americans, the opportunity for an Asian Canadian minority voice to share or add is evidence of inclusiveness, a commitment to diversity. For though there are many commonalities that transcend national boundaries for Asians on this continent, Canada as a nation does have a distinct history, a geographical reality, and social characteristics of its own.

Even my Chinese heritage has its own "slant." "Home" for me in childhood has included sojourns in Vietnam and Macao as well as my birthplace, Hong Kong. Yet the Confucian formation in my youth and young adulthood was eventually subsumed under the pervasive Western cultural shaping of a British colonial educational system. Similarly, the Christianity that I adopted was mainly the version brought and practiced by Catholic and Protestant missionaries from Italy, England, and the United States. The resulting mentality is one that could lead to the paradox of a weird sense of culturally "coming home" when certain images one has imbibed from study but never actually witnessed appear before one's eyes. One powerful instance was the young green buds of spring on hedges, bringing to life Chaucer's unforgettable lines in the Prologue to the *Canterbury Tales* about such green "ysprongon on everith holt and heath."

Another was the sight of real daffodils that justified Wordsworth's enthusiastic, almost mystical description of them learned by heart as one of the earliest efforts of getting into the rhythm of a new [i.e., English] language. Other emotional homecomings would include experiences such as finally setting foot in Westminster Abbey, or catching the first glimpse of Niagara Falls and picking up discarded pieces of gem-streaked rock in the cave of an abandoned mine near Bancroft on the Canadian shield—these latter two experiences having been duly learned in global geography class in junior high.

Are there similar parallels of a sense of homecoming theologically? The reply would have to be yes and no. For someone baptized in Hong Kong's China Congregational Church, it certainly felt as if I were entering a related branch of the ecclesial family when I joined the United Church of Christ during graduate school and, later, the United Church of Canada, which has the Congregational Union as one of its founding denominations in 1925. It was satisfying to be actually crunching snow underfoot when walking to the Christmas Eve service "in the bleak mid winter" (though, ironically, Christina Rossetti's lovely images had already been contextualized from a Middle Eastern to a Northern European landscape and climate). But on the whole, it was not so much the known as the new that broadened my personal theological horizons. For the days of the good Pope John XXIII (late fifties to early sixties) were heady ones for a former convent schoolgirl enjoined never to darken a Protestant church, and contacts between budding Maryknollers and Union Theological Seminarians blossomed into daring acts of sharing at more than just the dinner table. Perhaps, even for a relatively young Christian as myself then, there was a beginning of chafing under the missionary yoke. The first stage of any process of conscientization is to entertain the possibility of one's subjugation/oppression.

Drinking from Our Own Wells: Acts of Claiming/Reclaiming

For first-generation, formerly colonized immigrant Asians like myself, therefore, the pain of coming face-to-face with our colonized mentality can constitute one of the higher rungs on a "hierarchy of pain," after the survival struggles of food, shelter, health, and employment have been more or less resolved. It is nothing less than a recognition of having been robbed of an essential part of one's identity. How to seek out that part and reclaim it constitutes a first act of resistance. In a way, such acts of "cultural recovery" can parallel the "search for roots" of *sensai,* or third-generation, American/Canadian–born persons of Asian heritage, and can become a common front on which to act together—for instance, in organizations/movements such as PACTS (Pacific Asian American Center for Theology and Strategies) or PAACCE (Pacific Asian American Canadian Christian Education

Ministries). For those in our midst who have grown up being hurt by ignorant racist taunts of "Why don't you go back where you came from?" such claiming may take the form of making the physical journey to our ancestors' native village for the first time. For others of us who have throughout our English-speaking schooldays been called by European saints' names given by well-meaning missionary teachers, it may take the form of taking back the use of our Asian language given names. The particular time in someone's life when these acts of resistance occur depends very much on the particular stage of one's racial-ethnic identity development.[3]

Asian congregations in North America have traditionally been committed to the preservation of heritage languages by operating or sponsoring Asian language classes. New activities in recent years have included other identity-strengthening initiatives such as the production by PAACCE of the resource "Pacific Asian American Canadian Cultural Literacy 101," which introduces basic texts of Asian North American life in the form of fiction, biography, and film, as well as suggested immersion experiences of sites connected with the painful history of the Asian presence in America, such as Angel Island in the San Francisco Bay area (where all entering Chinese nationals were detained, sometimes for unreasonably long periods) and the Japanese American Museum in Los Angeles (with numerous artifacts from the relocation camps). Such resources, together with the actual life stories of Asian North American Christians and their communities, can aid in theological reflection and indeed in the formation and articulation of both story theology[4] and autobiographical theology.[5]

In matters of spiritual and liturgical practice, cultural recovery can take a variety of forms, although most of these run the danger of raising the spectre of syncretism for church members still under the sway of a "Western/ missionary practice equals orthodoxy" syndrome and therefore need to be embarked on with great sensitivity.[6] Some of those with which I have experimented include:

(a) Introducing Asian hymnody—making available either through translation from original Asian languages or by indigenous production hymns depicting Asian and Asian North American experiences and theological perspectives;

(b) Incorporating (appropriately, of course) the use of symbols from heritage Asian cultures on liturgical occasions, such as the color red for Chinese weddings and "New Year couplets" as banners;

(c) Reflecting on the connections between Asian religio-cultural traditions and festivals and Western Christian traditions (for instance, having an Asian winter festival for the lunar new year using the winter festival aspects of Christmas, or combining the annual commemoration of the dead/ancestors with All Saints Day);

(d) Adopting some religio-cultural practices, such as embodied *Taiji* movements or yoga meditation, into one's personal spiritual practice.

This dimension of a bamboo theology may be seen as the North American parallel to the movement of indigenizing liturgy and theology of the young churches of East and Southeast Asia in the sixties and seventies and continued by the contextualizing approaches of Asian theologians within the Ecumenical Association of Third World Theologians (EATWOT) and the Programme for Theologies and Cultures in Asia (PTCA). It can be summarized thus:

Growing a bamboo theology is a process–
…gathering the resources of one's own culture,
one's own community, one's own life and loves–
~ stories, myths, legends, operas, nursery rhymes,
~ mid-autumn festivals, Chinese New Year
~ dragons and jade pendants and tofu and rice
~ Daoist paintings hung on drawing room walls in one's childhood
~ Taiji movements one adopts without knowing
~ calligraphy script…
~ red paper couplets on either side of an ancestral tablet
~ graveside commemorations every spring and fall.[7]

Cultural Identity in Diaspora: Confronting the Danger of Orientalism

Empowering as this journey of claiming/reclaiming may be, a cautionary note needs to be sounded regarding the very real danger immigrants often fall into, that of either (for first generations) trying to preserve cultural patterns and values as they knew them when they left their lands of origin, or (for subsequent generations) that of believing that if only they went back far enough, they would be able to recover the "pure" heritage of their ancestors. But since cultures are never static but forever evolving according to political and socioeconomic contextual necessities, there really is no mythical "pure" original tradition to return to. There simply is no cultural essentialism. For Asians in diaspora like myself, this is a hard lesson to learn, but a crucial one if we are to avoid the Scylla of cultural negation only to fall into the Charybdis of Orientalism. Edward Said in his postcolonial theory has helped us see that "Asia," with its many colorful, exotic (and for us nostalgic) cultural entities, was actually a construction of the West, especially of Western intellectuals and scholar "experts," a construction maintained to function as "Other" for the West's domination and consumption. This is especially tempting in these days of the early twenty-first century, when everything from "authentic Asian cuisine" (Korean, Thai, Vietnamese, and Indonesian, as well as the more well-known Japanese and Chinese) to *feng shui* (the art of location according to direction and the positioning of furniture and interior decoration to channel *qi,* or energy flow) is gaining in popularity among the general population. In our enthusiastic journey of cultural recovery, we must be sophisticated enough to exert vigilance, lest we succumb to a new type of "reverse cultural imperialism" through cultural misappropriation–something of which Native peoples also have unhappy experiences.

What then, are we to do? As minorities in North America who daily experience the need to cross boundaries, we might have to adopt a strategy of "hybridity" in this age of globalization, like our contemporaries in Asia and Africa, who are daily bombarded with multimedia representations from powerful, usually American-based, multinationals, sometimes find it useful to do. Perhaps we can insist on heritage symbols and/or values (all those Confucian ones–work ethic, respect for elders, preserving harmony in home and community–for which our neighbors envy us) where it is strategic to do so and where it will be helpful to the rest of society, and to resort to more "globalized" (read, "homogenized" as a Western norm) ones where necessary or appropriate. Cultural hybridity straddles more than one culture as norm. Here is where the flexible bamboo, which bends with the wind at the height of a storm, learns to survive while the more rigid trees around them are felled by the force of hurricanes and typhoons. The only additional caution is to be critically aware of what principles besides expediency guide our choices. I would suggest as a theological criterion that of liberatively abundant life as, for instance, when trying to discern how far the traditional injunction to "obey your elders" should go in matters of cross-generational relating in our faith communities and in our own families. This is especially relevant where women are concerned, because one of the sad consequences of too uncritical a reversion to traditional (read "Confucian") values is a condoning of male dominance and the primacy of male heirs to continue the ancestral line, resulting in the devaluing of daughters and all females, so that they become, in the words of sociologist of religion Jung Ha Kim, cross-bearers as well as bridge-makers.[8]

Recently, sociologists and cultural anthropologists have been arguing that the phenomenon of globalization, which affects the "stay-at-homes" as well as the ones that move/migrate, seems to have brought about more porousness in several areas in contemporary life. The migration of labor is dictated more by a response to demands for cheap labor rather than by a deliberate choice of desirable host locations. Then there is flexible citizenship, a term coined by anthropologist Aihwa Ong to apply to Asian investors and capitalists who fly the "Pacific shuttle" as modern-day astronauts (breadwinners who have established households in foreign soil but fly back and forth to places of origin to do business) as a new breed whose chief loyalty may be to more than the land where they have settled their families.[9] What kind of effect does such straddling of more than one nation-state by Asians in the North American diaspora have on the rest of us, either locally born or more permanently settled? Does the attendant concept of deterritorialization, put forward by John Tomlinson as a cultural condition of globalization, apply in some degree to us too?[10]

What tensions does it set up for the biblical tradition of identity and its close ties with "land"? How does the concept of diaspora keep "home" and dispersion in tension for more settled immigrants, whose "homing desire" may have already been transferred to the fixed locality of adoption?[11]

One consequence that I have personally experienced is that of an increasing awareness of the inevitability of one's connections with Asia and its ideas, because "settledness" in North American soil/society can become loosened from time to time by happenings in the lands I left so many years ago. This is definitely so for all immigrants still with close family ties or members in our places of origin. At the same time, theological developments in those lands become part of our theological resources.[12] Our lives in North America have often been influenced by the dynamics between national states in Asia and the U.S. or Canada—we only have to recall the racist killing of Vincent Chan in Detroit, who was mistaken for a Japanese, at the time of intense rivalry between the American car industry and Japan's. The dramatic increase of immigrants from Asia in the late twentieth and early twenty-first centuries is leading to a fear of the "thirdworldization of American cities."[13] Sri Lankan British scholar Avtar Brah calls this aspect, which affects all host societies, "the diasporising of home" in juxtaposition with the "homing of diaspora" produced by the settling down process.[14] Whether we like it or not, "crossing oceans" has become for Asian North Americans a repeatable act both actually and metaphorically, not just a time-frozen migratory journey.[15]

Biblical Journeys from the Other Side

The Asian North American journey intersects with the biblical journey in interesting ways. Consider the following vignettes:

(a) The year was 1980; the occasion, the first Ontario Women's Conference in Canada. More than two hundred women in table groups listened intently as three Bible study leaders reflected on the well-known story of Sarah and Abraham, intrigued by the prominence given to Hagar by one of the leaders, but also feeling somewhat disconnected. It was only when the third leader, a Chinese Canadian woman, told them of the practice of concubinage in China, of how in her congregation she was even then ministering to more than one family with children born of "second mothers" impacted by the material and psychological consequences of such lesser status, that they began to catch a glimpse of the "realness" of the very human dynamics of that ancient biblical family. This was a perspective they had not heard from before. With a connection established, they were then more ready to accept the suggestion that the Divine actually chose to reveal itself to this "minority" female, and not to just send her a birth announcement like that received by Mary of Nazareth many centuries later.

(b) Fast forward to the latter years of the same decade, when a select group of Asian American "church bureaucrats" and lay denominational representatives from both sides of the border gathered in San Jose to consider their antiracism work. For Bible study they were invited to consider in their own context (and that of their communities) Jeremiah's exhortation in his letter to the exiles in Babylon: "Build houses and live in them…[S]eek the welfare of the city where I have sent you…and pray to the LORD on its behalf, for in its welfare you will find your welfare"(Jer. 29: 5a, 7). The energy that filled the hall from the engaged buzz of sixty-odd earnest minds and hearts was proof enough that even staid male Asians who expected to receive straight lectures on which to reflect individually as the only legitimate form of Bible study were able to open up and share reflections and struggles with one another when given encouragement to deal communally with issues they had personal insight into.

(c) When asked, "And what was the name of Naomi's other daughter-in-law?" only a few voices responded from among many, in an ecumenical group studying the Bible to be better preparing themselves for the end of the World Council of Churches Ecumenical Decade of Churches in Solidarity with Women. And no wonder, for Orpah's point of view had seldom made the regular commentaries. It remained to another minority woman, an African Canadian in the group, to point out how the Moabite community might have looked on Orpah, the one who remained loyal, rather than Ruth, the deserter, as the faithful one. In fact, this same member was so excited about this unusual angle of looking at the Bible that she eventually signed up to enter theological school on a part-time basis.

Thus,

Growing a bamboo theology is
engaging the Judaeo-Christian scriptures
through the eyes of the neglected, ignored,
unnamed, silent and silenced ones,
from the perspective of the servant girl,
the oft-maligned "enemies of Israel,"
the other daughter-in-law.
It is learning to choose from among
Graeco-Roman-Euro-Anglo-German…traditions
which strands to discard
which strands to preserve
which to weave into our new fabric…[16]

One of the realities of being Asian/Asian American-Canadian is that of being a "minority" and, as a minority, to exist on the margins rather than at the centers of power. As a woman in a society still fairly patriarchal, as a racial-ethnic minority in a predominantly Anglo-European institution and nation (albeit it is a nation with an official multicultural policy), as a pastoral/ministry theological educator in an academic climate still giving centrality to the "classical disciplines," I have existed on a complex of margins in spite of my majority status given by my education, profession, and socioeconomic class. And yet being on the margin, as Korean American theologian Jung Young Lee has argued, can give one an "in-both" advantage, not only the "in-betweenness" that is often seen as problematic and undesirable.[17]

One such "privileging," as the above vignettes have shown, is the perspective people on the margin can gain into scripture by approaching it from "the other" side, much as feminist interpreters have been doing. Not the side of the victors who eventually remembered the stories, passed them on, and eventually wrote them down, but the side of the defeated or unimportant. As "voices on the margin"[18] engaging and being engaged by Christianity's sacred texts, Asian North American Christians are often drawn to those on the margin, wondering what their side of the story might have been and how God might have acted in their lives and helped them survive. In daily scripture readings and sermon preparation, we begin looking for hints of such stories, imagining feelings and struggles and, where such stories are absent, to ask why. In reflecting on such stories and exploring them with others, we may come to insights that mainstream biblical commentators may not arrive at. A related task is then to share the results of our research and reflection with others in the faith community, whether in the form of Bible study leadership, published articles, or church school curricula.[19]

Such a journey is, of course, not limited to Asian North Americans alone, but very much one that is shared by our brothers and sisters in the Native American/Canadian, African American/Canadian, and Hispanic American communities. For instance, a group from these communities who felt they had something unique to contribute to the church and its theology met over several years in the 1980s in a "Roundtable of Ethnic Minority Theologians" under the sponsorship of the United Methodist Church. In their exploration of the relationship between the Bible and their cultural backgrounds and ethnic experiences and what new insights the latter might have for the former, they came to agree on a few general points:

1. The Bible has been used in the past (by dominant group interpreters) as a tool of oppression to minorities and the powerless (hence, justice must be central in all biblical interpretation).

2. A new hermeneutics is needed, to be based on an approach quite different from the traditional/dominant (Western) one.

3. There is a great deal in these traditional cultures that allow members to come closer to the biblical worldview than much Western theology (a more holistic worldview, an extended family structure—in a word, sharing with the Bible a more "high-context" culture).

4. "Community" occupies a central place in such new hermeneutics.[20]

5. It is exciting to watch the development of this new hermeneutics,[21] one of the elements of which is that the traditional struggle between fundamentalist/conservative and liberal interpretation is something these interpreters are not too much concerned about, since issues of oppression and liberation, marginalization and justice, hardship and survival matter so much more in the lives of these communities.[22] Along the same lines, salvation to these communities lies not so much in the niceties of atonement theory, but stark, mere survival to the next day or, as Asian American feminist theologian Rita Nakashima Brock puts it so well in a christological study based on one of the protagonists in Amy Tan's *The Joy Luck Club*, "losing your innocence but not your hope."[23]

We will reflect more of the shared aspects of the Asian American journey with others below.

Intersecting Journeys within and with Other Nondominant Communities: Toward a Theology of Solidarity

Thus, the Asian North American journey, albeit with many specificities, is never taken in isolation but in community—the individual with her family, a family with other families within their own ethnic group, one ethnic group in relation to other ethnic groups. The kind of relations that exist and evolve between and among them, however, can vary, ranging from the much-vaunted "family/clan solidarity" of Confucian-oriented groups, to the mistrust and hostility that could erupt in south central Los Angeles between nondominant racial-ethnic groups. I use the term *nondominant* here instead of the more traditional *minority* to combat the derogatory connotation of "minors in tutelage" pointed out by Avtar Brah in discourse pertaining to women, working classes, and subjugated peoples.[24] Even within the same ethno-cultural group, younger generation members in asserting themselves to achieve their 1.5- or second-generation identity may be perceived as rebellious by their elders; female members of the first generation may have roles and functions thrust on them rendering them equal or even chief breadwinners, roles that unsettle age-old gender role expectations; long-time settlers may resent what to them looks like all-too-easy acceptance of more recent immigrants by the host society.[25] To eliminate conflict altogether is impossible, and perhaps not even desirable, in spite of the supreme value of harmony still carried by many of us. Perhaps a more attainable goal is to try to understand the underlying causes for some of these power dynamics in order that just dealings may ensue. In this concluding section, I will confine my exploration to (a) relations between the major existing groups within Asia America, and (b) relations between Asian Americans/Canadians and members of other nondominant racial ethnic groups.

(a) It has generally been accepted that variations in immigration history (period, socioeconomic circumstances, the political atmosphere influencing the attitude of reception by the host country, etc.) can render different the lives within their own ethno-cultural group, but may render common the lives of groups crossing geophysical homelands or ethno-cultural lines. Thus, there is probably more in common among late twentieth-century "capitalist" emigrants from South Korea, Hong Kong, Taiwan, or Singapore than between them and the pre-1965 or even pre-1980s immigrants (recruited laborers, skilled artisans, students, employed professionals) from the same ethnic group. However, there is also no denying that historical occurrences in their home nations or places of origin can sometimes subtly color how one immigrant group relates or reacts to another group even when they are now in North America, far from their homelands. One only has to recall the conquest and colonization by Japan of Korea, Taiwan, and almost all of Southeast Asia, plus the war with China, to acknowledge that strong feelings could linger even among Christians, sometimes unconsciously. As a rule, Asians everywhere usually preserve "face" by not letting such feelings rise to the surface–a style of conflict management described by Alban Institute researcher Virstan Choy as "ginseng over aspirin."[26] But psychologically, will there come a time in each person's journey when the past, including one's communal past, must be exorcised before an effective common stand can be embarked on?

In my own experience as a theological and church educator, one strategy with some promise is getting to know one another's history on this continent, usually a history of oppression, in order to induce empathy and forge a common bond of resistance and justice seeking. This can come about by researching and making accessible historical accounts in existing texts, by facilitating face-to-face meetings (for instance, survivors of World War II Japanese American/Canadian relocation/internment camps or their descendents), and, where such meetings are impossible to arrange, by being introduced to the powerful portrayals of such lives found in autobiographies, fictional accounts, or on film/video. In Canada, for instance, Joy Kogawa's *Obasan* has become a classic work of fiction in this genre, while more recent Chinese Canadian women writers Sky Lee *(Disappearing Moon Cafe)* and Denise Chong *(The Concubine's Children)* have filled with female and family perspectives the gap left by earlier or other male accounts such as those by Paul Yee *(Salt Water City, Ghost Train,* etc.) and Wayson Choy *(The Jade Peony, Paper Shadows).* Together with more well-known Asian American writers (Maxine Hong Kingston, Amy Tan, Gish Gen, and others recommended in the PAACCE Pacific Asian American Canadian Cultural Literacy 101 list), contemporary Asian North Americans are given a chance to develop some empathy with another Asian group as they encounter that group's pain and struggle on this continent. These can include both struggles of forebears, such as Chinese railroad workers and Filipino, [East] Indian, and Korean sugar-cane workers in Hawaii in the mid-nineteenth and early twentieth centuries, as well as the struggles of the Vietnamese boat people in the seventies and eighties, and those of the most recent boat people from China's Fujian Province to American and Canadian shores.[27] Hopefully, such exposure can be the means of conscientizing one another into a common history of discriminatory, exclusivist, racist treatment by government and the dominant society. It can challenge us not to be complacent, but ever to be vigilant. As Fumitaka Matsuoka reminds us, dealing with racism has been a steady theme in the life of Asian American churches.[28]

A similar challenge facing us as Christian faith communities is how to claim some measure of autonomy in denominational structures without ghettoizing ourselves or shirking our contribution to the whole. In the Presbyterian system, for instance, Korean presbyteries have been set up on both sides of the border. Another model is that of the Ethnic Ministries Council of the United Church of Canada with a mandate of supporting the ministries of congregations other than Anglo-Francophone and Native/ Aboriginal ones. To recognize ethno-cultural distinctiveness, "Associations" of Chinese, Japanese, Korean, and Filipino Canadian [United] churches meet annually for support and intra-group decisions. The model thus takes into account the history, distinctiveness, and needs of each group without sacrificing the mandate of working together as a much-needed core group within the larger framework of a mainstream Anglo-Canadian church structure and membership. The Council's ministry of empowering the leadership of women and their ministries is manifested concretely in a biennial conference, "Sounding the Bamboo," that recognizes and honors the multiplicity of its own makeup by its slogan "We are Many, We are One."

(b) Such a recognition and honoring of difference and diversity while pursuing common goals should also stand at the heart of intergroup relations between Asian North Americans and other nondominant groups. It also stands in contrast to a bland, neutral, naive, tolerant kind of multiculturalism that aims at utopian inclusion without acknowledging the very real and sharp divisions that can exist between such groups. The fact that, in the United States at least, Asian Americans have come to be perceived as the "model minority" must cause resentment among non-Asian groups whose histories of subjugation (slavery for African Americans, conquest and then discriminatory immigration sentiments for Mexican Americans, cultural genocide against Native Americans, etc.) are different enough to make it hard for such "pulling oneself up the one's bootstraps" efforts to work as effectively. The carry-over of a historical attitude of cultural superiority on the part of "civilized" East Asians like the Chinese, who were wont to look on all other ethno-cultural groups as Barbarians,[29] does not help matters because it allows for a residue of prejudice toward non-Asians on this continent, sometimes leading to the charge of "reverse racism" or racism pure and simple.

On this issue, however, it is helpful to realize that genuine racism is prejudice plus power—control of others' lives, power over, not simply prejudice, as pointed out by Virginia Harris and Trinity Ordona in their essay in the epoch-making volume *Making Face, Making Soul.*[30] A more accurate phrase, they suggest, is "cross-racial hostility," which they characterize as prejudice plus trying to feel powerful, which much more accurately defines relationships that can exist between Asians and non-Asian nondominant groups in North America. We need to be aware that this is a by-product of the kind of structural racism that has played one group against another by differentiating the treatment given to these groups. We must also guard against the trap of relating only to the dominant group each on our own and thus not learning to find out the intergroup dynamics among us for more horizontal relating.

Horizontal relating will not eliminate existing differences, but it can attempt to accord just treatment to one another while respecting and indeed celebrating the differences. Sometimes just treatment will mean acknowledging past wrongs in which some of us have become implicated, such as the cultural genocide and physical or sexual abuse perpetrated on Native residential school students by the employees of those mainline denominations that operated the schools.[31] Only then can we be linked in solidarity (thus has Korean Minjung theologian Kim Young Bok described acts of solidarity) as we attempt to address what Fumitaka Matsuoka calls "the monopoly of imagination" and "domestic colonization" expressions of racism on this continent,[32] to release the *han* of historically and contemporary oppressed groups.[33] The challenge, then, is for those, even within those groups, with greater power not to force even well-intentioned acts of solidarity on those with less power, to be vigilant in what womanist social ethicist Emilie Townes refers to as a refusal to dominate as well as to be dominated. For, as Townes realistically puts it, "solidarity and differences are messy...[W]e will not always agree...[W]e may not be able to work/ together on everything or every issue."[34] Yet we do not give up because of "the hope that is in us," because of our faith in that supreme act of solidarity, the incarnation, when the Godhead took on human identity with all its restrictions and vulnerability for humanity's sake.[35] It is this faith that enables Asian North American Christians to cling to a stubborn conviction that the God of our ancestors, the *Dao,* the Great Spirit, ultimately wills that bamboo clusters can hold their own among taller though not necessarily stronger maples, oaks, and cedars in this vast land:

> Maker of oak and maple and cedar
> as well as of bamboo,
> you will show us how.[36]

Notes

[1]From G. A. Wenh-In Ng, "Bamboo Theology," *Journal of Asian and Asian American Theology* 2, no. 1 (Summer 1997): 126, 128.

[2]ABC is a nickname for "American-born Chinese," and CBC for "Canadian-born Chinese."

[3]For an interesting explication of the theory of racial-ethnic identity development as applied to Asians in America, see David Sue and Derald Sue, *Counseling the Culturally Different: Theory and Practice,* rev. ed. (New York: John Wiley & Sons, 1990).

[4]The "guru" among Asian theologians in advocating story theology is Chao Sang Song, beginning with *The Tears of Lady Meng: A Parable of People's Political Theology* (Geneva: World Council of Churches, 1981), through *Tell Us Our Names* (Maryknoll, N.Y.: Orbis Books, 1989), to *The Believing Heart: An Invitation to Story Theology* (Minneapolis: Fortress Press, 1999).

[5]See Peter C. Phan and Jung Young Lee, eds., *Journeys at the Margin: Toward an Autobiography Theology in American-Asian Perspective* (Collegeville, Minn.: Liturgical Press, 1999).

[6]I deal with these matters in more detail in the following: "The Asian North American Community at Worship: Issues of Indigenization and Contextualization," in *People on the Way: Asian North Americans Discovering Christ, Culture and Community,* ed. David Ng (Valley Forge, Pa.: Judson Press, 1996), 147–75; "The Dragon and the Lamb: Chinese Festivals in the Lives of Asian Canadian/American Chinese Christians," *Religious Education* 84/3 (Summer 1989): 368–83; and "One Faith, One Baptism—One Liturgy? Worship in a Multicultural, Multifaith Context," *Reformed Liturgy and Music* 30, no. 3 (1996): 146–49.

[7]G. A. Wenh-In Ng, "Bamboo Theology," 129.

[8]Jung Ha Kim, *Bridge-Makers and Cross-Bearers: Korean American Women and the Church* (Atlanta: Scholars Press, 1997). Issues of how both tradition and the Christian scriptures can be oppressive and/or liberative for Asian and Asian North American women are also discussed in Greer Anne Wenh-In Ng, "Asian Sociocultural Values: Oppressive and Liberating Aspects from a Woman's Perspective," in *People on the Way,* 63–104; Young Lee Hertig, "Asian North American Women in the Workplace and the Church," in *People on the Way,* 105–28; and Greer Anne Wenh-In Ng, "Toward Gender Justice: Challenges in Human Living from a Confucian-Christian Perspective," *Ching Feng* 41/3-4 (September-December 1998): 345–61. A recent volume delineating Asian American women's struggles within ethnicity, identity, and other issues and their eventual resolution can be found in psychotherapist Claire S. Chow's many verbatim accounts in *Leaving Deep Water: Asian American Women at the Crossroads of Two Cultures* (New York: Plume Books, 1998).

[9]Aihwa Ong deals with this issue specifically in "The Pacific Shuttle: Family, Citizenship, and Capital Circuits," in *Flexible Citizenship: The Cultural Logics of Transnationality* (Durham and London: Duke University Press, 1999), 110–36. The whole volume is illuminating on the phenomenon of transnationality as experienced by Asian nationals-turned-immigrants.

[10]John Tomlinson deals with the issue of deterritorialization specifically in "Deterritorialization: The Cultural Condition of Globalization," in his fascinating study *Globalization and Culture* (Chicago: University of Chicago Press, 1999), 106–49. Multilocality is dealt with in the final chapter, "The Possibility of Cosmopolitanism," 181–207.

[11]This question is stimulated by issues discussed by Avtar Brah's critical thinking in "Diaspora, Border and Transnational Identities," in *Cartographies of Diaspora: Contesting Identities,* Gender, Racism, Ethnicity series (London: Routledge, 1999), 178–210.

[12]Such resources would include the following periodicals: *Asia Journal of Theology,* the *CTC Bulletin* (Committee on Theological Concerns, Christian Conference of Asia), *In God's Image* (Asian Women's Resource Centre for Culture and Theology), *Ching Feng* (Christian Centre for the Study of Chinese Religion and Culture), *Voices from the Third World* (Ecumenical Association of Third World Theologians), and *Inter-Religio* (Network of Christian Organizations for Interreligious Encounter in East Asia).

[13]Brah, *Cartographies of Diaspora,* 190–95.

[14]Ong, *Flexible Citizenship,* 100.

[15]See Greer Anne Wenh-In Ng, "Crossing Oceans, Crossing Disciplines: Doing Theology as Asians in Diaspora," in *Ecumenism in Asia: Essays in Honour of Feliciano Carino,* ed. K. C. Abraham (Bangalore: Board of Theological Education–Senate of Serampore College, and the Association of Theological Education in South East Asia, 1999).

[16]G. A. Wenh-In Ng, "Bamboo Theology," 130.

[17]See especially chapters 2 and 3 in Jung Young Lee, *Marginality: The Key to Multicultural Theology* (Minneapolis: Fortress Press, 1995), 29–76.

[18]R. S. Sugirtharajah, ed., *Voices from the Margin: Interpreting the Bible in the Third World* (Maryknoll, N.Y.: Orbis Books, 1995), has been seminal in the development of my own interpretive approach over the years. Helpful works from Asia include Christian Conference of Asian Women's Concerns Unit, *Reading the Bible as Asian Women* (Singapore: 1986); Lee Oo Chong et al., eds., *Women of Courage: Asian Women Reading the Bible* (Seoul: Asian Women's Centre for Culture and Theology, 1992); Kwok Pui-lan, *Discovering the Bible in the Non-Biblical World* (Maryknoll, N.Y.: Orbis Books, 1995); and Kwok Pui-lan, "Racism and Ethnocentrism in Feminist Biblical Interpretation," in *Searching the Scriptures: A Feminist Introduction,* vol. 2, ed. Elisabeth Schüssler Fiorenza (New York: Crossroad, 1993); as well as the work of Western feminist biblical interpreters such as Schüssler Fiorenza, Phyllis Trible, and others.

[19]One of the most innovative attempts in the way of Christian education curricular resources is the two sets of biblically based curricula (five volumes each from Kindergarten to College-Adult) produced by the Presbyterian Church (USA) under its Asian American Christian Education Curriculum Project with Wesley Woo as project director: *Choosing Sides: The Book of Judges from An Asian American Perspective,* and *One in Christ: The Letter to Galatians from An Asian American Perspective* (El Cerrito, Calif.: San Francisco Presbytery, 1988).

[20]Based on the summary of the four papers presented and the discussion that followed, contained in Justo L. Gonzalez, "Visions of the Word," in *Out of Every Tribe and Nation: Christian Theology at the Ethnic Roundtable* (Nashville: Abingdon Press, 1992), 38–56.

[21]See, for instance, the communal effort by African American biblical scholars in Cain Hope Felder, ed., *Stony the Road We Trod: African American Biblical Interpretation* (Minneapolis: Fortress Press, 1991).

[22]Gonzalez, *Out of Every Tribe and Nation,* 49ff.

[23]See Rita Nakashima Brock, "Losing Your Innocence But Not Your Hope," in *Reconstructing the Christ Symbol: Essays in Feminist Christology,* ed. Maryanne Stevens (New York/Mahwah: Paulist Press, 1993).

[24]See especially the section "Diaspora and Minority" in Brah, "Diaspora, Border and Transnational Identities," in *Cartographies of Diaspora,* 186–90.

[25]See Aihwa Ong, "Chinese Modernities: Narratives of Nation and of Capitalism," in *Ungrounded Empires: The Culture Politics of Chinese Transnationalism,* ed. Aihwa Ong and Donald Nononi (New York/London: Routledge, 1997); as well as Ong, *Flexible Citizenship.*

[26]Virstan B. Y. Choy, "Ginseng Before Aspirin: Acupuncture Instead of Surgery: Insights from the PAACE West Event on Conflict Management in Asian American Congregations,"

PAACE Newsletter 7, no.4 (October 1991); Choy, "Asian American Conflict Management," in *Yearbook of American and Canadian Churches, 1995* (Nashville: Abingdon Press, 1995), 17–19, and Choy, "Conflict and Decision-Making in [Asian American] Congregations," in *People on the Way,* 239–79.

    [27]Two informative and analytical volumes on the history of Asian Americans are Sucheng Chan, *Asian Americans: An Interpretive History* (Boston: Twayne, 1991); and Karin Aguilar-San Juan, ed., *The State of Asia America: Activism and Resistance in the 1990's* (Boston: South End Press, 1994).

    [28]See his account and analysis in Fumitaka Matsuoka, *Out of Silence: Emerging Themes in Asian American Churches* (Cleveland: United Church Press, 1995).

    [29]For an informative introduction to this attitude, see Tu Wei-ming, "Cultural China: The Periphery as the Center," in *The Living Tree: The Changing Meaning of Being Chinese Today,* ed. Tu Wei-ming (Stanford: Stanford University Press, 1994), 1–34.

    [30]See Virginia Harris and Trinity Ordona, "Developing Unity Among Women of Color: Crossing the Barriers of Internalized Racism and Cross-Racial Hostility," *Making Face, Making Soul: Creative and Critical Perspectives by Women of Color,* ed. Gloria Anzaldua (San Francisco: Aunt Lute Foundation, 1990), 304–15.

    [31]The Roman Catholic, Anglican, and United Churches in Canada are currently (closing years of the 1990s and into the early 2000s) in the turmoil of being sued by former students of residential schools. These students were taken from parents and Native communities to be educated and socialized to become "white." These schools were operated on behalf of Canada's federal government between the 1920s and the 1970s.

    [32]Fumitaka Matsuoka, *The Color of Faith: Building Community in a Multicultural Society* (Cleveland: United Church Press, 1998), especially chap. 3, "Racism as a Monopoly of Imagination," 57–96.

    [33]Korean American theologian Andrew Sung Park's *Racial Conflict & Healing: An Asian American Theological Perspective* (Maryknoll, N.Y.: Orbis Books, 1996) deals with this in detail from the experience of Korean Americans involved in the racial riots in south central Los Angeles in 1992.

    [34]Emilie M. Townes, "Women's Wisdom on Solidarity and Differences (On Not Rescuing the Killers)," *Union Seminary Quarterly Review* 53/3–4 (1999): 153–64.

    [35] See G. A. Wenh-In Ng, "Toward a Theology of Solidarity," *Groundswell* (Summer/Fall 1996): 1–2.

    [36]G. A. Wenh-In Ng, "Bamboo Theology," 130.

7

From Context to Context

Cognitive Dissonance

ROY I. SANO

Introduction

Asians in North America have undergone many changes. First, they came from many parts of Asia to a very different world in North America. Their trip across the Pacific Ocean, the largest body of water on this earth, dramatically depicts drastic changes involved. Second, after their arrival, they moved across a variety of economic, social, and cultural barriers and terrains. Third, interpretations of their experiences have undergone changes. Indeed, the Asian North American pilgrimage from context to context involved changes in geography, experiences, and interpretations.[1]

We will focus on steps that altered interpretations of Asian American contexts in the midst of recent changes.[2] The procedure, which is sometimes called "contextualization," seeks to align interpretation with current realities and thus to clarify courses of action and their rationale. The steps will begin with experiences and then move to critical reflections on the traditions that process them.

The purpose of the process is to empower people to take charge of their own lives and improve the lives of their people, to offer contribution to the welfare of others and renew the environment–a "vision of hope." The purpose summarizes what Christians mean by "making disciples" of Jesus Christ who participate in God's mission.

Elaborating the Purpose

A brief elaboration of the purpose may be important at this point. Described succinctly, a disciple is attuned to who God is and what God is doing and saying. The brief statement requires an explanation on two points.

First, being "attuned" involves our cognitive, affective, and volitional functions. The cognitive functions include activities of the mind, such as thinking and knowing, understanding and imagining. The affective functions include the full range of feelings in hating and loving, fear and confidence, sadness and joy, as well as revulsion and resolution. Finally, the volitional functions appear in the choices we make as an individual or with others. If we say the cognitive, affective, and volitional functions are involved in being attuned to God, it represents one way to assert that the whole person is fully engaged in being attuned to God. Such persons share those qualities with others and thus improve the human and natural ecology.

The brief description requires a second explanation. The reference to God is vague. Described more comprehensively, a Christian is attuned, through the Holy Spirit, to who God is and what God does and says, as revealed in Jesus Christ. It is, after all, the Holy Spirit, the living and acting Divine Presence, who empowers and guides us to grow in being attuned to God (Jn. 16:13; Rom. 8:14). Finally, Jesus Christ reveals in telling ways who God is and what God does and says (Jn. 14:9; Col. 1:15). The presence and actions of the triune God make it possible to "make disciples."

Start with Experiences of Pathos and Anguish

We will begin with pathos and anguish in Asian American experiences.[3] They lead us into the depths of our experiences. Pathos combines pain with possibilities; anguish combines anger with aspirations. Pain can cut deep and become destructive with self-pity, blaming, and a drive for vengeance. In pathos, however, our pain does not smother the flickering possibilities for vindication that is restorative for victims and perpetrators. Similarly, anger by itself can eat us up. In anguish, however, anger stirs aspirations to rectifying what has gone awry. Pathos and anguish do not immobilize us into acquiescence. Rather, they induce restlessness and longings. With nurturing, pathos and anguish generate a resolve: We will "not be overcome by evil, but overcome evil with good" (Rom. 12:21), whether it is overcoming lies with truth, injustice with justice, hate with love.

Pathos and anguish occur in any number of settings. Chinese Americans, for example, experience pathos and anguish when they visit Angel Island in the San Francisco Bay and read those poems written on walls by immigrants confined for months and years within sight of their destination. Japanese Americans experience the same in their pilgrimage to the site of windswept, abandoned, wartime concentration camps in the desert. The list goes on and on of other Asian Americans who rehearse histories through anecdotes, poems, and songs. With reminiscences in symbols and stories, they liturgically reenact the past, which illuminates the present. Indeed, we are referring to hallowing moments permeated with pathos and anguish.

Reason in Critical Reflection

If they are not nurtured, pathos and anguish can degenerate into maudlin, sentimental nostalgia. Critical reflections on modes of interpreting these experiences enhance the cognitive aspects of being attuned to God and, consequently, the affective and volitional aspects. Critical reflections employ reason in several ways. Reason clarifies concepts, contexts, and questions. Reason also develops cogency through consistency in a system of concepts, coherence in a narrative, and correspondence of concepts, systems, and narratives to facts. With reference to concepts, religious discourse adds symbols and stories, doctrines and dogmas. With reference to narratives, religious discourse speaks of metaphors and myths made visible in drama and rituals. With reference to facts, we will note in our reflections on theology and scriptures two levels of the facts important for religious discourse.

Reason fulfills these functions in descriptive and prescriptive tasks. In the descriptive task, reason describes the concepts, systems, and narratives that are actually operating when we interpret a specific context and thus perceive what we can do and why. In the prescriptive task, reason explores other concepts, systems, and narratives that are more appropriate to interpret a given situation and thus specify better options for action and improve the rationale.

Reason turns to a number of resources for the descriptive and prescriptive tasks to fulfill its functions. We will highlight the "scientific" and cultural resources that have proved particularly crucial to improving a reading of our situation, as well as clarifying what we can do and why. In both resources, we will turn beyond them to traditions in the scriptures (the Bible) and see how our spiritual ancestors were attuned to God in comparable settings. The critical and constructive "communion with the saints" therefore reshapes our cognitive function and thus energizes our affective and volitional functions toward better ends. A "vision of hope" permeates our America of the heart.

Traditions in the Social Sciences

Integrationist Traditions

In the descriptive task of reason, we begin with an examination of the modes of perceiving and interpreting our situation that are currently operating in us. Because we have appropriated them from the prevailing values, these modes of perception and interpretation come under the classification of traditions.

In the ethnic studies movements of the late 1960s and early 1970s, racial minorities became conscious of the disparity between the expectations that we inherited from the 1940s and 1950s and the actual outcome. The broken promises generated pathos when we remembered those who had sacrificed so much for us. The same discoveries evoked anguish in us because we had gullibly accepted false hopes. The pain and the anger did not destroy us because critical reflections improved our reading of the situation. New readings revealed neglected possibilities and stirred aspirations to take charge of our lives.

Critical reflections also uncovered a serious conceptual confusion that obscured the disparity between the purposes of integration strategies and the actual results. Milton Gordon exposed the flaw. In his 1964 study *Assimilation in American Life,*[4] Gordon distinguished between acculturation of racial ethnic minorities into the behavior and values of the prevailing culture in the U.S. and their assimilation into existing sectors of society. Just because immigrants and their children, for example, were acculturated into the "American way of life" at the point of language, residence, employment, and so forth, it did not mean they were assimilated into existing social and economic, political and cultural enclaves still dominated by whites. Once we identified the conceptual confusion of acculturation with assimilation in the integrationist hopes and strategies, we rejected the false promises of the "melting pot" theory. In effect, the promises said to people of color, "if you become like us, we will like you and welcome you into our sacred precincts."[5]

The concept of marginalization, which suggested a horizontal axis, proved inadequate to describe our place in society. While it appropriately indicated people of color were kept at the margins of society, it did not adequately describe the stratification that the power arrangements created and maintained.

Several studies accumulated the data and explained why stratification, and its implicit vertical axis, more accurately described our context. First, the Kerner Commission studies of the racial upheavals of the mid- to late-1960s rightly concluded that white racism in the U.S. had created "two societies, one white, the other black."[6] Second, for many Asian Americans, Harry H. L. Kitano and Roger Daniels, in their book *American Racism,* confirmed the division but included other people of color and provided a conceptual schema.[7] They named prejudice, discrimination, segregation, and domination with possibilities of genocide as that which created and maintained the "two category system" where whites were on top and racial ethnic minorities were below.[8] Individuals, of course, play important roles in creating and perpetuating the racial divide.

Even more, however, clusters of institutions and their backup systems created various patterns of inequities in residence, education, employment, income, wealth, and cultural opportunities. These sectors of society virtually acted like a chain of causation. Unless exceptional personal qualities or circumstances intervened, the chain of causation sent people of color into a downward and narrowing spiral of diminishing resources and privileges. While focusing our corrective action on key institutions in this chain made sense, a third study gave us cause for modesty and realism. In his book *Racial Oppression in America,* Robert Blauner reminded us about the intractability of racism. He said that advocates for racial justice and harmony had falsely assumed that "racism and racial oppression are not independent dynamic forces but are ultimately reducible to other causal determinants, usually economic or psychological."[9] Elaborating Blauner's view in the affirmative, racism is an independent force and as such is able to find new expressions even if we transform individuals and improve social and cultural, economic and political institutions.

Given the contributions of these sample studies, critical reflections in our struggles for racial justice and harmony prescribed concepts, analytical frameworks, and narratives in line with our actual situation. They explained what was happening as our communities experienced pathos and anguish in our struggles. At the same time, we expanded the scope of our reflections in two ways. One dealt with class, and the second with international human rights struggles in South Korea and the Philippines.

Expanding the Picture, Developing Coalitions

First, in the 1970s, we had to take seriously a measure of social and economic advancements on the part of Asian Americans and, therefore, address the issue of class. We did so while we challenged the popular media picture of Asian Americans as "model minorities." The stereotype held the promises of the "log-cabin-to-White-House" mythology over us, but covered up growing numbers of our elderly and new immigrants who did not enjoy comparable advances.

Beth E. Vanfossen offered a promising option to interpret the operations of racism within a larger framework. After she had participated in the struggles of the 1960s and 1970s for racial justice, peace in Southeast Asia, and equality for women, Vanfossen sensed that much was still amiss and that a lot of the advances had gone awry. She pursued graduate studies in order to analyze what had actually happened. In 1979, Vanfossen produced the results of her studies in *The Structure of Social Inequality.*[10] She offered a careful critique of the then-prevailing structure-function approach in social analysis associated with Max Weber and Talcott Parsons. They essentially depicted the subjects and objects in the social environment on a horizontal axis.

In place of the Weber-Parsons tradition, Vanfossen located people on a vertical axis in a stratified society. On top are the determinative institutions, especially in economic systems with "junior partners" in political systems. The determinative institutions are supported in their pursuits from "below," on the one hand, by control systems in law, military, and intelligence agencies, and, on the other hand, by social systems in family, education, media, and religion. Vanfossen correctly lists religious bodies among support systems. We sadly know that too many religious groups socialize people into the structures and simply sanctify the power arrangements.

The dynamics of power arrangements allow, for example, the educational and religious support systems to challenge and force alterations at some points in the economic and political institutions. The determinative institutions, however, still remain determinative in the end. They resist fundamental changes despite all the efforts to change them through the legislature, judicial procedures, executive orders, and other public means such as through the media.[11] The determinative institutions, with the help of support systems, allocate the resources of society, including the necessities in housing, medical care, welfare, and transportation that affect income, wealth, and prestige.

With her analysis, Vanfossen explained what was amiss and why her involvements went awry. The "structures of inequality" upstage the struggles and understandably induce the pathos and anguish in a widening body of people. Others, such as William Domhoff, also highlighted the role of universities, think tanks, and foundations that develop the rationalization or ideologies for these power arrangements.[12] These analyses offered a better reading of our context by naming the *individuals, institutions,* and *ideologies* that give this power arrangement such coherence it operates without a single center in total control. Advancements in technology and shifting organizations strengthen its hold. People, regardless of color, gender, or orientation in middle and lower classes, now move to form coalitions. They could see the distinct contributions of various movements for change within a broader conceptual framework and a wider sweep of the course of events.

The second expansion of our analyses emerged out of our international struggle for human rights in the 1970s. Asian Americans, along with some *personas non grata* living in exile here, focused on dictators in South Korea and the Philippines. Dictators acted as elites in their society and as tools in U.S. development and national security ideologies during the Cold War era. They exploited their own people and wreaked havoc on their countryside with transnational corporate ventures. Our involvements uncovered an international network of intelligence agents operating with impunity in their homelands and in the U.S. If indigenous repressive efforts failed, oppressors launched counterinsurgency forces, trained and supported by the U.S. Where those measures failed, armed forces, amassed in the Cold War, entered the fray. In essence, the analytical model proposed for "internal colonialism" of class, gender, and race was extended in its basic outline to "neo-colonialism" in the international scene. In the post–Cold War era, we need a further round in the spiral of critical reflection on the positive and negative impact of the structures and operations of globalization.

Shift in Consciousness

Critical reflection described the inadequacies of the prevailing modes of interpreting our context and prescribed better modes of perception, courses of action, and rationale. New perspectives called for a shift of consciousness. Progressive middle-class Asian Americans in various denominations worked with the prevailing liberal middle-class notion. Living above the poverty line, they saw themselves pushing a button here or pulling a lever there to improve society. They essentially became technocrats managing the machinery of this society and steering it toward greater justice.

Liberals worked with this consciousness because a bourgeois mythology in our civil religion assumes that nothing prevails over us. The bourgeois had overturned the "three estates" of the royalty, the nobility, and the clergy in the eighteenth-century democratic revolutions. They therefore had access to responsive decision makers as peers. Together they could alter our context at basic points in the "post-revolutionary" setting.

The analysis above suggests, however, that even if we were living "above the poverty line," we still live "under the power line." We no longer live in the "post-revolutionary" era, where powers did not exist over us. We now live in a "pre-revolutionary" era, with new powers "over us." Those powers manage, if not manipulate, us and even outwit and outmaneuver our brightest and best efforts.[13] As evidence, "mainline denominations" that many Asian Americans worked with from the 1960s through the 1990s are now "sidelined," and other religious bodies are the "mainline." If the middle class fails to make a shift in consciousness and learn to work from "below the power line," they will live with a "false consciousness." To acknowledge the realities in our situation, however, does not need to lead us to despair. Pathos combines pain with promise; anguish combines anger with aspiration. On what grounds can we see possibilities and work for basic changes–a vision of hope?

The Theological Tradition and the Bible

To provide "an account of the hope that is in us" (1 Pet. 3:15b, paraphrased), we turn our critical reflection to our theological tradition. We do so because it can help describe a second level of facts. We have dealt with the first level in the social realities visible to everyone. The biblical writers, however, reported at another level who God is and what God is doing and saying in the course of those events. The doctrine of salvation summarizes what God does to rectify what has gone wrong. Critical reflection on this "tradition of the elders" exposes the way they have muffled neglected strands of the biblical tradition that speak more appropriately to our situation (Mt. 15:6; Mk. 7:9).[14]

Critical Reflection on the Order of Salvation

In the usual picture of this doctrine we find no sustained theological strand that deals with the social realities as intermediaries that hamper God's saving activities. Efforts that sought to overturn the political or economic domination appear in separate ethical considerations subsequent to the experience of salvation. If the drama of salvation deals with anything beyond the experiences of individuals, the doctrine of atonement, as the interpretation was called, refers to suprahuman transactions between God and the devil or Satan.

The evolution of the doctrine of salvation illustrates a preoccupation with reconciling individuals to God. Medievalists, at least from the Protestant perspective, said that by doing what is right, we get right with God. In the early sixteenth century, Martin Luther taught Protestants to reverse the order. We get right with God by trusting God's gracious forgiveness and are therefore able to do what is right (Eph. 2:8). Speaking doctrinally, justification, or forgiveness that makes us right with God, precedes sanctification, or the changes in us whereby we can do what is right. Because he concentrated so much on justification, Luther was reluctant to say that much change could actually occur through sanctification. John Calvin, shortly thereafter, expressed confidence that justification by God would lead to improvements in us through sanctification (Rom. 5:1–5). In the eighteenth century, John Wesley dared to add a third step in the process. The biblical witness, in the command to be perfect, actually expected us to be perfect (Mt. 5:48; Heb. 2:10; 12:23). Recognizing the resistance to accept this challenge, Wesley carefully circumscribed the scriptural understanding of perfection. The doctrine of salvation therefore developed into a process with three steps: justification, sanctification, and perfection of individuals. The doctrine noticeably excludes references to historical forces of oppression and exploitation over us and between ourselves and God. The Latin title for the doctrine, *ordo salutis,* "the order of salvation," has given this narrow focus a sacrosanct status.

Because tradition confined the experience of salvation to individuals, participation in struggles for social justice is a secondary, if not a secular, consideration. From this perspective, those who advocated stands on social issues or participated in political activities were less religious and pursued profane commitments. Amidst the heat of "culture wars" in the 1970s and 1980s, religious critics from the right said that participants in and supporters of liberation struggles in the last half of the twentieth century against classical European colonialism, internal colonialism, and neocolonialism were stirred by an evil spirit. Something serious is at stake. According to Jesus Christ, anyone who says that the stirring of the Holy Spirit comes from an evil spirit is committing blasphemy, an unforgivable sin (Mt. 12:22–32; Mk. 3:19b–30; Lk. 12:8–12).

Critical Reflection on the History of Salvation

Decades of biblical studies suggest that the Holy Spirit, and not an evil spirit, prompted people to join those struggles for liberation. These studies uncovered a number of "histories of salvation" in the Hebrew and Christian Scriptures that see God directly involved in rectifying social, economic, and political evils. Furthermore, these activities of God are integral to salvation itself. They cannot be reduced to one-dimensional secular affairs. Indeed, these histories of salvation depict the religious dimension of the Divine Presence that people experienced in their struggles for racial justice and equity for women and men below the power line, as well as restoration of human rights and health to the environment.

We can only review one of the histories of salvation in Ezekiel's prophetic words to the children of Israel in exile. In the early sixth century B.C.E., invading forces took many of the children of Israel into captivity in Babylonia. During their captivity, Ezekiel announced that God would stage a course of events reminiscent of (1) the exodus from Egypt, (2) the uniting of the people before their God at Sinai, and (3) the eventual building of a society in a new land.[15] Three words in the English translation summarize the story in three stages: take, gather, and bring. They appear together with a slight variation seven times and sound something like a creedal formula that abbreviates the sweep of the history of salvation.[16] (1) "Take" describes a new exodus, or a liberation from the oppression and exploitation of the Babylonian captivity. (2) "Gather" depicts the reuniting of the people who had been scattered after the destruction of the nation and is reminiscent of the covenanting at Sinai. (3) "Bring" summarizes all that is required to create a new livable space by rebuilding the nation and the countryside, their capital city and the temple.

According to Ezekiel, the Sovereign Savior, Yahweh, says that the course of events "will vindicate the holiness of my great name" (Ezek. 36:23, paraphrased). Furthermore, Yahweh says "[T]he nations [Gentiles] shall know that I am the LORD" (36:23c), meaning they will be converted after they see the "taking, gathering, and bringing."[17] If the holiness of the divine name is vindicated and Gentiles come into an intimate relationship with Yahweh, we are speaking of a sacred, not secular, history of salvation. Because Yahweh prompts people to promote this story (36:23a), it indeed becomes blasphemous to say that an evil spirit is ultimately behind these struggles, however much their actual expressions distorted God's intentions (Mt. 12:22–32; Mk. 3:19b–30; Lk. 12:8–12).

Joining a Holy God in the Order and History of Salvation

Ezekiel establishes the sanctity of the "history of salvation" despite all of its apparent secular trimmings. This sanctity in the "history of salvation," however, does not mean we can neglect conversion and transformation of individuals. The outrageous behavior of indigenous leaders in liberated societies in the last half century points to the importance of Ezekiel's integrating the transformation of individuals with the "order of salvation" into the larger "history of salvation." Nelson Mandela represents a vivid example of integrating a personal transformation during twenty-seven years in prison into the longer view of liberation, union of disparate people (whites and black), and nation building. According to Ezekiel, within the larger social movements for transformation (36:24), the conversion of individuals occurs through justification or forgiveness of sin as a cleansing of their guilt (v. 25), sanctification as a new heart in place of a heart of stone (v. 26), and perfection as fulfilling the commands of God (v. 27).[18]

As we noted, Ezekiel says that the holiness of the divine name will be vindicated through the three stages of the history of salvation (Ezek. 36:23).The Sovereign Savior, the Lord or Yahweh, is therefore a Holy God. We surmise from the biblical witness that the Holy God is offended by sin, evil, and death. "Offended" is too mild a word. We are more accurate to speak of the outrage of the Holy God. Furthermore, this Holy God who is offended and outraged goes on the offensive to rectify what has gone wrong. Biblical references to the "wrath" and "jealousy" of God combine the outrage that fuels the actions to overcome evil with good in the creation God loves.

We notice a fascinating and promising correlation between the twofold qualities in pathos and anguish, on the one hand, and, on the other hand, in the holiness of God. The pain we experience in pathos recalls the offense in God; the anger in anguish evoked by false promises and injustices recalls the outrage of a Holy God at sin, evil, and death. At the same time, we notice a further analogy between the possibilities we see and the aspirations to make a difference with the God who goes on the offensive to rectify wrongs. These correlations and analogies suggest an adumbration of the Divine's presence and activity in the pathos and anguish that individuals and communities experience. This should not surprise us. The Holy Spirit stirs in us sighs and groans for liberation too deep for words. Their pulsations reverberate throughout creation (Rom. 8:22–23). Even if pathos and anguish are at times unintelligible sighs and groans, they offer a starting point that we can nurture into being attuned cognitively, affectively, and volitionally to who God is and what God is doing and saying in a given context. As disciples, we offer tangible evidence of being attuned when we actually experience and spread the order and history of salvation.

Bicultural Strands and Their Biblical Precedents

The reflections here have offered steps we might take to uncover in our changing contexts the energizing religious dimensions that empower us to make a difference in our situations. We may ask what is distinctly Asian American in this proposal?

At the most basic point, the exploration illustrates the operations of a bicultural ingredient in Asian American identity. On the one hand, acculturation to the European American traditions appears in welcoming critically and constructively cultural strands in the host society. The functions and tasks of reason, which are applied to the social sciences and the Bible, come from the lengthening tradition of twentieth-century ordinary language philosophy in the U.S. and England.

On the other hand, the treatment of traditions is traceable to strands of Asian cultures. First, filial piety, reminiscent of the Confucian reverence for elders, appears in the respect for existing traditions. Reflection probably began with pathos and anguish because of a powerful melancholic force in Japanese cultural history shaped by elements of Buddhism. Furthermore, even if we criticize what we have received, we acknowledge some values for the long haul in integrationist strategies and streaks of benefits in the short term from developmental ideologies. Second, filial piety operates in an even deeper way by recovering neglected strands in the tradition, such as in the recovery of the biblical history of salvation for Christian doctrine. Third, a strand from the Taoist heritage appears in recasting tradition. Taoism says that we are comparable to water. We therefore fit into the shape of existing containers as we make our way downstream in time, in this case, into European American and Asian traditions. But by assuming the shape of the container, we reshape the it. Quite by contrast, an iconoclastic understanding of creativity in the U.S. calls us to break the container and create *de novo,* a different mold.[19] Fourth, the Taoist heritage readies a person to bring together the yin of one viewpoint and the yang of a quite different viewpoint and reshape them into a new ongoing process. This inclination appears in being bicultural as well as in combining into a new whole the order and history of salvation, the personal and the social, which are so often at odds in U.S. Protestant theology and ideology. Hence, Asian elements in the bicultural identity *respect* traditions, *recover* neglected ones, and *reshape* them into an evolving whole.

The procedure described in this chapter may warrant further observations concerning cultural factors. The combination of Jewish and Christian religious insights with Confucianism and Taoism recalls Paul Tillich's prediction. He said once, almost in passing, that the combination of European linear perspective and the Asian attraction to circles will produce a course of action best depicted in a spiral. The method outlined here calls for a spiral moving from experience through critical reflection on traditions, with the Bible as the final arbiter in the samples cited, and returning to action and experiences. As contexts change, however, we have noted the need for another round in the spiral, especially in processing globalization in the post–Cold War era. Rather than return to the same level, as in a circle, each round of the spiral will hopefully return us to a better plane of being attuned to God so we will make a greater difference in this world as disciples of Jesus Christ.

These bicultural patterns that combine religious traditions must address a long-standing rejection of syncretism. How can we answer this insistence in the tradition? Again, we can respect the rejection of syncretism that is done uncritically or shoddily. At the same time, we recall biblical models of "syncretism" in bicultural persons, such as David with a Moabite and Hebrew ancestry, as well as Esther's and Daniel's biculturalism and the "socially amphibious" skills that allowed them to operate in two worlds. The genealogy of Jesus in Matthew carefully includes Gentile women among the Jewish ancestors (Mt. 1:1–12). Jesus came from a mixture of "races," or culturally distinct ancestries. Scholars regularly remind us of the Jewish and Gentile cultures functioning in the time of the apostle Paul and other early Christians. Finally, in Revelation we hear that Jews and Gentiles will be in the fullness of God's reign and realm (Rev. 7:1–12), and that the Gentiles will bring their "glory and...honor" into the culmination of God's work (21:24, 26). Their "glory and...honor" surely includes their distinct values, unique social orders, and different cultures, including the arts created by religious forces beyond Judaism and Christianity. Thus, the biblical witness balances the exclusive resistance to syncretism at certain points, but also includes an inclusiveness that leads to a combination of hitherto different elements.

Conclusion

We have explored a procedure to interpret the journey of Asian Americans from context to context. Contextualization as summarized here found early expressions in the 1970s and assumed its basic shape in the 1980s. The vision of hope, therefore, needs review and revision in light of the changing context of the new millennium. It requires broader participation from a welcomed proliferation of interpreters who have emerged subsequently. We can look forward to creating forums where we further develop methods along a number of fronts that will make disciples attuned to God. God, help us. Amen.

Notes

[1]These reflections cannot address the same issues among Pacific Islanders and Asian immigrants to North American generally, nor to the Caribbean Islands and Central and South America. The author regretfully cannot claim sufficient familiarity with these histories to interpret their experiences and hopes others can speak more broadly.

[2]While we interpreted our journey during the integrationist era of the 1950s, interpretations underwent major changes from the late 1960s during the multicultural ethnic studies strikes and the Black Power movement.

[3]By focusing on action or practice *(praxis)*, Latin American liberation theologians pay more immediate attention to the outcome of pathos and anguish. While attention to experience does not focus directly on action or practice, attention to pathos and anguish discloses the interactive aspects of human experience that lead to action. As noted, we may suffer indignities and injury, but pathos and anguish as outlined here generate action.

[4]Milton M. Gordon, *Assimilation in American Life* (New York: Oxford University Press, 1964).

[5]We dealt in part with the demeaning and empty integrationist promises with gallows humor. We told the story about an upstart at a research center. The ambitious honors graduate in zoology announced he would produce a new species. By crossing an abalone with a crocodile, he claimed he could produce an "abodile." After months of humiliating failures, he posted an announcement one morning. Colleagues rushed to see the results at the appointed hour. Alas, they found the cross between a crocodile and an abalone did not produce an abodile, but a crock of baloney.

[6]National Advisory Commission on Civil Disorders, *The Report of the National Advisory Commission on Civil Disorder* (New York: Grosset & Dunlap, 1968), 2.

[7]Harry H. L. Kitano and Roger Daniels, *American Racism: Exploration of the Nature of Prejudice* (Englewood Cliffs, N.J.: Prentice-Hall, 1969), 11–13. Kitano expanded this thesis to cover the national scene in *Race Relations* (Englewood Cliffs, N.J.: Prentice-Hall, 1974). The concept of internal colonialism was also employed by Albert Memmi in *The Colonizer and the Colonized* (Boston: Beacon, 1965). Joe R. Feagin, in his *Discrimination American Style* (Englewood Cliffs, N.J.: Prentice-Hall, 1978) and his *Racial and Ethnic Relations* (Englewood Cliffs, N.J.: Prentice-Hall, 1978), provided further confirmation and data. While the studies by Thomas Sowell, for example in his *Ethnic Minority* (New York: Basic Books, 1981), tried to give a brighter history, he has not provided sufficient data nor a conceptual scheme that can replace stratification.

[8]Reference to "genocide" or "extermination" is not excessive. The Native American population had been reduced to less than a million in 1960, down from various estimates of 20 to 40 million before the European invasion from the sixteenth century.

[9]Robert Blaunder, *Racial Oppression in America* (New York: Harper and Row, 1972), 2.

[10]Beth Ensminger Vanfossen, *The Structure of Social Inequality* (Boston: Little, Brown and Company, 1979).

[11]Earlier works included C. Wright Mills, *The Power Elite* (New York: Oxford, 1956); and G. W. Domhoff, *Who Rules America?* (Englewood Cliffs, N.J.: Prentice-Hall, 1967). By the 1980s, however, we saw publications from the university presses, including, in chronological order, Manuel Castells, *The Economic Crisis and American Society* (Princeton, N.J.: Princeton University Press, 1980); Paul Blumberg, *Inequality in an Age of Decline* (Oxford: Oxford University Press, 1980); Edward S. Herman, *Corporate Control: A Twentieth Century Fund Study* (Cambridge: Cambridge University Press, 1981); and Joel I. Nelson, *Economic Inequality: Conflict Without Change* (New York: Columbia University Press, 1982). Although Herman's study sponsored by the Fund for the Republic did not garner the attention of the earlier study by the Fund, A. J. Berle, Jr., *Organization Revolution* (New York: Harper, 1949), it nevertheless was as substantive. In the post–Cold War era, we now need to pursue studies beyond domestic, or internal colonialism (Albert Memmi) and classism and develop concepts and analytical frameworks for globalism largely led by the U.S.

[12]See William Domhoff's schematic in his, "State and Ruling Class in Corporate America," *The Insurgent Sociologist* 4, no. 3 (Spring 1974): 9.

[13]The Hebrew Scriptures provide instructive analogies for newcomers who are climbing the social ladder in a host society. While Joseph, for example, rose to a position of power in one generation and made an enormous contribution to the welfare of Egyptian society, the next Pharaoh forgot his contributions. The Pharaoh proceeded in the very next generation to enslave and exploit the Hebrew people (Ex. 1:7–11). Esther, a Jew living in captivity, concealed her ethnic identity, won a "beauty contest," and married the emperor. Although she lived in the palace, Esther had no access to the royal court unless invited. She risked her life after reclaiming her ethnic identity. Esther broke the law, barged into the court, and convinced the emperor to reverse the decree that threatened to exterminate her people (Esth. 4–7). Finally, in exile, Daniel and his friends outlearned the Babylonians and quickly assumed prominent positions. Those positions did not, however, protect his friends from a crematorium when adherence to their own God meant they could not worship the idols required by the captors

(Dan. 3:8–30). Daniel might have functionally become the emperor (5:29), but Babylonians fed him to lions because of trumped-up charges leveled by hirelings (6:10–28). Daniel wore his status and prestige lightly. After all, Daniel "read the handwriting on the wall" concerning the empire he governed (5:5–28) and saw visions of its imminent demise (chaps. 7–8). Even if we treat these stories as folktales, versions of them actually occurred repeatedly throughout Jewish history, thus urging Jews to walk humbly with their God. Despite the contributions Jews may have made in host societies, and despite the comforts and privileges that their achievements brought, their people did not automatically enjoy the benefit, nor did they obtain the security, some thought they gained. Upwardly mobile Asian Americans are duly forewarned by our Jewish spiritual ancestors.

[14]The shift of consciousness led us to change the biblical models to interpret our situation. The classical eighth-century B.C.E. prophets who spoke to rulers and priests during nationhood were no longer adequate by themselves. We therefore turned to prophets of the sixth century and later who addressed the situation in captivity and exile. The apocalyptic developments of prophetism in Jeremiah, Ezekiel, and Daniel became particularly relevant.

[15]The story is rehearsed in 2 Isaiah and Jeremiah, albeit not as succinctly nor explicitly.

[16]"Take," "gather," and "bring" are used with only a slight variation in Ezek. 20:34–35, 40–42; 34:13; 36:24; 37:21; 39:27–28.

[17]In the last half of the twentieth century we have seen a phenomenal growth in Christian groups in many Third World countries, namely those groups who (1) gained liberation from classical and neocolonialism, (2) brought together scattered people into a new nation, and (3) participated in many facets of nation building. In U.S. history we saw such new denominations as Methodism grow most rapidly after they (1) participated in the Revolutionary War (our exodus), contrary to the wishes of their founder, John Wesley, (2) supported the Constitution (covenant), and (3) promoted nation building (creating livable space), albeit with profound moral ambiguities and problems.

[18]We notice in Ezekiel that the three stages in the transformation of a person support the sequence in the *ordo salutis*. By contrast, Jeremiah's "new covenant," which is generally cited as a foundation for the *ordo salutis,* obscures the sequence and actually appears to reverse the order (Jer. 31:33–34, cited in Heb. 8:10–12)!

[19]Because of this emphasis on fitting in or assuming the shape of the container before reshaping it, creative and constructive efforts by some Asian American theologians will not be conspicuous and startlingly different and distinct. Given the stereotype of things Asian, the wider theological public is inclined to wait for something that is exotic, if not quaint. Sadly, it is even tempting to be cute in order to meet expectations.

PART 3

Visions of Hope

Realizing the America of Our Hearts

8

The Korean Immigrant Church and Naked Public Square

YOUNG LEE HERTIG

In the age of "sound bites," we suffer not so much from the absence of diverse perspectives but from the dearth of sustained syntheses and interpretations. In the absence of alternative frameworks, a dominant frame emerges to "make sense" of various voices, while muffling other voices and interpretations.

−Nancy Abelmann and John Lie[1]

This chapter originates from my own theological, social, cultural, and psychological struggles in dealing with the violence of the Los Angeles riots during the period of 1992 through 1998. My academic career is somewhat connected to the L.A. riots in 1992 as the violence against minorities exploded. Possibly because of a need to respond to the escalating awareness of a lack of diversity, I was hired to teach at an institution where I studied in the Los Angeles area.

Now that I live in Dayton, Ohio, and have experienced another case of urban violence caused by similar racial profiling in Cincinnati, I am all the more motivated to see how churches can fulfill their mission−being a social witness in the bleeding cities of America.

Because racial profiling is so common and often fuels the tension between race and class, I want to reflect on the burning of the City of Angels in 1992, its aftermath, and the pulse of the Korean immigrant church. During several visits since my departure from Los Angeles, life in Los Angeles seems to have gone back to business as usual, and the quiver has submerged.

Richard John Neuhaus, in his award-winning book *The Naked Public Square,* rightly asserts that neither church nor state has a monopoly in the public square and promotes complementarity of church and state in the public square.[2] The separation of church and state unnecessarily draws boundaries in the public arena and thus creates a vacuum of ecclesiastical voice and action. Therefore, this chapter seeks to analyze the Korean immigrant church's reticence in the public square despite the rude awakening of the 1992 L.A. riots. The community felt powerless during the burning of their mom-and-pop stores in 1992. While that memory still is vivid, proposal after proposal has passed since the L.A. riots that serve the interest of the mainstream rather than the ethnic minority that now makes up the majority in number. Therefore, the major goal of this chapter is to explore ways in which the Korean immigrant church might find its presence and voice in the public arena.

Burning of the City of Angels

The much-publicized beating of Rodney King by policemen touched the raw nerves of African Americans and triggered a remembrance of their whole history in America. The subsequent riots called attention to the accumulating inequalities, fear, prejudice, greed, and injustice that have long lurked beneath the surface of the City of Angels.

On March 3, 1991, Rodney King, a twenty-five-year-old African American living in Altadena, California, was speeding down a highway in San Fernando Valley, when he was stopped, shot by a stun gun, and repeatedly kicked and beaten by police officers. What distinguished this episode of police brutality was that the "excessive force" used against King was videotaped by George Holliday, a nearby resident, and repeatedly shown on television news shows throughout the United States. Yet on April 29, 1992, twelve Simi Valley jurors–ten European Americans, one Latino, and one Asian American–acquitted all four officers standing trial: Stacey Koon, Laurence Powell, Timothy Wind, and Theodore Briseno.[3]

Tension was brewing in the air. The American legal system was on fire while the city itself was burning. Racialized justice divided Los Angeles into a tale of two cities. Taking the black's justice to the all-white jury in a majority white county, Ventura ignited a flame in the majority/minority region. The nearly all-white jury verdict found the police not guilty in the brutal beating of a black man, Rodney King. A huge uproar broke out on the delivery of the verdict. Korean American mom-and-pop storeowners were caught in the crossfire.

The media's depiction of rage among the poor African Americans on the one side and the powerlessly militarized Korean American mom-and-pop merchants on the other only increased the stereotyping. Yet the pain that hit the Korean American community was very complex. On the one hand, the burning of the Korean American businesses was a burning of their hopes of achieving the American Dream. On the other hand, confronting the naked public square caused another sort of pain and despair.

Without the approved tool to express what they were going through—the language of the powerful, English—a deep sense of alienation and powerlessness imbued the Korean immigrants.

One of the most frequently raised questions during that time either through the media or in person was, Why are these people burning their own neighborhood? Why don't they go to the rich neighborhoods and burn? Somehow, the white mass media attributed the burning and looting of the Korean mom-and-pop stores to the conflict between blacks and Korean Americans. Korean American churches alone numbered more than one thousand in 1992, but in these cities full of huge churches, where is the reconciling power of the gospel?

During and after the riots, many Korean immigrant churches came to the fore, acknowledged the violence, and attempted to address the meaning of this experience. Once the emotional media hype and rhetoric subsided, only empty promises confronted the victims whose lifelong sweat and tears melted down in split seconds along with their American dream.

The first generation's vicarious dreams of their children's success through their hard work evaporated before their eyes. Furthermore, their dreams turned out to be illusory. The fundamental truth that everyone's well-being is connected to everyone else's struck them harder than the earthquakes.

Was the American Dream on trial in the Los Angeles eruption? Are traditional systems breaking down? Is there a role for the religious institutions? Does it take a crisis to unite minority groups in urban America? What perceived and real roles have Korean American churches adopted in response to the victims? What are the theological and ecclesiological narratives that hinder the Korean immigrant church from public engagement?

Now that the heat is off, where are they and what have they accomplished? Undoubtedly, Korean immigrant churches were awakened during the burning of the city and yet moved back to their pre-crisis dormant position as quickly as the flames were extinguished. Meanwhile, since the riots, proposition after proposition that protects not the victim but the power elite has passed. Instead of empowering the victims, Proposition 187 divided minority groups into two classes—documented and nondocumented. The flag flown by Proposition 187 symbolized the divided lives of the documented and nondocumented, the suburbanites and urbanites. A wave of minority bashing has come into fashion after decades of affirmative action practice, now on the wane in the University of California schools, despite the opposition of all nine chancellors. Initiated by the so-called California Civil Rights Initiative, Proposition 209, the rollback of affirmative action found its way to the ballot in November 1996. Funded by rich corporate America, it reversed affirmative action using the language of the civil rights movement.

What is the role of the churches in this political climate? Does Martin Luther King, Jr.'s, famous statement that the most segregated hour of the week is 11:00 a.m. on Sunday morning still stand true? Where are the Korean immigrant churches in light of their relatedness to the wider society?

This chapter first seeks to interpret the mainstream ideology from the aftermath of the L.A. riots through Proposition 209, the California Civil Rights Initiative. Second, it seeks to explore the Korean immigrant church's dominant narratives and underlying ethos that cause it to be silent regarding the social activism aspect of God's mission. Third, it seeks to thaw and redefine frozen narratives of what it means to be the church in racially diverse contexts. Part 1 will be devoted to Proposition 209 in order to assess the dominant themes of the mainstream ideology. For example, themes such as equality, justice, uniformity, and fairness, which arose again during the November 2000 presidential election, will be examined. Part 2 will focus on the Korean immigrant church's self-understanding and core theological narratives. Part 3 will explore an alternative epistemology that will unleash the Korean immigrant church from dualistic frames into the holistic understanding of the church and its public witness.

The Underlying Belief System of the California Civil Rights Initiative

After numerous meetings dealing with racial reconciliation, churches returned to their usual business of worshiping. Meanwhile, quietly, a movement that hijacked the 1960's civil rights movement was brewing. The California Civil Rights Initiative (CCRI), Proposition 209, is violence dressed in the rhetoric of equality and nondiscrimination. It is violent because it does not consider the conditions certain groups are under and assumes that everyone from child, adolescent, adult, to elderly run the same race equally. CCRI launched a wholesale approach to equality, ignoring the diverse realities of California. At the core of affirmative action lies pursuit of equality with diversity. At the core of CCRI, however, lies personal anger misdirected at diversity. Its ideology is steeped in competition and success. It promotes individualistic, acultural, ahistorical, fragmented values. CCRI views the human being in a vacuum and, worst of all, redefines the discriminator as an avid advocate for equality. The very notion of equality is so unilateral that it violates the realities of human diversity and condemns diversity as a cause for discrimination. Conformity and equality are not necessarily the same. How should individuals and institutions practice the CCRI version of equality without denigrating the dimensions of diversity?

> You do not take a person who for years has been hobbled by chains, liberate him, bring him to the starting line of a race and then say, "You are free to compete with all others," and still justly believe you have been completely fair.[4]

After thirty years, affirmative action is charged by CCRI, through its microscopic lens, as discriminatory. As long as you can keep diversity in its exotic place at cultural celebrations and food festivals and at the same time ignore structural levels, it is manageable and tolerable. Ironically, the call to end discrimination in the name of equality is nothing more than an attempt to institute discrimination based on race, class, and gender.

Hijacking the Language of the Oppressed

Language is powerful because it connotes meaning. The group that defines and controls the meaning of words, therefore, owns power. And the groups whose identities are defined by the powerful group are powerless simply by being subject to a self-fulfilling prophecy. In other words, the groups that are negatively defined are trapped and thus become victimized by the very categories superimposed onto them. As testified in human history, it takes a great deal of courage and consciousness for the subordinate group to recreate the meanings of the definitions given to them. Slavery and even genocide were justified when the powerful simply defined the other as less than human.

The deception and oppression of CCRI is found in its hijacking of the language of the victim and its application of that language to the members of the dominant group. They hijack the only power of the underprivileged, words that authentically describe their reality, and apply them to the dominant group for its own interest and benefit:

> The state shall not discriminate against, or grant preferential treatment to, any individual or group on the basis of race, sex, color, ethnicity, or national origin in the operation of public employment, public educational or public contracting (California Civil Rights Initiative, 1995).[5]

The word *discrimination* here contradicts with equality and derives solely from the micro-individual perspective. Its perspective, therefore, is not only untruthful but also dangerous considering the interdependent nature of human beings. Through this lens uniformity is seen as equality. Therefore, any deviation from upper- and middle-class white parameters is perceived as a diminishing of quality. Regretfully, the examination at the level of the parameter itself is inconceivable because it is labeled immediately as disruptive.

CCRI simply reduces already unequal realities of a great number of people to a color-blind policy as if race, ethnicity, and gender as social constructs cease to intersect in American experience today. Stanley Fish emphasizes that "a distinction must surely be made between the ideological hostility of the oppressors and the experience-based hostility of those who have been oppressed."[6] Former California Governor Pete Wilson's usage of the term *color-blind* and Martin Luther King, Jr.'s, term *color-blind,* therefore, must surely be distinguished. Wilson's use of the term refers to the ignoring of inequalities; King's use of the term referred to overcoming inequalities.

Fairness, according to the forerunner of CCRI, is perceived as fair only when the measure of the upper-middle-class is enhanced, regardless of huge discrepancies of cultural and social locations of various people. Any adjustment of the measurement itself is perceived as troublesome. Thus, they dare to use the terminology of the recipients of discrimination, words such as *justice, discrimination, color-blind,* and *equal opportunity.* By reversing the position and hijacking the language of the victims, CCRI not only discounts the victims' daily lives but also distorts their realities.

Gender-based affirmative action gave white women more opportunity than minority men and women in academic employment. As the number of white women's representation in academia reached a critical mass, the proposal of rolling back the carpet was initiated. This excluded opportunities for many, including Asian Pacific American women faculty, when they are still not properly represented in comparison to the many Asian American students at the University of California. Thus, further marginalization is legitimized in the name of nondiscrimination and equality. The ideology of blaming the victim persists in the twenty-first century.

Is Uniformity Equality?

Does equality mean uniformity? If so, then whose uniform should people wear? While America as a whole is demographically diversifying, the power structure continues to be held mainly by the white power elite. Similarly, the policy-making and decision-making levels do not correspond with the diverse face of California. The insistence that all people follow the same criteria regardless of their history and culture does not accommodate equality. Ironically, CCRI deceptively claims to reverse discrimination when, in fact, it institutes discrimination.

The underlying ideology of CCRI advocates equality based on sameness and thus distorts uneven realities. How does the power structure serve equality in such an unevenly ranked society? Whose justice is more important? Unilateral equality is inequality because the very practice of equality in decision making, whether in college enrollment or in employment, contains a value-ridden criteria that predetermines who the insiders and outsiders will be.

When the very social construct is unjust, can we even diagnose realities justly? What group does the existing social construct serve, and what group does it victimize? The times are changing drastically when the language of the oppressed, the only tool the underprivileged own, is stripped away in the name of justice and equality. Meanwhile, its victims are hidden in silence.

The champions of CCRI must reflect on the ultimate goal of "equality" that they claim. If their equality destroys the circle of humanity, it is mutually self-destructive. Equality does not mean sameness with a uniform measure.

Equality is a balance that is crucial as illustrated in keeping the diverse human body parts whole. The Chinese diagnosed human anatomy holistically based on the dynamic balance between yin and yang; their imbalance causes harm and sickness.[7] Likewise, the body of higher education, when lacking a balance in its diversity, will become dysfunctional.

When they seek more opportunity for whites, they use the term *discrimination.* When they mean justice for one kind of group, they make it sound as if it means justice for all groups. When diverse representation is viewed as discrimination of the already over-represented group, the language becomes a powerful means to enhance the existing domination. Since diversity connotes in their minds lowering the quality, the very purpose of affirmative action–that is, diversifying representation–is disregarded.

Justice Harry A. Blackmun warns against the equation that sameness equals equality: "In order to get beyond racism, we must first take account of race. There is no other way. And in order to treat some persons equally, we must treat them differently. We cannot–we dare not–let the Equal Protection Clause perpetuate racial superiority."[8]

The Bush versus Gore election court case also depicts an ideology of the uniformity as equality. The Equal Protection Clause of the Fourteenth Amendment, which was enacted to give equal status to newly freed black slaves, was reversed to protect the wealthy, white, Ivy League–educated political candidate.[9] Once again, in the name of equality, justice was stripped from the poor but served the wealthy. The fusion of equality with uniformity continues to advocate for the power elite at the expense of the poor.

Whose Rights Count?

Was CCRI a counterattack on the verdict in the O. J. Simpson criminal trial? One of the most widely telecast trials of the century signaled that the justice system no longer serves the dominant group. While there are many cases of injustice, such as the Rodney King case, it only took one losing case for the political mobilization of a proposition such as CCRI. The strong belief system here is that white people are superior and are thus entitled overall rights in preference to the rights of other people. If white rights are not ensured, all the political and economic resources can be mobilized to make sure this matter is rectified.

In contrast to more than two hundred years of slavery, the California Civil Rights Initiative (Proposition 209), with only one stroke, redefined and overturned the civil rights movement. It took only six federal court cases from 1990 to 1994 to come up with the CCRI:

> [A]ccording to the Department of Labor, affirmative action has caused very few claims of reverse discrimination by white people. Fewer than 100 of the more than 3,000 discrimination opinions in federal courts from 1990 to 1994 even raised the issue of reverse

discrimination, and reverse discrimination was actually established in only six cases.[10]

Yet by mid-1995, affirmative action was the focus of the presidential campaign. The true meaning of the language of the underprivileged was successfully abducted because there was not even a major resistance expressed by the very people whose lives are being affected. Therefore, the advocates of CCRI did not need to exercise force.

"Race no longer matters"

The increase of minority groups' affluence is regarded as the end of racial discrimination as well. However, more well-to-do minority groups share that their social location is predetermined by their skin color as someone who is lower than others. An affluent African American male says, "You walk down the street with a suit and tie and it doesn't matter. Someone will make determinations about you, determinations that affect the quality of your life."[11]

How can we deal effectively with racial and ethnic diversity with integrity? First and foremost, the decision makers' and administrators' own individual lenses, as well as their institutional belief systems, must shift for ongoing changes to occur.

In summary, CCRI is more violent than blatant racism because stealing the language of the underprivileged is legitimized. Even the victim may naively dance to the CCRI tune, believing that it would also represent them. The language that gave rise to the civil rights movement has now become the language of the dominant.

Undoubtedly, CCRI is violent because it marginalizes the other, distorting affirmative action as reverse racism. CCRI is violent because it dismisses diversity and replaces it with assimilation and conformity at the expense of sacrificing diversity. CCRI demonstrates how the dominant ideology can be mobilized as a social force filling the vacuum of the public square.

Is the American Dream really accessible to everyone in the United States? As long as American society remains obsessed with dividing and segregating people according to false social constructs of race, class, and gender, affirmative action must persist. Against such an organized exercise of power, anointed by right-wing Christian groups, is any Korean immigrant church aware of the consequence of its silence in the public arena? With what are the Korean immigrant churches consumed? Would it take another crisis to bring them up from their frozen state?

The Korean Immigrant Church's Response

While the large scale of reversal of the civil rights movement sweeps the nation, where are the voices of Korean immigrant churches in the public square? In light of the pains and hopes of Asian Americans, what are the religious and theological resources that we can tap? What kind of balm does the Christian tradition have to offer to the wider society in need of healing?

Because the Korean American community centers on the church, I want to pursue where the pulse of the Korean immigrant churches is and what underlying theological narratives they espouse. Once these questions are answered, then we can move onto proactive steps and strategies.

The number of Korean immigrant churches in the Los Angeles area alone is estimated at more than one thousand. Therefore, exploring the fundamental belief system, the ethos, is significant in answering the key question this chapter raises. Why does the Korean immigrant church remain socially mute while the anti–affirmative action force has been mobilized as a major social force? What are the theological and cultural ideals that the Korean immigrant churches uphold? There are several reasons as to why immigrant churches face a naked public square.

Theological Polarity

The Korean Protestant immigrant church's main role is limited to being an ethnic sanctuary with ethnic island mentality. Preoccupied with its otherworldly theology and programs on the one hand, and this-worldly materialism on the other, the dominant theme of the sermons preached on Sunday mornings focuses on "If you obey and serve the church by giving all sorts of offerings and tithes, you and your children will be blessed."

With dualistic theology as an underlying assumption, the core beliefs are in this world against the other world, the church against the world, faith against social action, and conservatives against liberals. The preceding lists are not in any way unique to the Korean American worldview. In fact, it is rather difficult to pinpoint such a theology as purely Korean.

On the contrary, the above dichotomies are also highly Western. The reason the Korean immigrant church lacks a public voice primarily lies on the theological bias. The doubly reinforced dualistic theology from Confucian and Puritan theology, which promotes otherworldly faith, promotes public disengagement. Fused with Puritan fundamentalism and Confucian fundamentalism, Korean immigrant churches still uphold the separation of proclamation and social action.

The Marxist critique of evangelicalism is on target, as the majority of the Korean immigrant churches espouse evangelicalism. It causes social disengagement by "channeling people's repressed energies, anxieties, and general social dissatisfaction into a spiritual obsession and attendant eschatological hope that preclude critical political thought."[12] This spiritual obsession and eschatological hope do not transform conflict, powerlessness, and anxieties within. In the case of the first generation, the language and cultural differences block them from any desire to venture into the mainstream.

Paradoxically, the specter of the naked public square faced by Korean immigrants turns their energy inward. The sense of powerlessness is manifested too frequently in power seeking and abusive behavior within the church. Because a lack of social positions and public roles, positions in the church are the only source for the social gratification of the first generation. Regrettably, the church's position of servanthood turns into a big political campaign. Furthermore, it is not surprising to witness more and more leaders in Korean churches tending to choose their son or son-in-law to be their successor.

Lucian W. Pye observes that Asian politics concentrates on the person, not the office. He writes, "Power is seen as residing in the person of high officials and not in their offices or in institutions."[13] Consequently, it draws no boundaries of accountability if leaders choose to abuse their power. The church power dynamic, also deeply rooted in Confucian practice of personalized as opposed to institutionalized power, frequently exhausts the energy of the body of Christ. Therefore, the external expression of faith in the public arena is vacant.

While theology is floating in midair, this world is left with a theological vacuum, which then is filled with materialistic values. The contradiction between otherworldly faith and materialistic practice demonstrates a serious lack of integration of faith and comprehensive theological narratives.

Even among the emerging generation such belief is prevalent. I was struck by the emerging 1.5-generation Korean American professionals in their political and religious fundamentalism. College ministry, occupied mostly by para-church organizations, replicates fundamentalistic faith that confines young people into a narrowly and exclusively defined faith. Particularly, gender disparity among the male and female Korean American has become a serious social problem as more women enter into the professional life and thus are liberated from the patriarchal value. They are on the margin of the Korean American culture. The Korean immigrant church censures such women and labels them as "the other."

What holds the Korean immigrant church together? What causes it to drift apart? Where does it stand in relation to public social witness?

The Need for Usness and the Challenge of Otherness

The Korean immigrant church is like an island of *usness* within the sea of the mainstream *otherness.* The very existence of the immigrant church is rooted in ethnicity, which forms its own static tribal value against the unfamiliar mainstream culture. The very need for the common heritage disconnects it from the public arena.

Victor Turner refers to this as *communitas,* a deep sense of oneness with other humans that runs deeper than surface social differences of gender, class, ethnicity, and office.[14] Turner defines three types of communitas: normative, existential, and ideological. What the Korean ethnic church experiences seems to include all three aspects. As an extended family, the Korean immigrant church's boundaries are consequently narrow, and it operates as a patriarchal Confucian family.

Kinship vs. Citizenship

If the Korean immigrant church operates like a Confucian family, how is the body of Christ made manifest? The dialectic tension between the need for *usness* and the challenge of *otherness* in relation to the wider society confronts the Korean immigrant church. The *usness* takes a form of a strong kinship, while otherness involves citizenship.

First-generation Korean Americans, despite their life history in America and American citizenship, still feel alienated. Their life depicts them as *forever guests* in the land of immigrants. The *otherness* against the mainstream norm also pushes Asian Americans toward a kinship type of *usness*. This perceived *otherness* by the mainstream society and self-perception by the immigrants themselves has been the driving force for Asian American churches' existence. Many first-generation Korean immigrants live in America as guests, not hosts. The guest consciousness strips the first generation from exercising any rights as citizens. The very notion of citizenship based on individual rights is a foreign concept to the kinship-oriented Asian American.

The crisis of the 1992 L.A. riots caused Korean immigrants for the first time to see realities beyond their own kinship. Somehow, kinship value as primordial consciousness persists stubbornly. Exercising citizenship remains a remote reality for first-generation immigrants as long as they live according to a *forever guest* script.

In summary, the calling and the mission of the churches today in a multicultural setting require a delicate balancing of the need for racially homogeneous community and the richness of heterogeneous unity. In balancing such unity in diversity, the very lens through which we see reality must be inclusive and holistic. The fact that the Korean immigrant church is weak in public expression of faith derives from its theological and cultural fundamentalism on the one hand and lack of internalization of faith on the other. Basically, the underlying theological and cultural dualism paralyzes the Korean immigrant church from engaging in the public witness. Therefore, reconciling them with a holistic paradigm is much needed. Reshaping the dominant theological narratives is crucial if indeed any public representation will be organized in the face of injustice and violence. Waiting for another crisis as a stimulus is as risky as the flames that charred the City of Angels.

Bringing in the theological dimension, what visions of dwelling are generated from the wells of Asian American pluralistic religious traditions?

Can we identify some theological motifs and metaphors that would adequately and responsibly address the plight of Asian Americans and their commitment to the wider well-being?

For this, I turn to Taoism as an alternative social activism model for the Korean and Asian North American church. People often raise the question, What does Taoism have to do with the public square? They often associate Taoism with passivity, tai-chi, and meditation–contrary to activism.

This chapter argues that Taoism offers an inner centering that allows outer expression of activism. I named it a *yinist* epistemology. One without the other is not authentic and thus binding. The internalization of faith– *yin*–needs to precede external expression of faith–*yang*–in public arena. Lacking the *yinish* internalization process of faith and simultaneously feeling powerless over the naked public square, Korean immigrants bring their reactionary *yangish* expression into the church. Heavily reinforced by externally defined success, the Korean immigrant church devotes its energy at whim on any and every program. Thus, the balancing of faith in both yin and yang aspects is crucial for any consciousness to emerge.

Yinist Ecclesiology

The following attempts to provide an alternative theological lens, *yinist* epistemology from Taoism, to reconcile dualistic, fragmented understandings of the gospel and the role of the church. The working definition of *yinist* epistemology is described below:

> The term, *yinist* is taken from the word, *yin,* the female energy in Taoism. This female energy is comprehensive because it encompasses gender, ecology, nature, health, and God. The *yin* is holistic, dynamic, synthesizing, and complementary with *yang*, the male energy...It seeks harmony but not without chaos. Her epistemology allows interconnected between the paradox of order and chaos. It seeks to understand reality through the lens of integrated wholes whose properties cannot be reduced to those of smaller units.[15]

The core of the *yinist* epistemology seeks the balance of yin and yang. It is thus nonlinear and dynamic. It understands nature as a dynamically interconnected network of relationships that include the human observer as an integral component.

> All life embodies yin
> And embraces yang,
> Through their union
> Achieving harmony.[16]

As an alternative to the predominant reductionist epistemology that contrasts and divides, *yinist* epistemology thus seeks to provide a lens that brings out the nature of interdependency and interconnectedness. Diane Dreher also critiques the limitation of the reductionist epistemology: "Our options limited by linear reductionism, we perceive reality as two opposite points on a line. Unable to find a synthesis or consider other alternatives, non-Tao people become trapped in the false dilemma of either/or."[17] Therefore, *yin* and *yang* polarity "is not to be confused with the ideas of opposition…The *yin-yang* principle is not what we would ordinarily call a dualism, but rather an explicit duality expressing an implicit unity," writes Alan Watts in his last book on Taoism.[18]

The scholar Jung Young Lee pioneered ecclesiology from Taoistic epistemology. Differentiating two terms used for the church, *Kirche* and *ekklesia,* Lee diffuses the boundaries between the secular and sacred. Stressing dual aspects of ecclesiology, Lee writes, "the inner quality of the *ekklesia* is *koinonia,* which means the community of love…The *koinonia* is then the inner essence of the *ekklesia* and the criterion of being the true Church."[19] The *koinonia* then can be referred to as *yin,* and *ekklesia* as *yang.* Likewise, justice and the life of love, or freedom and justice, are also two sides of one coin.[20]

According to *yinist* epistemology, the immigrant church cannot remain silent as an island before injustice because it offers duality, not dichotomous practice of Christian faith. Justice and love ought to be the core of the church. When the church chooses to split rather than integrate, the church ceases to be the body of Christ.

Yinist epistemology, as one of the primordial consciousnesses of Asians and Asian North Americans, also has parallels with the Pauline concept of wholeness. It is an old concept and yet new because it engages today's postmodern realities.

The Body as a Unit

The mosaic of multicultural realities can be likened to a living organism. For the sake of the health of the body, all of its parts need to be well attended. Both Jesus and the apostle Paul use this body analogy to describe Christian identity and unity. On the evening of the Passover, Jesus offered his body as a lamb: "Take; this is my body…This is my blood of the covenant, which is poured out for many" (Mk. 14:22c, 24). Jesus laid himself down in order for us to be whole, a radical contrast to the culture of hegemony and the culture of lip service. Such qualities correspond to *yinist* epistemology.

When our lens is expanded, we will be able to finally see the whole picture. Policies accompanied by a kaleidoscopic value will serve all segments of the society relatively fairly, not maximally fairly. Everyone must yield to make a whole circle possible. Everyone must realize that we all are beautiful parts in the design of a kaleidoscopic circle. The apostle Paul in 1 Corinthians 12 lays out the principle of affirmative action by encouraging the church to attend to the weaker parts of the body more.

Connectionism, not fragmentation; mutual plurality, not conformity, are the keys to being the body of Christ.

1. The body is one and has many members...
2. All the members of the body, though many, are one body...
3. The body does not consist of one member but of many...

> The members of the body that seem to be weaker are indispensable, and those members of the body that we think less honorable we clothe with greater honor, and our less respectable members are treated with greater respect; whereas our more respectable members do not need this. But God has so arranged the body, giving the greater honor to the inferior member, that there may be no dissension within the body, but the members may have the same care for one another. If one member suffers, all suffer together with it; if one member is honored, all rejoice together with it.

> Now you are the body of Christ and individually members of it. (1 Cor. 12:12, 14, 22–27)

Thus, the alienation of certain parts jeopardizes the whole body. Yet in today's multicultural capitalistic world of local and global competition, the weaker, who lack a power base of protection, often fall prey to the stronger.

The term *holistic,* from the Greek *holos* ("whole"), refers to an understanding of reality in terms of integrated wholes whose properties cannot be reduced to those of smaller units. This fits Paul's analogy of the human body for what it means to be the church. The Pauline metaphor of the church is applicable to today's diverse setting, illuminating the escalating dark side of today's competitive realities.

Tao Teh Ching: Fusion of Faith and Action

In the Eastern mind, the very essence of learning takes place when there is a fusion between idea and being. Fung Yu-Lan states this as "sageliness within and kingliness without."[21] In the discipline of the sage, the idea and deed are one, and thus, the Western quest for practical theology stemming from the dichotomy of the two is not necessary.

The perpetual cycle of split knowledge and theology is transmitted through seminary education, inhibiting seminarians from actively engaging in their social realities. Many pastors who have gone through theological education are crippled by the lack of holistic education. *Tao Teh Ching* offers a theological model that will connect mind, body, and spirit. In the concept of *Tao Teh Ching* there is no separation of theory from the action. "*Tao* means the integral truth of the universe, *Teh* means the virtuous application of such high, subtle knowledge, and *Ching* means serious spiritual guidance."[22]

In the concept of *Tao Teh Ching* lies the paradigm that can bridge a split Christianity—sacred versus secular, and private versus public. In living out the faith, the Korean immigrant church needs to reclaim the Asian wisdom of *Tao Teh Ching.* The naked public square may be filled by the Korean immigrant church as theological polarity is overcome with Asian epistemology.

Conclusion

As the 1992 Los Angeles riots sounded the alarm for a restoration of human connectedness, the Korean immigrant church needs to reinterpret who it is and who it ought to become. A fixated self-understanding only rotates the problems, exhausting rather than revitalizing the body of Christ. Only when the Korean immigrant church balances its inward and outward journey can a healthier connection with the transforming power of the gospel be represented.

For this endeavor, the ongoing theological reflection of the 1992 Los Angeles riots needs to be processed to fill the void in the public arena with the body of Christ. The theological lens of *yinist* epistemology overcomes the pitfalls of the dualistic, dichotomous paradigm that divides rather than connects the diverse parts. It bridges both *usness* and *otherness* to become whole.

For carrying out God's presence in the public arena as the body of Christ, the Korean immigrant church must dare to reexamine and remember its own perspective through which we see ourselves and neighbors. Otherwise, the vacuum of the public arena will continue to distort and exploit the lives of the powerless. The aftermath of several propositions needs to be revisited so that the organism may not be subsumed by the organization.

The embodiment of the holistic theological epistemology is crucial for bringing the immigrant church's voice to the public arena. It is the split theology, not the Asian culture, that incarcerates the Korean immigrant church. In fact, many who are sitting in the pews are members of the generation of student demonstrators in Korea. It is not the Korean culture that hinders anyone from social activism. Rather, it is Christian fundamentalism, with its dualistic separation of this world from the other world, liberal from conservative, that puts the brakes on people's consciousness.

In *yinist* epistemology with *Tao Teh Ching* praxis, knowledge and application are not separable. Therefore, it reconciles a false dichotomy of belief and action. As an epistemology of interdependency and wholeness, the *yinist* lens can bring the Pauline concept of the body of Christ into reality, offering hope of recovering the broken dimensions of humanity and nature, the church and the world, the other world and this world, and male and female.

Notes

[1]Nancy Abelmann and John Lie, *Blue Dreams: Korean Americans and the Los Angeles Riots* (Cambridge, Mass.: Harvard University Press, 1995), xi.

[2]Richard John Neuhaus, *The Naked Public Square: Religion and Democracy In America* (Grand Rapids, Mich.: Eerdmans, 1984), 175.

[3]Nancy Abelmann and John Lie, *Blue Dreams,* 2.

[4]President Lyndon Johnson announced Affirmative Action in 1965.

[5]For the full text of the initiative, see http://vote96.ss.ca.gov/Vote96/html/BP/209text.htm.

[6]Stanley Fish, "Reverse Racism or How the Pot Got to Call the Kettle Black?" *Atlantic Monthly* (November 1993): 130.

[7]Frijof Capra, *The Turning Point: Science, Society, and the Rising Culture* (New York: Bantam Books, 1983), 36.

[8]Quoted in Vincent N. Parrillo, *Strangers to These Shores: Race and Ethnic Relations in the United States* (Boston: Allyn and Bacon, 1997), 93.

[9]*Time* (25 December 2000): 78.

[10]"Reverse Discrimination of Whites Is Rare, Labor Study Reports," *Time* (March 31, 1995).

[11]Fish, "Reverse Racism," 135.

[12]Quoted in R. Stephen Warner and Judith G. Wittner, eds., *Gatherings in Diaspora: Religious Communities and the New Immigration* (Philadelphia: Temple University Press, 1998), 164.

[13] Lucian W. Pye, *Asian Power and Politics: The Cultural Dimensions of Authority* (1985), 23.

[14]Victor Turner and Edith Turner, *Image and Pilgrimage in Christian Culture: Anthropological Perspectives* (New York: Columbia University Press, 1978), 13.

[15]Young Lee Hertig, "The Asian-American Alternative to Feminism: A *Yinist* Paradigm,"*Missiology: An International Review* 26 (1998): 16, 21.

[16]*Tao Teh Ching:* 42.

[17]Diane Dreher, *The Tao of Inner Peace* (New York: HarperPerennial, 1990), 7–8.

[18]Alan Watts, *Tao, The Watercourse Way* (New York: Pantheon Books, 1975), 19, 26.

[19]Jung Young Lee, *The I: A Christian Concept of Man* (New York: Philosophical Library, 1971), 116.

[20]Ibid., 120–21.

[21]Fung Yu-Lan, *A Short History of Chinese Philosophy: A Systematic Account of Chinese Thought from Its Origins to the Present Day* (New York: The Free Press, 1948), 8.

[22]Hua-Ching Ni, trans., *The Complete Works of Lao Tzu: Tao Teh Ching & Hua Hu Ching* (Santa Monica, Calif.: Seven Star Communications, 1995), 3.

9

Faith Practices for Racial Healing and Reconciliation

DEBORAH LEE

In 1999, on the eve of Martin Luther King, Jr., Day, Truong Van Tran, a Vietnamese immigrant, erected a Vietnamese communist flag and a poster of Ho Chi Minh inside his Hi Tek TV and VCR video store in Little Saigon, Westminster, in southern California. He claimed it was an exercise of his freedom of expression. The following day, an angry crowd of ten thousand South Vietnamese supporters gathered in protest. News reports depicted high emotions, angry shouting, and threats of physical violence. Two hundred city police in riot gear were called in to protect the store owner's "freedom of expression" from the angry group of Vietnamese community members. This Westminster incident sparked similar protests in San Jose, California; New Orleans; Los Angeles; and Houston, Texas.

A few weeks later, the store owner, Truong Van Tran, was arrested by the police (perhaps the same ones who had protected him just a few days before) on charges of video piracy. Three days later the Hi Tek TV and VCR video store was closed, and Truong pleaded guilty on felony charges, facing up to five years in prison.[1]

A second dispute has since erupted in Westminster, this time between Vietnamese and white community members, over the flying of the U.S. and South Vietnamese flags in tandem along the strip malls of Little Saigon. City council members and several patriotic American organizations allege that hanging the two flags at equal heights fails to show proper respect for the U.S. flag and the notion of U.S. citizenship. Howard Skeen, one white community member of Westminster, says:

> They've been in the country now going on twenty-five years, and
> they've been given plenty of rope to adjust...people living around

are just absolutely fed up with it...What they don't understand is that they're not still Vietnamese, they're Americans...That's not in my estimation... practicing good citizenship. There's been an undercurrent of rebellion ever since I moved in here in '84.[2]

This snapshot of the controversies in Westminster illustrates the current complex and multifaceted state of race relations in the U.S.: the painful past between North and South Vietnamese; the complicated power relations between state police and immigrants; and the historic prejudices and racist attitudes of white Americans toward immigrants and people of color. U.S. society is racially more diverse and more complex today than at any previous time in its history, and the trend is that this will continue.[3] Nationwide the white population has declined almost 10 percent from 1970 to 1990; the black population has risen slightly; the Hispanic population has doubled; and the population of Asians and other non-whites has tripled.[4] In the last decade, Asians and Pacific Islanders have had a higher rate of population growth (45 percent) than any other group.[5]

Among these broad racial groupings there are further layers of complexity. For instance, the racial category of Asians/Asian Americans includes more than forty different national and ethnic heritages, including Asians of Filipino, Vietnamese, Laotian, Thai, Cambodian, Korean, Indian, and Chinese descent, just to name a few. Furthermore, Hawaiians and Pacific Islanders, a grouping that includes Samoans, Tongans, Tahitians, Fijians, and other ethnicities, are often lumped together with Asian Americans, even though in many cases their experiences and concerns have more in common with Native Americans. The 2000 census marks the first census that Pacific Islanders and Asian Americans have been treated as separate categories. The fact that these groups are generally aggregated is a "racially based process," for no other reason than because "the majority of Americans cannot tell the difference between members of these various groups."[6] The rash of racial scapegoating and hate crimes against people of Middle Eastern and South Asian descent, and those mistaken for them, in the wake of the World Trade Center attacks is evidence of the dangerously arbitrary nature of racial construction based on "popular" perception. In addition to the ethno-cultural differences within a racial group, such categories fail to account for the diverse experiences, religions, classes, languages, historical animosities, as well as generation of immigration. Recognizing the "multiplicity, hybridity, and heterogeneity" among Pacific and Asian Americans is a critical aspect.[7]

The drama that unfolded in Little Saigon in 2001 displays the level of distrust, to the brink of violence, that exists within one mono-ethnic community that shares linguistic, cultural, and historic ties. It points to the fact that the challenge of reconciliation in U.S. society is not only to address the painful wounds of racism embedded in our domestic history and context, but also to address the pains and scars that people bring with them. The task of reconciliation and healing is not only between whites and groups of color but also between and within groups of color themselves. The complex racial context in which we live has some profound implications. We can no longer afford a too simplistic view of the reality of racial relations and racial woundedness today. This increasing complexity poses a strong challenge to established civil rights and racial justice movements. Can they adequately address and support the issues of groups that have historically been made invisible by racial classification? The complexity poses a strong challenge to faith communities, particularly multicultural and ethnic-specific congregations and bodies. Can they promote the development of pertinent theologies that illumine and respond to our current racial context?

Sociological Approaches

Approaches to rectify the injustices, inequalities, and injuries rendered by racism have varied in assumption, focus, strategy, and vision. The spark of widespread race consciousness in the early 1960s emphasized overcoming attitudes of racial prejudice, promoting tolerance, and prohibiting discriminatory practices in the arenas of public access, jobs, housing, and education. The strategies were primarily that of litigation, and the vision one of integration. Later that same decade emerged the recognition of racism's deeper roots and the degree to which racism was embedded into all structures of U.S. society, a "product of centuries of systematic exclusion, exploitation, and disregard of racially defined minorities."[8] People of color themselves began to rearticulate race into new constructions of racial and ethnic power.

Today, nearly forty years after the United States' official civil rights project began, we are in the midst of a public backlash against affirmative action and all other race-based programs aimed at rectifying historical racial injustices. At the same time, the popular pronouncement has been made that racism is no longer a social problem and in fact has now been replaced by "reverse-racism." The word *racism* itself has been replaced with vague and depoliticized language of diversity, multiculturalism, pluralism, and globalization. These assertions could not be further from the truth, for racism, exacerbated by dimensions of class, gender, sexual orientation, and citizenship status, persists in structurally entrenched forms, as made evident by the criminal justice system, wages, poverty, and education. Race was, is, and continues to be central to American politics and life.[9]

Racism can be defined as "those social projects which create or reproduce structures of domination based on essentialist notions of race."[10] Racism's reduction to essentialist notions corresponds with "generalizing" and "homogenizing," described as forms of violence by Robert Schreiter.[11] Omi and Winant's theory of racial formation claims that racial categories are socially constructed and politically contested, thus changing and transforming across time and social historical contexts.[12] An example of race as a socially constructed concept was shared with me by a Colombian American friend. Wherever she has lived, she has been mistaken for the most-hated group in that area. In Texas she was presumed to be Mexican; in New York she was mistaken to be Puerto Rican; in New Mexico she was treated as a Native American. To fight against racism, we must become more "color-conscious" rather than "color-blind," and fight against reducing and idolizing any notion of racial "essences" that serves the needs and purposes of domination.[13]

A Personal Approach

Racism is a societal and at the same time deeply personal issue for me. My family was one of the only Chinese American families in a small, white Ohio suburb in the early 1970s. Race was my defining experience of "otherness." Though being middle class and belonging to the majority religion of Christianity certainly mitigated some of the harshness of racism, racism has made and continues to make an indelible mark on my life. It has shaped my personality, my opportunities, my friendships, my marriage, my dreams, and many other dimensions of my daily existence.

I remember in recent years a conversation with my mother (a Chinese Indonesian immigrant to the U.S.) in which she remarked, "I don't understand how you could grow up with white people, and now you hate them." Caught off guard, I immediately denied the assertion, but after reflecting a few days, I had to admit that some aspect of her comment was true. Perhaps hate was too strong of a word, but I had to admit that my heart remained closed toward white people. I no longer hoped, no longer believed, no longer had faith that I could trust white people and that racial inequality could be overcome. Bitterness and cynicism had fossilized my hurts.

My experience working with community groups organizing and educating for racial and economic justice has shown me the importance and the limitations of this work. These groups tend to define the "problem" as ignorance and inaction. Thus, the strengths of their strategy are the dissemination of information and promoting involvement. The limitation of this paradigm that I have experienced is that knowledge, information, and action do not necessarily lead to reconciliation and healing. Healing's goals are defined differently. The goals of healing and reconciliation are to move hearts, give hope, heal scars, rebuild trust, and restore faith in the *possibility* of reconciliation. The legislative, litigious, and educational strategies are a necessary part of public policy, yet they also demonstrate that it is not possible to legislate respect, affirmation, acceptance, trust, and love between people, much less between former enemies. Healing the deep roots of racism requires more complex ways than we could have imagined. The challenge is not how we will live together, beyond merely surviving and not harming one another, but how we will heal the deep generations-long wounds to spare the next generation from the brokenness and painful divisions that separate us.

A Theological Approach

Spirituality and theology can be powerful resources to bring about healing and reconciliation. A theological approach to the problem applies "depth thinking" and "depth feeling" to the roots of suffering, oppression, and alienation. It asks the questions, How do we heal at the roots? How do we begin to feel again? Theology and faith practices can enable us to engage the issue at the level of the heart, where the depths of distrust, fear, and pain reside. This does not equate a theological strategy to the psychological or therapeutic, but it is part of the necessary inner healing in tandem with the healing of the wider society's structural and systemic manifestations of racism.

A theological stance approaches racial reconciliation with the vision of wholeness. Its vision includes seeking the prerequisites of justice, redress, and liberation. Yet beyond remedy, healing seeks wholeness and building right relationship.[14] This may refer to a fractured relationship or, in many cases, a relationship that never existed. Robert Schreiter challenges that, "Reconciliation is not just restoration. It brings us to a place where we have not been before."[15] Reconciliation brings forth a new relationship, unrecognizable and previously unexperienced. According to Schreiter, reconciliation is more of an "attitude" than a "skill." It is a "stance assumed before a broken world rather than a tool to repair that world...more spirituality than strategy."[16] How does a victim or group of victims cultivate this disposition, this "stance," this spirituality? How do they become reconciling agents moving us all toward a "place where we have not been before?"

One of the prerequisites for the victim of injustice is forgiveness, and indeed it is the victim who must forgive, for the tormentor cannot forgive himself or herself. Forgiveness is no easy task. One must be willing to give up "certain claims" and grievances against another.[17] Losing a longtime enemy can be disorienting to one's worldview and self-conception. To be open to reconciliation is to be open to the idea of trusting again. It is to be open to the possibility of living in new ways with one another. Reconciliation is the willingness to let go of rigidly constructed racial categories and to take on the task and promise of rearticulating them. Most importantly, according to Schreiter, reconciliation is not *performed*, but *discovered* by the victims who experience "the power of God's grace welling up in one's life."[18]

Ritual and Faith Practices

The promise of theology and spirituality to healing and injustice is gaining recognition beyond the religious community. Activities of secular political movements display a greater openness toward the inclusion of religious symbols and ritual. Whether it is an opening blessing, a moment of silence, meditation, or the use of altars, there is an openness to the religious and spiritual dimension in people's lives. Much can be attributed to the influence of the youth and young adult generation to these movements, which, though still counterinstitutional, are less influenced by dialectical materialism and are more open to spiritual and creative expression.

I identify two main resources that theology can contribute to processes of racial reconciliation: ritual and faith practices. The creation of sacred space through ritual and liturgical process offers a powerful space where healing can take place. It is a space for honesty, humility, vulnerability, self-reflection, safety, and listening before the Creator and in the context of community. Creating sacred space means creating the emotional, spiritual, and physical space necessary to allow room for God to do the reconciling.[19] It is making room for compassion.

Symbols used in ritual play a powerful role in transforming pain and mediating healing. Schreiter claims that deliverance from suffering into a new mode of relating requires symbols that are "strong...complex, something able to hold the contradiction of the situation together."[20] In addition, symbols are a particularly powerful form of expression where words may be inadequate but where a simple action can penetrate to a deep level of consciousness and heart. According to anthropologist Clifford Geertz, ritual or "consecrated behavior" is the moment or space where "the world as lived and the world as imagined, become fused under a single set of symbolic forms."[21] Ritual thus provides moments for the contradiction of the world as it is and the world as it should be to come together in a simple but powerful act that opens the heart to the notion of possibility and the mounting of hope. Liturgical process is an art form, and like art and creative expression, it works at the conscious and subconscious levels, with often unforeseen and spontaneous effects. Ritual, particularly in a secular setting, provides an opening for the power of the Spirit to transform the world.

In *Practicing Our Faith: A Way of Life for a Searching People*, Dorothy Bass and the contributing authors articulate and develop identified Christian practices drawn from Alistair MacIntyre's work on social practices. Faith practices are defined as daily practices or "concrete human acts" that address "fundamental human needs and conditions."[22] Concrete practices make values and ideals lived and real. The repeated and communal practice of these ordinary human activities deepens one's understanding and "involvement in the redemptive practice of God in the world."[23] It is the small gestures repeated over and over that uncover the "deepest expression in the activities of God."[24] As the significance of these gestures are transformed, so are we. The contributing authors of *Practicing Our Faith* offer twelve practices, including hospitality, household economics, testimony, forgiveness, healing, and dying well. I now offer two additional "concrete human acts" that I believe through their practice can help promote racial healing and lead to a "new way of life."[25]

Talk Story as a Practice of Faith

"Talk story," or "talking story," is the Asian American pigeon word for storytelling activity. There are individuals whom I have come to trust, despite racial lines between us, because I have come to know and appreciate their stories. Through story, I have been opened and my heart has been moved by their struggle and spirit, or God's spirit. I have come to see their humanness, and in the process, they have seen mine. Talk story as a faith practice, as a form and process for relating, can be a powerful practice to heal the pain of racism. Talk story is a way of framing depth thinking. It allows us to move beyond rigid boundaries of theology to a language that expresses depth and allows theology to emerge. It is at this deep level that we become connected. It is a form that does not reduce the storyteller; it is a form that is big enough to hold the contradictions and the whole picture. Talk story as a form allows for sharing in a cultural context, which does not call for censoring out the cultural and spiritual that often happens in the secular world. Talk story shares similar principles to that of testimony and narrative theology. Testimony has many forms of "words, works, actions, and lives which attest to an intention, an inspiration, an idea at the heart of experience and history which nonetheless transcends experience and history."[26] Narrative theology takes the position that people's life stories "are the text, and the bible and the Christian church are the context of our theology."[27]

Talk story directly counters racism's process of reducing racialized "human experience to an essence attributed to all without regard for historical or social context."[28] For in talk story there are real, individual, and grace-filled stories. There are no colors, only shades. Talk story provides a process for the "rearticulation" of race and life experience, the deep honoring and respect for an individual's journey, struggle, and survival in the midst of violence. Storytelling is seen as an important tool by critical race theorists, as it challenges "versions of reality put forward by the dominant culture."[29]

If racism is the diminishment of being a "relational self" with one another, then talk story allows one to get beyond the baggage, to engage in "entering into relation," the defining act of being human.[30] Talk story creates a space for vulnerability, the opening up of one's life, pains, struggles, prayers, and hopes. Through talk story, people share biographies of their living conditions, class, race, and gender experiences rooted in the community and societal context of their time. Talk story reflects on key moments and everyday events that are forever imprinted in the memories of the mind and body. Talk story reflects on defining moments that have shaped lives and asks, What have I learned? How have I, my people, or my community been transformed? What have I learned through my experiences about love, loss, God, and goodness? Where has there been evidence of the Spirit on the way?

Talk story includes the task of the listener to "be" in holy presence, with body and spirit, to the sacred process that is shared. Like testimony, it is a shared practice. But talk story and the storyteller are living testimony to goodness, survival, courage, and God's grace. Leonardo Boff calls these "testimonies charged with hope," testaments to faith, truth, justice, love, and life that is stronger than death, not just hatred.[31] Both listener and teller through talk story are able to transcend barriers of separation and touch deeply.

Family and Kinship as a Practice of Faith

I was raised in and am still part of a family full of contradictions. Yet I also learned, from an early age, that despite all the contradictions, we still love one another, for we are always family. My family was an extension of myself. Their needs were my needs, their pain my pain. Interestingly, when my family was playing mah-jong, we would only gamble money when playing with one another because it was assumed that it was all the same pot of money anyway, and should anyone be in need, the family would be there.

A second practice to promote racial healing and reconciliation, I would suggest, is the practice of family or kinship. Fumitaka Matsuoka names family as a "subsidiary institution" that can be one of the "agents of transformation" in the face of racism.[32] Of course, families have both positive and negative traits, but as a model for reconciliation, what would be the best values of family and kinship practice? First, there is assumed relationship, and it is an eternal one. In life and long after death, whether you like it or not, in some form, there is relationship. Second, there is unconditional love and the ability to embrace differences and yet still love. Third, there is the sharing of rituals to maintain and reinforce the kinship, such as the sharing of food, history, time, and resources. Kinship, I believe, is a model and symbol broad enough to embrace the realities of difference, hospitality, love, and sacrifice.

There is often little choice regarding into what family you are born and who becomes part of your extended family. Fate, or this random sorting process, has brought us together. What if we took these fateful ties seriously and used our relationality, inherent in kinship, as a starting point to break down barriers and promote deeper understanding? What would it mean to go deep and really embrace and reconcile with the differences and tensions in our own families? Take the inherent relationships in my own extended family, for example. I recently participated in a political protest in downtown San Francisco, and my brother-in-law was on duty in the line of police blockading protesters. In my family are members who are affected by the new anti-immigration legislation. They have been incarcerated for twenty-five-years-to-life under the Three Strikes Law. Some members have grown rich from the stock market boom of the 1990s, and some have gotten poorer. We are already related and connected; what would it mean for us to practice "deep feeling," compassion, and reconciliation in these inherent relationships?

Further opportunity and possibility is being embodied by racially mixed families. Interracial marriages in the U.S. now number 1.5 million.[33] For the first time in census history, responders to the 2000 census had the option to "mark one or more" races. Among those who opted, 6.8 million reported more than one race.[34] I believe that racially mixed families offer a glimpse of hope and an opportunity for rearticulating new stories about racial categories and racial barriers. I myself am a child of a bicultural marriage. My own immediate family is multicultural, which includes my spouse, who is Japanese and African American; my stepdaughter and two stepsons, who are Japanese, African, and Chinese American; and an extended family that includes Caucasians, African Americans, Asians, and Latinos. What would it mean if we took our "togetherness" and our relationship seriously as an opportunity to cross the barriers of racial lines and love deeply?

This is not to glorify families, for certainly there are some families from whom it is sometimes necessary to distance oneself. This is sometimes by choice, as an act of health, and sometimes not by choice. Ironically, the family institution can also be a great perpetrator of racism and violence "in the most entrenched fashion."[35] In these cases, kinship can be practiced by creating new families, which are bound, if not by blood, then by some other value or experience. These new families can also share in rituals and practices of giving, sharing, eating, praying, and singing. Despite and because they are places of complexity and, at times, contradiction, family and kinship provide an opportunity to confront racism and "move past the culture of distrust, climate of alienation–toward a new dynamic human interaction, a new vision of human relatedness."[36]

Conclusion

The 2000 census projects that by the year 2050 the white population will have declined by almost 20 percent, to 53 percent of the total population. The black population will have risen slightly to 15 percent of the population, while the Hispanic population will have doubled to 24 percent of the total population. The Asian American and Pacific Islander population is projected to have increased the fastest, tripling to 9 percent. The number of foreign-born is expected to have increased from 26 million to 53 million.[37] By 2050, the number of interracial marriages and mixed-race persons may complicate these limited racial projections. As our society moves toward a society where there will be no racial majority numerically, it remains to be seen whether numeric democracy necessarily leads to power democracy. In states that are already ahead of the rest of the country in terms of diversity, such as California, there is striking evidence that despite greater racial diversity, the white population continues to "over-vote" their population percentage, and minority groups (because of citizenship status and other factors) highly "under-vote" and remain underrepresented. It is clear that we cannot rely on numeric democracy as a simple answer to racism. Indeed, we will need new visions and strategies, as the tensions of diversity are likely to increase and multiply. Theological and spiritual approaches will play a critical role in addressing racial, interracial, and intraracial conflict in addition to civil rights and structural reforms. Ritual, symbols, faith practices of talk story, and depth relationship of kinship can be catalysts for new ways of relating and healing the wounds of race relations and difference in our society. A more racially diverse and complex United States will not just bring increased tension and challenge, but will bring forth new gifts of wisdom, experiences, knowledge, and intellectual and spiritual resources. Most of all, we hope for new possibilities and ways of being human. As we move toward this end, I pray:

> O, Sacred breath,
> give us the courage to let go
> to hurl ourselves into the holy spirit.
> melt our hearts of stone
> fossiled hurts.
> lead our hearts to begin to dance again
> to remember what joy it is to reach for another
> to embrace an enemy.
> may we fear not
> or fear anyway
> push us beyond my own inclination
> remind us how wonderful it is
> to love
> forgive
> risk
> hold out for hope in wholeness
> Turn enemies into friends.

Notes

[1]Janet Dang, Perla Ni, Joyce Nishioka, "Poster Protest Aftermath," *Asian Week* 8 April 1999, 7–9.

[2]Quoted in Scott Martell and Harrison Sheppard, "The Controversy Continues," *Nguoi Viet: Vietnamese American Weekly Review,* 18 April 1999, A5.

[3]Michael Omi and Howard Winant, *Racial Formation in the United States: From the 1960's to the 1990's* (New York: Routledge, 1994), 152.

[4]Charles Aaron, "Black Like Them," *Utne Reader* (March-April 1999): 69.

[5]Population Estimates Program, Population Division, U.S. Census Bureau, Washington, D.C.

[6]Omi and Winant, *Racial Formation,* 23.

[7]See Lisa Lowe, "Heterogeneity, Hybridity and Multiplicity: Asian American Differences," in *Immigrant Acts: On Asian American Cultural Politics* (Durham and Linden: Duke University Press, 1996), 60–83.

[8]Omi and Winant, *Racial Formation,* 69.

[9]Ibid., 2.

[10]Ibid., 194.

[11]Robert Schreiter, *Reconciliation: Mission and Ministry in a Changing Social Order* (Maryknoll, N.Y.: Orbis Books, 1992), 53.

[12]Ibid., viii.

[13]Omi and Winant, *Racial Formation,* 159.

[14]Schreiter, *Reconciliation,* 22; and John Koenig, "Healing," in *Practicing Our Faith: A Way of Life for a Searching People,* ed. Dorothy C. Bass (San Francisco: Jossey-Bass, 1997), 149.

[15]Schreiter, *Reconciliation,* 60.

[16]Ibid., 26.

[17]Gregory Jones, "Forgiveness," in Bass, *Practicing Our Faith,* 135.

[18]Schreiter, *Reconciliation,* 26.

[19]Ibid.

[20]Ibid., 48.

[21]Clifford Geertz, *The Interpretations of Cultures* (New York: Basic Books, 1973), 112.

[22]Bass, *Practicing Our Faith,* 6.

[23]Ibid., xiii.

[24]Ibid., 7.

[25]Ibid., 11.

[26]Ibid., 101.

[27]Chung Hyun Kyung, *Struggle to Be the Sun Again: Introducing Asian Women's Theology* (Maryknoll, N.Y.: Orbis Books, 1990), 111.

[28]Omi and Winant, *Racial Formation,* 159.

[29]Fumitaka Matsuoka, *The Color of Faith: Building Community in a Multiracial Society* (Cleveland, Ohio: United Church Press, 1998), 49.

[30]Ibid., 60.

[31]Ibid., 102.

[32]Ibid., 60.

[33]U.S. Bureau of the Census, Current Population Reports, Series P20–514, "Marital Status and Living Arrangements," March 1998 (update).

[34]U.S. Bureau of the Census, U.S. Department of Commerce, Overview of Race and Hispanic Origin, Census 2000 Brief, March 2001 Issue.

[35]Matsuoka, 60.

[36]Ibid., 60–61.

[37]Population Projections Program, Population Division, U.S. Census Bureau, Washington, D.C.

10

The Dragon and the Eagle

Toward a Vietnamese American Theology

PETER C. PHAN

Like the American population, the ranks of the Christian churches in the United States are constantly swelled by a steady stream of refugees and immigrants. This is particularly true of the Roman Catholic Church, whose membership has been dramatically increased in recent years by the coming of Asian and Spanish-speaking people. Among Asians, there is no doubt that the Vietnamese and Vietnamese Catholics form a most significant group.[1]

In this chapter, I will first give a brief report on the Vietnamese Catholics in the United States. Then I will delineate the social, cultural, and ecclesial condition of immigrants as the context in which a Vietnamese American theology is to be constructed. The last part will offer suggestions as to how a Vietnamese American theology can be formulated. In this way it is hoped that the dragon *(Lac Long),* which, according to Vietnamese mythology, is the god from whom the Vietnamese descended, can live in harmony with the eagle, the symbol of the United States. Metaphors aside, these reflections are intended to contribute to the process of healing and reconciliation between the two peoples who for various reasons were caught for decades in a disastrous war against each other.[2]

Vietnamese American Catholics

The victory of Communist North Vietnam over South Vietnam in April 1975 provoked the largest ever exodus of Vietnamese, and in particular Vietnamese Catholics, to the United States of America. Vietnamese refugees settled in various parts of the world, in particular Canada and Australia, but the country of choice was and is the United States, partly because it had the best organized resettlement programs (in particular, the agencies of the United States Catholic Conference) and partly because it was perceived as offering the greatest opportunities for educational and economic advancement.

Vietnamese in America

To date there have been no exact statistics of the Vietnamese population in general and on Vietnamese Catholics in particular in the United States. After a quarter of a century since their settlement on these shores, the number of Vietnamese is estimated at slightly over one million. Before 1975, 18,000 Vietnamese people were living in America.[3]

Their number was dramatically increased by refugees from communism after the fall of South Vietnam. Their flight from Vietnam occurred in five waves: The first consisted of about 130,000 who arrived in the immediate aftermath of the collapse of South Vietnam in April 1975; the second of ethnic Chinese who left in 1978–1979; the third of 300,000 "boat people" who came between 1978 and 1982 after being temporarily sheltered in various refugee camps–mainly in Thailand, the Philippines, and Hong Kong; the fourth of a much smaller number of people who were reunited with their families through various official programs such as Orderly Departure Program and Humanitarian Operations between 1983 and 1989; and the fifth of those who came after March 14, 1989.[4]

In terms of education and professional training, Vietnamese of the first wave were noticeably superior to those of the four later groups, which consisted mostly of students, small-business owners, farmers, fishermen, craftsmen, unskilled laborers, young men fleeing the military draft for the war against Cambodia, and children sent out by their parents to have a better life. These people had much lower levels of education, fewer job skills, and practically no knowledge of English, and therefore experienced much difficulty in adjusting to the new environment.[5]

In terms of religious affiliation, Vietnamese refugees and immigrants represent the whole spectrum of religious traditions in Vietnam, from the indigenous religion, often called animism, to the three ancient imported religions–that is, Buddhism, Confucianism, and Taoism–to the native religion of Caodaism, and, of course, Christianity (Catholic and Protestant).[6] Though Catholic Christianity constitutes only 8 percent of the total population in Vietnam, in the U.S., they make up 30 percent of Vietnamese Americans. The reason for this high proportion is that many Vietnamese Americans are Catholics who had fled North Vietnam to the South in 1954 to escape communism. Having had firsthand experiences of the evils of communism, they had much greater incentive to emigrate in 1975.

Like most other recently-arrived ethnic groups, the Vietnamese tend to settle close to one another. California has the largest number of Vietnamese and Vietnamese Catholics (especially in Orange County, which has a city named Little Saigon, and San Jose), followed by Texas (Houston, Dallas/Fort Worth, and Port Arthur), Louisiana (New Orleans), and Virginia/Washington, D.C. As a whole, the Vietnamese have done well in the new country, as testified by the high educational achievements of their young and their economic successes.[7]

Vietnamese American Catholics

In general, Vietnamese Catholics are deeply attached to their Vietnamese churches and hold their pastors in high esteem. They spare no resources to have their own churches and their own priests so as to be able to worship in their mother tongue and to preserve their religious and cultural customs. Most dioceses where there is a sizeable number of Vietnamese Catholics have at least one, and in many cases several Vietnamese parishes (e.g., San Jose, California; Atlanta; New Orleans; Dallas and Fort Worth; Arlington, Virginia; and Washington, D.C.). Even where there are no Vietnamese parishes, Vietnamese Catholics often have the opportunity to worship together, using the facilities of the American parishes.

By and large, the relation between Vietnamese American Catholics and the hierarchy of the American Catholic Church has been marked by mutual respect and friendly collaboration. Only extremely rarely has the relationship between the Vietnamese Catholic community and the local bishop been marred by controversies (e.g., in San Jose, California; and Port Arthur, Texas). Fortunately, these conflicts have been peacefully resolved.

There are currently some five hundred Vietnamese priests (diocesan and religious), some twenty permanent deacons, and several hundred sisters. Even among the clergy, there are "success stories": A good number of Vietnamese priests are pastors, responsible for not only the Vietnamese but also American parishes; a few of them hold the office of vicar general; and some have even been made monsignors! Vietnamese vocations to the priesthood and religious life have been numerous. In some dioceses (e.g., Orange, California; and New Orleans), Vietnamese priests constitute a significant percentage of the clergy; and in some religious societies (e.g., the Society of the Divine Word), a high number of members are Vietnamese.

Among the dozens of male religious orders, the largest is Congregation of Mary Coredemptrix *(Dong Dong Cong),* which was founded by a Vietnamese priest and is headquartered in Carthage, Missouri. Every August, the society organizes a celebration in honor of Mary, regularly with some forty thousand participants. There are about twenty female religious societies, the largest of which is the Congregation of the Lovers of the Cross *(Dong Men Thanh Gia),* also an indigenous congregation, founded by Bishop Lambert de La Motte in the seventeenth century and divided into groups according to the dioceses to which the members belong in Vietnam (e.g., Ha Noi, Hue, Thanh Hoa, Vinh, Cho Quan, Qui Nhon, and Phat Diem).

Two of the several official organizations for Vietnamese Catholics in the United States deserve mention: The Vietnamese Catholic Federation in the United States of America, whose general assembly meets every four years; and The Community of Vietnamese Clergy and Religious in the United States of America, whose general assembly meets every two years. Within the National Conference of Catholic Bishops there is the committee on migration, with responsibilities for refugees and immigrants.

Like many other ethnic groups, Vietnamese Catholics are deeply concerned with preserving their language, culture, and religious traditions. To achieve this goal they publish numerous newspapers, magazines, and journals, among which the most important are *Dan Chua* (People of God), *Duc Me Hang Cuu Giup* (Our Lady of Perpetual Help), *Thoi Diem Cong Giao* (Catholic Periodical), and *Hop Tuyen Than Hoc* (Theological Selections). Other activities include Vietnamese language classes and catechetical instruction in Vietnamese. (There is a well-attended biannual national catechetical conference.) Occasions on which Vietnamese cultural traditions are solemnly celebrated are weddings and funerals. Other more public occasions include the lunar New Year *(Tết),* the commemoration of the fall of South Vietnam (April 30), and the feast of the martyrs of Vietnam (November 24). Vietnamese American Catholics also contribute generously to the church in Vietnam, especially for the restoration of old churches or the building of new ones and for assistance to victims of natural disasters.

A Different Way of Being a Christian

When Vietnamese Catholics came to the United States, they brought with them their own ways of living the Christian faith. To understand Vietnamese Catholicism, it is important to remember that it developed in dependence on the growth of missionary activity since the sixteenth century. The type of church organization and Christian life that were brought to Vietnam by missionaries unavoidably mirrored those of contemporary Europe, today often referred to as post-Tridentine Catholicism, that is, shaped by the Council of Trent (1545–63). It has, of course, been renewed in various degrees by the reforms mandated by Vatican II. Vietnamese American Catholics stand, then, between a more conservative post-Tridentine Catholicism and a more progressive Vatican II Catholicism. Which side they favor largely depends on their particular regions of origin, being generally more open in the south and more traditional in the north. In spite of regional differences, the following traits seem to be common to Vietnamese Catholicism.

1) In terms of ecclesiological model, Vietnamese American Catholics tend to see the church primarily as a social institution. This model exaggerates the role of visible and canonical structures and the importance of the hierarchy. It has often led to the error known as institutionalism characterized by clericalism, juridicalism, and triumphalism. This

ecclesiological model is strongly buttressed by the Confucian culture, with its emphasis on deference for authority and tradition. It also responds well to the Vietnamese church's need to strengthen its corporate identity and social cohesiveness, given its minority status in Asia.

2) Connected with this emphasis on the institutional aspects of the church is the relatively passive role of the laity. Despite the fact that the Vietnamese American Catholic laity, especially the younger ones, are highly educated and successful in various professions, they have as yet no effective voice in the day-to-day operation of parish life. The local priest most often wields absolute power. Besides excessive reliance on the clergy, the laity's lack of competence in matters theological may account for the minimal role of the laity in church organization, because training in nonsecular fields is generally regarded as inappropriate for the laity.

3) Another consequence of institutionalism is an excessive concern with the internal problems of the church and neglect of the dialogue with other believers. Vietnamese American Catholics still look on the followers of other religions with suspicion, despite Vatican II's insistence on the necessity of interreligious dialogue. Furthermore, they have barely begun to reflect on, much less enact, the task and ways of inculturating the faith into their own cultures, in spite of ample resources available in their adopted country for this purpose.

4) Vietnamese American Catholics are also reluctant to take upon themselves the challenges of social justice, even if most of them are vigorously opposed to communism, and understandably so, because many of them have been victims of communist oppression. In general, Vietnamese American Catholicism is still heavily shaped by individualistic pietism, with insufficient knowledge of the social teaching of the church and, consequently, with little engagement in the sociopolitical and economic realms in the spirit of the gospel.

The above four observations are not intended to convey a negative evaluation of Vietnamese American Catholicism. On the contrary, on any showing, Vietnamese American Catholics form a vibrant and vigorous community that has already made invaluable contributions to both the American society and the church, not only from their cultural traditions but also from their Catholic heritage.

5) One area in which Vietnamese American Catholics have already visibly transformed the American church is the number of priestly and religious vocations they have produced. Beside hundreds of Vietnamese priests who came in and after 1975, many dioceses (e.g., Orange, California; and New Orleans, Louisiana) and religious societies (especially the Divine Word Society) have been enormously enriched by new Vietnamese vocations. Also to be mentioned are hundreds of sisters of various orders, some of which are of Vietnamese origin (e.g., the Lovers of the Cross), who are serving generously in many dioceses and who can easily raise

vocations in the hundreds if they have the resources. This large number of vocations could be attributed to the high respect in which priests and the religious are held among Vietnamese (which has, of course, its own negative side), but certainly it has roots in the devout faith of Vietnamese American Catholic families.

6) This fervent faith is nourished, no doubt, not only by the sacraments but also by popular devotions. Indeed, the cultivation of popular devotions is a distinguishing characteristic of many Vietnamese American communities and constitutes an important contribution that Vietnamese American Catholics make to the American church. While post–Vatican II Catholics tend to downplay popular devotions for their alleged superstitious character and their tendency to alienate people from this-worldly concerns, Vietnamese Catholics have continued to foster practices of popular devotion (e.g., Marian devotions, pilgrimages, novenas, Benediction, prayers to the saints, etc.) and derive much spiritual nourishment from them. Every August, the Marian celebrations organized by the Congregation of Mary Coredemptrix in Carthage, Missouri, draw an astonishing crowd of some forty thousand Vietnamese Catholics. These popular devotions will play a much more significant role if their tendency toward excessive sentimentalism and individualism can be minimized and their potential for community building, liberation, and social justice can be retrieved.

7) Intimately connected with popular devotions is another major characteristic of Vietnamese American Catholic communities and parishes– that is, the flourishing of communal activities, often in tandem with sacramental celebrations (especially baptism, marriage, and funerals), certain calendrical feasts (e.g., the New Year), and cultural customs (e.g., death anniversaries). In addition, there are a large number of pious associations (e.g., confraternities, sodalities, youth groups) that provide the laity with the opportunity to exercise leadership and be actively involved with the community, especially in its liturgical and spiritual life. Recently, more modern associations have been added, such as Bible study groups, charismatic prayer groups, RENEW, Cursillo, and so forth. These associations, with their manifold activities, are reliable indices of the vibrancy of Vietnamese American Catholic communities.

8) In addition to being nourished by sacraments and devotions, the faith of Vietnamese churches has been tested in the crucible of suffering and even persecution. The memory of martyrdom is still fresh in the minds of Vietnamese American Catholics, especially that of 117 martyrs (of whom twenty-one were foreign missionaries) canonized in 1988. More recently, many Vietnamese Catholics have suffered for their faith under the communist regime and as a result have chosen exile in the United States and elsewhere. While such an experience might have rigidified their conservative political views, it has no doubt enriched and fortified their faith in a way not available to those enjoying religious freedom.

9) Asia is the birthplace of almost all world religions (including Christianity!). In Vietnam the three main religious traditions are Confucian, Taoist, and Buddhist. Scratch the surface of every Vietnamese Catholic and you will find a Confucian, a Taoist, and a Buddhist, or more often than not, an indistinguishable mixture of the three. Vietnamese Catholics live within a cultural framework undergirded by Taoist, Confucian, and Buddhist values and moral norms. They are socialized into these values and norms not only though formal teachings but also, and primarily, through thousands of proverbs, folk sayings, songs, and, of course, family rituals and cultural festivals. Many Vietnamese Catholics do not find it strange or difficult to inhabit different religious universes. It is this rich and varied religious heritage, latent but pervasive, that Asian American Catholics bring with them to the United States, and it will be one of their most significant contributions to the American church.

10) Lastly, most if not all first-generation Vietnamese immigrants in the United States experienced socioeconomic deprivation, extreme in some cases, before they came here. This experience of poverty makes Vietnamese American Catholics sensitive to the sufferings and needs of their fellow nationals and generous in their financial support for the church as well as their relatives back home. This sense of solidarity with victims of poverty and of natural disasters is also a characteristic of many Vietnamese American Catholic communities and should be fostered with care, since the struggle against poverty and oppression is an essential part of the inculturation of the gospel, especially in a society whose economic and military policies have caused sufferings in many parts of the world and in Asia in particular.

Vietnamese American Catholics live between two cultures and between two churches. Neither fully American nor fully Vietnamese, they are *both* Vietnamese *and* American. Being both, they have the opportunity and the challenge to fuse both worlds, their own cultural values and Catholicism and the American culture and the American Catholic Church, into something new, so that they stand not only *between* these two cultures and churches, but also *beyond* them.

Dwelling in the Interstices Between Two Cultures and Two Churches

As refugees forced to flee their country or as immigrants voluntarily seeking a better life in the United States, Vietnamese Catholics face a double challenge: how to maintain their cultural heritage in a foreign land and how to forge a new Christian identity in a new ecclesial environment. In a very short time they have made a disconcerting journey from their predominantly premodern society to the modern and postmodern culture of America. As Catholics, the Vietnamese have brought with them ecclesial experiences to a church that bears resemblance to their Catholicism but most of the time baffles them. The remaining issue is how to envision the space Vietnamese American Catholics occupy both as citizens of American society and as members of the American Catholic Church. From this space flow the tasks that are incumbent on them as citizens and church members as well as those of American society and the American church toward them.

Betwixt and Between

Despite profound personal and spiritual differences, Vietnamese American Catholics share one common trait and fundamental predicament: They are all immigrants. And being immigrant means being at the margin, or being in-between, or being betwixt and between.[8] To be betwixt and between is to be neither here nor there, to be neither this thing nor that completely. Spatially, it is to dwell at the periphery or at the boundaries. Politically, it means not residing at the centers of power of the two intersecting worlds, but rather occupying the precarious and narrow margins where the two dominant groups meet and clash, and being denied the opportunity to wield power in matters of public interest and self-determination. Socially, to be in-between is to be part of a minority, a member of a marginal(ized) group. Culturally, it means not being fully integrated into and accepted by either cultural system, being a *mestizo*, a person of mixed race. Linguistically, the betwixt-and-between person is bilingual but may not achieve a mastery of both languages and often speaks them with a distinct accent. Psychologically and spiritually, the person does not possess a well-defined and secure self-identity and is often marked with excessive impressionableness, rootlessness, and an inordinate desire for belonging. In short, an American Vietnamese will never be American enough; because of his or her race and culture, *American* will function only as a qualifier for the noun *Vietnamese*. On the other hand, a Vietnamese American is no longer regarded by his or her compatriots in Vietnam as authentically Vietnamese; she or he has "left" Vietnam and has become an American for whom *Vietnamese* functions only as a qualifier. In fact, Vietnamese Americans have been given a special name by the Vietnamese government, that is, *Viet kieu* (Vietnamese foreigners).

However, to be betwixt and between is not totally negative and need not cause cultural schizophrenia. Paradoxically, being neither this nor that allows one to be *both* this *and* that. An American Vietnamese or a Vietnamese American is American in a way no "pure" American can be, and he or she is a Vietnamese in a way no "pure" Vietnamese can be, precisely because she or he is both Vietnamese and American.

Of course, the process of rapid and extensive globalization and internationalization has compressed the geographical and cultural boundaries and made them exceedingly porous, so that there is today little connection between the passport one holds and the languages one speaks, the clothes one wears, the foods one eats, the music one listens to, the views one professes, and the religion one practices. The constant flow of persons, technologies, finance, information, and ideology across continents and countries has brought about deterritorialization and multiple belongings and loyalties. While this is true of almost everyone in the modern world, only the immigrant experiences this "both-and" situation of multiple identities and loyalties as a permanent, day-to-day, existential condition that she or he must constantly negotiate, often without the benefit of clear guidelines and helpful models. Furthermore, the believing immigrant must consciously accept this predicament as his or her providentially given mission and task, and must devise ways to create a space in which to live a fruitful life and not to fall between the two at times conflicting and competing cultures. Belonging to both worlds and cultures, immigrants have the opportunity to fuse them together and, out of their respective resources, fashion a new, different world, so that they stand not only *between* these two worlds and cultures but also *beyond* them. Thus, being betwixt and between can bring about personal and societal transformation and enrichment.

Between Two Churches

What has been said of the destiny of immigrants between the two cultures, their own and the American culture, applies equally to their ecclesial situation. Here, too, they stand in-between two churches, at the boundary between the American Catholic Church and the churches of their native countries. Belonging fully to neither, they feel estranged in both and do not occupy positions of power in either church. For most American Catholics, Vietnamese American Catholics' religious practices seem to be a throw back to their own Catholicism of the fifties, with clerical dominance and lay submissiveness, with colorful processions and pious devotions. On the other hand, Vietnamese American Catholics, both clerical and lay, do not fare much better when they return home for a visit. While welcoming them, the local hierarchy often looks on them (especially the clerics) with suspicion, fearing that they have been contaminated by the liberal, and even heretical, ideas and lax morality of the American church.

Nevertheless, while belonging fully neither to the American church nor the Vietnamese church, Vietnamese American Catholics belong to both. Vietnamese American Catholics live a Catholic life in a way no "pure" American Catholic can because of their indelible Asian religious traditions, and they live a Catholic life in a way no "pure" Asian Catholic can because of the distinctly American Catholic ethos that they have willy-nilly absorbed through sheer contiguity and symbiosis with the American society and Catholic church. Here, again, their betwixt-and-between position should be viewed not only as a negative asset producing marginalization but also as an opportunity and a task to create a new way of being Catholic. Here lies their unique contribution to the church.

In the Interstices Between Two Worlds

But in order to accomplish this mission, where should Vietnamese American Catholics stand? What is their social location, the specific space they occupy within American society and the church? How should they be part of the societal and ecclesial realities? In speaking of the inculturation of an immigrant into the modern and postmodern culture, scholars have outlined three possible strategies, which Robert Schreiter, following Jonathan Friedman, terms antiglobalism, ethnification, and primitivism.[9] The first is a total retreat from the ideals and values of globalization to defend and preserve one's cultural identity, either through a complete rejection of modernity as found in fundamentalism, or through strategies of hierarchical control as in revanchism.[10] The second is the attempt to rediscover a forgotten cultural identity through a retrieval of real or imagined cultural traits, with the result that often a hybridized culture is constructed through the process of ethnogenesis.[11] The third is the attempt to select a period or an aspect of one's previous, premodern culture and use it as a framework for dealing with globalization.[12]

None of the these three strategies, I submit, would be a satisfactory solution for Vietnamese Americans. In light of what has been said about the existential condition of the immigrant, I would argue that the reason they are unsatisfactory lies in their common presupposition that an immigrant must be either completely inside or completely outside American culture. Anything less than a complete opposition against or absorption into American culture conceived as an integrative system is unacceptable. Antiglobalism is in favor of the first option, whereas ethnification and primitivism are implicitly in favor of the second. Whereas antiglobalism rejects inculturation altogether, acknowledging no common space whatsoever between American culture and Vietnamese cultures, ethnification and primitivism accept absorption into the American culture as an ideal by means of a retrieval either of an allegedly lost culture or a forgotten normative cultural dimension or period.

In contrast to these three strategies, I propose that we view the predicament of Vietnamese Americans as neither completely inside nor completely outside Vietnamese and American societies, but as belonging to both but not entirely, because they are *beyond* both.[13] The same thing should be said about Vietnamese American Catholics. They are neither completely outside the American Catholic Church and their native Asian churches nor completely inside them; they belong to both but not completely, because they are also *beyond* both. In other words, they live and move and have their being in the interstice between the American culture and their own, between the American church and their Asian churches. Because of this inalienable interstice, there should be no attempt to incorporate Vietnamese Americans into American society and

Vietnamese American Catholics into the Catholic church as if it were into a melting pot, in such a way that they would lose their distinct identity both as Vietnamese and as Vietnamese Catholics. Nor should there be an attempt to keep them apart from American society and the American church in a kind of ghetto, in such a way that they would be marginalized from church and society.

Furthermore, given the present reality of culture in the United States as globalized, conflicted, fragmented, and multiple, this space is not some preexisting no-man's-land, peacefully and definitively agreed on in advance by the powers that be of the two cultures and the two churches. Rather, the interstice is to be carved out by the Vietnamese American Catholics themselves, in everyday living, by trial and error, in creative freedom, over the course of a lifetime. Its boundaries, quite porous to be sure, are ever shifting and are subject to being redrawn and renegotiated as new circumstances and needs arise. What remains indisputable is that Vietnamese American Catholics have a right to this cultural and ecclesial interstitial space where they can fulfill their God-given mission of being the bridge between East and West, between the church of Asia and the church of North America.

Interculturation

This does not mean that inculturation or interculturation is an arbitrary and haphazard process, bereft of guiding principles, theological and canonical, or without a supervising authority. Indeed, in the process of interculturation between Vietnamese culture and American culture, all the three dimensions (i.e., signs, message, and codes)[14] and the three levels of culture (i.e., the surface, the intermediate level, and the mentality)[15] must be brought into play. Interculturation is the process whereby the American culture and the Vietnamese culture are brought into a reciprocal engagement in such a way that both of them are transformed from within. Essential to interculturation is the *mutual* criticism and enrichment between the American culture and the Vietnamese culture. The expressions of all these cultures are transformed as the result of this process.

Strictly, interculturation is a three-step trajectory. First, what Louis Luzbetak calls "individual building-blocks of culture"—that is, the signs and symbols—of one culture are assigned functional equivalents in another culture. Here, obviously, *translation* plays a predominant role.

Then comes the stage of *acculturation,* in which one culture acquires certain elements of another culture, which, in its turn, adopts certain elements of the other culture. However, often such mutual borrowing still operates at best at the intermediate level. Furthermore, because of the unequal power relations between the American culture and the immigrants' cultures, there is the danger that the latter will be dominated and absorbed by the former. Also, in this cultural exchange there are plenty of opportunities for mutual misunderstanding, because the codes through which the meaning of the signs of culture are carried may be hidden and different. Often, acculturation may lead to either juxtaposition (elements of both cultures are unassimilated and are allowed to operate side by side) or syncretism (the basic identity of both cultures is lost or diluted).

The third stage, the level of *inculturation* proper, engages the deepest level of the two cultures together, their worldviews, their basic "message," as expressed in their philosophies and religions. Obviously, this task requires that immigrants achieve a measure of intellectual sophistication and institutional autonomy that would enable them to confront the American culture as equals in a truly multiethnic and pluralistic society.

What has been said about the encounter between the American culture and the Vietnamese culture applies as well to the encounter between the American church and Vietnamese American Catholics. A similar three-stage process of interculturation takes place. There is the first and essential phase of translating significant religious texts in English into Vietnamese and vice-versa, a work largely still to be done for and by Vietnamese American Catholics.[16] Whereas many classics of Asian philosophy are available in English, very few Christian classics have been translated into Vietnamese. I am thinking not only of the Bible but also of patristic and medieval classics as well as works on spirituality. As a result, many Vietnamese American Catholics are deprived of the theological and spiritual heritage of Western Christianity and therefore do not possess the necessary resources to enter into a fruitful dialogue with the Western church.

There is next the phase of finding the ways by which both the American church and Vietnamese American Catholic communities can critique and enrich each other on the ten (and other) characteristics listed above. For example, from the perspective of the American church, Vietnamese American Catholics will be challenged to correct their predominantly institutional model of ecclesiology by means of other models in which the role of the laity is duly recognized and their active participation fostered, dialogue with followers of other religions undertaken, and social justice seriously pursued. On the other hand, through the experiences of Vietnamese American Catholics, the American church may rediscover the importance of priestly and religious vocations, popular devotions, pious associations, martyrdom, and solidarity with the poor and the oppressed. No less importantly, in a religiously pluralistic world, which the United States has become, the manifold non-Christian heritage of Vietnamese American Catholics will be a springboard for the church to learn from the spiritual riches of other religions.

The mention of non-Christian religions brings us to the third and deepest level of interculturation, which is also the most difficult and challenging. Connected with this level of inculturation are some of the most controversial themes in contemporary theology, such as religious pluralism, the salvific values of non-Christian religions, the uniqueness of Christ, the necessity of the church, praxis for liberation, and interfaith dialogue.[17] This is not the place to broach these theological issues, but there is no doubt that the presence of Vietnamese American Catholics will bring them to the fore. Furthermore, Vietnamese American Catholics are in a privileged position to help their fellow Catholics in Vietnam deal with these thorny issues, because they have at their disposal, and hence are duty-bound to take advantage of, opportunities for theological education that have been denied to their fellow Catholics for more than fifty years in their own country.

Three Theological Tasks

Theologically, Vietnamese American Catholics have to perform the three tasks that Anselm Kyongsuk Min prescribes for Korean American theology.[18] The first is to retrieve both the Western and the Asian traditions for the needs of Asian communities in America, whose needs and circumstances as immigrants are different from those of their fellow Asians in Asia.

The second task is to reflect on the theological significance of the Asian American experience itself. Such an experience, Min points out, has at least four dimensions: separation, ambiguity, diversity, and love of the stranger (xenophilia). The Asian American experience is first of all that of separation from the old, familiar, ancestral ways of doing things: "For a people so devoted to the tradition, living in America brings with it pain of radical separation, the repression of nostalgia for the old culture and old identities, dying to old self and being born again, born to the truth of human life as pilgrimage of the *homo viator,* the wayfaring human being."[19] Second, the experience of separation is also that of ambiguity. "It means no longer having the certainties of the home tradition available for every moment of decision and crisis, but rather meeting such a moment in a creative, inventive way, improvising, compromising, agonizing, and in any event learning to live with a large dose of ambiguity, the very ambiguity of life itself."[20] The third experience is the pain of diversity. Coming from a relatively homogeneous culture, Asian Americans must learn to live with the ethnic others—those who are different in ethnicity, language, religion, and culture. They must learn to overcome ethnic prejudices and narrow nationalism. From this comes the fourth experience, that of learning to love the stranger. Min suggests that the event of April 29, 1992, in Los Angeles, in which Korean businesses were systematically looted and burned by African and Hispanic Americans, should teach Korean Americans that they cannot live just for themselves but must learn to live with others with some solidarity of interests.[21]

The third and last task is to elaborate a political theology appropriate to Asian Americans as citizens of the United States who have both domestic responsibilities toward the common good and international responsibilities as part of the sole surviving superpower in an increasingly globalizing world. Min warns against the danger of focusing on only ethnic and cultural issues and forgetting the duty of prophetic criticism: "As citizens of a country with the historic burdens of colonialism, slavery, and imperialism," Asian Americans "too need particular sensitization to this international dimension of U.S. power. They cannot simply disallow all political responsibility for what their political, military, and economic representatives do overseas in their names."[22]

Toward a Vietnamese American Theology

In line with Min's three suggestions, I would like to sketch the contours of a Vietnamese American theology. Such a theology has barely begun, and what follows is nothing more than a series of unsystematic reflections on how Vietnamese Christians must make full use of *both* American and Vietnamese cultural and religious resources to understand and express the Christian faith. In their *both-and* and *beyond* social and religious situation, they cannot do otherwise.

Resources and Methodology

With regard to cultural resources, there are in Vietnamese philosophical tradition no writings by Vietnamese thinkers that have achieved the canonical status similar to that of the Chinese Five Classics and Four Books with which a Vietnamese Christian theology could enter into dialogue or which it could use as its resource. This does not mean that there is not a Vietnamese philosophy or no philosophical writings in Vietnamese. On the contrary, there is a substantial body of these writings.[23] Unfortunately, however, they still remain mostly unknown and are not readily accessible because they are not yet transcribed into the national script.

While recourse to these writings remains necessary, a Vietnamese American theology should not be limited to a dialogue with these ancient philosophical texts. It must bring into play other resources of Vietnamese culture. Among these, the pride of place must be assigned to literally thousands of proverbs, sayings, and traditional songs. This body of Vietnamese popular or oral literature, which has been carefully collected and studied, is rightly regarded as the most authentic treasure of Vietnamese wisdom and worldview.[24] Among contemporary philosophers, the numerous writings of Kim Dinh present a rich plethora of insights into the Vietnamese cultural heritage and can serve as a valuable basis for a Vietnamese American theology.[25] Vietnamese literature, past as well as contemporary, is also a fertile source for theological reflection. Among literary works, Nguyen Du's epic *Doan Truong Tan Thanh,* more popularly known as *Truyen Kieu,* remains an indispensable source of Vietnamese worldview.[26] But this chef d'oeuvre should not be allowed to eclipse other literary works, especially contemporary poetry and novels, which embody a different but no less important understanding of the Vietnamese ethos. In addition, life stories of ordinary Vietnamese, especially those who suffer from poverty and all forms of oppression, provide a rich ore for Vietnamese American theology. Finally, Vietnamese American theology must enter into dialogue with the sacred texts and ritual practices of Vietnamese Buddhism, Confucianism, Taoism, and indigenous religion.[27]

A Vietnamese-American theology, however, must not confine itself to reiterating the past wisdom of the Vietnamese culture, but must bring this wisdom into a fruitful confrontation with the experiences of Vietnamese immigrants in the United States. These experiences are unique to Vietnamese expatriates struggling to survive in the interstices between two cultures and churches. They are unavailable to those living in the native country, even though, as has been mentioned above, Western and American ideas and values have been exported to all corners of the world through the process of globalization. In this way, what is true, good, and beautiful in Vietnamese culture can be enriched further by the truths and values found in American culture, just as what is defective in it can be corrected. For example, the communitarian ethos, characteristic of the Vietnamese worldview, by which the individual is subordinated to the collective welfare of the family and society, can sometimes lead to the suppression of the individual's autonomy and dignity. Here, it should be corrected by the typically American respect for and promotion of the individual's inalienable rights. Thus, a Vietnamese American anthropology will be a dialectical fusion of communitarianism and individualism that is a genuinely new *tertium quid* emerging from the encounter between two different cultures.

Theological Themes

It is, of course, impossible to develop at length here the various themes that a Vietnamese American theology must attend to. In the remaining pages I would like simply to highlight a list of themes, by no means exhaustive, that I consider essential to a Vietnamese American theology.

1) Basic to the Vietnamese worldview is what is called the "three-element philosophy" *(triet ly tam tai)*.[28] The three elements are Heaven, Earth, and Humanity, *(thien, dia, nhan* or *troi, dat, nguoi)*, forming the three ultimates constituting the whole reality. "Heaven" refers to the firmament above humans (as opposed to the earth), to the law of nature, and to the Creator, endowed with intellect and will. The firmament is the place where the Creator dwells; the law of nature is the Creator's will and dispositions; and the Creator is the supreme being who is transcendent, omnipotent, and eternal. "Earth" refers to the material reality lying beneath humans (as opposed to heaven above), to that which gives rise to entities composed of the five constituents *(ngu hanh)* of metal, wood, water, fire, and earth; and

to matter in general, which is essentially directed upward to Heaven. "Humanity" refers to human beings, "whose heads carry Heaven and whose feet trample upon Earth" *(dau doi troi, chan dap dat)*—that is, humans as the link or union between Heaven and Earth. Humans express the power of Heaven and Earth by being "the sage inside and the king outside" *(noi thanh ngoai vuong)*, that is, by orienting upward to Heaven *(tri tri)* through knowing Heaven, trusting in Heaven, and acting out the will of Heaven on the one hand, and by orienting downward to Earth *(cach vat)* through the use of material things for the benefit of all. As the center connecting Heaven and Earth, humans as the microcosm unite the male and the female, the positive and the negative, light and darkness, spirit and matter *(yin* and *yang)*, and the characteristics of the five constituents: subtlety (water), strength (fire), vitality (wood), constancy (metal), and generosity (earth). In this way humans practice the "human heart" *(nhan tam)* and the "human way" *(nhan dao)*.

The most important principle of the *tam tai* philosophy is that all the three constitutive elements of reality are intrinsically connected with one another and mutually dependent. Heaven without Earth and Humanity cannot produce or express anything. Earth without Heaven and Humanity would be an empty desert. Humanity without Heaven would be directionless, and without Earth it would have nowhere to exist and to act. Each of the three elements has a function of its own to perform: Heaven gives birth; Earth nurtures; and Humanity harmonizes *(Thien sinh, dia duong, nhan hoa)*. Consequently, human action must be governed by three principles: It must be carried out in accord with Heaven *(thien thoi)*, with the propitious favor of Earth *(dia loi)*, and for the harmony of Humanity *(nhan hoa)*.[29]

It is clear that a Vietnamese American theology can and should make use of this *tam tai* philosophy to construct not only a theology of the Trinity but also an integral anthropology. First, with regard to the Trinity, it is possible to correlate God the Father with Heaven, God the Son to Humanity, and God the Spirit to Earth and to elaborate their roles in the history of salvation in the light of those of Heaven, Earth, and Humanity.[30] The Father's role is to "give birth" through "creation"; the Son's is to "harmonize" through redemption; and the Spirit's is to "nurture" through sanctifying grace. These roles are truly distinct from one another (hence Trinitarian and not modalistic) but intimately linked with one another (hence one and not subordinationist or tritheistic). Like Heaven, Earth, and Humanity, the three divine Persons are united in a *perichoresis* or *koinonia* of life and activities. In this Trinitarian theology, God's transcendence and immanence are intrinsically related with each other. God, though transcendent, is conceived as internally connected with and dependent on Humanity and Earth to carry his activities in history. Indeed, the Trinity is conceived as inscribed in the structure of reality itself.[31]

Second, a Christian anthropology constructed in light of the *tam tai* philosophy will offer an integral understanding of human existence. In this anthropology there is no opposition between theocentrism and anthropocentrism, nor between theocentrism and geocentrism, nor between geocentrism and anthropocentrism. Indeed, *tam tai* philosophy is opposed to any *ism* that is exclusive of any other perspective. The human is understood neither as subject nor object but as intrinsically *related* to the Divine and the ecological, just as the Divine is intrinsically related to the ecological and the human, and the ecological is intrinsically related to the Divine and the human. This anthropology will be an important corrective to the American culture, which tends to view, under the influence of modernity, God and humanity as competitors and humans as unrelated to their ecology.

2) Any Christian philosophy must, of course, reflect on Christ as both Divine and human. In Vietnamese American theology, I would highlight two aspects of Christ. First, Jesus can be regarded as the Immigrant par excellence, the Marginalized One living in the *both-and* and *beyond* situation.[32] This in-between, on-the-margin status is foundational to the Incarnation as well as to Jesus' entire ministry, including his death and resurrection. But Jesus' being on the margin creates a new circle with a new center, not of power but of love, joining and reconciling the two worlds, human and divine. Vietnamese Americans can readily relate to this figure of Christ the Immigrant from their experiences, sometimes painful, of living as marginalized immigrants in the United States. But like Jesus, they are called to create a new circle, made up of both Americans and Vietnamese, with a new center, not in order to exclude anyone but to help both Americans and Vietnamese to move *beyond* their ethnic identities and create a new reality of *both* Vietnamese *and* American.

Second, from the Vietnamese religious perspective, Jesus can be regarded as the Eldest Brother and the paradigmatic Ancestor. As is well known, the veneration of ancestors is one of the most sacred duties for Vietnamese. It is also common knowledge that this religious practice constituted one of the serious problems for missionary work in Asia.[33] A christology that presents Jesus as the Eldest Brother and the Ancestor has much to recommend it not only for missionary purposes but also for fostering Vietnamese ethics, especially familial, at the center of which lies filial piety. This latter aspect is all the more urgent for Vietnamese Americans who are encountering tremendous difficulties in preserving the rite of ancestor veneration, especially at weddings and funerals.[34]

3) The theology of the church in Asia, especially in the Roman Catholic Church, has been for a long time characterized by an excessive focus on the church's institutional aspects, in particular the hierarchy and its power. Asian ecclesiology, in other words, has been ecclesiocentric. In recent years, thanks to the work of the Federation of the Asian Bishops' Conferences,

theological attention has been turned away from intra-ecclesial issues to the mission of the church toward the world, especially the world of Asian peoples.[35] Ecclesiology is now focused on the reign of God as its goal: The church exists for the sake of the kingdom of God. The church's evangelizing mission is now understood in terms of the threefold task of inculturation, interreligious dialogue, and liberation.[36]

Such a kingdom-centered ecclesiology is called for in Vietnamese American theology. As Min has correctly pointed out, Asian immigrants cannot be oblivious to the fact that politically and economically, they, immigrants though they are, belong to the only surviving superpower exercising an enormous influence and not infrequently an unjust and oppressive control over the rest of the world through the process of globalization. The task of sociopolitical and economic liberation, which is a constitutive dimension of evangelization, becomes all the more urgent for Vietnamese Americans. Furthermore, because Vietnamese Americans are religiously diverse, the need for interreligious dialogue is no less pressing in the United States than in Asia. Finally, for Vietnamese Americans the inculturation of the Christian faith is no doubt a much more challenging and complex task in America, because they are confronted with not only one but at least two very diverse cultures. Of course, these tasks of inculturation, interreligious dialogue, and liberation cannot be separated from the other aspects of evangelization such as proclamation, personal witness, and worship.[37]

4) Another area that Vietnamese American theology must attend to is liturgy and sacramental worship. It is well known that, in most Asian Roman Catholic churches, liturgical and sacramental celebrations are largely determined by officially approved books composed in Latin by the experts in Rome and then translated into the vernaculars. These translations in turn have to be approved–again by Rome–before they can be used. Little input by the local churches has been made, though liturgical "adaptation" within prescribed limits is allowed. Recently, some liturgical inculturation has been carried out in Vietnam. Noteworthy are the expanded prayers for the dead in the Eucharistic Prayers of the Mass to mention explicitly the ancestors and the liturgies in celebration of the lunar New Year *(Têt)* and for burial. Nevertheless, these adaptations still remain timid and pallid attempts to make worship culturally and religiously meaningful to the Vietnamese. A major task of liturgical inculturation is still to be carried out by Vietnamese American theology by taking into account, among other things, what has been described as Vietnamese popular religiosity.[38]

5) The last aspect of Vietnamese American theology concerns ethics and spirituality. Asians are often viewed as embodying such values as love of silence and contemplation, closeness to nature, simplicity, detachment, frugality, harmony, nonviolence, love for learning, respect for the elders, filial piety, compassion, and attachment to the family. While these

characteristics may be exaggerated and even caricatured, there is no doubt that there is a core of truth in this description of what has been called the "Asian soul." Vietnamese cultural critics have often pointed out how Vietnamese philosophy and literature, especially Vietnamese proverbs and popular songs, have prescribed as moral ideals total harmony with Heaven, Earth, and Humanity; equilibrium and balance in mind and body; psychological wholeness and integrity; interior peace and calm; solidarity and sharing.

Obviously, these ideals are hard to practice in a culture such as that in the U.S., which prizes professional competition, material success, individual autonomy, democratic egalitarianism, and personal self-fulfillment. However, there is little doubt that these ideals can correct the excesses of the American way of life. On the other hand, challenged and enriched by the American moral ideals, Vietnamese Americans can avoid the risk of yielding to leisurely quietism, political and social withdrawal, avoidance of public responsibilities, and spiritual escapism. Vietnamese American moral and spiritual theology is called to develop a way of uniting the best of the two cultural and moral traditions, while avoiding the excesses of both.

The Vietnamese have chosen the bamboo tree as their national symbol. Vietnamese villages are typically surrounded by high rows of bamboos bonding the villagers with one another and shielding them from natural disasters and human invaders. Bamboo shoots provide poor people with nourishing food. Bamboo canes are used to build houses and the leaves for roofing. Bamboo wood is woven into the most common utensils. Above all, bamboos are extremely resilient; they bend but cannot be easily broken, like the Vietnamese spirit during centuries of oppression and colonialism. For Christians, the cross is the symbol of God's unconditional love for humanity and final victory over evil. Vietnamese Americans, as Vietnamese and as Catholic, live in the shadow of the bamboo and the cross in a new country, now gratefully adopted as their own. If they are faithful to both their cultural heritage and their Christian faith, their cruciform bamboo will grow and prosper in the soil of the New World. A Vietnamese American theology is an indispensable fertilizer to bring about the flourishing of this cruciform bamboo.

Notes

[1] The first two parts of this essay are adapted from my earlier essay, "Vietnamese Catholics in the United States: Christian Identity Between the Old and the New," *U.S. Catholic Historian* 18/1 (2000): 19–35. See also my "Asian Catholics in the United States: Challenges and Opportunities for the Church," *Mission Studies* 16/2, no. 32 (1999): 151–74.

[2] For reflections on the meaning of the so-called American War in Vietnam and its aftermath, see Peter C. Phan, "Escape to Freedom: 25 Years After the Fall of South Vietnam," *America* 182/15 (April 29, 2000): 12–14.

³See Ruben Rumbaut, "Vietnamese, Laotian, and Cambodian Americans," in *Asian Americans: Contemporary Issues and Trends,* ed. Pyong Gap Min (Thousand Oaks, Calif.: Sage, 1995), 232–70.

⁴See James M. Freeman, *Changing Identities: Vietnamese Americans 1975–1995* (Boston: Allyn and Bacon, 1995), 29–41.

⁵See Darrel Montero, *Vietnamese Americans: Patterns of Resettlement in the United States* (Boulder, Colo.: Westview Press, 1979); Nathan Caplan, John K. Whitmore, and Marcella H. Choy, *The Boat People and Achievement in America: A Study of Family Life, Hard Work, and Cultural Values* (Ann Arbor: University of Michigan Press, 1989); and Paul James Rutledge, *The Vietnamese Experience in America* (Bloomington and Indianapolis: University of Indiana Press, 1992).

⁶For information on these religions, see Peter C. Phan, *Mission and Catechesis: Alexandre de Rhodes and Inculturation in Seventeenth-Century Vietnam* (Maryknoll, N.Y.: Orbis Books, 1998), 13–28.

⁷On the educational achievements of Vietnamese Americans, see Nathan Caplan, Marcella H. Choy, and John K. Whitmore, *Children of the Boat People: A Study of Educational Success* (Ann Arbor: University of Michigan Press, 1991); and James Freeman, *Changing Identities,* 69–86. Freeman writes, "The academic achievements of Vietnamese schoolchildren in America are almost legendary: valedictorians of high schools and colleges, a Rhodes scholar, winners of science competitions, high grade point averages, high scores on the Scholastic Aptitude (now Assessment) Test" (69).

⁸On this understanding of being an immigrant, see Jung Young Lee, *Marginality: The Key to Multicultural Theology* (Minneapolis: Fortress Press, 1995); and Peter C. Phan, "Betwixt and Between: Doing Theology with Memory and Imagination," *Journeys at the Margin: Toward an Autobiographical Theology in American-Asian Perspective,* ed. Peter C. Phan and Jung Young Lee (Collegeville, Minn.: Liturgical Press, 1999), 113–33.

⁹See Robert Schreiter, *The New Catholicity: Theology between the Global and the Local* (Maryknoll, N.Y.: Orbis Books, 1997), 21–25. The work of Jonathan Friedman referred to is *Cultural Identity and Global Process* (London: Sage, 1994).

¹⁰Fundamentalism is found of course in all religions, from Judaism to Islam to some Catholic and Protestant conservative groups. Revanchism is present in the restorationist policies of the post-Vatican II era in the Catholic Church.

¹¹This strategy is proposed, for example, by some African Americans or Native Americans who attempt to recover their lost or suppressed cultural or tribal traditions, or to construct their cultural identity by means of some celebration, e.g., Kwanzaa.

¹²This practice is found, for example, among Catholics who choose the patristic or medieval periods as benchmarks for the renewal of the church and theology. Some Asians have made certain practices, such as veneration of ancestors, the defining trait of their cultures.

¹³On the concept of the immigrant as being "in-beyond," see Jung Young Lee, *Marginality,* 55–70.

¹⁴On the semiotic interpretation of culture as composed of sign, message, and code, see Robert Schreiter, *Constructing Local Theologies* (Maryknoll, N.Y.: Orbis Books, 1985), 49–73.

¹⁵On the three levels of culture, see Louis Luzbetak, *The Church and Cultures: New Perspectives in Missiological Anthropology* (Maryknoll, N.Y.: Orbis Books, 1988).

¹⁶For an account of how profoundly translation affects the work of inculturation, see Lamin Sanneh, *Translating the Message: The Missionary Impact on Culture* (Maryknoll, N.Y.: Orbis Books, 1989).

¹⁷For an excellent presentation of these issues, see Jacques Dupuis, *Toward a Christian Theology of Religious Pluralism* (Maryknoll, N.Y.: Orbis Books, 1997).

¹⁸See Anselm Kyongsuk Min, "From Autobiography to Fellowship of Others: Reflections on Doing Ethnic Theology Today," in *Journeys at the Margin,* 148–51.

¹⁹Ibid., 149.

[20]Ibid., 150.

[21]The need for racial reconciliation and solidarity is impressively developed by Andrew Sung Park, *Racial Conflict & Healing: An Asian-American Theological Perspective* (Maryknoll, N.Y.: Orbis Books, 1996).

[22]Min, "From Autobiography to Fellowship of Others," 151. In this context Min develops his concept of "solidarity *of* others": "The model I propose, solidarity of others, is an inherently dialectical model and must be grasped in all its dialectic. Opposed to all particularism and tribalism, it is not opposed to particularity as such. It advocates solidarity of others, not unity of the same. This is crucial, especially in view of the fact that global interdependence and universalization have historically been purchased by making victims of individuals, but most often of groups, based on gender, ethnicity, status, culture, and religion, by excluding and marginalizing them as others whose otherness must be either repressed or reduced to the same" (155–56).

[23]For a list of writings belonging to the Vietnamese *ju chia* ("School of the Literati") tradition (in Vietnamese, *nho*), see Vu Dinh Trac, *Viet Nam trong Quy Dao The Gioi* (Orange, Calif.: Lien Doan CGVN tai Hoa Ky, n.d.), 51–60. See also his two dissertations, *Triet Ly Chap Sinh Nguyen Cong Tru* (Orange, Calif.: Hoi Huu Publishers, 1988); and *Triet Ly Nhan Ban Nguyen Du* (Orange, Calif.: Hoi Huu Publishers, 1993).

[24]See the monumental, four-volume study (a total of 2,360 pages) by Nguyen Tan Long and Phan Canh, *Thi Ca Binh Dan Viet Nam* (Los Alamitos, Calif.: Xuan Thu, 1969–1970). Other useful works include: Nguyen Van Ngoc, *Tuc Ngu Phong Dao*, 2 vols. (Hanoi: Vinh Hung Long Thu Quan; reprinted by Xuan Thu, 1989); Vu Ngoc Phan, *Tuc Ngu Ca Dao Dan Ca Viet Nam*, 11th ed. (Hanoi: Nha Xuat Ban Khoa Hoc Xa Hoi, 1998); and Nguyen Nghia Dan, *Dao lam nguoi trong tuc ngu ca dao Viet Nam* (Hanoi: Nha Xuat Ban Thanh Nien, 2000). There is a slim volume of 95 pages by Huynh Dinh Te, *Selected Vietnamese Proverbs* (Oakland, Calif.: Center for International Communication and Development, 1990).

[25]Kim Dinh (1914–1997) has published more than thirty books on Vietnamese *ju chia* and Vietnamese philosophy. More than anyone else, Kim Dinh was responsible for retrieving the sources of the Vietnamese *ju chia* (which he terms "original *ju chia*") and constructing a Vietnamese philosophy. Another important contributor to the retrieval and elaboration of Vietnamese philosophy is Tran Van Doan, professor of philosophy at National Taiwan University. See his "Tu Viet triet toi Viet than," *Dinh Huong* 11 (1996): 16–22; "Tong hop ve Triet hoc va Viet Triet," *Dinh Huong* 12 (1997): 41–90; "Viet Triet di ve dau," *Dinh Huong* 13 (1997): 4–43; and "Viet Triet kha khu kha tung," in *Viet Nam: De Ngu Thien Ky,* ed. Vuong Ky Son (New Orleans: Trung Tam Van Hoa Viet Nam, USA, 1994), 69–116. For Tran Van Doan, Vietnamese philosophy is humanistic *(vi nhan)* but not anthropocentric *(duy nhan)* in so far as humans are conceived as the center or the Archimedian point of reality and as self-realizing (though not self-creative); it champions the "human way" *(dao nhan)*. In addition, Vietnamese philosophy advocates balance and harmony *(trung dung)* as well as self-transcendence *(sieu viet)*. In other words, the nature of Vietnamese philosophy is characterized by humanism *(nhan)*, balanced harmony *(trung)*, and self-transcendence *(viet)*. Finally, according to Tran Van Doan, Vietnamese mode of thinking is relational *(tuong quan)*, dialectical *(vien viet)*, dynamic *(dong tinh)*, wholistic *(toan the tinh)*, pragmatic *(thuc tien)*, and symbolic *(bieu tuong)*.

[26]Nguyen Du (1765–1820) is universally regarded as the greatest Vietnamese poet. For an English translation of this epic, see *The Tale of Kieu,* trans. Huynh Sanh Thong (New Haven, Conn.: Yale University Press, 1983).

[27]One of the most important studies on Vietnamese Zen is by Cuong Tu Nguyen, *Zen in Medieval Vietnam: A Study and Translation of the Thien Uyen Tap Anh* (Honolulu: University of Hawaii Press, 1997).

[28]For an elaboration of this *tam tai* philosophy, see in particular Vu Dinh Trac, *Triet Ly Chap Sinh Nguyen Cong Tru,* 203–213; and *Triet Ly Nhan Ban Nguyen Du,* 91–144.

[29]This philosophy is claimed to be represented on the upper surface of the bronze drum,

especially the one discovered at Ngoc Lu in 1901 and now preserved at the Center for Far-Eastern Antiquities *(Vien Dong Bac Co)* in Hanoi. This philosophy has been elaborated by Kim Dinh in his *Su Diep Trong Dong* (San Jose, Calif.: Thanh Nien Quoc Gia, 1984). See also Vu Dinh Trac, "Triet ly truyen thong Viet Nam don duong cho Than Hoc Viet Nam," *Dinh Huong* 11 (1966): 23–47. Vu Dinh Trac believes that traditional Vietnamese philosophy is constituted by *tam tai* philosophy, *yin yang* metaphysics, and agricultural philosophy. These three strands are illustrated by the various symbols on the upper surface of the Ngoc Lu bronze drum.

[30]For an attempt to construct a Trinitarian theology on the basis of *yin yang* metaphysics, see Jung Young Lee, *The Trinity in Asian Perspective* (Nashville: Abingdon Press, 1996).

[31]For an attempt at conceiving reality in Trinitarian terms, see Raimon Panikkar, *The Cosmotheandric Experience: Emerging Religious Consciousness* (Maryknoll, N.Y.: Orbis Books, 1993).

[32]For an elaboration of Jesus as the Immigrant par excellence, see Jung Young Lee, *Marginality*, and Peter C. Phan, "Jesus the Christ with an Asian Face," *Theological Studies* 57 (1996): 399–430.

[33]For an account of the so-called Rites Controversy, see George Minamiki, *The Chinese Rites Controversy: From Its Beginnings to Modern Times* (Chicago: Loyola University Press, 1985).

[34]For a christology of Jesus as the Elder Brother and the Ancestor, see Peter C. Phan, "Jesus as the Eldest Brother and Ancestor? A Vietnamese Portrait," *The Living Light* 33/1 (1996): 35–43; and Phan, "The Christ of Asia: An Essay on Jesus as the Eldest Son and Ancestor," *Studia Missionalia* 45 (1996): 25–55.

[35]See the documents of the Federation of Asian Bishops' Conferences and its various offices in *For All the Peoples of Asia: Federation of Asian Bishops' Conferences. Documents from 1970 to 1971,* ed. Gaudencio Rosales and C. G. Arévalo (Maryknoll, N.Y.: Orbis Books, 1992); and *For All the Peoples of Asia: Federation of Asian Bishops' Conferences. Documents from 1992 to 1996,* ed. Franz-Josef Eilers (Quezon City, Philippines: Claretian Publications, 1997).

[36]See Peter C. Phan, "Human Development and Evangelization: The First to the Sixth Plenary Assembly of the Federation of Asian Bishops' Conferences," *Studia Missionalia* 47 (1998): 205–227; and Phan, "Catechesis as an Instrument of Evangelization: Reflections from the Perspective of Asia," *Studia Missionalia* 48 (1999): 289–312.

[37]See Peter C. Phan, "Kingdom of God: A Theological Symbol for Asians?" *Gregorianum* 79/2 (1998): 295–322.

[38]See Peter C. Phan, "How Much Uniformity Can We Stand? How Much Unity Do We Want? Church and Worship in the Next Millennium," *Worship* 72/3 (1998): 194–210; and Phan, "The Liturgy of Life as 'Summit and Source' of the Eucharistic Liturgy: Church Worship as Symbolization of the Liturgy of Life?" in *Incongruities: Who We Are and How We Pray,* ed. Timothy Fitzgerald and David A. Lysik (Chicago: Liturgy Training Publications, 2000), 5–33.

11

Lessons for a New America

An Anglo American Reflection on Korean American Christian History

RANDI JONES WALKER

As an Anglo American Protestant Christian living in the culturally diverse and basically secularized social environment of the North American West Coast, specifically in the San Francisco Bay area (with its history as a cultural meeting place), I enter this conversation with my Asian American brothers and sisters with a sense of anticipation, but also a sense of trouble and anxiety.

My own ancestors, of course, were immigrants to North America. It is ironic that my people, who experienced both welcome and rejection as newcomers in this land, have learned so little about hospitality. I am also aware of the tensions in Anglo American Protestant churches about the influx of Protestant Christians from Asia (particularly from Korea, the Pacific Islands, and the Phillippines). Our vision of what it means to be an American Protestant is circumscribed by language, a traditional role in society, shared theological themes from the Reformation and the American Revolution (even if our people did not participate in it), as well as by our traditional animosities toward each other. While Asian American Protestants have been shaped by many of the same factors, Asian Christianity is quite different from what Anglo American Protestants expect.[1] Both vision and reality of what it means to be American become changed and contested in unpredictable ways as both Asian and Anglo American Protestants settle in with each other in what is relatively new terrain for both. For the purposes of this chapter, I propose to limit my reflections to Korean American and Anglo American Protestants because these are groups I know best. The situation is, of course, more complex.

180

As I reflect on what it means to be American in this setting, and as I develop a theological framework for understanding the meeting places of Anglo American and Asian American Christians, my own vision of America changes. Every culture sees itself as the center of the universe. Some over the course of history have imposed themselves on or have been adopted by a wider portion of humanity. At no time has a culture been as pervasive as that of the North Atlantic European American West. But that culture will, as all cultures do, break down over time. On the Pacific Coast of North America, Anglo American and Asian American Christians over the next few generations have the opportunity to help forge a new America born, not from the West, but "from Above," from the heart.

I enter this part of the chapter with uneasiness because it is one thing to recite and analyze the history of some Christians in a particular part of the world, and it is quite another to say what "we" ought to do in the future, especially when it is an open question whether I am a welcome part of the "we" my ancestors did not want to claim. I am also aware that as an Anglo Protestant woman scholar from a liberal mainline tradition, I have multiple communities of accountability, few of which contain large numbers of Asian Americans. My tradition (the United Church of Christ) has a complex history, and it contains discouraging elements. Its congregational polity allows individual churches to go their own way without consulting anyone else, though that is not theologically what congregationalism stands for. Its missionary history consists of efforts to justify cooperation with American foreign policies that proved harmful to the peoples of Asia. Its pronouncements against racism have not always been followed by effective action. However, it has also a history of radical efforts to put the gospel of Jesus Christ into effect in the world, from abolition of slavery to labor law reform to work for racial justice and world peace.[2]

My Christian commitment to the gospel compels me to take seriously the theological issue of hospitality primarily for those regarded as strangers in our land by virtue of race and culture. All concern for liberation is, for me, rooted in issues of hospitality, the foundational hospitality of God to us human beings on this earth. We did not, any of us, decide on our own to inhabit this earth. We were invited by Somebody. Though we have not always been received with hospitality by others, God's fundamental invitation to us to exist constitutes the ground for us to extend hospitality to others. All others are in reality strangers to us, even our own family. We cannot ever know them fully. But one essential sign of love is that we place their interests and needs alongside our own and live so that they may live. In a world where the movement of people is the rule, and in a history where my people both felt and inflicted the pain of inhospitality, for me the America of our hearts brings us back to the fundamental hospitality of God, and in the power of that divine grace, locates us in a crucible where a new humanity might be born. It is, however, an America that will change us all profoundly. In this chapter, as I trace the history of interaction and influence between Korean American and Anglo American Protestants on the West Coast, I want to learn both the possible shape and the inherent difficulties of such a new vision.

History, Hospitality, and the Migration of Peoples

Throughout the cities on the West Coast of North America, Korean-language church signs appear next to long-standing English-language signs. They denote shared space. They also denote a complex and difficult intercultural experience. Having been one of the pastors of such an English-speaking Protestant church in southern California and knowing many other such situations, I know that the English-speaking congregation is most often ambivalent about the arrangement. On the one hand, they do not hesitate to cite the biblical mandate of hospitality to the stranger, especially the Christian stranger, as the fundamental theological premise of their decision to share their building, their house, with another congregation. On the other hand, the English-speaking congregation is not sure what to do about language difference, theological or cultural, and finds it hard to curtail its own free use of the place in order to accommodate the guests. Also, while theologically they see themselves offering hospitality to guests, the English-speaking congregation would often prefer the more controlled economic relationship of landlord to tenant.

Layers of complexity haunt the efforts of the two congregations to live together in harmony. Host and guest, landlord and tenant, these terms have theological meaning within Christianity, and they have different cultural meanings both within Korean American cultures and Anglo American cultures and between Anglo and Korean Americans. The construction of the relationship as one between host and guest or as one between landlord and tenant puts a definitive shape to a corresponding relationship between needs and resources. The relationship exists in the realms of power and economy as well as culture and theology.

Equally complex is the problem, theological and practical, of whether the individuals in these congregations see themselves as sojourners or citizens, outsiders or insiders. With what self-understanding does each find herself or himself to be a Christian person in this particular location? How long does one need to be in a place to be at home? Or rather, how many and how deep do ones roots need to be before one can say one belongs to the place? What does it mean to be a Christian in America? Can a Christian ever really be a citizen of any but the realm of God? If that is the case, how can these host and guest, landlord and tenant, sojourner and citizen relationships give birth to a sense of *oikos*, where we are "no longer strangers and aliens, but..." (Eph. 2:19a)?

The history of Korean and Anglo American Protestant interaction is now over one hundred and fifty years old. I turn to four historical frames for understanding the cultural meeting places of Korean and Anglo American Protestants, particularly on the Pacific Coast. The mission frame lodges the story of Korean American Protestantism within the Anglo Protestant home and foreign missionary projects of the nineteenth and twentieth centuries. The theologies and strategies of the missionaries profoundly shaped Asian Christianity and, consequently, Korean American Christianity. A clear division among Korean American Protestants emerges in the divergence of mainline American Protestant understanding of missions. The evangelical Protestants continued the approach of emphasizing evangelization, whereas the liberal Protestants turned more toward an emphasis on social service and social justice, with evangelization as a secondary concern. Though both of the emphases can be found in the Reformation tradition and are rooted in biblical ideas, the theologies lying behind them are different, and the splits between evangelical and liberal Protestants are deep and lasting. For both Anglo groups, the purpose of evangelization and social justice work remained similar—that is, to guard the Anglo American Protestant way of life by converting the outsider to its ways. The Asian American Protestant community is divided along the same lines.

The second frame useful for understanding the history of Korean American Protestants is the immigrant frame. Religion plays an important role in forming American identity among immigrant people. Protestant churches serve two purposes in this frame: Either they may be the portal through which the immigrant enters mainstream American life, or they may be the source of strengthened identity in the culture left behind, preserving one's native language and customs. Often they serve both purposes.

The third frame for the history of Korean American and Anglo American Protestant interactions derives from the 1960s and the move by mainline Protestant denominations toward what one of them terms a multi-racial, multicultural church.[3] While this has sometimes played out as cultural sampling or a patchwork showcase of all the different kinds of people in the denomination, and while the integration it calls for has been questioned as simply another version of a melting pot, the model has the potential for real change. Within this frame it is possible to imagine a new culture where real change born of real relationship is possible. The question of how this real change might be possible shaped from different value systems, languages, and histories—and what it would look like—can only be explored briefly here. One mind cannot imagine it sufficiently. Finally, the frame of Anglo Protestants' own immigration history sets the stage for this interaction. After looking at the history noted here in these frames, I would like to venture some theological themes that can move us toward a new vision of America "born from above" or from within our hearts as sojourners in this place.

The Missionary Frame

Outside the scope of this chapter is the early presence of Christians in Korea from the Roman Catholic communion. The Protestant presence in Korea, for all practical purposes, dates from the nineteenth century. In most current historical discourse, these Protestant missions are connected with the imperial expansion of various North Atlantic nations and the rise of modernity. Within North America, the missionary movement of Protestant churches moved both outside national boundaries and within the nations themselves, particularly in the United States, the focus of this chapter. This twofold mission was well established before the arrival of Korean immigrants to the United States, to Hawaii, and later to California. Korean people as objects of the "foreign" missionary movement in Asia represented a puzzle to American Protestants within the borders of the United States. Should they continue to be treated as objects of foreign mission because of their language and culture differences, or should they be regarded as part of the "home" mission because of their location within the boundaries of the home nation? Most Protestant churches, assuming that the Korean immigrants did not intend to stay, put their work under the rubric of foreign missions at first. One example of such an assumption from the *Pacific Christian Advocate* concerns the hopes of the workers at the Methodist Japanese Home in San Francisco for a little girl in their care. "This little girl when asked at the public school what she expected to be, when grown, stood before the school and said, 'Missionary.' I pray that she may some day return to her native land and there lead many souls to Christ."[4]

As time wore on and Korean people made their homes in the United States and established churches, the home missionary societies found it difficult to place them under the rubrics of a mission strategy designed to support and encourage congregations duplicating the cultural ethos of East Coast Anglo Protestant churches because they did not fully share that culture's forms, language, or purpose. The question of what it means to be Christian in America became acute in the Korean American churches.

Debates were common among Anglo Protestant church people over whether new immigrants should be encouraged to integrate into already established churches or whether they should be encouraged to establish homogeneous churches of their own culture and language. As had been the case when European immigrants arrived in the United States, the first generation's ethnic language churches did not appeal to the second-generation children who grew up knowing mostly English, adopting American culture. The racism already operating in American Protestantism with regard to black church members and in the southwest with regard to Hispanic[5] members affected Koreans as well. A chief result of this racism was a missionary paternalism that required the objects of its care to manifest perpetual childlikeness and dependency. This dependency ensured a purpose for the missionary institution. Full equality for these churches would require a willingness, in full partnership, to shape a new kind of church. The missionary societies and their mission personnel were not able to imagine such a relationship for many years; some are still not able to imagine it. This is not to say that no American Protestants had the imagination to recognize the problems of racism and try to remedy them. The same missionary publication that encouraged the Korean little girl to think about going back to Korea as a missionary, twenty years later reported discouragement that this is precisely the only option the girl would have:

> A girl of Korean parentage, born in Honolulu, educated as a doctor in the United States, finds all doors of opportunity closed against her; a student at one of our great universities with two generations of American living behind her is learning Chinese and says she will have to go to China for a job because her grandparents came from that country and there's no chance for her here.[6]

By the middle of the twentieth century, the missionary theology and strategy of several mainline Anglo American churches had changed. Several factors influenced this change. The liberal optimism of the Progressive era turned focus from the individual to society in solving social problems. The progressive churches reshaped their missionary enterprise into social service rather than individual conversion. Those missionaries who had lived a long time among the people with whom they worked brought a more sophisticated understanding of other cultures to bear on missionary policies, making them less likely to favor the kind of assimilation that aimed to turn everyone into English-speaking, if not white, middle-class church members.[7] In addition, among the liberal churches from the old nineteenth-century evangelical heritage, engagement with modern historical criticism of the Bible, the compelling worldview of science, and encounters with other world religions as equal partners in conversation led to a reassessment of the need to convert the world to Christianity. Among those evangelical churches who rejected, or were critical of, both of these intellectual movements, individual salvation and the goal of converting the world to Christianity remained strong.

From these cultural and theological divisions the missions also became further divided until the Korean immigrant, whether Christian or not, faces an array of missionary pressures upon arriving in the United States. David Yoo, in his introduction to *New Spiritual Homes: Religion and Asian Americans,* points out the contested nature of the religious scene facing new immigrants. Should they remain in their own religious tradition or convert to a new Americanized one? If they already are Christian, should they join a congregation that speaks the language of home or assimilate more quickly by joining an English-speaking congregation? The fact that these multiple options exist suggests the deep tensions within American Christianity.[8]

Other divisions complicate the religious choices of Korean American immigrants. The interests of university-educated professionals differ from those of the Korean war brides without higher education but with bicultural children to raise.[9] Though both are Christian, they need and want very different things from the churches. Earlier Korean immigrants faced the political problem of nationalism as well, with the churches divided on the questions of means for the independence struggle.

The Korean experience of Christian missionary activity was not a unified one. Western Christian missionaries from different churches, particularly the Presbyterians and Methodists, vied with one another and with missionaries sent from nondenominational missionary societies. Each presented their version of Christianity as the true one in contrast to the others. However, from a non-Christian point of view the differences seemed minor. Similarly, the American Christian missionaries tended to miss distinctions among Asian peoples, thus collapsing the Japanese and Koreans into a single group because they were under one national umbrella (the Japanese). Such divisions within Western Christian missions fit themselves into already existing divisions within the communities hosting the missionaries, thus strengthening those differences among the new Korean converts. Christianity developed differently in different parts of Asia as well. In some cases missionary Christianity from the West had the upper hand; in other places native developments of Christianity took the initiative and became more pervasive than those forms started by missionaries. In Korea, Christianity had initially been introduced by Korean Catholics in the eighteenth century. Though Protestantism was introduced from outside Korea, Koreans quickly made the religion their own and started their own fast-growing churches.

Protestantism entered Korea in the late nineteenth century at a moment of political turmoil. Faced with pressures from China, Japan, and the United States, Koreans struggled for a sense of national self. For many reasons, some Koreans saw Protestantism as a vehicle for the cultural transformation necessary for them to survive as a people under the pressures they faced. Protestantism continued through the Japanese occupation of Korea to provide one means of countering the efforts of Japanese hegemony. However, Protestants in Korea differed deeply about the means of maintaining national identity and resisting the Japanese.[10] They continue to differ deeply about the question of national reunification since World War II. These divisions of Korean Protestantism superimposed on American Protestantism's many divisions have created a complex tapestry of Korean American churches.

Historians and other scholars of Christianity have widely assumed that the missionary impulse is implicit in Christianity, but recent work on the connections between Western Christian missions and the rise of modernity have challenged that idea. Dutch historian Peter van Rooden suggests that, at least among Protestants, the missionary movements developed, not because they are intrinsically Christian, but because they served a symbolic function for these churches as they navigated the transition from the medieval to the modern world. The vision of the global spread of Christianity became a way for them to imagine the position of Christianity in their own societies. Thus, the ambiguous connection between Protestant missions and Western national cultures becomes more clear.[11] Certainly, American Protestant missionaries considered themselves to be ambassadors of both their religion and their culture. They thought of American culture as the inevitable result of the application of Protestant principles to society and considered it to be the highest development of human culture. It did not occur to them that any people, once enlightened about its qualities, would disagree.

The cultural aspect of the missionary project in the United States is even more apparent in the Protestant Home Missionary movement of the nineteenth century.[12] Fueled by the nativist response to an influx of European Roman Catholic immigrants and the growing movement of American Protestants west, the home missionaries worked to establish as many Protestant churches as they could to stem the tide of "Romanism" and secularism. Considering a virtuous, pious citizenry as the basis of the republic, and seeing both Roman Catholicism and secularism as dangerous idolatries, they connected the future of the nation with the expansion of the Protestant churches.[13] In spite of their efforts, the American West became steadily less "churched" as one moved away from the East Coast. Coupled with their anxiety about the disinterest of the gold rush population in California in Protestant institutional religion, fear about the influence of "Oriental" immigrants, whose religions were largely unfamiliar but increasingly interesting to Americans, fueled the desire to convert them as quickly as possible both to Christianity and to the white, middle-class American way of life. Protestant home missionaries tended to view culture and religion as so closely bound that they could not separate conversion to Christianity from conversion to their own way of life.

Therefore, it particularly puzzled them to find a few Korean immigrants who came to the United States with indigenous forms of Protestant Christian practice rooted in a different cultural mode. Familiar missionary Christianity was wedded to Confucian philosophical and cultural forms. When the people coming were already converted to evangelical Christianity in Korea, they often then began to convert people in the United States and form churches of their own. Many of these were recognizably Protestant, such as the Presbyterian Church of Korea. Others, however, such as the Reverend Moon's Unification Church, were less recognizable. The home missionary approach to both was to attempt to incorporate them into the American denominational structures, not realizing fully the importance to both Americans and new immigrants that Christianity come in their own comfortable cultural forms. The connection of Christianity with specifically Korean political agendas startled Anglo Protestants who assumed often that new immigrants would simply adopt the Protestant style of American civil religion. That the Korean Americans would have an equally compelling agenda from another culture was hard for the home missionaries to accept. The Korean political agendas associated with Korean American churches also created problems between the first and second generations within the Korean American community itself.[14]

While the missionary picture of America included the Korean immigrant, it was a fully Americanized Korean immigrant. The missionaries too often presented their dream of America rather than its reality. Disconnections between American missionary motives and ambiguities about whether cultural conversion was as important as religious conversion affected the appeal the American Protestants made to the new immigrants. R. Laurence Moore, in his work on religious outsiders in American religion, suggests that the cultural form of religion is important for helping people to understand themselves as American. Indeed, Moore suggests that outsiderhood is characteristic of Americanness.

Despite what Frederick Jackson Turner wrote, most people who lived in this country did not gain a sense of what it meant to be an American by going to the frontier.[15] Far more of them gained that sense by turning aspects of a carefully nurtured sense of separate identity against a vaguely defined concept of mainstream or dominant culture.[16]

With this understanding, let us turn to view the history of Asian and Anglo Protestant interaction from the immigrant's point of view.

The Immigrant Frame

Another way to frame the history of Korean American and Anglo American Protestant interaction is almost like viewing the picture from the other side of the mirror.[17] Like Alice in Wonderland, the world on the other side of the mirror is the same, yet disturbingly different. Koreans who came to the United States already converted to Protestantism reported their surprise that people in the United States, a land they had been taught was Christian, did not behave toward strangers as Christians should. Even if they were not Christian and did not have expectations of their reception here, America's loud claim to be a Christian nation rang hollow under the harassment Asian people received.

The immigrants came expecting hospitality in a Christian country after being (often persecuted) minorities in their own countries. They were shocked at being treated as second-class citizens when the American missionaries had encouraged them to come to America because it was a Christian country. The missionaries painted a picture of America and its churches as a place of equality, democracy, and being classless and racially integrated. The immigrants discovered instead the moral ambiguities of

American life, the "mechanization of human work, the importance of money, specialization of reality which makes wholeness of life impossible."[18] Sang Hyun Lee, a Korean American theologian, paints a clear picture of the theological situation of the immigrant:

> Like Abraham, we have been called by God to leave our homeland with dreams for "the land of promise." Like Abraham, we live in a wilderness "as in a foreign land," as "strangers and exiles," not feeling wholly at home where we are, nor being comfortable any more about returning to where we came from. We are not wandering, aimless nomads, however. We are a pilgrim people who are on a sacred journey. We have been freed from the hold of one culture or one society; we have been called "to go out" with visions for "a better country" that would be a true homeland not only for ourselves but for all.[19]

While immigrants of all kinds came to the United States to benefit from the economy and free society, the Christian claim that American wealth was a reward for the nation's adherence to Christian principles and that the free society was derived from biblical mandates was hard to reconcile with the exploitation of workers and the racism that prevented everyone from having access to political rights. American Christians seldom seemed to acknowledge that American wealth was often extracted from the land and the people simply by using increasingly sophisticated technology, which might be considered a reward for human cleverness, but not for superior morality.

Korean immigrants found the churches provided critical services, especially English classes, but the missionary project to make them into American Christians was not shared by the majority of those who learned English in these settings. However, the Korean clients of these church programs were not as welcome as members of the white churches. More helpful were the various Korean American churches already established, some under the auspices of white churches but others independent. Here immigrants, as Moore shows, found a place to forge an identity within the American context that included their previous language, political agendas, and culture, as well as the adoption of the English language and American ways.

The immigrant experience of exclusion along with racism complicated the Korean American experience of success in many economic endeavors in the United States.[20] Like most immigrants, the process of coming to a new home was an ambivalent one. Whether fleeing as a refugee from danger, searching for better economic opportunity, or attracted by America as an ideal, Korean American immigrants had many reasons for staying, and slowly began to participate in the creation of institutions and social forms that allowed them a safe place in a strange land.

Though the majority of Korean Americans were Christian, by the end of the twentieth century, many Christian immigrants from Korea viewed the United States as a mission field, a secular culture in need of the gospel. With this missionary spirit churches such as the Presbyterian Church of Korea have shown enormous growth in the United States. They first recognized Korean immigrants as objects of mission, but soon also attracted non-Koreans. Their missionary strategies have attracted the attention of those concerned about Protestant church growth in America. In addition, Korean immigrant Christians challenge mainline American Protestantism's liberal theological positions. Here, the encounter of the theology taught by nineteenth-century mainline evangelical missionaries confronts the changed theology of those same churches in its adoption of modern approaches to the scriptures and issues of social and personal morality.

The interaction of theological and generational issues in the Korean American churches is a perennial issue. Particularly after the change in immigration laws in the 1960s, the strong contrasts between the first and second generations introduce language and culture questions into the churches. While some in the second generation leave the church, influenced by the surrounding secularism of American society, others are attracted to new forms of church life, a few to English speaking mainline churches, but far more to the thriving evangelical youth movements such as the InterVarsity Fellowship.[21] The conflict between the Korean American churches' desire to promote Korean culture and continue to support various political interests among Korean immigrants and the need of the second generation for a church supportive of their new Korean American identity creates challenges to Korean American Christian unity. In many ways the Korean immigrant experience parallels that of the European immigrants. The danger of cultural loss is significantly the same.

The frame of European Protestants' own immigration history completes the setting for the interaction of Anglo and Korean American Protestants. Those European Protestants who immigrated to the United States and other parts of North America generally experienced hostility from English-speaking American Protestants. The pressures to preserve their language and culture within their churches fostered the development of ethnic Protestant churches either within or outside of the already existing American denominations.[22] Similar generational problems arose in the European immigrant churches as in the Korean immigrant churches. The second generation, more Americanized and tending to speak only English, became alienated from their parents and from the churches that fostered the preservation of their specific language and culture. The generations also differed in their sense of themselves as Americans. Given the Anglo-American emphasis on race, European immigrants fared much better than their Asian counterparts because they were considered to be white–or

Anglo—even if their original language was not English. If they were Protestant, the transition to American citizenship was substantially easier than if they were Catholic. A new vision of America, born from the heart, requires Anglo Protestants to revisit and acknowledge our own immigrant history, its tragedies and its privilege. Sooner or later we must decide what we are going to do about ourselves.

Returning to my own family history, some were among the colonial immigrants to North America from Great Britain. They were initially received with hospitality by the native people of the Atlantic Coast. Using theological ideas derived from the scriptures, they chose the theological stream that views the native people as Canaanites, whom God's people seek to supplant, and against whom God's people define their identity. They ignored the theological stream that measures the faithfulness of God's people by the quality of their care for the stranger, the alien, because they were once strangers in Egypt. Viewing the native people as Canaanites, the United States conceived its Manifest Destiny[23] and justified to itself the theft of their land.

For Christian Americans tracing our ancestry to Europe, this history involves us at every turn in the consequences. One of them, though by no means the greatest, is that after the first generation, our people were met with hostility rather than hospitality on these shores and in the heart of the continent as well. As a historian, I will not claim a direct relationship between this hostile reception and the hostility toward newcomers so often shown by European Americans. Too many factors, economic and social, lie behind xenophobia in any culture. However, as a theologian, I cannot help but wonder if American Christianity's participation in this history and consequent sharing in the experience of hostility served to strengthen certain theological ideas about who God favored and what God intended. As sin seems to visit itself on the next generations, themselves innocent of the original transgression, so this imperial theology serves to undergird the next generation's natural ambivalence toward the stranger and turns us away from the prophet's call to hospitality. Lest Anglo Americans think this propensity is superficial and easily overcome, I think it is important to note the strength of its hold on the American psyche. Carl Jung, the Swiss psychologist, reported this conversation with a Taos Indian leader in New Mexico.

> "See," Ochwiay Biano said, "how cruel the whites look. Their lips are thin, their noses sharp, their faces furrowed and distorted by folds. Their eyes have a staring expression; they are always seeking something. What are they seeking? The whites always want something; they are always uneasy and restless. We do not know what they want. We do not understand them. We think they are mad."

I asked him why he thought the whites were all mad.

"They say they think with their heads," he replied.

"Why of course. What do you think with?" I asked him in surprise.

"We think here," he said, indicating his heart.

I fell into a long meditation. For the first time in my life, so it seemed to me, someone had drawn for me a picture of the real white man. It was as though until now I had seen nothing but sentimental, prettified color prints. This Indian had struck our vulnerable spot, unveiled a truth to which we are blind.[24]

Jung went on to recite the history of imperial expansion in European traditions from the Roman legions to the Crusades to the conquest of Mexico by Cortes.

It was enough. What we from our point of view call colonization, missions to the heathen, spread of civilization, etc., has another face—the face of a bird of prey seeking with cruel intentness for distant quarry—a face worthy of a race of pirates and highwaymen. All eagles and other predatory creatures that adorn our coats of arms seem to me apt psychological representatives of our true nature.[25]

It is a well-known psychological phenomenon that we human beings tend to see in the other the most disturbing aspects of our own behavior. Perhaps that is why Anglo Americans so often assume that immigrants want our jobs, our land, or to impose their way of life on us.

As Jung suggests, the traditions of inhospitality to the stranger, especially the stranger of a different religious tradition, go back further than the European movement to the Americas. But so also do the European experiences of hostile reception. Most Europeans are descended from the Germanic and Slavic nomadic peoples who moved into Europe during the last centuries of the Roman Empire. There they met inhospitality and sometimes forced conversions to Christianity. Such legacies of both conqueror and conquered came with the European to North America where they played themselves out, justified by elaborate theologies derived from another culture whose experience was remarkably similar. After hundreds of years, a cultural pattern of inhospitality developed and prevails to this day.

The majority of expressions of immigrant experience in America, however, is not filled with either the desire of conquest or hostility toward those who already live here. It is filled instead with a dream of a better life, a new beginning. Freedom—religious freedom, economic freedom, political freedom—is a main theme, as is the desire to join in a great human project of creating a free society where every individual can prosper and contribute. This is understandably a vague dream; it rarely contains a specific project, nor does it express the reality of American life. It is also a dream marred by the hypocrisy of conquest and enslavement of others. But it is the vision, the American of our hearts. Given the vast problems facing humanity–poverty and exploitation, intolerance and hatred, greed and violence toward the earth and its people, a crisis of meaning in a technologically sophisticated society, and the disillusionment of the very people who hold the dream in their hearts–it is perhaps a waste of time to try to recreate the dream. However, I believe one solution to a crisis of meaning and loss of dreaming power is to deliberately recreate a meaningful life and to spend time deliberately sleeping so as to be able to dream again.

The Multiracial, Multicultural Church Frame

With this frame we move into the contested territory of the American Dream–or dreams. Could it be that to bring about a truly multiracial, multicultural church, those used to being in control must deliberately sleep so that everyone may dream, not of a melting pot or a salad, but of something as yet unimaginably different? If the American Dream is truly to be a dream shared by all, each individual dreamer must be willing for his or her own dream to die or to live so that it may contribute fully to the new dream of an America born from the heart, as a phoenix rises from the ashes of the fire that consumes it.

The grand vision of America as the "phoenix grave" of denominational or sectarian differences envisioned by the Swiss immigrant Philip Schaff is the classic expression of America as melting pot.[26] Schaff wrote:

> America seems destined to be the Phoenix grave not only of all European nationalities…but also of all European churches and sects, of Protestantism and Romanism. I cannot think that any one of the present confessions and sects…will ever become exclusively dominant there; but rather, that out of the mutual conflict of all something wholly new will gradually arise.[27]

Under this rubric, something new and American will arise as all Christian groups meet and mix in North America, especially in the United States: They will lose the distinctions that Schaff regarded as vestiges of the many national and class divisions of Europe and return to a more pure Christian form. Schaff meant the denominational distinctions in Christianity, but he could as easily have been discussing cultural differences, that Christians from all cultures would lose their cultural distinctions in an American Christianity. The trouble was that as time went on, this American Christianity bore a distinctively Anglo stamp. It was not really devoid of cultural attachments at all.

Robert Handy, in his history of the failure of Protestants to achieve their nineteenth-century dream of a Christian America,[28] delineated the Anglo Protestant view of what it meant to be Christian in America. They placed American Protestants squarely within the national political and economic interests. They also involved themselves in conflict when national policies were opposed to Christian teaching. Anglo Protestants generally assumed that the God the United States claimed to stand under in "One nation, under God" was their Protestant God. They took it for granted that the Providence of God had placed them in this land and inspired a constitution that protected them from encroachments by the government. This was how Protestants were meant to live. That they failed is not generally acknowledged by those of us who are their heirs. For the Anglo Protestant, though, being Christian in America is not as simple as it used to seem to be. With the rise of industrial and technological economies, the religious ideas we like to think undergird the creation of this nation no longer influence culture outside our churches. In the twentieth century, Protestants have been divided among ourselves about the degree to which we can continue to regard our nation as Christian. Even when we agree that it is not, we disagree profoundly about why and about what we should do. To be Christian in America, from an Anglo Protestant point of view, is to experience Christian life in a larger culture that has a Christian form, but no Christian substance. We feel at home and yet alien. America has not proved to be the location of Christ's second coming, but it has turned out to be as corrupted by worldly concerns as Europe was.

For the Korean American, being Christian in America is also complex. Just as Anglo American Protestants often combine their religious and political interests, so too do Korean American Protestants. For Korean Americans, however, there are extra layers of complexity. For one thing, the issue of what it means to be Christian in Korea is contested. Christianity has played several roles in Korean history. The earliest Catholics in Korea forged a Confucian Christianity that served to open up a conservative and moribund system as well as to introduce Western ideas into Korean thought. The earliest Protestants were welcomed because they seemed to offer a way to understand Korea's experiences of the modern world and the rapid Westernization of the Pacific Rim. In addition, though many American Protestant missionaries and their Korean congregations welcomed Japan's takeover of Korea because it seemed the most likely way to achieve stability for the growth of Christianity, others saw Protestantism as a vehicle for anti-Japanese independence movements. Protestantism entered Korea in a time of stress and provided a variety of new forms of identity for a people experiencing rapid change. Korean Protestants then came to the United States expecting to enjoy participation in a Christian society, but were profoundly divided among themselves about the proper role of Christianity in their own culture.

Given the encouragement they had received from American missionaries, the inhospitality they faced from American Christians was a stunning disappointment. The question of what it meant to be Christian in America was complicated not only by what it meant to be Christian in Korea but by what it meant to be Korean in America. Was there any sense to be made of these dilemmas of identity? For some, the answer was to remain Korean, though living in America. The Protestant church provided a social center for maintaining Korean life, and the Korean Protestant churches served as a comfort for the stranger as well as a critique of that larger society's hypocrisy. For others, the answer was to try to assimilate. For them, the Protestant church was a bridge into Anglo American society. Korean American congregations in Anglo Protestant denominations sometimes served this purpose. But rarely did the immigrant pilgrim find real welcome and hospitality among Anglo Christians. The America of my heart requires an active hospitality. It is the customary kind of welcome that says to the immigrant, although you are welcome to become like us, it is not enough. That limited welcome requires the conversion of the other and allows continued pride of place and privilege on the part of the host. It sustains the maternalism and paternalism of the missionary movement requiring the other to be a perpetual guest and never a fellow citizen.

By the twentieth century, after the First Amendment to the Constitution had been firmly tested and the World Parliament of Religions had established a place for non-Christian faiths in American consciousness, another version of the American Dream began to develop. Though it made Christians nervous, by the end of the twentieth century, one heard of American religion being described as a salad bowl. All kinds of religions tossed together yet each retaining its distinctiveness, the image formed a more accurate picture of what actually happened and perhaps a better ideal of American religious life than the phoenix grave of difference reborn into uniformity. However, this vision has serious flaws for those who see religion as a unitive force in human society or those for whom there is only one true religion.

Lately a third vision has arisen to shape the lives of some mainline Protestant denominations. That is the vision of a multiracial, multicultural church. Within this vision, the phoenix grave is not for difference, but for claims of exclusive privilege, priority, and self-sufficiency. While differences are valued and celebrated, and theoretically each group is welcomed and encouraged to continue its own traditions and practices, the vision also contains the dream that all groups will, in living together, learn from one another, and so all will be changed. So the phoenix grave will operate as well, but more slowly and without so much sense of inevitability. Understanding that this vision, too, has its flaws, it can serve as a jumping off point for some theological reflections on what it might mean to be Christian in America.

Toward an American Protestant Christian Theology of Hospitality

Developing a theology of hospitality requires not only a renewed look at the Bible, it also requires practice. It is not enough to say welcome. The disciplines of hospitality require listening, using new languages, and having an open spirit. They demand flexibility in stiff people. Making others feel at home does not mean changing them to fit our ways, but changing ourselves to fit their ways. Most of all, hospitality requires a Christ-like spirit. Hospitality always carries the risk that one will have to go without in order to provide for one's guest. It may also entail the risk of reaction from one's surrounding community. Jesus ate with all kinds of people rejected by the community around them. He ate with tax collectors, prostitutes, and other questionable associates. He offered hospitality to his disciples regardless of their potential for loyalty or service to him. For this and other transgressions based in his understanding of God and divine love he received the hostility of the community and eventually lost his life. This would be discouraging to us except that the gospels all end with a resurrection—an affirmation that the very thing that seems to lead to death in fact is filled with life, a life beyond death that takes death into itself and transforms it into something newly alive, a phoenix grave.

Jesus thought with his heart. In our hospitality to the other—the stranger particularly, the least one—we move our vision from our brain to our heart. Not that we cease to think clearly about how things are or how they need to be, but that our thought serves our heart. Jesus was himself not free from human propensity to discount the stranger. His initial rejection of the Canaanite woman placed him clearly in the mainstream Jewish response to their neighbors, those from whom they had wrested the land. But he caught himself and in the end offered her the same generosity he offered his own people. His identification of the good neighbor with the Samaritan, another outsider, places Jesus more clearly in the tradition of the prophets who advocated hospitality to the alien and stranger, because "we were slaves in Egypt." The tradition that placed this hospitality at the heart of the life of faith also pointed to a future of the people beyond the limited boundaries of its own clans and race, to the whole of humanity.

A vision of the America of our hearts, from my perspective, takes shape only when there is a multitude of voices and each one is given time to speak. It is molded from the vast pool of dreams yet unrealized from, among others, people who bring their Asian worldviews and values into play. The vision is not an easy one. I cannot see beyond the initial conflicts and painful recognitions. I cannot see beyond the complex changes that are required of everyone. This sense that everything will be reshaped and that no one can see how dominates my vision and sometimes makes me afraid to try to see further. I know that the new vision is connected to the age-old idea that these American lands are a country where God's future is located. The golden mountain, the beautiful land, the new Jerusalem—these eschatological images fill the thought of Americans of many cultures. I took these in unconsciously as a child and cannot help expecting to see this vision come into being. Only as I come to understand how strongly we resist truly loving our neighbors do I understand that only God can bring it into being. This vision of an America where everyone is at home also fails to account for the just restitution due the native people because we live on land taken by somebody without permission. We cannot just declare ourselves to be at home and welcome others into it when we are not ourselves welcome.

The relationship between Korean American churches and Anglo American churches with which I started this chapter is complicated by all these historical factors. Strangers and sojourners, citizens, householders, landlords, and tenants: The images that will serve us best in building the American of our hearts are those that recognize God as the landlord, the householder, and we, all of us, the strangers and sojourners, tenants. However, as Christians we understand ourselves to be invited by God's profound hospitality to be citizens of the realm of God. We cannot speak for those of other faiths, but our faith calls us to hospitality. Though we read in our scriptures about the rejection of the alien, the destruction of those whose land we believe God has given to us, we know from our knowledge of the prophets and of Jesus that the God revealed in their words is not that kind of God—that those directives have to be mistaken impressions of God, that God requires us to care for the stranger and sojourner in our midst because God has cared for us as strangers and sojourners. We share this faith across many cultural lines as Christians. God's intention is that we all be one in Christ—not all the same, but all one in our love. From this stance, America could become the crucible for God's hospitality to work the transformation of the phoenix grave until we all find ourselves at the resurrection feast with Christ.

Notes

[1]Robert Handy, *A Christian America: Protestant Hopes and Historical Realities* (New York: Oxford University Press, 1971).

[2]Our tradition of concern for justice and liberation in the United Church of Christ has led into more controversial directions in the ordination and full equality of women in the church and the reception of lesbian and gay church members into full participation in the ministry of the church, including ordination. Clearly, the issue of a multiracial and multicultural church cuts across some of these other agendas. Just as not all Anglos in the United Church of Christ agree on these issues, not all Asian American UCC members do either. Not only in my denomination but also in others, such as the Presbyterian or United Methodist churches, similar issues arise. Within the more conservative evangelical Protestant churches, many of my theological commitments to openness and liberation are held to be antithetical to the gospel.

[3]The United Church of Christ adopted this as a core value and mark of identity in 1993. Its document "Toward Becoming a Multi-Racial, Multi-Cultural Church," adopted by the

Nineteenth General Synod in St. Louis in 1993, reads in part, "The Nineteenth General Synod calls upon the United Church of Christ in all its settings to be a true multiracial and multicultural church. A multiracial and multicultural church confesses and acts out its faith in the one sovereign God who through Jesus Christ binds in covenant faithful people of all races, ethnicities and cultures. A multiracial and multicultural church embodies these diversities as gifts to the human family and rejoices in the variety of God's grace."

⁴Margarita Lake, "News From the Japanese Home," *Women's Home Missions* (April 1908): 68. There is little evidence that the workers at the Japanese Home noticed the tensions between Japanese and Korean clients in the home. The Methodist Episcopal Church supported the Japanese de facto colonization of Korea.

⁵*Hispanic* is another word that needs definition. In work on Spanish-speaking peoples in the United States, a variety of terms are employed, each favored by particular groups and criticized by other groups. Within the Hispanic Protestant communities in the Southwest in the late nineteenth century, *Hispanic* is more likely to be the word recognized by both the people referred to and the scholars. *Latino/Latina* tends to de-emphasize the Spanish colonial associations of *Hispanic; Mexican American* is too specific; and *Chicano/Chicana* has political overtones from the 1960s. *Hispanic* is still the more common word among mainline American Protestants (The United Church of Christ has the Council for Hispanic Ministries, for instance).

⁶Katherine Gardner, "Church Women's Work in Race Relations," *Women's Home Missions* (February 1935): 5.

⁷Recent works that discuss this change, particularly among women missionaries, are Susan Yohn, *A Contest of Faiths: Missionary Women and Pluralism in the American Southwest* (Ithaca, N.Y.: Cornell University Press, 1995); Sarah Deutsch, *No Separate Refuge: Culture, Class and Gender on the Anglo-Hispanic Frontier in the American Southwest, 1880–1940* (New York: Oxford University Press, 1987); and Peggy Pascoe, *Relations of Rescue: The Search for Female Moral Authority in the American West, 1874–1939* (New York: Oxford University Press, 1990).

⁸David Yoo, "Reframing the U.S. Religious Landscape," in *New Spiritual Homes: Religion and Asian Americans,* ed. David Yoo (Honolulu: University of Hawaii Press, 1999), 6–7.

⁹Jung Young Lee, *Korean Preaching: An Interpretation* (Nashville: Abingdon Press, 1997), 23.

¹⁰Kenneth M. Wells, *New God, New Nation: Protestants and Self-Reconstruction Nationalism in Korea 1896–1937* (Honolulu: University of Hawaii Press, 1990), is an excellent work on this complicated development. In addition, see Yu Tong-sik, *Hawai'i Hanin kwa kyohwe: k'lis'toyenhapkamlikyohwe 85nyonsa* [Hawaiian Koreans and the Church: Christ United Methodist Church 85ᵗʰ Anniversary] (Honolulu: K'lis'toyenhapkamlikyohwe, n.d.); chapter 3 discusses at length the relationships between these divisions within the churches in Korea and the ways they manifested themselves as divisions in the American Korean congregations.

¹¹Peter van Rooden, "Nineteenth-century Representations of Missionary Conversion and the Emergence of Missions in Modern Western Christianity," in *Conversion to Modernities: The Globalization of Christianity,* ed. Peter van der Veer (New York: Routledge, 1996), 65–87.

¹²Still the best general history of this movement is Colin B. Goodykoontz, *Home Missions on the American Frontier* (Caldwell, Idaho: Caxton Printers, 1939).

¹³Van Rooden, "Nineteenth-century Representations," 80.

¹⁴Sucheng Chan, *Asian Americans: An Interpretive History* (Boston: Twayne Publishers, 1991), 116.

¹⁵Frederick Jackson Turner, "The Significance of the Frontier in American History," in American Historical Association, *Annual Report for 1893* (Washington, D.C.: American Historical Association, 1893), 199–227. In this essay, Turner gave the frontier experience defining significance for American culture and social structures. His essay continues to be a force in the study of American history. For recent engagements with Turner, both arguments against and arguments in favor of his continued relevance, see John Mack Faragher, "The Frontier Trail: Rethinking Turner and Reimagining the American West," *American Historical Review* (February 1993): 106–17.

[16]R. Laurence Moore, *Religious Outsiders and the Making of Americans* (New York: Oxford University Press, 1986), xi.

[17]I am borrowing a somewhat modified metaphor from Ronald Takakai, *In a Different Mirror* (Boston: Little, Brown, 1993).

[18]Chansoo Lee, "A Study on Historical Experience of Koreans in America: Perceptions of America and Self-Definition" (master's thesis, Pacific School of Religion, 1997).

[19]Sang Hyun Lee, "Called to Be Pilgrims: Toward a Theology within the Korean Immigrant Context," in *The Korean Immigrant in America,* ed. Byong-suh Kim and Sang Hyun Lee (Montclair, N. J.: Association of Korean Christian Scholars in North America, 1980), 37.

[20]The complicated question of the relationship of political and economic marginality and racism is an important one; however, there is not room in this chapter to engage it fully. A good introduction to the debate can be found in Anselm Kyongsuk Min's review of Jung Young Lee, *Marginality: The Key to Multicultural Theology* (Minneapolis: Augsburg Fortress Press, 1995), with the author's response in *Journal of Asian and Asian American Theology* (Summer 1996): 82–96.

[21]A particularly interesting account of this latter movement is Rudy Busto, "The Gospel According to the Moral Majority?: Hazarding an Interpretation of Asian American Evangelical College Students," in David Yoo, *New Spiritual Homes,* 169–87.

[22]See H. Richard Niebuhr's *Social Sources of Denominationalism* (New York: Meridian Press, 1957) for theological as well as sociological reflections on this situation.

[23]This phrase was first used by John O'Sullivan in an article in the *Democratic Review,* July 1845. "[Foreign interference with U.S. efforts to annex Texas] exists for the avowed object of...checking the fulfillment of our manifest destiny to overspread the continent allotted by Providence for the free development of our yearly multiplying millions." The phrase became famous almost overnight. The idea, however, has roots in more general imperial theories, held by most great empires, that the deities ordained the spread of their power.

[24]C. G. Jung, "America: The Pueblo Indians" (extract from an unpublished manuscript), in *Memories, Dreams, Reflections,* recorded and ed. Aniela Jaffé, trans. Richard and Clara Winston (New York: Vintage Books, 1965), 247–48.

[25]Ibid., 248–49.

[26]I am indebted to Catherine Albanese for pointing out this image in the writings of Philip Schaff in her essay, "Religion and the American Experience–A Century After," *Church History* (September 1988): 337–51.

[27]Philip Schaff, *America: A Sketch of the Political, Social and Religious Character of the United States of America* (New York: Scribner, 1855), 97. Quoted in George Schriver, *Philip Schaff, Christian Scholar and Ecumenical Prophet* (Macon, Ga.: Mercer University Press, 1987), 41.

[28]Robert Handy, *A Christian America: Protestant Hopes and Historical Realities* (New York: Oxford University Press, 1971).

12

America of the Broken Heart

SHARON G. THORNTON

The Adoption

Not flesh of my flesh
Nor bone of my bone
But somehow miraculously
My own
Don't ever forget
For a single moment
You didn't grow under my heart
But in to it.

–Author Unknown

I approach this reflection from the perspective of being the daughter of an immigrant. This point of view is enhanced by my experience of serving as the pastor of a Japanese American church. It is further enriched by my commitments within an intercultural and interracial marriage. This is to acknowledge that my thoughts and words here are confessional in nature, therefore limited in scope, but imbued with a deep sense of gratitude. Themes of adoption, loyalty, trust and the betrayal of trust, forgiveness, and the giving of new identities permeate the way that has led me to this writing. A theology of the broken heart emerges as a critical faith posture.

America of My Mother's Heart: "My Country, 'Tis of Thee"

I was born the daughter of immigrant parents. Weren't we all? Except for native peoples, indigenous tribes, we all came to these North American shores from different parts of the world. My mother was born in Manchester, England, during a time of tremendous upheaval in the world. My

200

grandparents brought her and their other seven children to Ellis Island by ship hoping for safer ports and more secure and steady work. They easily accommodated to American optimism and the belief that if you work hard enough, you can accomplish just about anything and become anyone you want to in the process. Their adopted home captured their imaginations and their hearts.

My family of origin quickly became loyal Americans. Anyone who has ever met my mother knows that she is not from the meek and docile strain of British gentility. No, she has more of the no-nonsense, "Woodhouse" characteristics (Mrs. Woodhouse starred in a recent PBS series on training your dog "the Woodhouse way"–obviously with authority and command!). It is an understatement to say that she is opinionated. And her "opinion" is that America is the best place on earth to live and that anyone who comes here should be grateful, drive a Chevrolet, and always exercise their privilege to vote–preferably Republican. Patriotism, not cleanliness, was next to godliness in our home.

I grew up going to parades every Fourth of July, Memorial Day, Labor Day, President's Day–whatever excuse there was to attend a parade celebrating our national life, we used it. It might have been simply a neighborhood gathering where the parents helped their children decorate their pull wagons and bicycles, or it was the whole city out to watch the marching bands and drill teams leading the proud veterans and city officials through the center of "downtown." I had my own little hand-held flag to wave as the dignitaries passed by us on the street, where hundreds of other boys and girls were jumping up and down, calling out their greetings. We never missed the magnificent fireworks display that lit up the sky over Green Lake, and later Lake Washington. Seattle knew how to throw a birthday party for her country.

Our home always flew the Stars and Stripes on national holidays, and at other times, too, when the weather was beautiful and the summer "good humor" wagon toured the neighborhoods, to every child's delight. I inherited my mother's "pride without question." It was part of being American. It was what it meant to be a member of our family. My tiny five-year-old heart burst open every time I placed my right hand over it to say the Pledge of Allegiance or sing the "Star-Spangled Banner."

The unquestioning loyalty that my mother presented was not unique to her. It seems to be a common theme amongst many immigrants who come with an unreserved trust in their new adopted home. I heard this same theme from many of the members of the Japanese American church I served in Chicago, and later from those in the Japanese American church I attend in Berkeley, California. There appears to be a special kind of bonding that occurs in any "adoption" process, whether of new family members or places of residence–"Don't ever forget/ for a single moment/ You didn't grow under my heart [or flag]/ But into it." At its best, adoption involves choosing and being chosen, a sense of gratitude for receiving something very precious and valued, or being received as someone precious and valuable; a willingness to trust first and put aside any hesitations or suspicions. There is a noticeable lack of any sense of entitlement. Adoption has more humble and holy origins. Paul talks about a spirit of adoption in his letter to the Roman church.

> For all who are led by the Spirit of God are children of God. For you did not receive a spirit of slavery to fall back into fear, but you have received a spirit of adoption. When we cry, "Abba!..." it is that very Spirit bearing witness with our spirit that we are children of God, and if children, then heirs... (Rom. 8:14–17a)

Here, it is not blood status that gives identity. Instead, identity and relationship are freely given—no strings attached. Under these circumstances adoption creates a bond where the agency of all parties is honored. Where each participant has a part in establishing relationships, gratitude wells up and illumines all of life. Perhaps this is why the metaphor of adoption has been such a powerful one for children who have been embraced by loving parents who are not the originators of their conception, and for hopeful immigrants who move to a new country and have learned to claim it as their "adopted homeland."

Yet the unquestioning loyalty of my mother never fully concealed some of her emerging questions about her new country. Loyalty never eclipsed her opinions. I remember most clearly a family discussion she led on the merits of our national anthem. It was her opinion that "bombs bursting in air" was too "bloody" harsh in a world now trying to recover from two World Wars, each one supposedly fought to secure a world peace that is still to come. This conversation took place when she had recently learned of the devastation to her childhood home in Urmston, outside of Manchester. German fighter planes had bombed northern England mercilessly in retaliation for the destruction of Dresden. Her thinking was that "My Country, 'Tis of Thee" should be our national anthem, and I believe she even wrote to then-President Truman to tell him so.

> My country, 'tis of thee,
> Sweet land of liberty,
> Of thee I sing;
>
> ...
> Let music swell the breeze,
> And ring from all the trees
> Sweet freedom's song...

"My country, 'tis of thee, sweet land of liberty" speaks of a vision in stark contrast to "bombs bursting in air." The music of freedom, not the noise of explosives, speaks in a persuasive way, hinting at a theology informed by something different than proof through power: one born of humility and reverence for the earth and her people. However, I am not completely certain that my mother's choice of "My Country, 'Tis of Thee" was simply because of the lyrics. Looking back, I realize it may have captured her imagination because it was written to the music of "God Save the Queen." One's roots remain intact in various ways.

It was also around this time that she began to teach me the correct posture and grace of the curtsy, "just in case." I really believed I would have occasion to use it! Either when the Queen came to visit the United States, perhaps even our house, or when we were invited to her home for tea. Such are the dreams of a five-year-old. Little did I know that this curtsy would later introduce me to the ceremonial bow I experience in my own adopted family and circle of friends.

Innocent loyalties and the thin line that protects dreams from reality do not last forever. I grew up. Mine was the generation that went to war on television. The image of a little girl running down a dirt road to escape the flesh-burning attack of napalm is forever seared onto my memory. Vietnam: a place, a people, and my country's shame. The flag I once honored became a flag from which I wanted to hide. No, I never personally put a match to it, but I did become deeply involved in the antiwar movement of the Vietnam era. I was a college student and young mother at the time. My children teethed on "Peace Now" political buttons, and my son took some of his first steps in an antiwar protest march. My daughter to this day will only wear Birkenstocks, the signature footwear of my generation. "My country, 'tis of thee…land of the pilgrims' pride" became the land of my "broken pride." The America of my child's heart became an America of my broken heart. How could my mother's dream have become such an illusion in so short a time?

Later, when I became an ordained minister in the United Church of Christ, I was asked to preach at a colleague's church on the Fourth of July. It was the most difficult sermon I ever remember offering. The scripture chosen for the day was 1 Peter 2:9:

> But you are a chosen race, a royal priesthood, a holy nation, God's own people, in order that you may proclaim the mighty acts of him who called you out of darkness into his marvelous light.

Since it was the Fourth of July, people were expecting a sermon that gave some assurance that our country was indeed a nation that had fulfilled such a calling and purpose. I couldn't do it. As I spoke, I felt my heart pierced by the broken promises of a country I had loved, but not known. I would face this conflict again in the years ahead.

The Adoption: "Getting to Know You"

I had not planned to serve a church in Chicago, and the thought of pastoring a Japanese American church had not even entered my mind. How it actually came about is a story for another time. That it did is the main reason for this rumination. Christ Church of Chicago called me to be their pastor and surprised me by "adopting" me into their community. Once there I began to learn the ways of the church family. In part, my acceptance was made easy because I am married to someone who is Japanese American. I was given an initial trust I had not yet earned. My calling became how to live into that trust.

Yet, I soon learned that acceptance is only part of the process of adoption. There is a certain relinquishment that is involved as well. As I grew within my new community, I was changed, not by choice or necessarily by design, but through a gradual process that involved having my previous worldview challenged, modified, and complicated. Becoming adopted by my new community involved relinquishing some of the assumptions I had grown up with. It meant hearing and seeing some of these assumptions through new eyes informed by the insights of others. But mostly it meant learning to see with a new heart. Seeing with a new heart not only expanded my thinking by exposing me to new customs and traditions, it also began to shift my very identity. Identity becomes formed, or re-formed, when we allow our interest and curiosity to deepen into the kind of commitment where we allow who we are to become known and, yes, loved.

At the same time, relinquishment is not an easy process. It is never smooth and seamless. Nor is it completely a voluntary and rational procedure, even if one enters into it freely. Because it involves change, it also includes loss—loss of what is given, stable, and secure. And loss means grief. But this kind of grief can be more than mourning over what is no longer there. It can be tremendously life-giving, kindling the imagination in a way that leads to new life. Relinquishment, then, is ultimately a gesture of faith. One enters it trusting in something that cannot be known in advance. This is to say, trust is everything. Through the eyes of people who loved and trusted me, I was invited into a new way of being in the world.

Trust either grows or it dies. Trust involves a gradual process of "getting to know you," as the old song from *The King and I* claims—"getting to like you, getting to hope you like me." This may sound trite or sentimental, but it is not. It is a very important part of learning to respect and honor new relationships. For me, in the beginning it meant learning to take off my shoes, to say "*arigato*," and to love sushi. It meant a new appreciation for the way flowers are arranged in a bowl, the power of silence, the weight of inference, and the significance of words not spoken. It also meant learning the importance of not just four-o'clock tea, but green tea and the way it is prepared and served. And I began to see an affinity between the curtsy of my youth and the bow of respect in my new community.

The curtsy and the bow speak to a ceremony of "meeting," where people come together in mutual regard without the intent to manipulate or control. They are hospitable gestures. Unlike a handshake, a bow can never "grasp"; its form contains its own restraint. Unlike the "stand at attention," a curtsy never frightens or intimidates; its movement communicates something different. A bow speaks of generosity and not greed. A curtsy shows benevolence and not ill will. These simple gestures reflect a theology of adoption where each person is viewed as an equal heir before God. These simple gestures reminded me of the promise of the day when relationships between people will honor and reflect this free and given status of people. As such, the bow and the curtsy have become for me unpretentious signs of hope. Some would call this grace.

Grace became the hallmark of my ministry in this community and became evident in many ways. Two in particular come to mind. One involved an incident around the American flag in the sanctuary; the other took place during an event commemorating five hundred years of history in America.

America of the Broken Heart

Early in my ministry there was a big controversy over whether or not to reinstall the American flag in the sanctuary. It had been in storage while the congregation moved to a new church setting. Some members wanted the flag in full view during worship. (This reminded me of my mother's patriotic pride.) Others were clear that they did not want the flag placed next to the altar. This controversy made me face, in some new ways, my own conflicted history of pride and protest toward the country that cradled my birth.

Veterans of World War II, particularly those who served in the 442, the all–Japanese American unit of the 100th Battalion, were of strong mind about the value of having the flag visible at the front of the church. Others, some who were in the American concentration camps and were more ambivalent about the role of the Japanese Americans serving in the armed services during the war, felt differently. Still others, some of the Sansei (children of the Nisei), had mixed feelings about their parents' experiences during the war and the ongoing impact of their mistreatment by the United States government. The congregation had divided reactions to the possibility of installing the flag in the sanctuary. I felt sick about it.

My own stance from my young adult years, and the personal experience of having friends die in what I believed to be an unjust war, made the thought of leading worship under the banner of the "Stars and Stripes" almost unbearable. However, gradually, and admittedly at first grudgingly, I learned a new meaning for the flag from the Nisei members of the church. Seeing the flag through their eyes began to transform my vision.

On February 19, 1942, President Roosevelt issued executive Order 9066 establishing the means to evacuate 120,000 Japanese and Japanese Americans from the West Coast of the United States. Even Peruvians of Japanese ancestry were abducted and transported to Crystal City in Texas. They were incarcerated in American concentration camps, euphemistically

called "internment camps," located in various parts of the Untied States
from Montana to Texas and as far east as Arkansas. The founders of Christ
Church were among these detainees. When they relocated to Chicago after
the war, one of the first things they did was to begin a Bible study class,
which eventually grew to become the vital and flourishing church it is today.
While in camp, some of them faced the question of whether or not to serve
in the United States military in the Pacific and in Europe. For many of
them there was no straightforward response. To serve or not to serve was
fraught with conflicting values and consequences.

Why would Japanese Americans imprisoned unjustly behind barbed-
wire fences be willing to serve the government that put them there in the
first place? This is the way I began to understand it. Some of them
volunteered because they were first of all "loyal Americans," period. But
by far the majority of those who enlisted were more circumspect. By serving
they would not so much defend their country as prove their captors wrong.
Indeed, they were not, and never had been, the threat to American security
they were suspected of being. However, more importantly, they went for
the sake of their family and friends and for the future generations that
would benefit from their service. By proving their loyalty, they hoped to
lift the shame and disgrace inflicted on those they loved and honored. The
442 Regiment of the 100th Battalion became recognized as the most highly
decorated fighting unit of World War II. Its motto was *Go for Broke.* "Go for
broke" meant to risk everything. "Go for broke" meant they fought without
reserve. Thirty-three thousand Japanese American soldiers gave their lives
to benefit the members of the community who remained on American
soil. National security was not a single aim when the identity and well-
being of a people were at stake. Service to country meant to serve in the
hope of providing a better life for the generations to come.

Go for Broke became the emblem of willing sacrifice for these Japanese
American soldiers. It spoke to their deep sense of commitment in the midst
of a painful conflict of values, a commitment they hoped would lead to
new life. Reverend Paul Nagano, a Japanese American Baptist minister
who was in the camps at the time, speaks of this commitment as an
expression of the cross. The theology of the cross became expressed as
"go for broke" in the lives of these soldiers who lived an experience of
"taking up your cross." For Christians, the cross represents the way of
authentic living. "Go for broke," too, offered the possibility for authentic
living even during a time of conflict, confusion, and great repression
of life.

The flag of the veterans of 442 and the flag of a Vietnam War protestor
represent very different points of view. Where one stands makes all the
difference in how one understands the meaning of an event, a symbol, a
story, a way of life. Although for various reasons we did not end up
displaying the flag in our sanctuary, my appreciation for what it represented

for the members of this community complicated and deepened my own perceptions. Today I cannot simply view this national symbol from my personal and limited history and point of view. The experiences of those I love and respect are now a part of my experience too. They contribute to my "conflict of values" and painfully reveal more fully the America of the broken heart. Perhaps this is another form of grace, the grace of truth telling and ambiguity.

The second event occurred in 1992 during one of the many commemorations to "celebrate" the five hundred years of history in the Americas. A group of racial/ethnic congregations on the north side of Chicago met to reflect on the meaning of this national anniversary. Japanese Americans, Korean Americans, African Americans, Filipino Americans, and Hispanics came together for an all-day program to discuss the impact of five hundred years in America on their various communities. As you might imagine, within this diverse gathering there was a broad spectrum of response, but historical injuries were critical features of each group's story. Feelings were strong as unhealed wounds were revealed and shared. Anger, hot debate, some tears, and extended periods of silence marked the hours of the day.

Perhaps a half-dozen folks attended from our church. The WWII internment experience was again the main focus of their reflections as well as the ongoing racial discrimination many continued to experience. However, even among our few members who talked there were different opinions about the meaning of these experiences. Someone felt that the 1988 Civil Liberties Act, which granted redress to the some sixty thousand surviving internees, hadn't gone far enough to fully acknowledge the suffering inflicted on families, especially the Issei. Another countered by saying that the camp experience really "wasn't all that bad." This statement evoked a quick rebuttal by yet another whose education had been interrupted and ultimately sacrificed by the years spent imprisoned behind barbed-wire fences.

Toward the end of the day, as conversations between groups became less guarded and more fluid, reinforcing the parallel painful histories, one of our church members said, "We have to forgive." There was silence. A very pregnant silence. It wasn't that everyone agreed with her, or even took her that seriously. But a few did. She went on to say, "We only hurt ourselves if we cannot find some way to forgive. It [racial animosity] will never change. We have to begin somewhere." I will never forget her words or the impact they had on me, the one white guest at this gathering. I didn't expect to hear anything like this, particularly after listening to the inexhaustible list of grievances that had been expressed throughout the day. She wasn't saying something naive, and she wasn't simply offering a pious platitude. In her own way she was searching for a real alternative even in the midst of a painful conflict of values.

Perhaps Donald Schriver, drawing on the work of Vincent Harding,[1] says it best in his reflection on the American civil rights movement. Referring to the 1865 Coloured People's Convention at the Zion Presbyterian Church in Charleston, North Carolina, he comments on the freed African American slaves' willingness to offer the hand of friendship to former slave holders, at great inner cost, in order to cooperate in building a new civil society. He asks, "Is there, in the culture of black Americans, a predisposition, an ingrained gift, for injecting the forgiveness of sins into their political negotiations with us, their white American neighbors?" He then makes this indicting observation about the outcome of these continuing overtures enacted throughout the long history of the early and later civil rights movement:

> The culture of black Americans is more hospitable to the forgiveness of America's sins than the culture of white Americans makes them hospitable to being forgiven. But the forgiveness of which many blacks are capable waits for the display of justice of which white society has yet to show itself capable.[2]

When my church member said, "We must forgive," I felt a similar response to the Asian American community that Shriver expressed about the African American community. Paraphrasing his words, "The forgiveness of which many Asian Americans are capable waits for the display of justice of which white society has yet to show itself capable." Redress was a partial response, and the apology by President Reagan made a deep impression on many Japanese Americans. But those gestures remain extremely limited.

As I write these words, I am aware of recent reports indicating a rise in hate crimes against Asians and Asian Americans in this country, along with renewed attitudes of suspicion and disrespect. A case in point is the recent indictment of Wen Ho Lee, a Chinese American physicist at Los Alamos who spent nine months in solitary confinement in jail for downloading old weapons-design files onto an unsecured computer. The FBI assumed he had passed weapons secrets to China, but were never able to document anything of the kind. The *New York Times,* in commenting on this case, noted,

> Mr. Lee is not the first government employee to find secure computers frustrating and inconvenient. John Deutch, former head of the Central Intelligence Agency, also loaded classified information onto his unsecured home computer. (He, however, has not been subjected to arrest and extended incarceration for doing so.)[3]

Today I am struck even more by my parishioner's statement "We have to forgive." This is no easy forgiveness she is talking about. It is not "cheap grace," as Dietrich Bonhoeffer would say. No, it is a costly offer, one filled with historical memories that do not disappear even as they are spoken and released into an air of hope and unfulfilled promises. If she is willing to forgive, if she is still willing to forgive in spite of everything, are there European Americans willing to hear and accept it? What would it mean for European Americans to really accept forgiveness for something that is part of our history? Such an offer of forgiveness is beyond my understanding. But again, as Bonhoeffer reminds us, "Abandonment of understanding is real understanding; not knowing where you are going is the right way to know where you are going."[4] This speaks to the power of relinquishment mentioned earlier, of letting go and accepting that the power of forgiveness does not ultimately rest within my own purview. It means relinquishing even this false sense of privilege and becoming open to something new. With all of the recent public apologies for various public indiscretions and historical crimes, I wonder if this aspect of reconciliation can be recognized.

Forgiveness invites us into a way of relinquishing all trappings of privilege. It is the "bow" that *precedes* reconciliation and expresses the wisdom of "unknowing." The wisdom of unknowing recognizes that knowledge originates in new and unexpected places, from people who have something to say that has never been said before—or if said, not heard before. In practice, this means dismantling the "known," "taken-for-granted" unjust and harmful ways of life. Such unknowing, or dismantling, is another expression of grace, "amazing grace," which ultimately leads us all home.

Theology of the Broken Heart

Forgiveness, grace, homecoming—these sound wonderful, and indeed they are the fruits of our longing. But we have not arrived there yet. We are a long way from home. We are in a period of longing for home, longing for the America of our hearts. In the meantime, the truth for many Americans is that America is a place where trust has been betrayed, hopes compromised, acceptance partially extended, and relinquishment required in a far too one-sided fashion. It is amazing that in such a climate trust perseveres and generosity is practiced.

In Adeline Yen Mah's autobiography, *Falling Leaves,* she writes about the Chinese character for endurance, *ren.* [5] The character for *ren* is made up of two components. The top one is *dao. Dao* means "knife," with a sheath in the center of the rapier. The bottom one is *xen. Xen* means "heart." Together *dao* and *xen* make the word *ren* (endurance). *Ren* communicates the poignant posture of someone who "wraps one's heart" around the instrument of pain. This speaks of living through incredible pain because of some deep love or commitment. Da Chen offers an example of this *ren* in a Father's Day article he wrote for *The New York Times*.[6] In his editorial he tells about his father's suffering during the Cultural Revolution in China. His father was hanged by his thumbs in their commune's headquarters when he refused to make a false confession. Da Chen was there peeping through a window. His heart broke as he watched his father scream while he was being beaten. However, when his father caught sight of him, he ceased his screams and threw his son a secret smile. He smiled a second time, this time as a warning for his son to go home. Da Chen writes, "The luxury of such a smile came at a high price. The cadres beat him till one of his fingers snapped"—*ren,* endurance for the sake of some deep commitment or love.

Ren suggests something to me about the unique longing that is involved when we talk about America of the heart. The spirit of endurance alluded to here also helps illumine a particularly Asian interpretation of theology of the cross that can be a helpful lens for viewing this "America of the heart."

Japanese theologian Kazoh Kitamori was one of the first to articulate a theology of the cross indigenous to the Japanese experience following the atomic bombings of Hiroshima and Nagasaki. In his seminal work *Theology of the Pain of God,* he talks about the God who endures pain in order to enfold us completely in love. Pain, for Kitamori, involves a realization that our reality is totally broken. This is an especially vivid theological truth for Kitamori in the aftermath of the devastation of Japan.

In the midst of incomprehensible destruction and the human agency involved in propagating it, Kitamori reminds us that God's love enfolds us completely. What a claim! Yet this all-embracing love is the very origin of God's pain because God wills to love the objects of God's pain. Kitamori contends that God is a suffering God because God embraces in this way. This is a powerful illustration of the anguish of acceptance, demonstrating complete love for what one is and not for what one might be, could be, and is not. It shows reality in conflict with love. Such love that embraces completely is painful and costly, again not what Bonhoeffer called "cheap grace." Grace is not soft; it involves anguish. In some ways to "love" America means to embrace the object of pain. If this is so, this is a costly expression of grace, not a soft grace but a painful grace.

Kitamori's notion of pain is deeply rooted in the Japanese experience and understanding of tragedy: *Tsurasa. Tsurasa* is neither bitterness nor sadness. It is realized when one suffers and dies, or makes someone else that one loves suffer and die, for the sake of loving and making others live. Such a God who knows *tsurasa* wills to love what is unlovable. This willingness to love means that God forgives and loves those who, for all good reason, should not be forgiven. Pain is deepened because the one who forgives bears the responsibility for the sinner and suffers because of it.[7] The pain of God, this *tsurasa,* is the very heart of forgiveness of sin. To "love" America in this fashion means to bear responsibility for what should not be forgiven for the sake of authentic life.

Tsurasa is not masochism, pain for pain's sake. *Tsurasa* enfolds what is opposite to win it to the side of love and life. This is how "love" of America becomes America of the heart. In this way, anguish gets translated into yearning and compassion and opens a way for something different–a new heart broken open by the pain of broken reality. Kitamori contends that human pain is to be put in service to God's pain. This is the meaning of bearing the cross–serving the pain of God by your own pain–and through this service your pain will be healed. Or in Kitamori's words: "Through our service in the pain of God, the wounds of our Lord in turn heal our wounds, thus our pain can actually be relieved by serving the pain of God."[8] This is the ethical and theological as well as pastoral implication for serving the pain of God. To serve this pain challenges us to be careful not to suffer human pain in vain.[9]

I wonder if there is a deep cultural and cross-generational formation through *tsurasa* that can help illumine the commitments, in spite of the conflict of values, that motivated those internees to enlist in military service and "go for broke." *Tsurasa* enfolds what is opposite to win it to the side of love and life. Those young Japanese American soldiers embraced military service in a country that mistreated them in order to create a better life for their families and friends and future generations. From a Christian point of view, they put their human pain into the service of God's pain, preparing the way for authentic living. Many died for this. They served at a level of excellence and sacrifice that opened a way for something different–perhaps the America of their hearts. To receive their sacrifice challenges us to be very careful not to let their suffering be in vain.

I hear my parishioner's plea to forgive historical injuries inflicted on Japanese Americans in light of this theological reading of Kitamori. Her plea for forgiveness echoes the plea from the cross, "Forgive them…" and addresses those who for all good reasons should not be forgiven. Forgiveness is not a "given," natural, or rational response to pain, especially when evidence of ongoing injustice continues. Yet forgiveness is everything. If forgiveness bears the responsibility for the sinner and suffers because of it, to serve this pain challenges *every one* of us to be careful not to allow any one person or community to suffer human pain in vain. The pain of offering forgiveness hints of *tsurasa,* of enfolding what is opposite to win it to the side of love and life. This pain awaits the display of justice of which white society has yet to show itself capable. The pain of God awaits a total recognition of its depth and our place in it, our own "enfoldedness" in the total love of God. What would it mean to really receive this?

In the meantime, trust endures–*ren*. In the meantime, *tsurasa* enfolds what is opposite to win it to the side of love and life. In the meantime, "America of the heart" is really "America of the broken heart." Yet the broken heart is a heart broken open, and here and there through this openness a generosity of spirit emerges again and again where human forgiveness becomes possible. The anguish involved in this opening and continual offering involves a *tsurasa* kind of grace, a most powerful expression of grace. To be sure, these gestures are yet to be realized, but they are holy signs that spring from a profound depth, saying, "God is love."

Conclusion

America of the heart—what does it mean? Does it mean pining for some unreal fantasy that has been fed to us by the manufacturers of commercial optimism? Does it mean putting away any dream for the "good life" that seems unrealizable and settling for the leftovers and hand-me-down versions that taste bitter and do not fit? We know what happens when people have no vision and when dreams evaporate in the noontime sun. America of the heart means something else. It involves recovering *our* communal memories that reveal themes of loyalty and trust, courage and the betrayal of trust, forgiveness and the possibility of new identities. But these new identities involve the painful process of adoption.

Adoption is a part of each one of us and includes the reality of relinquishing aspects of a former way of life. However, for those who have been a part of the dominant society, relinquishment carries some particular obligations, above all a willingness to engage in some very specific ways of "not knowing." It will involve adopting other interpretations of history than the governing ones and allowing them to impact and change our lives. For those who have not experienced historical injuries, it will mean receiving the tears of others who have—until those tears wear away all false pretensions of ever being free from the legacy of historical atrocities. It will mean realizing that there is no such thing as historical innocence. These aspects of adoption mean that not one of us can ever "go home" again, and our new "home" is still a future-leading image.

In a way, America of the heart is really sort of a joke. It could be a cynical joke, or it could be an ironic joke—the kind that evokes laughter until you almost want to cry. Laughter can be a good thing. So can tears. When laughter is honest, it emanates from that deep place where newness begins. Laughter means that all is not as it appears to be. Something more needs to be said. It pokes fun at "taken-for-granted" ways of knowing. Something else is true. Tears tell the truth, cleanse the mind, and kindle a kind of tenacious strength that some call survival. Together laughter and tears provide a window of hope that pierces what Douglas John Hall calls our society's "official optimism," an optimism that cannot deliver. Optimism soothes. Hope endures. *Ren* says there is a new horizon that is only dimly coming into view. It may involve a painful arrival, this America of the heart, but it is coming nonetheless. In the end, laughter and tears lead us to eat together, to forgive one another, to endure one another in order to build what Martin Luther King, Jr., called "the beloved community." This, too, is about learning to bear the cross together.

When I listen to the words of our two "national anthems," it seems to me as though many Americans live out the vision of "The Star-Spangled Banner." It is a vision of triumph, of pride in success, that communicates a certain confidence and assurance. This is the hymn of a proud heart. It is a heart unable to be touched by the pain of God. The vision of the second doesn't seem so clear. "My country, 'tis of thee, sweet land of liberty," suggests a place where the climate of true civility thrives. This hymn of letting freedom ring sings of a vision still to be realized. Therefore, it is a hymn of the broken heart.

My mother was wise in her own way. "My Country, 'Tis of Thee" is closer to the nature of American life as a hymn of the broken-hearted. To sing "My Country, 'Tis of Thee" means to cry, so we might learn to laugh together, a laughter filled with longing, compassion, and "getting to know you." And "Getting to Know You" is so much more than the song from *The King and I.* It is more than rational knowing, for it has to do with compassion, endurance, practicing forgiveness, and relinquishing worn-out ways of getting on with life. "Getting to know you" really means learning to sing together, in a new way, "My Country, 'Tis of Thee." It means to let our hearts become broken so that we might become America of the broken heart in service to the pain of God. It is a hymn that embraces a worthy vision and "enfolds" completely all of America, even in her brokenness. Broken and yet beloved, she might one day know her true identity and become the home for all her people. Perhaps we can learn to sing this hymn in a way that brings all that opposes its vision over to the ways of justice, love, and authentic life.

Notes

[1] Vincent Harding, *There Is a River: The Black Struggle for Freedom in America* (New York: Vintage Books, Random House, 1983).

[2] Donald W. Shriver, Jr., *Forgiveness and Politics: The Case of the American Black Civil Rights Movement* (London: New World Publications, 1987), 12.

[3] Richard Rhodes, "The Myth of Perfect Nuclear Security," *New York Times,* 24 July 2000.

[4] Dietrich Bonhoeffer, *Meditations on the Cross* (Louisville: Westminster John Knox Press, 1998),18.

[5] Adeline Yen Mah, *Falling Leaves* (New York: Broadway Books, 1997), 76.

[6] Da Chen, *The New York Times,* 17 June 2000.

[7] Kazoh Kitamori, *Theology of the Pain of God* (Richmond, Va.: John Knox Press, 1965), 40.

[8] Ibid., 53.

[9] Ibid.

PART 4

Asian Americans and Global Connections

Challenges and Prospects

13

The Stranger in Our Midst

Diaspora, Ethics, Transformation[1]

LESTER EDWIN J. RUIZ

Our age is one in which...the very activities of their own states—combined regimes of sovereignty and governmentality—together with the global capitalism of states and the environmental degradation of many populous regions of the planet have made many millions of people radically endangered strangers in their own homes as well as criminalized or anathemized strangers in the places to which they have been forced to flee. The modern age's response to the strangeness of others, indeed, the scale of its politically instrumental, deliberate, juridical, and governmental manufacture of estrangement, necessarily calls into question, therefore, its very ethical and political foundations and accomplishments—particularly those of the state and of the international state system.

—Michael Dillon[2]

I trust no text that is not in some way contaminated with negative theology, and even among those texts that apparently do not have, want, or believe, they have any relation with theology in general.

—Jacques Derrida[3]

I pray God to rid me of God.

—Meister Eckhart[4]

Beginning with a Dilemma

The "pursuit of the 'body politic'" today is situated within a seemingly intractable dilemma. On the one hand, how does one begin to speak about, much less experience, his or her body, not to mention the *political* body, when for the most part, one has been *dis*embodied—banished from, excluded from that very body and the *vita activa* and *vita contemplativa*[5] —not only by modern politics[6] but also by academia and the church? On the other hand, how does one pursue this body when the conditions for its articulation require not only the dissolution of this body but also its articulation as a body "beyond" space, time, and place (or at least, a transformed space, time, and place)? This dilemma, which at its core is a profound limitation, must be both celebrated and mourned for the sake of the future, namely, the "recovery of the 'body politic.'" It must begin with one's body even though this body is limited by that very body itself. At the same time, it means, beginning where one finds that body, namely, in the spaces, times, and places of those dispersed, the displaced, and the dislocated—in short, the diaspora.

In fact, the diaspora is, fundamentally, about "the body"—all kinds of bodies: what they are, who they are, what is happening to them. This essay explores the pursuit of the "body politic" in the context of the assertion that such an exploration involves a rediscovery of "the body" *under the conditions of diaspora.*

Identifying the Body: A Filipino Diaspora

Historically, Filipinos were always a "migrant" people: The "original" inhabitants of the islands later called *Las Islas Filipinas* were nomadic; the first "settlers" were "boat people" from the Malayo-Polynesian region.[7] Under Spanish colonialism, the "natives" migrated to Europe, especially to Spain; under U.S. colonialism, to the U.S. In the late nineteenth century and throughout the twentieth century, migration and immigration to the U.S., despite a painful Philippine-U.S. war, was virtually unbroken. In fact, Filipinos, whether prominent or not, were part of the woof-and-weave of American life:[8] Filipinos in the Hawaiian pineapple and sugar cane plantations,[9] Filipinos claiming World War II veterans benefits promised by the U.S. government in return for their role in the USAFFE,[10] Filipinos going to the U.S. to study, Filipinos joining the U.S. military, Filipino nurses, Filipinos in exile in the U.S.[11]

Such migrations to the U.S. and elsewhere could simply be the consequence of an ineradicable colonial experience—the inevitable "return" of the colonized to the home of his or her colonizer.[12] However, such a "journey," particularly in the last twenty years, could very well be the apotheosis of modernity, the effect of the fundamental transformations that are occurring under the sign of a *globalizing* transnational capitalism.[13] Perhaps the most innovative of all metaphors deployed for such fundamental transformations has been that of turbulence, suggesting by its use not mere motion, activity, or movement, but disruptive, unpredictable, volatile speed.[14] Of migration, Nikos Papastergiadis notes:

The flows of migration across the globe are not explicable by any general theory. In the absence of structured patterns of global migration, with direct causes and effects, turbulence is the best formulation for the mobile processes of complex self-organization that are now occurring. These movements may appear chaotic, but there is a logic and order within them…As Manuel de Landa noted, "a turbulent flow is made out of a hierarchy of eddies and vortices inside more eddies and vortices."[15]

Such turbulent flows have produced new forms of belonging and identity, not to mention novel understandings of contemporary politics and culture. They evoke and provoke images of "border crossings" as well as invasions. They reveal global trajectories of deterritorialization as well as local surges (insurgencies?) of reterritorializations. They underscore contradictions and antagonisms, while intensifying the asymmetries, of political, economic, and cultural structures and processes.[16] Surely, such flows affect directly any "pursuit of the 'body politic.'"

Epiphanio San Juan, Jr., writing on the "condition of the Filipino," particularly in the United States, observes their contemporary experience as one of the

> …fusion of exile and migration: the scattering of a people, not yet a fully matured nation, to the ends of the earth, across the planet throughout the 60s and 70s, continuing up to the present. We are now a quasi-wandering people, pilgrims or prospectors staking our lives and futures all over the world–in the Middle East, Africa, Europe, North and South America, in Australia and all of Asia, in every nook and cranny of this seemingly godforsaken earth…A whole people dispersed, displaced, dislocated.[17]

So significant has this experience of displacement, dislocation, and dispersal become in the past twenty-five years that some Filipinos have come to refer to this, not so inaccurately, as a "Filipino Diaspora," much in the same way that *diaspora* has been used in the Jewish and African American contexts. This experience encompasses immigration, migration, and exile– from overseas contract workers (OCWs) to political exiles, from the "undocumented" to the variously "documented" (students, businesspeople, overstaying tourists, "regular immigrants," and "expats")–under conditions ranging from the voluntary to the coercive to the oppressive.[18] In fact, such an experience has called forth–provoked/invoked–the vocabulary, in addition to what has already been noted, of estrangement, border, and hybridity, as well as of subjectivity, identity, and agency, particularly under the conditions of transnational capitalism.[19]

In this sense, the Filipino experience of diaspora is not exceptional. William Safran, for example, using the Jewish Diaspora as a model, has

identified a number of defining features of diaspora that resonate with the
Filipino experience:

1. dispersal from an original "center" to two or more "peripheral" places;
2. retention of a "collective memory, vision, or myth about their original
   homeland";
3. belief that they are not and perhaps cannot be fully accepted into
   their host society;
4. belief that they or their descendants would or should eventually return
   to their homeland when conditions are appropriate;
5. collective commitment to the maintenance or reestablishment of their
   homeland;
6. collective consciousness and solidarity "importantly defined" by this
   enduring relationship with the homeland.[20]

However, the name itself may reflect a fundamental transformation in
the "condition of the Filipino." For while the experience of Filipino
migration and immigration is not new,[21] the speed and scope, not to mention
the character, of this movement has certainly accelerated alongside the
transformations in the structures and processes of *global* capitalism itself.[22]
While the dynamics of Filipino migration and immigration continue to
reflect the political, economic, and cultural character of "traditional"
immigration–that is, the centrality of the "homeland" in the identity of the
immigrant–these dynamics have been thoroughly recast by the experience
of modernity: (1) the separation of time and space (including the emptying
of time and space), (2) the development of disembedding mechanisms,
and (3) the reflexive appropriation of knowledge.[23] One could say, in this
context, that "diaspora" is, in fact, a creature of modernity. The very
dynamics of modernity, which is unavoidably a "globalizing" experience,
create the very reality of "diaspora."

However, as a creature of modernity, "diaspora" is not only a
"condition" that has gained some level of autonomy at the global level,
which is sustained by the movements and flows of capital, people, goods,
information, ideas, and images, and which alters the conditions under which
communities and identities are enacted.[24] "Diaspora" is a social construction
constituted by those who are "in diaspora," by the actions and/or activities
of these individuals and communities situated in different parts of the world.
In short, diaspora is also, and fundamentally so, the "practice of subjects,"
the *imagined* transnational *relations* between and among the minority and
its homeland, as well as its counterpart overseas communities throughout
the world.[25] James Clifford has noted that these relations include cultural,
economic, and social linkages evident in the circulation of people, money
and consumer goods, and information and ideas, though not necessarily in
reference to their original homeland.[26] Diasporas, in other words, produced
and reproduced as they are by "collective human agency," which are at

once multiple and polyarchic,[27] also sustain what we call globalizing capitalism.

At the same time, diasporas are more than creatures of modernity. The very experience of dispersal, displacement, and dislocation, in the context of the trajectories of globalization noted earlier,[28] have created, among other things, conditions of borderlands and border-crossings, of hybridity and contingency, of contradiction and antagonism, that are articulated, not only in academic life but also in political, economic, and cultural life.[29]

The reality of a Filipino Diaspora, then, raises at least three fundamental questions that have a direct bearing on the pursuit of the "body politic." First, the Filipino Diaspora raises a critical question about the nature of the social totality of which we are a part. By recognizing that the Filipino experience is a *pastiche,* an *assemblage,* of political, economic, cultural, religious, and historical specificities and pluralities, and not a singular, let alone unitary, totalized reality, this foregrounds issues about the meaning and significance of the historicity of being, the contingency of human thought and action, and the plurality of human life for the pursuit of the "body politic." Equally important, the reality of a Filipino Diaspora challenges us to intentionally negotiate the linkages—the connections—of these perspectives, especially since what is at stake is not only the historical specificities and pluralities of Filipino experience but also their inextricable and contingent relationships. In fact, the boundaries of politics, epistemologies, and academic disciplines are now constantly being negotiated and renegotiated especially in terms of their long-held correspondences with nation, culture, identity, and place.[30]

Second, the reality of a Filipino Diaspora also raises a question not only about subjecthood but also about subjectivity. This is the question of "the Subject": not only *who* the subject is, but also *what* being a subject entails.[31] This is particularly important because the very reality of a diaspora undermines any notion of a "unitary" subject—even, as noted above, a "collective human subject"—which modern politics requires.[32] The plurality of subjects and subjectivities presupposed by a diaspora directs us not only to the question, What is to be done? but also to: Who are we? For what do we hope? Where do we go? In short, What does it mean to be a people under the conditions of diaspora? This has momentous implications for the recovery of the "body politic."

Third, the reality of a Filipino Diaspora identifies—indeed, it situates— the locus of the pursuit of the "body politic" at the *nexus* of a people's political, economic, and cultural life and work. In fact, starting with a Filipino Diaspora situates Filipino experience within a *relational,* and therefore political, *whole.* This is of no small significance. For to locate the question of politics at the heart of a people's life and cultural practices (defined broadly as those concrete, sensuous realities embodied in rhetorical forms,

222 Lester Edwin J. Ruiz

gestures, procedures, modes, shapes, genres of everyday life: discursive formations and/or strategies, if you will, that are radically contingent arenas of imagination, strategy, and creative maneuver[33]) not only challenges the narrow confines of conventional politics. Such a concept of the diaspora also foregrounds the most comprehensive point of departure of politics: a people's pluralistic, plurivocal–and therefore, always and already contradictory–antagonistic, and *agonistic* histories (political, economic, and aesthetic) expressed in their stories, songs, poetry, arts; embodied in their political struggles; and articulated in their economic institutions. In so doing, this recognition of the diaspora safeguards the adequacy and relevance of politics, particularly, an *embodied* politics.[34] To celebrate the possibility of "the whole," particularly one that invites us beyond "ourselves," is to refuse to capitulate to the illusion of modernity that there is nothing beyond "self-interest."

Recovering the Body: Learning from a Feminist Diaspora

If the first part of this chapter suggests that the locus of the pursuit of the "body politic" is the *nexus* of a people's political, economic, cultural life and work; the second part suggests that recovering the "body politic" could depend on what might be learned from feminist struggles to regain not only control of their bodies, but to recuperate the *place* of the body in political life.[35]

In the first place, feminist struggles to recover the place of the body in political life involve different ways of producing and reproducing knowledge (epistemology). Here, not only is this about situated knowledges and partial perspectives, but also of subjugated and insurrectionary knowledges and agents of knowledges, and the ways in which they are related. Such struggles have consistently focused, among other things, on the necessity, if not desirablity, of rethinking "the relationship between knowledge and emotion and construct[ion of] conceptual models that demonstrate the mutually constitutive rather than oppositional relationship between reason and emotion."[36] At face value, this may be a straightforward, even simplistic, if not obvious, statement about the nature of knowledge. However, when one understands that these claims are set in the context of the historical pretensions about the universality of (masculinist) reason as opposed to say, feminist desire, and of the reality that emotion is associated with subordinate groups–particularly women–and deployed to discount and silence those realities deemed to be irrational, then one begins to realize how these epistemologies actually explode patriarchal myths about knowledge in political life.[37]

In the second place, feminist struggles to recover the place of the body in political life involve different modes of being (ontology). Here, this is not only about thinking, feeling, and acting–as relational practices–but also about "volatile bodies"–that is, of refiguring and reinscribing bodies, of moving through and beyond the conventional divide of gender as socially contructed, on the one hand, and of sex as biologically-given, on the other hand, to "our bodies our selves." Elisabeth Grosz has suggested that the "male (or female) body can no longer be regarded as a fixed, concrete substance, a pre-cultural given. It has a determinate form only by being socially inscribed."[38] She continues,

> As a socio-historical "object," the body can no longer be confined to biological determinants, to an immanent "factitious," or unchanging social status. It is a political object par excellence; its forms, capacities, behaviours, gestures, movements, potential are primary objects of political contestation. As a political object, the body is not inert or fixed. It is pliable and plastic material, which is capable of being formed and organized.[39]

Michel Foucault, who argues, himself, that the body is an "inscribed surface of events," shares this profound insight.[40] Thus, the body becomes "malleable and alterable," its surface inscribed with gender, appropriate behavior, and standards of, for example, femininity. The significance of such an understanding cannot be underestimated. This means, for example, not only that politics is about "who gets what, when, where, and how" but also that its "what, when, where, and how" are inscribed–written on, embodied–in our very bodies.

An example of Latin and ballroom dancing illustrates what I understand by the "body." Those who dance know that the dance floor and, I would say, the ceiling are constitutive elements of the dance, along with the beat of the music (to which most dance) and the melody of the music (to which the best of the best dance). Latin dancing, with its characteristic "hip motion," is achieved by one pressing from the waist down *into the floor*–actually, one of the reasons for the sensuous, earthy intensities of Latin movement. In contrast, the gliding, soaring, almost ethereal movement of the ballroom waltz is accomplished, in part, by stretching one's body toward the ceiling. Both floor and ceiling are, in this sense, constitutive of the dance in the same manner that heaven and earth are constitutive of human life. To put the matter rather starkly, ceiling and floor are part of the dancers' bodies.

In the third place, feminist struggles to recover the place of the body in political life involve different forms of "consciousness" (subjectivity): Here, not only is this about consciousness arising out of concrete and sensuous reality, but it is also about spirituality as always and already *embodied* experience–not only what subjectivity is, but what is entailed in becoming subjects. If it is true that human beings are more than *logos,* but also *eros, pathos,* and the *daimon,* then consciousness, and the structure of spirituality that accompanies it, must also be about touching, feeling, smelling, tasting, eating. Theoretically put, *spirituality* refuses, on the one hand, the temptation of a disembodied transcendence and, on the other hand, rejects its articulation as a totalized immanence. To say that "spirituality" is about "touching, feeling, smelling, tasting, eating" is to acknowledge not only the inadequacies of the received traditions of "spirituality," but to affirm that this "spirituality" is about a people's concrete and sensuous *experience* of self, of other, and, for the religiously inclined, of God. *Babette's Feast* may very well be the metaphor for such spirituality.[41]

In the fourth place, feminist struggles to recover the place of the body in political life involve different *empowering* practices (politics): Here, not only is this about the importance and power of self-definition, self-valuation, or self-reliance and autonomy, it is also about transformation and transgression, of finding safe places and voices in the midst of difference, particularly where the asymmetries of power are mediated through these differences.[42] In fact, what contemporary feminist struggles have contributed, in my view, is an interpretation of the complex and interdependent relationship between theory, history, and struggle as now being emphasized in the light of women's struggles, focusing on the intricate connections between systemic and personal relationships and the directionalities of power. Thus, for example, Dorothy Smith introduces the concept of "relations of ruling," where forms of knowledge and organized practices and institutions, as well as questions of consciousness, experience, and agency, are foregrounded. Rather than positing a simple relation, say between colonizer and colonized, capitalist and worker, male and female, this perspective posits "multiple intersections of structures of power and emphasizes the process or form of ruling, not the frozen embodiment of it."[43] Chandra Mohanty summarizes this point quite well. She notes,

> ...third world women's writings on feminism have consistently focused on (1) the idea of the simultaneity of oppressions as fundamental to the experience of social and political marginality and the grounding of feminist politics in the histories of racism and imperialism; (2) the crucial role of a hegemonic state in circumscribing their/our daily lives and survival struggles; (3) the significance of memory and writing in the creation of oppositional agency; and (4) the differences, conflicts, and contradictions internal to third world women's organizations and communities. In addition, they have insisted on the complex interrelationships between feminist, antiracist, and nationalist struggles.[44]

"Pursuing the 'Body Politic'": A Work of Ethics—of Spirituality, Cultural Politics, and Transformation

Pursuing the "body politic," then, may be read as having to do with the return of "the body" from its forced exile by the patriarchal rituals of modernity. Such a task involves the laying out of a modest agenda for "being and knowing" that may allow us to pursue the "body politic" in our own time. Here, the pursuit turns out to be a work of ethics—of spirituality, cultural politics, and transformation, within the context and framework of a *Filipino* Diaspora. One might ask, What does a politics and ethics of diaspora look like—at least, as an initial matter?

It has long been argued, rightly, I believe, that "ethics," or the "ethical relationship"—that is to say, its structure—is primarily that of the relationship between a mutually constituted and constituting Self and Other.[45] Beyond the *modern* notion of ethics as a set of rules and regulations adopted by pregiven, autonomous subjects, or of responsibility grounded in a command or imperative, ethics is primarily responsibility to/for the Other and *others*. In fact, without capitulating to some of the dangers of a metaphysics of total otherness that he is often accused of, Emmanuel Levinas may be read, quite appropriately, as arguing that ethics ought to be understood as something insinuated within and integral to subjectivity itself: Ethics "does not supplement a preceding existential base; the very node of the subjective is knotted in ethics and understood as responsibility."[46] In other words, one's identity, one's subjectivity, one's responsibility—that is, the "self"— are always and already *ethically situated*. Making judgments about conduct depends less on what rules are invoked as regulations and more on how the interdependencies of our relations with others are articulated.[47]

However, extending the arguments of those who write in this vein, this "self" is not only ethically situated, it is also and already *ecologically* situated. By this I do not mean to only highlight the multiple "ecological therapies" that underscore the importance of ecology for ethics and politics: from ecotechnology to ecopolitics, from human and social ecology to mental ecology, from ecological ethics to radical or deep ecology.[48] To be sure, these critical therapies call for "ethical practices" such as speaking out on behalf of those nonhuman voices that are not included in human decision-making, or following Aldo Leopold's early lead—for example, redefining community to include "soils, waters, plants, and animals, or collectively: the land,"[49] or adopting "environmentally sustainable" lifestyle choices (e.g., restraint, simplicity, reduced consumption). Rather, I want to suggest that this "ethical relationship" is largely about new ways of knowing and understanding, of engaging and being, of perceiving and communicating with Self, Other, and World. The insight on corporeality noted elsewhere in this chapter bears repeating. "Reason," Leonardo Boff writes, "is neither the primary nor ultimate moment of existence. We are also affectivity, desire, passion, turbulence, communication, and the voice of nature speaking inside us."[50] This is the sense in which I read the notion that to be ethically situated is at the same time to be ecologically situated. Moreover, to be ecologically situated is to gesture unavoidably toward a *planetary community*—which is not to assume that such a community already exists historically or is "pregiven" metaphysically, but rather, to indicate only what the trajectory and reach of the conditions of possibility for ethics today are and to suggest the need for cultivating an ecologically situated, *fully corporeal*, ethical sensibility.

In this context, because ethics has to do primarily with this situated responsibility, a responsibility for the Other whom we encounter face-to-face, the question, Who is my neighbor? becomes a question about the relationship of ethical responsibility to community.[51] In fact, ethics has always gestured simultaneously toward and away from "community." That is to say, ethics as a "responsible, non-totalizing relation with the Other"[52] has not, and cannot, end with the individual; indeed, it does not even begin with the individual; but rather, it is always and already in community.[53] Here, the primarily one-on-one structure of ethics gestures toward the communicative and, therefore, to a political relationship—that is, a "relation to...all others, to the plurality of beings that make up the community."[54] Ethics may not be synonymous with politics, but politics is inescapably ethical even if it is not yet the "pursuit of the good, the true, and the beautiful." The issue is not whether some politics are "ethical" and others are not; rather, all politics pre-suppose their own "ethics." The task is to discover what those ethics are. At the same time, with the constant aggregation, disaggregation, and reaggregation of these communities, due in large part to the transformations of space, time, and place brought about by (economic and political) migrations, "border crossings," "foot wanderers," and exiles—in short, of diaspora, the reality of a territorially circumscribed community is no longer self-evident. Thus, the question, Which community?—and therefore, Which ethics? Or whose ethics?—becomes a pressing issue.[55]

Moreover, this question is of particular importance, not only because what Levinas calls "the third party" always and already interrupts the primary ethical relation of the face-to-face and, by virtue of this interruption, renders the relationship "political," but also because this "third" who is simultaneously other than the other makes one one among others.[56] So Levinas asks, "When others enter (the relationship), each of them external to myself, problems arise. Who is closest to me? Who is the Other?"[57] In fact, Levinas is not only asking, To which community do I belong? nor simply, To whom and for whom am I accountable? nor even, Which community bears responsibility for "the world"? but also, *Why?* and, In what ways are these Other and others conditions of possibility for politics and ethics—or the pursuit of the "body politic"?

There is no doubt that difference is central to any politics and that plurality is intrinsic to the ethical relation. When situated not only in a deeply divided, contested world but also in a *globalizing* world under the sign of transnational capitalism, the question, How then shall I live? which is another way of posing the (normative) ethical question, challenges, as well as is challenged by, those who, in their very existence, demand it in the first place–namely, those who have become "radically endangered strangers in their own homes as well as criminalized or anathemized strangers in the places to which they have been forced to flee."[58] These are the Other and others in the contemporary world. "For the stranger," Dillon writes,

> by his or her very nature as stranger, is out of the settled modes of questioning, and the received understandings of truth and identity, as well as the laws, of which the community is comprised. And yet, the stranger is there not only in all of the mystery that provokes the question, but also in all of the inescapable and shared facticity that demands a response.[59]

These questions and challenges are rendered even more problematic when one understands that the political relation does not exhaust the "interruption" of the ethical relation. In fact, the question of community is also "interrupted" by what I have called the "ecological relation."[60] Surely, ethics cannot merely be anthropocentric. However, since ethics is tied mainly to human subjectivity–although it is an ecologically situated subjectivity–the burden of the ethical relation–that is, responsibility for the Other and others–still rests with human beings.[61] In this sense, ethics is returned to its original home, namely, human agency, only now it turns out to be less of a set of rules and regulations–whether tradition, law, or common practice–to which one commits oneself by implementing its demands. Rather, ethics turns out to be a fundamental structural relationship, among subjects and subjectivities–ecologically situated–which has to do not only with the capacity to decide but also, perhaps even more importantly, with creating the (ecological) conditions under which peoples and communities are able to decide.

These ecological conditions, and their corresponding subjectivities, include the aggregation, disaggregation, and reaggregation of political subjectivities; in short, the reality of human community under the conditions of global capitalism's dissolution of communities (of which the Filipino Diaspora is one specific form)–for example, in the context of immigration and emigration, or cross-border and internal refugees (economic or otherwise), or ecological disasters and degradation. While such political subjectivities are not overdetermined, and while it is not possible to reduce them to mere particular and discrete subjects, the multiplicity of subjects and subject positions, each relatively autonomous, even antagonistic of the other, but all connected by virtue of their respective struggles against violence, insecurity, and avoidable harm, and each constituted not a priori but in the context of these very struggles[62]–remain constitutive for the ethical relation. Here, the question of difference becomes central to the ethical relation. For without genuine alternatives or choices, there can be no genuine decision, only the implementation of an already existing or preexisting "technology." To put the matter differently, justice, nature, and difference are constitutive of the ethical and political relation.[63]

More than the multiplicity of subjects and subject positions is at stake here, however. For one's space, time, and place is of fundamental significance to the question, not only of ethics but to transformation—that is, the creation and nurture of the fundamentally new that is also fundamentally better.[64] Pluralism, even a normative pluralism, has no inherent virtue or efficacy. Who the subjects are, what they hope for, and how they get there are decisive not only to the nature and character of ethics but also to any transformative practice. This, to my mind, is what the discourses that go under the sign of postcolonialism, understood broadly as "oppositionality which colonialism brings into being,"[65] are addressing, as when Gayatri Spivak asks, "Can the subaltern speak?"[66] Ethics is tirelessly and relentlessly reminded that, in this context, it is inextricably related to the singular and specific opposition to all forms of domination by concrete "subjects of history" and struggle. That is, ethics is "concrete, sensuous" practice that both "refuses to turn the Other into the Same" and challenges those that would deny Otherness.

Critical to this "oppositional challenge" is an affirmation of the necessary, though insufficient, role that transgression plays in any ethical practice.[67] In her essay "A New Type of Intellectual: The Dissident," Julia Kristeva argues that it is only in becoming a stranger to one's own country, language, sex, and identity that one avoids "sinking into the mire of common sense."[68] "Writing," she adds, "is impossible without some kind of exile…[which is] already itself a form of dissidence."[69] At the heart of dissent—as exile and sites of difference and contestation—is both the recognition of limits and the practice of transgression of those limits. Borrowing from Richard K. Ashley and R. B. J. Walker, one might therefore suggest that ethics-in-diaspora is about

> the questioning and transgression of limits, not the assertion of boundaries and frameworks; a readiness to question how meaning and order are imposed, not the search for a source of meaning and order already in place; the unrelenting and meticulous analysis of the workings of power in modern global life, not the longing for a sovereign figure…that promises deliverance from power; the struggle for freedom, not a religious desire to produce some territorial domicile of self-evident being that men of innocent faith can call home.[70]

In the concreteness, contingency, and oppositionality of their differences, this plurality of subjects and subject positions not only widens and deepens the challenge to global capitalism, and provides a larger ethical/political perspective, but more importantly, it creates a fundamental structure of undecidability (which is not to say it is "groundless") that makes possible genuine political choices. The joining and conjoining of different movements in civil society, for example, speak eloquently to this aggregation, disaggregation, reaggregation of political communities; and so do those communities of resistance and solidarity: the excluded, the marginal, those rendered redundant. Without genuine, even antagonistic, perspectives, which admit their contingency and recognize the desirability, if not the necessity, of fundamental transformation, there is no possibility of what Jacques Derrida calls the "theoretico-ethical decision."[71] Moreover, without the recognition not only of the alterity of these different struggles but especially what Ernesto Laclau underscores as the *contingency* of their connections, and the contingency of their *connections,* there can be no possibility of constituting our own political identities.[72] For Laclau, this "theoretico-ethical decision" stands between the undecidability that lies at the heart of plurality is the "terrain of the radicalization of the decision," and the undecidability that is the "source of an ethical injunction."[73] Without it, there can be no ethics or politics. As Derrida puts it, "There can be no moral or political responsibility without this trial and this passage by way of the undecidable."[74] Indeed, if everything were reduced to the decidable, and if the undecidable were avoided, there would be no ethics, politics, or responsibility–only a program, technology and its irresponsible application.[75]

However, while "the passage by way of the undecidable" is necessary, it is not sufficient. There is no virtue as such in plurality or difference. Moreover, the profound problems confronting those who would pursue "the 'body politic'" today–violence, insecurity, avoidable harm–will not be resolved by mere appeals to formal notions of the ethical, political, and ecological relation. Indeed, borrowing from Simon Critchley, I want to suggest that the context and challenge today is whether we can "navigate the treacherous passage from ethics to politics"[76]–since the ethical is for the sake of politics, that is, for the creation of the fundamentally new that is also fundamentally better. As David Campbell observes, "The theme of undecidability gives us the context of the decision, but in and of itself undecidability does not provide an account of the (ethical) decision."[77] Indeed, "decisions have to be taken. But, how? And in virtue of what? How does one make a decision in an undecidable terrain?"[78]

To this question there can be no teleologically satisfactory answer, save the cultivation of a particular sensibility: that is, in the words of Campbell, to struggle for–and on behalf of–alterity, and not a struggle to efface, erase, or eradicate alterity;[79] to gesture, as Derrida would, in opposite directions at the same time without capitulating to quietism to resist the intolerable, to experience and experiment on the possibility of the impossible, to recognize and respect the limits and possibilities of the *aporia,* of the decision within the undecidable.[80] In other words, there can be no politics of resistance, solidarity, and vision without the existence not only of multiple struggles but also of a recognition and affirmation, if not celebration, of a *structural unrepresentability* at the very heart of these struggles. This, I suspect, is what is at the heart of the *experience* of (Filipino) Diaspora.[81]

However, precisely because of this fundamental unrepresentability, it therefore becomes necessary to "return to the body," in other words,

> to ecologize all that we do and think, to reject closed ideas, mistrust one-way causality, to strive to be inclusive in the face of all exclusions, to be unifying in the face of all disjunctions, to take a holistic approach in the face of all reductionisms, and to appreciate complexity in the face of all over-simplifications.[82]

A Return to the "Body Politic": The Religious Rediscovered?

The practical and theoretical leap from this basic structural unrepresentability to a "return to the body" cannot be made thoughtlessly, unfortunately. For the former is much more than an inability to comprehend the world, and the latter is much more than the reconciliation of the "body" to its estranged "mind." In fact, this "structural unrepresentability," which a Laclau, a Derrida, or a Caputo have sought to identify, and which they locate at the "center" of the political, has a much more profound significance. It may be that it is a marker for what might be called a "return of the 'religious moment'" that will challenge both religion and politics as we know them on the same grounds of "the religious" reinterpreted as *the moment of unrepresentability*–and not, as it has heretofore been conventionally understood, either as the symbolic-institutional expression of an eternal or essential truth, or as the representation of what is merely a *camera obscura*.[83] Not unlike the apocalypticisms of old, or of the mystics' *via negativa* or "negative theology," this reinterpretation will call forth, if it has not yet done so, not only a different religious practice, but a different *political* practice as well.

Indeed, it is well to be reminded that arguments for "relationality" (and therefore embodiment), transcendence (and therefore spirituality), and difference (and therefore "incommensurability"), particularly as they are deployed in what might be called a politics of diaspora, are not new. The religious traditions of the world, as much as contemporary feminism, have contributed their own share of these "counter-traditions": Christianity had its mystics, Islam had its Sufis, Judaism had its *kabbalists*.[84] These traditions addressed the inextricable connections between work, love, and politics as questions of the "religious."[85] As well, the argument of "difference" is not simply about what is not "the same," but rather about what is "incommensurable," "Wholly Other," "impossible," "apocalyptic"–in other words, that which is "yet to come."[86]

In fact, the realities of the past thirty years–from the return of "culture to international relations,"[87] to the religious wars of the post–World War II era (those conflicts waged in the name of supposedly eternal, transhistorical values, e.g., between India and Pakistan, Israel and its Arab neighbors, and "the West and the Rest"), to the failures of U.S. public policy not only in the Balkans but in Africa, as well as in the U.S. (in relation to "Black America," for example); indeed, even to the prognostications of a Samuel Huntington[88] concerning the future fault lines of international and civilizational conflict or the almost religious optimism of a Francis Fukuyama[89]–all may be read as the refusal of *homo religiosus* to go away, even if they may be explained as traces of an earlier, if primitive, world. My suspicion, which is not terribly original, to be sure, is this: Modernity failed to take seriously the reality of *homo religiosus* and, therefore, failed in its own obsession to enthrone humanity. If we follow its example, we will, without a doubt, do so at our own peril.

What has this have to do with the pursuit of the "body politic"? Perhaps nothing, perhaps everything. However, a number of things might be said. First, under the sign of modernity, both the "body" and the "religious" were banished, at least, to the margins of mainstream discourse. Second, religious communities have continued, if not increased, to be at the forefront of change in the last half of this century; and religions, ethnicities, and cultures have become increasingly prominent in the political, economic, and military life of individuals, peoples, and states. Third, "the religious"– whether as "belief" or as "faith," to borrow Wilfred Cantwell Smith's nomenclature[90]–is located, if not rooted, in the actual bodies of people. Often, those who have been excluded from the benefits of modernity have often found meaning and hope, even courage, in their beliefs or their faiths: for example, the *comunidades eclesiales de base,* millenarian movements, and, unfortunately, cults and paramilitary groups.

Thus, one might say that a return to the "body"–including the political, institutional body–is nothing less than a return to the rediscovery of the excluded, if not overlooked, dimensions of human experience–to grasp, as it were, the root of the matter–"man [sic] himself," as Karl Marx would have put it.[91] The radicality of this assertion, unfortunately, has been lost to many, not least to those who proclaim their indebtedness to Marx. In fact, to grasp "the root of the matter" is to understand the experience of "the people," to be thrown, if not invited, into their spiritualities. Moreover, this means, more than ever, not only to grasp people's spiritualities–their concrete and sensuous *experiences* of self, other, and world–but also to cultivate that sensibility of *nonrepresentability* ("the religious" in my language) that arises not when one escapes "the root of the matter," but rather, and precisely, as one moves even more fully to grasp it. To put the matter differently, rediscovering the body eventuates in the recovery of the spirit, and discovering the spirit leads to the recovery of the body.[92]

Here, Marx's critique of *materialism* becomes even more decisive; it bears revisiting. Conventional wisdom turns to Marx's "Theses on Feuerbach," particularly the Eleventh Thesis ("The philosophers have only interpreted the world, in various ways; the point is to change it"), to ground its argument for the primacy of action and, therefore, it is asserted, for the return of "the body" to politics. This, in fact, is a deceptive, if not seductive, argument, not least because the argument for the primacy of action vis-à-vis thought already accepts the dichotomy between action and thought, theory and practice. Such an argument also wrongly equates "action" with the "body." In fact, it is the question of materialism, posed by Marx in his Theses on Feuerbach, particularly the First Thesis, that provides the fundamental opening, not only for the return of "the body" but also for the return of "the religious." He writes,

> The chief defect of all hitherto existing materialism—that of Feuerbach included—is that the thing, reality, sensuousness, is conceived only in the form of the *object or of contemplation,* but not as *sensuous human activity, practice,* not subjectively. Hence, in contradistinction to materialism, the *active* side was developed abstractly by idealism—which, of course, does not know real, sensuous activity as such. [93]

Feuerbach wants sensuous objects, really distinct from the thought objects, but he does not conceive human activity itself as *objective* activity. Hence, in "Das Wesen des Christenthums," he regards the theoretical attitude as the only genuinely human attitude. Hence, he does not grasp the significance of "revolutionary," of "practical-critical," activity.

Surely, Marx faults Feuerbach for failing to grasp the significance of "revolutionary," "practical-critical activity." I want to suggest, however, that this failure is not, in the first instance, about the primacy of the "ideal" over the "real," the "material" over the "spiritual." Rather, the failure is in the articulation of a materialism that *separates* "objectivity" from "subjectivity" or "theory" from "practice"—that is, mis-recognizing "revolutionary," "practical-critical" activity. Marx's "Contribution to the Critique of Hegel's Philosophy of Law," written during the end of 1843 through January 1844 and published in the *DeutschFranzösische Jahrbücher,* makes this even more clear. He writes,

> The weapon of criticism cannot, of course, replace criticism by weapons, material force must be overthrown by material force; but theory also becomes a material force as soon as it has gripped the masses. Theory is capable of gripping the masses as soon as it demonstrates *ad hominem,* and it demonstrates *ad hominem* as soon as it becomes radical. To be radical is to grasp the root of the matter. But for man [sic] the root is man [sic] himself...As

philosophy finds its material weapons in the proletariat, so the proletariat finds its spiritual weapons in philosophy...The only practically possible liberation...is liberation that proceeds from the standpoint of the theory which proclaims man [sic] to be the highest being for man [sic]...The head of this emancipation is philosophy, its heart is the proletariat. Philosophy cannot be made a reality without the abolition of the proletariat, the proletariat cannot be abolished without philosophy being made a reality.[94]

It is this "revolutionary," "critical-practical practice" that "grasp[s] the root of the matter," which I call here the "religious moment." In fact, the significance of the "religious" is not only in its being a moment of "unrepresentability" that is encountered when one is brought face-to-face with the "root of the matter" but also in the fact that by this very unrepresentability, it is a condition for all criticism–criticism that aspires to the transformative.

Conclusion: Spirituality, Diaspora, Transformation

(Re)reading and (re)writing politics and ethics in the context of such a *religious* sensibility returns us to its heart–namely, the "body politic," which, I have argued, albeit in an indirect manner, has been forced into diaspora by the patriarchal rituals, racialized Eurocentricities, and classist pretentions of modernity itself. To insist on its return is to acknowledge that politics as we know it today has failed to bring forth the good, the true, and the beautiful, especially for the majority of the peoples of the world. It is also to suggest that the kind of ethical/religious sensibility discussed in the preceding section challenges, as feminist struggles have, political theory and practice on at least four grounds: epistemology, ontology, subjectivity, and politics–which, taken together, turns out to be a part of the work of culture, politics, and ethics.

This ethics-in-diaspora, which I understand as having to do with the joyful, even playful, striving *toward* thoughtful action and moving *against* or away from actionless thought, aspires toward the transformative–*the creation and nurture of the fundamentally new that is also fundamentally better,* without which, it is of no significance.

Having asserted this, I must hasten to add that by "play," I most certainly do not mean–just because it is play–that it is unimportant or devoid of profound seriousness or radical significance. *Au contraire.* Play, with its ludic quality (from the Latin, *ludere,* "to play"), in my view, is what the universe is about: play as in "the play of life" or "the *dance* of life." It is humor, laughter, conviviality. It is frivolity, but not frivolousness. In fact, to speak of play is to understand what Heraclitus already understood long ago: that the universe is a cosmos of continuous, meaningful creation; that is, it is motion, energy, speed–just as modern revolutions, be they socialist or capitalist, are specific, if oftentimes antagonistic, trajectories of this continuous creation, or transformation. The realm of music and dance demonstrates the character of transformation: from the improvisation that lies at the heart of American jazz to the conflicting, not to mention contested, passions that permeate the *Tango Argentino*.[95] Such improvisations are not accidental or autonomous, nor are the conflicts simply innocent or benign. Interestingly enough, the tango is directly related to exile and diaspora.[96] Jorge Luis Borges, in his description of the tango, states the equivocal, if unstable (or contingent), relationship between play, struggle, and transformation very well. Of the *Tango Argentino* he writes: "The tango is a direct expression of something that poets have often tried to state in words: the belief that a fight may be a celebration."[97]

By transformation, then, I mean not only constant movement but also improvisation, passion, and struggle. However, this is only one side of the coin. The other side is that this so-called movement of the universe is always and already also a transformation of movement into particular forms. If one is to employ the metaphor of language and meaning, one might say that meaning (as movement) is transformed into language (as form). Without this transformation, there can be no "intelligibility," no understanding. Hans-Georg Gadamer's notion that the interpretive act aspires to "the transformation of play into structure" does, in fact, point us in this direction.[98] Thus, one might say that human histories–including histories of struggle–are hermeneutical, interpretive acts that seek to render the universe intelligible or meaningful. However, if there is this reciprocity between movement and form–if, as Martin Heiddeger says, language (as form) is both the "house of being" and the "shepherd of being" (as movement)[99]–then, precisely because of this reciprocity, not only do our interpretive acts guide, if not direct, transformation, they also can overcome that transformation. It also means that interpretation cannot be reduced to mentalistic, cognitive acts. Thus, wherever structure dominates play, it is necessary to set the latter free. In other words, if particular forms, such as ideologies, institutions, and bureaucracies–political and religious–are specific structures, which is another way of saying they are specific forms or languages, if they dominate the "movement of the universe," they need to be brought into a reciprocal, dynamic, and critical relationship with this movement.

In this context, the contours of an ethics-in-diaspora will need to include

- first, the recognition of the profound limits of one's territorially-defined identities; the dangers of unrepentant, not to mention unbridled, eschatologies and apocalypticisms; and the indomitable human yearning for justice, peace, and security throughout the planet;
- second, the acknowledgement that politics and ethics must travel through the "passage by way of the undecidable" (in my language,

the politics and ethics of diaspora), even as it admits to the "uncertain reach of (its own) critical theory" while faithfully reaching through and beyond this uncertainty;

- third, the insistence on the limits of human thought and action as constitutive of the activist and scholarly commitment, even as one refuses the temptation of yielding to the luxury of hopelessness for the sake of those without hope;
- fourth, the appreciation not only of the inextricable relationship between politics and ethics, but of their fundamental "estrangement"– that is, their rootedness in "dissidence and exile"–and their inscription on human bodies, which are the conditions of politics and ethics as we enter the new millennium;
- fifth, the passionate refusal to capitulate to the nihilism that accompanies the so-called triumph of transnational capitalism, even as it risks a decision to discern, create, and nurture the connections among the different communities of resistance, solidarity, and vision that are in diaspora–not only in the global South, but in the global North as well–that are, today, exploring ways in which these differences are constitutive of the very struggles against transnational capitalism and its discursive strategies, as well as human and humane alternative pathways into the future.

Epilogue: The Promise of the Spirit

This chapter has repeatedly explored pathways–intellectual, moral, and political–filled with refusals, oppositions, and challenges. It embodies, without a doubt, a rhetoric of opposition. This is not surprising, given the displacement, dislocation, and dispersal of individuals, communities, and peoples by structures and processes that are often inhospitable to those aspiring towards "the good, the true, and the beautiful." However decisive, not to mention necessary, a rhetoric of opposition, resistance, even rebellion, is to an ethics-in-diaspora, it remains insufficient, even though the very act of resistance, when fully embraced, gives rise to practices that affirm and celebrate that which is fundamentally new that is also fundamentally better. In this context, one's diaspora cannot be one's "final" destination. It remains a condition of possibility–which is not to say it is without "ultimate" significance. Indeed, without this rhetoric of opposition, the destinations we desire will be severely compromised.

The temptation, on the one hand, is to secure the present by colonizing both the past and the future. The inevitable arrival of some promised land, if not the unavoidable return to some past garden of Eden, has been deployed precisely for this reason: to escape, if not overcome, the displacement, dislocation, and dispersal that accompany diaspora. Destinations have been turned–endlessly–into incarcerations, if not domestications, of hope, passion, and desire. On the other hand, the temptation is to turn displacement, dislocation, and dispersal–diaspora, in short–into a permanent condition of human life. Destinations are rejected for fear they will incarcerate or obliterate. Hope, passion, and desire are turned into expressions of individual self-interest without obligation or accountability, exacerbated by the creation of masterless people by modernity's obsession for itself.

The challenge, then, is to find an answer to the question, What is the promise that not only makes diaspora bearable but also transforms it into the journey of our lives? In other words, what will allow us to live fully and faithfully while we are in diaspora?

The answer is "the religious moment." The Spirit.

> And so the incarnation of God is the absolute and yet the obvious
> mystery…But when the longing for the absolute nearness of God,
> the longing, incomprehensible in itself, which alone makes anything
> bearable, looks for where this nearness came–not in the postulates
> of the spirit, but in the flesh and in the housings of the earth: then
> no resting-place can be found except in Jesus of Nazareth, over
> whom the star of God stands, before whom alone one has the
> courage to bend the knee and weeping happily to pray: "And the
> Word was made flesh and dwelt among us."[100]

Notes

[1]Part of this essay was published in Lester Edwin J. Ruiz, "Culture, Politics, and the Sense of the Ethical: Normative Challenges for International Relations Theory and Practice," in *Principled World Politics: The Challenge of Normative International Relations,* ed. Paul Wapner and Lester Edwin J. Ruiz (New York: Rowman & Littlefield, 2000), 322–48.

[2]Michael Dillon, "Sovereignty and Governmentality: From the Problematics of the 'New World Order' to the Ethical Problematic of the 'World Order,'" *Alternatives: Social Transformation and Humane Governance* 20, no. 3 (1995): 323, 357–58.

[3]Jacques Derrida, *Psyche: inventions de l'autre* (Paris: Galilee, 1987), 81.

[4]Meister Eckhart, quoted in John D. Caputo, *The Prayers and Tears of Jacques Derrida: Religion without Religion* (Bloomington: Indiana University Press, 1997), 1.

[5]See Hannah Arendt, *The Human Condition* (Chicago: University of Chicago Press, 1958), 248–326.

[6]By "modern" I mean, with Anthony Giddens, those practices characterized by "the separation of time and space and their recombination in forms which permit the precise time-space 'zoning' of social life; the disembedding of social systems…and the reflexive ordering and reordering of social relations in the light of continual inputs of knowledge affecting the actions of individuals and groups." Anthony Giddens, *The Consequences of Modernity* (Stanford, Calif.: Stanford University Press, 1990), 16–17.

[7]Teodoro Agoncillo and Milagros Guerrero, *History of the Filipino People*, 5th ed. (Manila: R. P. Garcia, 1977).

[8]Carlos Bulosan, *America Is in the Heart* (Seattle: University of Washington Press, 1973).

[9]From the 141 Filipinos recruited by the Hawaii Sugar Planters Association in 1908 to the 108,260 Filipinos, mostly farm workers, concentrated on the West Coast by 1930, Filipino workers were a significant part of the U.S. expatriate labor force. See Carey McWilliams, *Brothers Under the Skin* (Boston: Little, Brown, 1964). In fact, "Filipinos provided most of the agricultural labor force in the islands [Hawaii] and all along the Pacific Coast," Sucheng

Chan, *Asian Americans* (Boston: Twayne, 1991), 87. It is interesting to note that the first Filipinos in the United States are reported to have entered through what is now New Orleans, in the 1750s. These were workers/laborers on Spanish galleons plying the "New World" trade routes who "jumped ship" and settled in what is now Louisiana.

[10]At least 7,000 Filipinos joined the U.S. armed forces in World War II. The claims of the survivors and their families continue to be pursued in U.S. bureaucracies.

[11]More than 40,000 Filipinos emigrate every year to the United States. U.S. census data suggest that Filipinos in the U.S. totaled more than 2.1 million in 2000 with most of the new immigrants being professionals (nurses, doctors, scientists, etc.). This does not include, of course, the "undocumented" Filipinos. In a different but related context, the 1993 UNHCR report *The State of the World's Refugees* notes that in 1970, there were 2.5 million officially registered refugees. By 1980, the number had risen to 11 million; and by 1993, it was 18.2 million.

[12]That the Philippines was the only "official" colony of the U.S. (although Puerto Rico and Hawaii could certainly make such a claim as well) suggests a significant difference in the dynamics of Filipino migration and emmigration to the U.S. vis-à-vis other emmigrations. Filipinos, by definition, are not immigrants, but rather members, if not citizens, of the U.S. nation (though definitely the "colonized"). Our identities, in other words, are constituted primarily in relation to U.S. colonialism, not, as other immigrants, in terms of the relation to both the "homeland" and the "host country."

[13]Dillon, "Sovereignty and Governmentality," 323–68. See also Sarah Anderson, ed., *Views from the South: The Effects of Globalization and the WTO on Third World Countries* (San Francisco: Institute of Food and Development Policy, 2000).

[14]Paul Virilio, *Open Sky,* trans. Julie Rose (London: Verso, 1997).

[15]Nikos Papastergiadis, *The Turbulence of Migration: Globalization, Deterritorialization, and Hybridity* (Cambridge: Polity Press, 2000).

[16]Papastergiadis, *The Turbulence of Migration.* See also Nevzat Soguk, *States and Strangers: Refugees and Displacements of Statecraft* (Minneapolis: University of Minnesota Press, 1999).

[17]Epiphanio San Juan, Jr., "Fragments from a Filipino Exile's Journal," *Amerasia Journal* 23, no. 2 (1997).

[18]William Safran, "Diasporas in Modern Societies: Myths of Homeland and Return," *Diaspora* 1, no. 1 (1991): 83–99; Peter Stalker, *Workers without Frontiers* (Boulder, Colo.: Lynne Rienner, 2000); Khachig Tololyan, "Re-Thinking Diaspora(s): Stateless Power in the Transnational Moment," *Diaspora* 5, no. 1 (1996): 3–36; Grace Chang, *Disposable Domestics: Immigrant Women Workers in the Global Economy* (Cambridge: South End Press, 2000).

[19]See, for example, Papastergiadis, *The Turbulence of Migration,* passim.

[20]Safran, "Diasporas in Modern Societies," 83–84.

[21]Pyong Gap Min, ed., *Asian Americans* (London: Sage, 1995).

[22]The term *global capitalism* used throughout this chapter is intended to be imprecise. My concern is less with a substantive definition of capitalism—clearly an impossibility given the plural forms of capitalism today—and more with specifying a region of discursive practices characterized by the globalizing trajectories of *modern* capitalism. In fact, it might be argued that "transnational capitalism" could very well be the more useful term to describe the many capitalisms at the end of last century. By *globalization* I refer to those processes of profound structural transformation that have gained some level of autonomy at the global level, which sustain the movements and flows of capital, people, goods, information, ideas, and images, and which are altering the conditions under which communities and identities are enacted. See Michael Featherstone, ed., *Global Culture: Nationalism, Globalization and Modernity* (London: Sage, 1990). Cf. Yoshikazu Sakamoto, ed., *Global Transformation: Challenges to the State System* (Tokyo: United Nations University Press, 1994); Saskia Sassen, *Globalization and Its Discontents* (New York: W. W. Norton, 1998.)

[23]Giddens, *Consequences of Modernity,* 16ff.

[24]Anthony King, "Architecture, Capital, and the Globalization of Culture," in Featherstone, *Global Culture,* 397.

[25]Jonathan Okamura, *Imagining the Filipino American Diaspora: Transnational Relations, Identities, and Communities* (New York: Garland, 1998).

[26]James Clifford, "Diasporas," *Cultural Anthropology* 9, no. 3 (1994): 306.

[27]Roger Rouse, "Mexican Migration and the Social Space of Postmodernism," *Diaspora* 1, no. 8 (1991): 11.

[28]This includes those processes of profound structural transformation that have gained some level of autonomy at the global level, which sustain the movements and flows of capital, people, goods, information, ideas, and images.

[29]Charles Lemert, ed., *Social Theory: The Multicultural and Classic Readings* (Boulder, Colo.: Westview Press, 1993).

[30]See, for example, Papastergiadis, *The Turbulence of Migration.* See also Bill Ashcroft, Gareth Griffiths, and Helen Tiffin, eds., *The Postcolonial Studies Reader* (New York: Routledge, 1995).

[31]Eduardo Cadava, Peter Connor, and Jan-Luc Nancy, eds., *Who Comes after the Subject?* (New York: Routledge, 1991).

[32]Simon Critchley and Peter Dews, eds., *Deconstructing Subjectivities* (Albany: State University of New York Press, 1996).

[33]Michael Ryan, *Politics and Culture: Working Hypotheses for a Post Revolutionary Society* (Baltimore: Johns Hopkins University Press, 1989), 97.

[34]See Seyla Benhabib, *Democracy and Difference: Contesting the Boundaries of the Political* (Princeton, N.J.: Princeton University Press, 1996).

[35]Lester Edwin J. Ruiz, "The Master's Tools Will Never Dismantle the Master's House: Some Meditations on Women, Culture and Politics," *Silliman Journal* 39, no. 2 (1998): 52–65.

[36]Allison Jaggar, "Love and Knowledge: Emotion in Feminist Epistemology," in *Feminisms,* ed. Sandra Kemp and Judith Squires (New York: Oxford University Press, 1997), 190.

[37]See, for example, Sandra Harding, *Whose Science? Whose Knowledge? Thinking from Women's Lives* (Ithaca, N.Y.: Cornell Univ. Press, 1991); and Sandra Harding, *Is Science Multicultural? Postcolonialisms, Feminisms, and Epistemologies* (Bloomington: Indiana University Press, 1998).

[38]Elisabeth Grosz, "Notes Towards a Corporeal Feminism," *Australian Feminist Studies* 5 (1987): 2. See also Elisabeth Grosz, *Volatile Bodies: Towards a Corporeal Feminism* (St. Leonard's, N.S.W.: Allen and Unwin, 1994).

[39]Grosz, "Notes Towards a Corporeal Feminism," 2.

[40]Michel Foucault, "Nietzsche, Genealogy, History," in *The Foucault Reader,* ed. Paul Rabinow (New York: Random House, 1984), 83.

[41]See Isak Dinesen (Karen Blixen), *Babette's Feast and Other Anecdotes of Destiny* (New York: Vintage Books, 1988). Cf. "Babette's Feast" (New York: Orion Home Video, 1988, 1989). See also Rubem Alves, *Poet Warrior Prophet* (London: SCM Press, 1990).

[42]Patricia Hill Collins, *Black Feminist Thought: Knowledge, Consciousness, and the Politics of Empowerment,* 2nd ed. (New York: Routledge, 2000), 273–90.

[43]Chandra T. Mohanty, "Cartographies of Struggle: Third World Women and the Politics of Feminism," in *Third World Women and the Politics of Feminism,* ed. Chandra T. Mohanty, Ann Russo, and Lourdes Torres (Bloomington: Indiana University Press, 1991), 14.

[44]Ibid., 10.

[45]See, for example, John D. Caputo, *Against Ethics* (Bloomington: Indiana University Press, 1993).

[46]Emmanuel Levinas, *Ethics and Infinity: Conversations with Philippe Nemo,* trans. Richard Cohen (Pittsburgh: Duquesne University Press, 1985), cited in David Campbell, "The Deterritorialization of Responsibility: Levinas, Derrida, and Ethics after the End of Philosophy," *Alternatives: Social Transformation and Humane Governance* 19, no. 4 (1994).

[47]Campbell, "The Deterritorialization of Responsibility," 459ff; Dillon, "Sovereignty and Governmentality," 349–50.

[48]For a discussion of these "ecological therapies," see Leonardo Boff, *Cry of the Earth, Cry of the Poor,* trans. Phillip Berryman (New York: Orbis Books, 1997).

[49]Aldo Leopold, *Sand Country Almanac* (New York: Ballantine Press, 1949), 177.

[50]Boff, *Cry of the Earth,* 12.

[51]By "encounter" I mean simultaneously an engagement and disengagement, continuity and change, conflict and collaboration with self, other, and world. Cf. Manfred Halpern's notion of "performance" in Manfred Halpern, "Transformation: Essays for a Work-in-Progress" (Princeton, N.J., unpublished manuscript).

[52]Simon Critchley, *The Ethics of Deconstruction: Derrida and Levinas* (Oxford: Basil Blackwell, 1992), 220.

[53]Enrique Dussel, *Ethics and Community,* trans. Robert Barr (New York: Orbis Books, 1988).

[54]Critchley, *The Ethics of Deconstruction,* 220.

[55]Cf. Michael Walzer, *Spheres of Justice: A Defense of Pluralism and Equality* (New York: Basic Books, 1983); and Charles Taylor, *The Ethics of Authenticity* (Cambridge: Harvard University Press, 1991).

[56]Emmanuel Levinas, *Otherwise than Being or Beyond Essence,* trans. Alphonso Lingis (The Hague: Martinus Nijhoff, 1981), xxxv.

[57]Emmanuel Levinas, "Ideology and Idealism," in *The Levinas Reader,* ed. Sean Hand (Oxford: Blackwell, 1989), 247.

[58]Dillon, "Sovereignty and Governmentality," 357–58.

[59]Ibid., 358–59.

[60]My use of the phrase "ecological relation," not unlike "ethical relation," is intended to be suggestive, not denotative or comprehensive. Such a relation suggests a dynamic, relational, holistic structure of self-other-world.

[61]Michel Foucault, *Ethics: Subjectivity and Truth,* ed. Paul Rabinow (New York: The New Press, 1997).

[62]See Oscar Campomanes, "The New Empire's Forgetful and Forgotten Citizens: Unrepresentability and Unassimilability in Filipino-American Postcolonialities," *Critical Mass* 2, no. 2 (1995): 145–200. See also Epiphanio San Juan, Jr., "Configuring the Filipino Diaspora in the United States," *Diaspora* 3, no. 2 (1994): 117–33; Epiphanio San Juan, *From Exile to Diaspora: Versions of the Filipino Experience in the United States* (Boulder, Colo.: Westview Press, 1998).

[63]See David Harvey, *Justice, Nature and the Geography of Difference* (Oxford: Blackwell, 1996). See also Iris Marion Young, *Justice and the Politics of Difference* (Princeton, N.J.: Princeton University Press, 1990); Ernesto Laclau and Chantal Mouffe, *Hegemony and Socialist Strategy: Towards a Radical Democratic Politics,* trans. Winston Moore and Paul Cammack (London: Verso, 1985).

[64]Manfred Halpern, "Choosing Between Ways of Life and Death and Between Forms of Democracy: An Archetypal Analysis," *Alternatives: Social Transformation and Humane Governance* 12, no. 2 (1987): 5–35.

[65]Ashcroft, Griffiths, and Tiffin, *The Postcolonial Studies Reader,* 117.

[66]Gayatri Spivak, "Can the Subaltern Speak?" in *Marxism and the Interpretation of Culture,* ed. Cary Nelson and Lawrence Grossberg (London: Macmillan, 1988).

[67]bell hooks, *Teaching to Transgress: Education as the Practice of Freedom* (New York: Routledge, 1994).

[68]Julia Kristeva, "A New Type of Intellectual: The Dissident," in *The Kristeva Reader,* ed. Toril Moi (New York: Columbia University Press, 1986), 292–99.

[69]Ibid.

[70]Richard Ashley and R. B. J. Walker, "Speaking the Language of Exile: Dissident Thought in International Studies," *International Studies Quarterly* 34, no. 3 (1990): 265.

[71]Cited in Ernesto Laclau, *Emancipation(s)* (New York: Verso, 1996), 89. See also Jacques Derrida, *Spectres of Marx: The State of the Debt, the Work of Mourning, and the New International,* trans. Peggy Kamuf (New York: Routledge, 1993).

[72]Laclau, *Emancipation(s),* 89.

[73]Ibid., 81–82. See also Ernesto Laclau, *New Reflections on the Revolution of Our Time* (New York: Verso, 1990).

[74]Jacques Derrida, *Limited, Inc.,* trans. Samuel Weber (Evanston, Ill.: Northwestern University Press, 1988), 116.

[75]Campbell, "The Deterritorialization of Responsibility," 477.

[76]Critchley, *The Ethics of Deconstruction,* 189.

[77]Campbell, "The Deterritorialization of Responsibility," 471.

[78]Critchley, *The Ethics of Deconstruction,* 199.

[79]Campbell, "The Deterritorialization of Responsibility," 477.

[80] Druscilla Cornell, Michel Rosefeld, and David Gray Carlson, eds., *Deconstruction and the Possibility of Justice* (New York: Routledge, 1992).

[81]One might argue, as an initial matter, that diaspora has at least two dimensions: *aporia* (à la Derrida) and estrangement (à la Dillon). Citing Derrida, Campbell notes: "With neither of the two available options being desirable, one confronts an *aporia,* an undecidable and ungrounded political space, where no path is 'clear and given,' where no 'certain knowledge opens up the way in advance,' where no 'decision is already made'…I will even venture to say that ethics, politics, and responsibility, *if there are any,* will only ever have begun with the experience and experiment of *aporia*…were there no *aporia* there could be no politics, for in the absence of the *aporia,* every decision would have been pre-ordained, such that 'irresponsibly, and in good conscience, one simply applies or implements a program…'" Campbell, "The Deterritorialization of Responsibility," 475.

Dillon writes, "Just as there is no identity without difference, so there can be no politics without this estrangement; that is to say, without the difference we bear within and in respect of our own selves as well as that between ourselves. It does so because that estrangement is a difference that, in both separating and joining (individuating yet also combining), poses the very problematic of the belonging together of human beings in their individuation and of the ordering of the relations between individuals so constituted. Quite simply, it poses the issue of human being's belonging together in its very apartness, and so of how it is itself to assume responsibility for that way of being." Dillon, "Sovereignty and Governmentality," 359–60.

[82]Boff, *Cry of the Earth,* 13.

[83]Karl Marx, "The German Ideology," in *The Marx-Engels Reader,* ed. Robert C. Tucker, 2d ed. (New York: W. W. Norton, 1978), 154.

[84]Cf. Hinduism's *Bhagavad-Gita,* trans. Juan Mascaro (New York: Penguin Books, 1962); and Confucianism's *Tao Te Ching,* trans. Stephen Mitchell (New York: HarperPerennial Library, 1988).

[85]For a compelling work that draws these traditions together, see Manfred Halpern, "Choosing Between Ways of Life and Death and Between Forms of Democracy," 5–35.

[86]Caputo, *The Prayers and Tears of Jacques Derrida,* 69ff.

[87]Josef Lapid and Friedrich Kratochwil, eds., *The Return of Culture and Identity in IR Theory* (Boulder, Colo.: Lynne Rienner, 1996).

[88]Samuel Huntington, *The Clash of Civilizations and the Remaking of World Order* (New York: Simon and Schuster, 1997).

[89]Francis Fukuyama, *The End of History and the Last Man* (New York: Free Press, 1992).

[90]Wilfred Cantwell Smith, *Faith and Belief* (Princeton, N.J.: Princeton University Press, 1979).

[91]Karl Marx, "Contribution to the Critique of Hegel's Philosophy of Law," *Deutsch Französische Jahrbücher* (1844), in http://www.marxists.org/archive/marx/works/1843/critique-hpr/intro.htm.

[92]Matthew Fox, *Breakthrough: Meister Eckhart's Creation Spirituality in New Translation* (New York: Image Books, 1980); Matthew Fox, *Sins of the Spirit, Blessings of the Flesh: Lessons for Transforming Evil in Soul and Society* (New York: Harmony Books, 1999).

[93]Karl Marx and Friedrich Engels, *Selected Works,* vol. 1, trans. W. Lough (Moscow: Progress Publishers, 1969), 13–15. (First published as "Appendix" to Engels' *Ludwig Feuerbach and the End of Classical German Philosophy* [Stuttgart: Verlag von J. H. W. Dietz, 1886]).

[94]Karl Marx, "Contribution to the Critique of Hegel's Philosophy of Law." Cf. Fox, *Sins of the Spirit, Blessings of the Flesh,* passim.

[95]The tango, one might say, is a metaphoric disclosure of what life is about. See Marta Savigliano, *Tango and the Political Economy of Passion* (Boulder, Colo.: Westview Press, 1995). Savigliano asks, "What is tango? Dance, music, and lyrics, of course, but also a philosophy, a strategy, a commodity, even a disease…from the brothels of Buenos Aires to the cabarets of Paris, and the *shako dansu* clubs of Tokyo" (207ff). In other words, tango is life itself.

[96]See, for example, Savigliano's *Tango and the Political Economy of Passion,* 169ff.

[97]Jorge Luis Borges, "A History of Tango," in *Evaristo Carriego: A Book about Old Time Buenos Aires,* trans. Norman Thomas di Giovanni (New York: E. P. Dutton, 1984), 131–48.

[98]Hans-Georg Gadamer, *Truth and Method,* trans. and rev. Joel Weinsheimer and Donald G. Marshall, 2d rev. ed. (New York: Crossroad, 1989), 100ff.

[99]Martin Heidegger, *Poetry, Language, Thought,* trans. Albert Hofstadter (New York: Harper and Row, 1971). See also Martin Heidegger, *On the Way to Language,* trans. Peter D. Hertz (New York: Harper and Row, 1971).

[100]Karl Rahner, *Spirit in the World,* trans. William Dych, S.J. (New York: Herder and Herder, 1968), 408ff.

14

Asian Americans and Global Connections

Challenges and Prospects

M. THOMAS THANGARAJ

The phrase "global connections" has taken on a new meaning and a vital significance in today's world due to two major reasons. First, we enjoy today an increased amount of mobility, thanks to great advances in communication and transportation, that has brought about dramatic demographic changes. Especially in the United States this has meant that people of various religious, cultural, national, linguistic, and ethnic traditions are now brought into closer proximity to one another than ever before. One does not have to travel thousands of miles to meet a person of differing cultural heritage. People of other religions and cultures live next door to us. We encounter them right on our streets, in our workplaces, and in our shopping malls. We live in neighborhoods that are becoming increasingly multicultural.

For example, the city of Atlanta, Georgia, now has approximately thirty thousand Hindus, thirty thousand Muslims, fifteen thousand Buddhists, and many from other religious traditions living within the metro area. There are many Hindu temples, Jewish synagogues, and Muslim mosques. This is not only true of big cities like Atlanta; it is becoming a reality in smaller towns as well. Prof. Diana Eck has been engaged in a project at Harvard University, called Pluralism Project, that maps out the religious landscape on a CD-ROM titled *On Common Ground: World Religions in America.*[1] On this disc, Eck has shown how diverse the religious traditions are within the United States. These demographic changes to which I am referring have increased the actuality of global connections.

Second, the processes of globalization have also contributed to this new level of global connections. *Globalization* is a complex phenomenon and cannot be confined to a simple definition because this word has been used to signify so many different processes that are at work in the world today. For example, some would mean by globalization the bringing together of the world under the workings of a so-called free market economy. For others, globalization signifies the devaluation of national borders and the homogenizing of cultures. For the purposes of this chapter, I am concerned mainly with the global connections engendered by religio-cultural changes, and I therefore find the description of globalization by Robert Schreiter very helpful. Schreiter describes globalization as both "extension" and "compression."[2]

The effects of modernity have been extended to every part of the world. The modern technological gadgets, such as computers, cellular phones, televisions, and so on, are now within the reach of many peoples of the world. This is closely tied to the spread and growth of capitalism. This can, and often does, force peoples of the two-thirds world into a process of cultural homogenization symbolized by Coca-Cola™, fast food chains, and Nike™ sneakers, to name a few.

Accompanying the extension of the effects of modernity is the phenomenon of compression. The technological innovations of today have compressed the sense of time and space, as Schreiter argues. Distance, as a category, has become irrelevant for today's communications and relations. For example, I received an e-mail from my nephew in India this morning, and I replied to his query right away. Within an hour, I found a reply to my letter in my e-mail. The fact that he and I are thousands of miles away from each other was irrelevant to this communication process. Such is the compressed sense of time and space. Thus, the processes of globalization have altered the nature of global connections today.

Given this picture of global connections, I address in this essay how one particular group of Asian Americans–people from India who have immigrated to the United States–deal with the new global connections. There are more than a million people of Indian origin living in the United States. Among them we find a variety of religious traditions, languages, and cultures. They also represent different regions of India. While I acknowledge this complexity, I limit this chapter to a consideration of how Hindus and Christians who have emigrated from India encounter the new global connections and what some of the challenges and prospects are that these two groups of people face today. Two issues are highlighted in this chapter. First, we shall examine how the processes of globalization and the emerging new global connections have enabled Hindus and Christians from India to be in touch with their homeland in newer and fuller ways than before. Second, we shall explore the changes that are brought about in the way in which Hindus and Christians from India shape their religious life in the United States.

Closer Connections with Homeland

Thanks to the recent advances in the field of information technology, Indians in the United States are able to maintain constant and sustained contact with people and organizations back in India. Friends, relatives, and family are only a telephone call away, or increasingly now they are only a computer screen away. When I first arrived in the United States in 1980, it was not easy to stay up-to-date on what was happening in India. One had to depend largely on local newspapers, which in general did not report much about events in India. Today in 2000, I can read the Tamil newspaper published in my hometown, Madurai, every morning on the computer screen. I simply have to type the Web site address—www.thinaboomi.com (*thinaboomi* is the name of the newspaper, literally meaning "daily earth")—and the local newspaper appears in the Tamil language on the screen. I can also access an audio version of the headlines for that day. Through e-mail one can exchange photographs of people and events back home. Even video recordings of weddings and other family celebrations are available to relatives and family living in the United States.

Writing about Indian Christians in the United States, Raymond Williams lists three factors that "make the relations of these immigrants with their families and churches in India significantly different from the relations of those who arrived before the lull of immigration."[3] First, the frequency of visitors and the fact that "a tremendous amount of information moves along the new information high-way with ever-increasing speed"[4] contribute to lively contact with folks back home. Second, the inexpensive cost of telephone calls to India encourages Indian families to be in touch with one another much more frequently than before. Third, family reunifications bring new immigrants "who revitalize contacts and nurture them even when members of the second generation might slacken off in efforts to preserve contacts."[5] Moreover, the number of visitors to and from India has increased over the years due to the availability and the affordability of international air travel. The very information technology industry that has brought the people in the two continents closer to one another has also become the source for increased travel to the United States from India for an additional reason. Bangalore, in South India, is now called the Silicon Valley of India, and Indians there with computer technological skills travel between these two countries much more often than before.

One of the effects of these closer contacts is the creation of what Raymond Williams calls "transnational families."[6] Families in India are no longer defined by their geographical location. Most middle-class families in India now have persons living abroad, either in Gulf countries or in the United States. It is interesting to note this in the stories of the most recent movies produced in India. For example, most of the movies produced in the Tamil language have in their storyline a character that is living abroad or visiting abroad. A typical scene is as follows: A village landlord's daughter is pursuing studies in the United States and returns home to meet her childhood boyfriend, which precipitates incidents that portray the clash between the two cultures. This reflects the way Indians are now forming transnational families in which members of the family live in different parts of the world.

Transnational families lead to transnational religious communities as well. Williams portrays this in the following manner. He writes,

> Tamil Christians gather for a Christmas celebration and offer up a special prayer "for our brothers and sisters in India, Sri Lanka, Malaysia, Singapore, the Gulf states, England, and America." The phrase "brothers and sisters" has a double meaning because family members of many of those present are living and working in other countries and because Tamil Christians are establishing churches and prayer groups in all the areas mentioned.[7]

Christians from India form new Indian Christian congregations in the United States and keep in close touch with the churches and organizations in India. For example, there are congregations created by members of the Church of South India in some of the major cities of the U.S., and those congregations relate to the Church of South India through exchange of preachers and financial and other support of the work of the Church of South India. Similarly, there are several Baptist congregations in Atlanta, including The First India Baptist Church, that offer religious community for Indian Christians who live in Atlanta and also engage in periodic support of evangelistic programs in India.

Such transnational religious community is present among Indian Hindus in the United States as well. Hindus have maintained their contacts with the religious communities in India through various contemporary Hindu organizations such as Vishwa Hindu Parishad and other charitable organizations. For example, the organization called Child Relief and You (CRY) is one organized and maintained by Indian leadership in the United States and is actively involved in promoting the cause of children in India. CRY supported nineteen projects in India throughout 1999, with a total budget of $600,000.[8] CRY is only one example of several such Indian-based organizations in the United States.

Economy in India has been substantially impacted by the new global connections. Since the liberalization of the economy in India, the presence of transnational corporations in India has been increasingly significant. This has enabled Non-Resident Indians (NRIs) to invest in Indian trade, real estate, and other commercial settings. There are several Web sites on the Internet that deal with the real estate industry in India and its desire to cater to the needs of NRIs. A quick glance through the pages of *NRI Times,* an Indo-American news fortnightly, will show the variety of economic

involvements of NRIs. In the May 20, 2000, issue of the *NRI Times* an ad
appeared calling NRIs to invest in a Techno Park (software facility) in
Karunya Nagar Valley, Coimbatore, India. In the same issue was also a
plea from the prime minister of India asking the Indians in the United
States to donate to the Prime Minister's National Relief Fund, which was
set up to help the victims of drought in India.

Indigenization of Religious Life

The new global connections have had their impact on the religious life
of Indians in the United States. I shall first deal with the challenges and
problems that Indian Christians face and then address those facing Hindus.
One would expect that Christians from India would find it easier to move
into existing Christian communities in the United States due to the "catholic"
character of the Christian church. Although on the surface Christians from
India recognize the dominance of Christianity in the United States, they
do not always find Christian communities that provide the same amount
of support and sustenance that they enjoyed back home in India.

There are several considerations here. First, Christians from India who
belong to the Eastern Orthodox traditions (Syrian Orthodox Church, Mar
Thoma Church, and others) have to create their own congregations in this
country to worship and socialize. Raymond Williams has traced their history
in his book earlier quoted. Thus, liturgical traditions of the Eastern Church
have to create their own niche in the cities and towns of the United States.
Protestant and Roman Catholic Christians from India can find their
counterparts in the United States without too much difficulty. But here
again, there are problems. First, the members of both the Church of South
India and the Church of North India belong to ecumenical churches that
include Anglicans, Methodists, Presbyterians, and Congregationalists.
Having been brought up in such ecumenical churches, Protestant Christians
from India feel it is a step backward to choose a denominational church to
become members of in this country. That is one of the reasons there are
Church of South India congregations in some of the major cities such as
Boston, Houston, and New York. Second, Indian Christians have worshiped
in their mother tongues in India and therefore find that worship in English
has a strong foreign character. Indian Christians miss the hymns, readings,
and prayers in their own mother tongues. They recognize the need for a
congregation that uses their own language. For example, there are several
language-based Indian Christian congregations in Atlanta, such as Telugu
Christian Fellowship. Third, Christian congregations in the United States
are more often organized on racial grounds than otherwise. Therefore,
Indian Christians must choose to attend and integrate into either white or
black congregations, which becomes rather strenuous. Also, Indian
Christians at times feel unwelcome in these congregations. Thus, Protestant
Christians from India tend to organize their own congregations. These

congregations are maintained primarily by new immigrants, since second generation Indians get assimilated into American society in such a way that their mother tongue (Indian language) is no longer their language of worship and socialization.

All these considerations point to the fact that Indian Christians have to discover ways of "indigenizing" their Christian faith such that their Indian traditions, language, and ethos are preserved within the worshiping community. As Williams observed, "the religion carried by the immigrant and its religious symbols are transformed and have new meanings and context, so that the Christianity of Asian Indians is 'assembled in the USA' from materials mainly processed in India."[9]

Another aspect of Indian Christians' religious life in the United States is the predominance of "evangelical" or "fundamentalist" theological views. Many of those who belonged to mainline Protestant denominations in India tend to join Pentecostal and evangelical churches in the United States. Even those who maintain their membership in mainline churches, as well, adopt highly "evangelical" lifestyles and ways of thinking. This is perhaps due to at least two reasons. First, the experiences of uprooting and resettlement have strong emotional ramifications, and therefore they result in "strong religious commitments,"[10] which may eventually lead to evangelical forms of Christianity. Second, the commonly-held view of the United States as a land "paved with gold," added to their own success and prosperity, demands a theology that legitimizes their prosperity rather than loading them with a sense of guilt about the grinding poverty in India. Narrowly evangelical interpretations of the Christian faith go well with such a view of prosperity.

A similar process of "indigenization" of the religious also occurs for Indian Hindus in the United States. It must be noted that the Hindu faith is lived out in the United States within a culture that does not support it in the manner in which Christian faith is supported. Therefore, many more adjustments must be negotiated and carried out for a Hindu from India to live out his or her faith. Another challenge that Hindus face in this country comes from the very nature of Hindu faith. Hinduism came primarily to be defined by its geography rather than by a founder, book, set of doctrines or creed, or paradigmatic event. It is basically defined by its location. It is a piety based on location and geography. One may call it "geo-piety." It is not only the naming of the religion of India by outsiders that has led to the geo-piety of Hinduism; the very local expressions of Hinduism lend it to this designation. For example, local traditions are largely influenced by mythologies that tell the mighty acts of a particular form of God in that locality. Piety at this point is clearly tied to the soil. It is in this sense that Hinduism may be called "geo-piety."

The Hindu faith is determined not only by geography but also by biology. *Dharma,* which is the central category in Hindu faith, can be translated as "duty" in two dimensions–the individual and the social. The social dimension is known as *varnadharma* (caste system), and the individual, *ashramadharma* (stages of Life). Being a Hindu is closely linked to one's place or status within the caste system. Each person's religious and social duty is defined by that person's place within this system, so religious life is intimately related and tied to one's "biological" relations. One striking example of this bio-pietistic character of Hinduism is the practice of endogamy, in which members of a particular caste or sub-caste are permitted to marry only those within their own caste. In this sense, one may call Hinduism "bio-piety."

Ashramadharma stratifies the individual's life into various stages. The four stages of life are *brahmacharya* (student), *grahasta* (householder), *vanaprasta* (forest-dweller), and *sanyasa* (wandering ascetic). Here again, one discovers a bio-logistic character of Hindu religion. One of the effects of such an understanding of the individual journey is on the manner in which the question of age is addressed. Age is a symbol of wisdom and growth in spiritual life, so the young are required to obey their elders precisely on the basis of such an understanding. The *dharma* of a person is tied to one's biological clock.

The portrayal of Hinduism as "geo-piety" and "bio-piety" is helpful in illuminating some of the implications of globalization on Hindus in the United States, for it is even more clearly noticed in their religiosity. While building Hindu temples in the United States, Hindus are conscious of a blurring of boundaries, and so they include a host of images within a single temple. In reporting the installation of a new Hindu temple in Malibu, California, the *Los Angeles Times* quoted the President of the Federation of Hindu Associations as saying, "In India, temples may be just devoted to Vishnu or just to Shiva, but in this country the trend is to combine deities in each place."[11] It also quoted an accountant who lives in Brentwood, California, who reiterated, "Our philosophy and approach is to satisfy all Hindus as well as other Americans."[12] This is true of almost all of the temples in the United States. The Hindu Temple of Atlanta, Georgia, which is basically a Vaisnavite temple with Sri Venkateswara as the presiding deity, has within its sanctuary the images of Shiva and Durga. Another temple in Atlanta has the image of Mahavir (the founder of Jainism) among the images of gods and goddesses.

New geographical locations for the practice of Hindu faith bring with them new ways of being a Hindu. The traditional, family-centered Hindu religious education is no longer adequate to nurture the young in the religious beliefs and practices. The pace of life is faster; the joint family system has broken down; and the religious education of Hindu children is at stake. New methods are now under construction for educating the future generations of Hindus. Comic books with Hindu mythologies are one of the major sources of educating today's young Hindus. The introduction of Sunday classes in the Hindu temples in the United States is another response to the need. Regular series of lectures are being arranged by Hindu organizations and temples in which "preachers" from India are invited to address the young and the old. Vishwa Hindu Parishad (VHP) has branches in several cities in the United States, and the Hindu Students Council (sponsored by VHP) holds conferences to educate and motivate Hindu youth into a living Hindu tradition. VHP has also initiated the formation of university campus groups in the United States and Canada. The theme of the 1996 conference of the Hindu Students Council was "Hindu Youth: Linking Ancient India to Modern America." The very theme suggests the pressure that is put on the geo-piety of Hinduism. The 2000 conference chose "One World, One Future: Hindu Identities in the New Millennium." Here again, one detects an emphasis on geo-piety.

The other way to deal with compression is to move in the direction of discovering new forms of inculturation. The path of inculturation will assist in the emergence of new identities among Hindus. Immigration has forced Hinduism to face this. The sacred rivers, mountains, and places are no longer available to the Hindu Diaspora. The American Hindu cannot depend much on "geo-piety" because it is difficult, if I may use Hebrew biblical language, to "sing the LORD's song in a foreign land" (Ps. 137:4). Therefore, there are attempts to find geo-pietistic accommodations. For example, the Hindu Temple of Atlanta is built on a hill by Highway 85 on the south side of the city of Atlanta, and the presiding deity in that temple is Lord Venkateswara, who resides on a hill at Tirupathi in South India. Here is an attempt to "recreate" the geography to enable geo-piety.

The process of inculturation in this displacement is very interesting, and informative as well. The Hindu temples in the United States have to follow the local county's ordinances with regard to safety, zoning, and other matters. Such requirements give the temples an ethos, which any Hindu who enters the temple is aware of right away. To cite one example, temples in India are not carpeted from wall to wall. It does feel different to enter a Hindu temple in Atlanta than to enter one in India.

The new global connections have a significant influence on the bio-piety of Hinduism as well. As the Hindu religious community becomes international in its character, it has to face the problem of redefining its ties to *varnadharma*. There are two specific areas of concern. First, a growing number of non-Indians, such as Europeans and North Americans, are embracing Hinduism in its different forms. These persons may belong to a sect headed by a guru, the International Society for Krishna-Consciousness, or local Hindu communities in the West. How does one fit these persons within the *varnadharma*? An attempt to define such persons' *varnadharma* would involve revising the caste arrangement as simply a system of a division of labor and purging it of its connection to birth, endogamy, and pollution. Hindus are under significant pressure to think along these lines. Such a rethinking will call into question and affect the bio-pietistic framework of Hinduism.

Hindus who marry across racial, ethnic, and cultural boundaries bring pressure to bear on the bio-piety of Hinduism. The resulting interreligious and interracial families bring a significant challenge to Hindu bio-piety as well. Children born in these families often find it difficult to negotiate their place within the caste arrangement. Invariably, many choose to function without any reference to the caste system at all. Clearly, Hindus from India are reinventing a Hindu faith that meets the challenges that come from a culture that is not Hindu in character.

A Theological Assessment

Let us first turn to the Indian Christian experience in this country. What are the theological metaphors/images that make sense of the experience of Christians from India in the United States? As shown by Williams, there are three dominant images that are operative among Christians from India, namely, "the Exodus with Moses wandering around the wilderness, the Exile with Daniel striving to be faithful in the lion's den, and the Promised Land of every pilgrim trying to reach Zion."[13] Though Indian Christian preachers use the exodus story as a template to interpret the Indian Christian existence in the U.S., it does not adequately describe their position here. These Indian Christians have not faced any oppression or persecution in India to migrate to the United States. Most of them have moved here to take advantage of the various economic and professional opportunities.

The motif of Daniel in the lion's den is appropriate when one notices the efforts that Indian Christians put into the protection of their children from the influence of the American culture and ethos. To quote Williams, "Christian immigrants feel under siege in an alien culture made all the more threatening because it appears as a 'false friend' wearing some familiar trappings of Christianity."[14] The motif that is dominant among most Indian Christians is the image of the promised land.

Second, we turn our attention to Hindus. How do they make sense of their experience in this country? It is becoming clear to many Hindus that they need new "catholic" metaphors that free them from the constraints of both geo-piety and bio-piety. This catholicity demands that Hindus ask themselves the question, What would it mean to say that Hinduism is a universal faith taking into account the historical particularities of our situation and the particularities of the Hindu faith-expressions?

In this area of concern a conversation between Hindus in India and those abroad has already begun. Non-Resident Indians (NRIs) bring to the forefront the need to move beyond geo-piety. A new form of inculturation is required of Hindus in the United States. As one of the Hindu thinkers puts it,

Rather than fall prey to the culturalist notion that all "races" must take their place on the American spectrum of high cultures, we must fight to forge complex cultures of solidarity. Rather than turn to "India" for the pure tradition, we must be able to turn to the complexity of "India" in order to take elements of the tradition which are meaningful solutions to our own local questions. Rather than graft on cultural components which make no sense in our New World, it would be far better to take those things Indian which we can place on our heads in order for us to raise hell globally.[15]

Another part of the puzzle is the way in which Hindus in India and the NRIs differ in defining Hindu faith and the clashes that generate. In commenting on the controversy over M. F. Husain's paintings of the Hindu goddesses, the newspaper *Hindu* criticizes the over-zealous NRI Hindus:

It is amusing to read in the newspapers letters written by the NRIs on the controversy about M. F. Husain's paintings of the Hindu Goddesses. While criticizing Husain, these people often also take the liberty to preach Hinduism to the Indians here. When the non-resident Indians speak of their version of Hinduism, to the so-called 'ignorant and pitiable' Hindus who live here in India, one becomes a little uneasy...They leave their motherland with the sole objective of fulfilling their material ambition, which itself is the antithesis of the true practice of Hinduism.[16]

The editor goes on criticize NRIs for their guilt complex and their "ostentatious places of worship to visit either during week-ends or at the time of distress." It further states that one should be an insider to understand the nuances of the Hindu faith, and to perceive Hinduism as a "single solid monolithic block, at times, hides its rich pluralistic dimensions." As one can see, the path to a new catholicity is fraught with many complex issues and questions. Hindus are in the process of forging new metaphors and images for understanding and enhancing their life in the United States.

What is common among Indians, whether they are Hindus or Christians, is that their theological imagination is linked to space and location. Hindus, with their geo-logistic piety, definitely operate with sacred sites and holy places. Christians use biblical metaphors, such as wilderness, exile, and promised land. Yet the new global connections have eliminated the sense of place and locale. People are beginning to spend more hours in cyberspace and virtual locale than in the real flesh-and-blood world. This means that both Hindus and Christians have to discover theological categories that are not governed by spatial dimensions. Are there metaphors, images, and categories available to us? Discovering such relevant images will perhaps be a major challenge for Hindus and Christians in the years to come as they face the challenges of global connections.

What we have described so far clearly demonstrates that there is a need for an intense and intentional dialogue and engagement among Hindus and Christians from India. Such a dialogue will contribute to the emergence of new forms of Hindu and Christian religiosity. It will, as well, promote a common vision that quests for a global community of justice and peace.

Notes

[1]Pluralism Project, *On Common Ground: World Religions in America* (New York: Columbia University Press, 1997), CD-ROM.

[2]Robert Schreiter, *New Catholicity: Theology between the Global and the Local* (New York, Orbis Books, 1997), 9–12.

[3]Raymond Brady Williams, *Christian Pluralism in the United States: The Indian Immigrant Experience* (Cambridge, U.K.: Cambridge University Press, 1996), 228.

[4]Ibid.

[5]Ibid.

[6]Ibid., 234.

[7]Ibid., 231.

[8]*CRYterion: CRY Annual Newletter '98-99,* 18.

[9]Williams, *Christian Pluralism in the United States,* 185.

[10]Ibid., 182.

[11]*Los Angeles Times,* 6 June 1998.

[12]Ibid.

[13]Williams, *Christian Pluralism in the United States,* 183.

[14]Ibid., 185.

[15]Vijay Prashad, "Forging a New Identity: We Must Forge Complex Cultures of Solidarity," *Little India* 7, no. 4 (30 April 1997): 56. This essay contains excerpts from *Contours of the Heart: South Asians Map North America,* ed. Sunaina Maira and Rajini Srikanth (New York: Asian American Writer's Workshop, 1996).

[16]*Hindu,* 14 July 1998.

America from the Hearts of a Diasporized People

A Diasporized Heart

ELEAZAR S. FERNANDEZ

After months of labor and patient waiting, it is such a heartwarming event to come to this point when I have to write a concluding chapter: a conclusion that is not a closure but a resolve to keep the conversation open. Yes, a resolution to remain open to a continuing heart-to-heart conversation regarding the America of our hearts. We need to pursue serious conversations regarding the America that we all care about if all are to flourish in this place where destiny has brought us together. As we have spoken from the depths of our hearts our pains, struggles, joys, dreams, and hopes, we also expect the wider public to take our stories, analyses, claims, and reflections to heart.

At the time when Fumitaka Matsuoka and I decided to collaborate on this project, not much time was given to the formulation of a book title. For the purpose of submitting a book proposal, I proposed the title, *The America of Our Hearts*. With the gift of hindsight, I may have come to think of the title because of my encounter with Carlos Bulosan's work: *America Is in the Heart*.[1] Sharon Thornton's apt articulation of the heart metaphor helped me realize that we made the right decision for a book title, and the contributors to this book have, indeed, given voice to the America of their hearts.

Thinking, Imagining, and Speaking Through our Hearts

Heart, like other rich metaphors, has been trivialized. In a world dominated by the materialist-calculative worldview, the heart metaphor is often relegated to the margins, while the mind (rationality) takes the center stage. With this discursive subordination of the heart, it is not a surprise that the mind is identified with the powerful and the successful, while the heart—commonly perceived as the realm of the affective and the emotive— is stereotypically associated with the weak and marginalized members of society. Given this prevailing association of the heart, it seems that the use of the heart metaphor in this volume would only perpetuate the marginalization of Asian Americans. I argue, however, that we need to reclaim the heart metaphor. Reappropriating the metaphor of the heart, I believe, is helpful in de-centering and re-centering what has been traditionally dualized and hierarchized.

In spite of the volumes of discourses against dualistic and hierarchical ways of interpretation, it is still jarring to envisage thinking through our hearts and feeling through our mental faculties. Yet this is precisely what we need to do, a point raised by some contributors in this volume and by the spiritual leaders of the church. In her essay, Randi Walker speaks of moving "our vision from our brain to our heart." By no means should this be interpreted, she argues, that we stop thinking clearly, but that our thought "serves our heart." This resonates with what the great spiritual leaders of the church advocated when they spoke of "keeping the mind in the heart." This means, following Tilden Edwards, keeping our "thoughts, bodies, actions, wills, and sense of identity connected with our spiritual heart day by day, moment by moment." Human "sanity and authentic discernment, love, and delight," Edwards continues, "depend on this connectedness."[2]

It is only when our thoughts, actions, wills, and bodies are connected to the heart that we can maintain our sanity, for *heart,* both in Latin and French (*cor* and *coeur,* respectively), means "core" or "center."[3] The heart is the center or the innermost core of who and what we are. As the "center of all vital functions," says Rita Nakashima Brock, heart "is the seat of self, of energy, of loving, of compassion, of conscience, of tenderness, and of courage."[4] Heart, as a metaphor for center or core, unites body and spirit, reason and emotion, thinking and acting. To find one's heart is to find the center that holds or integrates the various parts without the imposing centralism. Finding heart is having that centering experience without being closed off. Finding heart is having that centering experience that propels one to reach out to the surrounding world without losing identity and dissipating one's energies.[5]

Is it not true that that which we know best, we "know by heart"? Is it not true that what we truly remember, we "remember by heart"? Is it not that when we take something seriously, we "take it to heart"? Is it not true that when we speak with passion and honesty, we speak "from the bottom of our hearts"? Heart-to-heart conversation means sincere and honest conversation. When one does something outrageously abhorrent, we ask,

"Where is your heart?" When we have gained courage, we also have found our hearts. When we are filled with joy, we feel it in our hearts. And when we have learned by heart, we act on what we know.

In the biblical sense, according to José Comblin, the human person does not *have* a heart, but the human person *is* heart. To speak of heart is to speak of "interiority, sensitivity, affectivity, emotion, thought, reflection, meditation, attention to reality and to other persons. By our heart, we know God." Heart is a place of encounter with God. "Through our heart, and in our heart," continues Comblin, "God acts in us. Our heart is the place of communion with God."[6]

What could be more apt for Asian Americans and their companions in the journey than to speak of the America of their hearts? They have known America by heart, remembered historic injuries by heart, suffered the breaking of their hearts, searched America's heart, experienced a changed of heart, and have found their hearts. In all these experiences, Asian Americans have remained committed to the America of their hearts and have claimed their right to participate in the making of America.

From the Hearts of a Diasporized People: Diaspora as a Condition and Discourse

A common thread that runs through the contributions of Asian Americans in this volume is their participation in the diaspora experience. Although diaspora (*diaspeiro,* to scatter or to spread about) is not a new phenomenon, the diaspora of people all over the world, especially from the Third World, has intensified in recent years. Due to political conflicts, economic hardships, job prospects, and media enticements to find a nice life somewhere else, people from the Third World become overseas contract workers, migrant workers, immigrants, and refugees to affluent countries. In 1995 alone, there were twenty-three million refugees that fled across borders, while twenty-six million were displaced in their own countries.[7]

Asians have contributed to this diaspora phenomenon. While Asian diaspora is worldwide, Canada and the United States have remained the primary destination of many Asians.[8] At the height of the United States' westward expansion (across the Indian lands and Mexican territory to a new Pacific frontier) and the building of its economy, Asians provided an army of "cheap labor." The U.S. government and private companies ordered Asian labor as if it were a commodity. The Chinese were among those first to participate in the building of the American empire. They named the land of their destination *Tan Heung Shan,* or "Fragrant Sandalwood Hills" (the Hawaiian Islands), and *Gam Saan,* or "Gold Mountain" (California).[9] In the Kingdom of Hawaii they worked for the booming sugar industry. The annexation of California in 1848 opened the floodgates for Asian labor. Aaron Palmer, a U.S. policy maker, recommended the importation of Chinese labor for the construction of the Transcontinental Railroad connecting Atlantic states to the western frontier, with the idea of cultivating the fertile lands of California and making San Francisco the "great emporium of our commerce on the Pacific."[10]

Other Asians arrived in waves in response to the need for laborers to build America: Japanese (1880s), Filipinos (1900), Koreans (1903), and Indians (1907). Their first area of destination was Hawaii. Over three hundred thousand Asians entered the islands between 1850 and 1920. These hordes of laborers helped transform the sugar industry into a "King" industry and helped themselves earn income, while at the same time displacing the Native Hawaiians.[11]

In the U.S. mainland, these later waves of Asian newcomers found themselves employed as railroad workers, canners in Alaska, and farm workers. The Filipino "old timers," being small in physical stature, were given jobs that, from their European American employers' point of view, "fit" their physical feature: planting and harvesting asparagus, iceberg lettuce, spinach, strawberries, and sugar beets.[12] Asian Indians found jobs as railroad workers in the Northern Pacific Railways and in lumber mills, and as fruit pickers in the orchards of California. Some of the early Koreans went to work in the copper mines of Utah, the coal mines of Colorado and Wyoming, and the railroads of Arizona. A few also found work in the Alaskan salmon canneries.[13] And the latest Asian wave to arrive is from Southeast Asia. This group (Vietnamese, Hmong, Laotian, and Cambodian) began coming to the United States in the 1970s as "refugees" from the war-torn places of Asia.

The flow of Asians to the U.S. still continues to trickle in after the major migration waves. Though mostly concentrated on the West Coast and in major cities, Asian American presence is scattered all throughout the continent. With the family farm crisis and the influx of huge agribusiness industries to the rural areas, it is getting more and more common to see Asian Americans in agricultural areas. Contributing to the significant increase of Asian American presence in the rural areas are the newcomers from the Southeast Asian regions, such as the Cambodians, Hmongs, Laotians, and Vietnamese.[14] My encounter with Asian Americans in a place like rural southwestern Minnesota made me think of writing an essay with the title "Little House on the Prairie Meets the Third World." Lester Ruiz and M. Thomas Thangaraj's chapters in this volume point to the connection between diaspora and the impact of globalization.

It is easy to associate diaspora experience with the first-generation Asian Americans. Among the first-generation Asian Americans, the experience of being scattered from one's original homeland and sown in a foreign place is direct. The memory of the original homeland is very much alive among the first generation; thus, there is an intense connection to the historic homeland. This connection nourishes a sojourner stance and a desire to return home at some right time. This is not quite the same with the next generations. Beyond the first generation, as Jeffrey Kah-Jin Kuan argues, "the attachment to a homeland and the desire to return home are often not present." This is much more so in the case of Kuan, who has experienced "double diaspora": from mainland China to Malaysia, and from Malaysia to United States. In this regard, in spite of its significant contributions to the diaspora discourse, William Safran's classic definition of diaspora is faulted by Kuan for not taking seriously generational differences in diasporic communities.[15]

There are generational differences in the experience of Asian American diaspora, but there is a common constellation of experience that makes it possible to speak of diaspora experience regardless of generational locations. Instead of putting the hinge on one mark of the diaspora experience—namely, the nostalgic longing to return to an original homeland—I would like to bring to our attention other dimensions, such as the experience of the diaspora people in their adopted country. More particularly, I would like to highlight the way they have been received by their host country and their perception of this experience, which certainly has direct bearing on the way they articulate their social place and identity. Second and ensuing generations may not strongly entertain the idea of return to an original homeland, but they all participate in the experience of being told to "go home" and in maintaining a sense of connection to their country of origin, though in varying intensity. With racial hostilities happening between nonwhites, even African Americans taunt Asian Americans to "go home." In other words, even those beyond the first generation participate in the diaspora experience because their presence in their adopted land remains a contested presence. Diaspora people, regardless of generational differences, face acute pressure to take account of their presence and identity in their adopted place. Also, diaspora people struggle to integrate their received cultural-religious heritage into the new context. In his chapter, Thangaraj brings to our attention how the Indian American Hindus have struggled to practice their religious way of life in a different land.

This diaspora experience has now taken an important place in the field of discourse, and rightly so. It has to be a significant part of discourse for diaspora people, if their "condition" is to be taken seriously and if the longings of their hearts are to be realized. As pointed out by Ruiz in his chapter, diaspora is not only a "condition" but also a discourse. Scholarly works under the aegis of diasporic studies are growing fast and are converging with postcolonial discourse. Diasporic studies have already invaded the field of biblical studies.[16] This volume seeks to articulate the experience and longings of a diaspora people—the Asian Americans. In the pages of this volume, the heart of a diaspora people is broken open so that we may see a diasporized heart. What is this diasporized heart of a diaspora people? The following two sections will attempt to answer this question.

Where Is America's Heart?

The question, Where is America's heart? is a profoundly deep and penetrating question. It is not a question of simple quest for geographical direction, though its importance cannot be taken lightly when one is lost. Where is America's heart? is a question that takes various angles. It calls us to examine America's heart or core in the midst of contestation on every side. It is also a cry of woundedness and anguish, a call for justice and accountability, and a call for healing. Macario Nicdao, a Filipino American World War II veteran, raised this poignant question. In 1990, after a long wait and struggle, Nicdao, along with other Filipinos who fought under the banner of the USAFFE (United States Armed Forces in the Far East), was granted U.S. citizenship. His arrival in the U.S. did not, however, entitle him the veteran's benefits. Nicdao could only cry out in anguish and desperation: "We offered our blood and lives. What have they done to us? Where is America's heart?"[17]

The Diasporized Heart Is a Wounded Heart

The question, Where is America's heart? is a question that comes from a wounded heart. Indeed, as Thornton beautifully puts it, the America of our hearts is the America of our "broken hearts." "The truth for many Americans," says Thornton, "is that America is a place where trust has been betrayed, hopes compromised, acceptance partially extended, and relinquishment required in a far too one-sided fashion." Pry open the hearts of Asian Americans and you see a wounded heart. The America of our broken hearts is an experience of broken dreams, scapegoat victimization, racism and other forms of discrimination, homelessness, humiliation, and marginalization.

Contributors to this volume have named in varied ways the Asian American experience of being wounded or broken. Andrew Sung Park in his chapter speaks of this brokenheartedness of Asian Americans in the notion of *han*. *Han*, for Park, is a "critical wound" brought about by "unjust psychosomatic, social, political, economic, and cultural repression and oppression." For her part, Deborah Lee names the wound in terms of deeply rooted racism and its intertwining with "dimensions of class, gender, sexual orientation, and citizenship status." Similarly, Greer Anne Wenh-In Ng points to "structural racism" that comes to expression not only between Asian Americans and whites but also in terms of "cross-racial hostility."

Where is America's heart in the killing of Vincent Chin and other Asian Americans? Vincent Chin's father served in the U.S. Army in World War II, but his loyalty to America did not spare his son's life from racist murderers acting with the collusion of the white justice system. In the aftermath of the brutal killing, Vincent's mother experienced shock and disillusionment. She came from a faraway country to find a better place for the family, but now her heart was crushed. With bitterness, Mrs. Chin cried: "My husband fought for this country. We always paid our taxes and worked hard. Before I really loved America, but now this has made me very angry."[18]

Likewise, where was America's heart in the internment of Japanese Americans during World War II? Speaking in particular of the Japanese American experience, Matsuoka's chapter focuses on the "historic injuries" that Japanese Americans experienced during their internment and how this has affected them as a people. All "injuries" are in a way "historic," but the internment experience is so deep a wound that it has defined present Japanese American experience in a way that the Holocaust has been the focal and defining experience for the Jews.

The South Central Los Angeles riots illustrate the deep wounds that people of color have suffered in general and Asian Americans in particular. What happened in South Central Los Angeles, where Asian Americans saw the years of their labor looted or turned into ashes, is an expression of a deep wound and many years of neglect and indifference by the system to the plight of all people of color in the U.S. Edward Chang sees what happened in South Central L.A. as "a culmination of years of neglect, abandonment, hopelessness, despair, alienation, injustice, isolation, and oppression that exploded."[19]

Both brazen and subtle, America continues to inflict wounds on Asian Americans. This is heightening in light of the perceived threat of the growing number of Asian Americans. Park points to the case of Wen Ho Lee, a Los Alamos scientist, as one of the most recent expressions of racism targeted against Asian Americans. The list of atrocities could go on and on, but even these few cases begin to show the deep wounds experienced by Asian American diaspora.

The Diasporized Heart Is a Homeless Heart: Aching and Longing for a Home

From the accounts of the contributors to this volume, one pervasive struggle of Asian Americans that has emerged is the experience of homelessness. They may try to recreate a replica of their former homes– like the Chinese with their Chinatowns, Koreans with their Koreatowns, or Little Saigon for the Vietnamese refugees–but it is not the same as their former homes. Deep down in the heart of Asian Americans is the feeling of homelessness and exile. Not even the passage of time would be powerful enough to erase this sense of homelessness. The accomplished novelist Jessica Hagedorn writes, "I will probably write about the culture of exile and homesickness in one form or another until the day I die; it is my personal obsession, and it fuels my work."[20]

Perhaps this pain of homelessness is more acute for Asian Americans who were violently uprooted from their former homes or who lost their homes, such as the refugees, and also have experienced in their adopted land a violent reception. Violently uprooted from their original homeland, refugees, unlike the regular immigrants, did not have time to prepare for their new life in the new place. Many of them left their original home countries with images of brutality. This is particularly true for the refugees in the aftermath of escalating wars in the Southeast Asian region.[21]

Jung Young Lee's theological autobiography gives us a glimpse of a heart broken and homeless. Even the home of his growing years (North Korea) was no longer a place he could return to after he crossed the 38th Parallel to South Korea during the Korean War and became a refugee in a country (U.S.) that played a significant role in dividing his beloved motherland.[22] He did return after forty years for a visit, but North Korea was no longer the same for him. He felt an abiding affection for the land; yet paradoxically, he also felt like and was considered to be a stranger. But if he had this paradoxical experience visiting his beloved motherland, his experience of America is as paradoxical. This is what Jung Young Lee said after years of living in the U.S.:

> I began to realize that for me the United States was no longer a land of promise. It had become a land of exile, and I was a stranger in the land where I now hold citizenship. The color of my skin, the shape of my face, and the peculiar character of my culture alienated me. People still ask, "When will you go back to your homeland?" I have no answer, because I have no homeland to return to.[23]

What will it take for Asians to find a home in North America? This question is both a cry of lament—of woundedness and homelessness—and a genuine quest for home that is so elusive. The pathos and quest are both intertwined in this question. They are intertwined even in such a horrible experience as the South Central Los Angeles riots. Pathos and longing for a better tomorrow is even present in the painful words of a Korean American who, upon seeing the fruits of his hard earned labor charred to the ground, raised his voice in anguish and disbelief: "What in the world am I doing here? And for what?"[24]

The Pain of Identity Diasporized

A diaspora's intense longing for a home goes along with the struggle to define identity. In my other chapter in this volume I argued that U.S. presence is as huge as God because it is palpably felt even in the country of my birth. Yet even as I internalized white colonization, I took my racial identity for granted, and my presence was not subjected to contestation. This is not so in the world of diaspora, especially in a white-dominated society. This is not so in a context in which every time I look at the mirror I am reminded that I belong to the "other" race. And it is certainly not so in my experience of being both an insider and an outsider. My identity was never problematized until I embodied the diaspora experience, more particularly the experience of living in a demographically multiracial-multicultural society in which my presence has become an issue of contestation.

Diaspora experience triggers an intense problematization of identity. This is certainly the experience of Asian Americans, whether first-generation immigrants/refugees or second-generation, and so forth. The experience of being uprooted and the struggle to find a new home creates a radical questioning of identity and belonging. Compounding the pain of the problem of identity for diasporized people is their encounters with hostility, some of which happens before their arrival in their newly adopted country. Recalling U.S. involvement in the division of his motherland Korea, Jung Young Lee expressed his troubled conscience about his American identity: "How can I be proud to be an American?"[25]

Diaspora experience, especially in a multicultural-multiracial and highly globalized context, raises the question of identity in a very acute way. Even first-generation Asian immigrants who have maintained a strong sense of identity connected with their country of origin face the issue of a new identity that is difficult to nail down. What seems to be a solid essence (identity), as diasporic studies have pointed out, is, after all, fluid, unstable, constructed, constantly shifting, and multiple.

Generally, however, our culture is still habituated into an either-or thinking. It still is not sure what to make of the experience of in-between-ness and mixture. Diasporized identity is often viewed with ambivalence, if not with indifference, by people in one's country of historic origin and by the dominant group in one's adopted land. On one hand, as Peter Phan pointed out in his chapter in this volume, "a Vietnamese American is no longer regarded by his or her compatriots in Vietnam as authentically Vietnamese; she or he has 'left' Vietnam and has become an American for whom 'Vietnamese' functions as a qualifier." In fact, continues Phan, the Vietnamese government has given a special name to Vietnamese Americans: *Viet kieu* (Vietnamese foreigners). On the other hand, a Vietnamese American is also qualified in North America by being Vietnamese. It is a terribly unsettling experience to be in the "betwixt and between." It is a lonely place to be because it is being both somewhere and nowhere. A hyphenated identity has continued to be a source of pain for Asian Americans.

Finding Our Hearts: The Diasporized Heart Finds its Center

In the first section I dealt with the question: Where is America's heart? This question explores the uprootedness, homelessness, brokenness, in-between-ness, and marginalization that Asian Americans have experienced. This second section articulates Asian Americans' experience of finding their heart, which is a significant dimension that is reflected in the chapters of the various contributors.

What does it mean when Asian Americans speak of finding their hearts? Finding heart is a metaphor for finding center, courage, a new vision, and new identity. It is finding a center after being de-centered through the diaspora experience, which could mean multiple displacements. Lest it be misunderstood, finding heart or center is not about arrival on solid ground after a long search, but it is about being able to live fully even in the midst of fluidity, ambiguity, hybridity, deconstruction and construction, and journey. Finding this center is finding home in the experience of being somewhere and nowhere, courage in the midst of risks, joy in the midst of pain, and hope even under the unswerving assault of hopelessness. It is also finding one's identity in the midst of fluidity and contestation. Moreover, it is gaining a new orientation that breaks petrified boundaries and re-centers what has been marginalized.

Finding Heart: Finding a Diasporized Identity

As I lifted up in the first section, diasporized experience triggers in an acute way the problem of identity. This problem of identity triggers intense crisis, a crisis that leads to pain but is also an occasion for seeking a new definition of identity that is adequate to one's experience. A sign that Asian Americans are finding their hearts with regard to their struggle for identity is their resolve never to surrender to white America their right to define what it means to be an American. Asian American preachers must preach "not only what it means to be [an Asian], but also what it means to be an American."[26] Let us be clear on this: European Americans do not have the exclusive right to define what it means to be an American.

Explicit and implicit throughout the chapters in this volume is the understanding that pain should not be negated but brought out into the open, if ever transmutation is to happen. There is no route to this new identity that pushes pain under the carpet of forgetfulness. That which has brought pain must also be a point of entry in reconstructing the new Asian American identity. This point of pain, as reflected in the essays, is the experience of in-between-ness that, in a world habituated to a binary way of thinking, is relegated to the margins.

But this experience of in-between-ness and "coerced liminality," as Sang Hyun Lee puts it in his chapter, has spurred a quest and an articulation of identity that transforms the world of binary opposition. It is an identity, following a Puerto Rican writer, not so much about "Where are you from?" as "Where are you between?"[27] But what is this new identity that is born in the crucible of the in-between?

For Jung Young Lee, this new identity embraces the negative experience of in-between-ness (being somewhere and nowhere) and a positive appropriation of the same experience, which is both/and, or being in two or multiple sites at the same time. Asian American identity is an identity that lies in two or more sites at the same time, which the centralist/ hegemonic group always seeks to push to the margin. So to be in-between is, in reality, to be in two or more worlds at the same time. It is to be in-both, which is an antidote to exclusivism. It is inclusive without being assimilative. The two or more components that comprise the new identity are not thrown into a "melting pot," but are allowed to fecundate each other so that what comes out is an identity that is authentically enriched by various streams. To pursue the transmutation, since the in-between is also the in-both, the new identity is in-beyond. It is in-beyond because something qualitatively new and different has emerged. It is an identity that has integrated the experience of in-between-ness and in-both-ness.[28] In this integration of the in-between and the in-both, I say that the diaspora person has found her or his identity. More particularly, this is the new Asian American identity.

Finding Heart: Finding Home in the Journey

The question, Where is America's heart? is a question raised by a homeless heart. For this homeless heart, finding home is finding heart; finding heart is finding home. The most basic notion of home, for a diaspora people, is a site (space) where they not only survive but also thrive. It is a place where they live with dignity, experience communal belonging, and dream dreams. In spite of all odds, Asian Americans in general are finding and making their homes in America. They have been told to "go home" many times to their historic homelands, but they have continued to claim America as their home. They have invested so much in the making of this country that they are not willing to give up the America of their hearts, for the America of their hearts is their home.

Home, if it were simply a place to rest, would not be difficult to identify. But home, to use postmodern thought, is a discourse about "sites." The various sites—which embrace economics, geopolitics, culture, and religion— are so inextricably intertwined that any attempt to treat them individually is artificial and solely for the purpose of explication. As a discourse about sites, home, for diaspora people, is fluid, dynamic, constantly shifting, and under contestation. The complex and fluid character of home for diaspora people is reflected in Steven de Castro's account, a second-generation Filipino American. While in the Philippines for a visit, he spoke of "going home" to the U.S. But "that's kind of funny," de Castro said, because "coming to the Philippines was also 'going home' of sorts."[29]

Another site for the discourse about home is the question of identity. A crisis of identity is an experience of homelessness. Conversely, finding one's identity is finding home. As I expounded earlier, this identity that has found its home, for Asian Americans, is characterized by the integration of the in-between and the in-both, which is the in-beyond. Asian Americans who have found home in their identity speak of this integrated identity. But the finding here of a new identity is not the finding of a finished product; it is the finding of an identity in the making.

The making of a home in the United States and Canada for Asian Americans does not simply unfold before them. It requires acts of deconstruction and construction. Moreover, as the forces of closure continue to thwart the construction of home, so struggle has become the constant reality of those who aspire to build a home. This constant reality of struggle for home by diaspora people has led to the important realization that there is no home outside of struggle and that they must find home in the struggle. As one activist puts it, "I guess our home is in the struggle."[30]

The struggle to find a home is long and arduous. As a site of intense contestation and construction, home is always in the making. That which is in the making is journeying still. It has not yet arrived at the port of destination. So how can Asian Americans speak of finding home in all its myriad of expressions if the journey is still going on? It seems contradictory to speak of home when one is still on the journey. But this is precisely the point. Asian Americans must find home in the journey. Or, following Nelle Morton, they need to affirm that the "journey is home."[31] Embracing the journey as home is part of a diaspora consciousness. It has not been easy, but Asian Americans are finding home in their journey, a journey characterized by dreaming and struggling. "My journey is not over yet," says Andrew Sung Park, "but I am at home; for home is everywhere God is and I am. And home is not only the place to relax, but also the place to struggle, challenge and grow."[32]

Finding home in the journey, to use Henry Nouwen's lines, is being "at home while still on the way."[33] This experience of feeling at home while still on the way, as Park suggests, is a profound spiritual experience: It is an expression of an encounter with the Divine, or more appropriately, God's indwelling. When a person experiences God's indwelling, she or he finds a home. When God fills the heart (*cor* and *coeur*), the whole being finds home. Even in the midst of a broken world, Asian Americans have found a home while still on the way because God has found a home in their hearts and they have found a home in God.

Finding Heart: The Wounded Heart as a Healing and a Healer Heart

Finding heart is both an experience of healing and a commitment to be a healer. Asian American heart has suffered historic injuries of tremendous magnitude, but it is a mending heart that has not given up on America. In spite of good intentions, people who are engaged in various forms of healing ministries have inflicted wounds on the people under their care because their wounds have not been dealt with properly. Mending, though wounded, is a condition for becoming a healer. Without the experience of healing from woundedness, one cannot be a healer. It is in this sense that we can speak of wounded-healer. Our own wounds are not a hindrance to our care for the other; rather, because we have known what it means to be wounded, we can understand the wounds of others and can become effective wounded-healers.

It is difficult to imagine how Asian Americans have experienced healing in spite of historic injuries. It is difficult to imagine that the word *forgiveness*– a manifestation of healing–would come from the mouths of World War II internment victims. This is not, however, a cheap forgiveness–not forgive and forget. It demands from those who have been forgiven that they show what it means to receive forgiveness. The burden to show what forgiveness means shifts to those who have been forgiven, in this case white America. In her transposition of Donald Shriver's lines, Thornton says, "The America of which many Asian Americans are capable waits for the display of justice of which white society has yet to show itself capable." Is the white society capable of displaying the demands of what it means to be forgiven? Asian Americans and other racial minorities in the U.S. are still waiting for white society to show that it is capable of doing justice.

As people who have experienced the healing process of their deep wounds, they are now reaching out for the healing of the wider American society. They are breaking their silence, articulating their dreams, and investing their lives to realize the America of their hearts. The wounded heart has become a healer heart, searching for that balm of Gilead that can heal the wounded soul of the American society. The wounded heart is reaching out to do the ministry of healing. Thornton expresses it well: "Yet the broken heart is a heart broken open, and here and there through this openness a generosity of spirit emerges again and again where human forgiveness becomes possible."

A body broken and broken up for the ministry of healing reminds me of the eucharist. The broken body of Jesus, symbolized in the broken bread of the eucharistic celebration, is also a symbol of being broken open for the many that all may experience healing and liberation. Here, the broken body is broken open as a symbol of openness and service. Out of a broken body has come the invitation to come together to a common table. The body broken by hostilities has become a symbol of hospitality. The eucharist shows the transcending of the experience of hostility and its conversion into a symbol of hospitality.

Asian Americans' experience of in-between-ness, in-both-ness, and in-beyond-ness portrays a movement from brokenness to reconciliation. Being in-both and in-beyond, an integrated Asian American identity embodies the reconciliation between two or more conflicting worlds. This qualitatively new identity embodies being both a reconciler and a wounded-healer at the same time. This new identity is a "symbol of creative nexus that connects different, often antagonistic worlds together, and a catalyst who inspires the creation of a beautiful mosaic of colorful people."[34] In the new Asian

American identity, the creative nexus has found its dwelling in the margin. Here, the margin is not converted into a new centrality/hegemony, but is embraced as a site of creative nexus where reconciliation becomes a possibility.

What we have here is an image of the great incarnation event in which the Sophia-Logos has chosen to dwell in the marginal person, Jesus of Nazareth, as a bearer of liberation and reconciliation. If Jesus, for Hispanic American theologians, is a *mestizo* (racial mixture), he is, for Asian American theologians, the Jesus that has embodied the in-beyond Asian American identity. In his in-beyond Asian American identity, Jesus not only bears the message of reconciliation, he also "bares" the possibilities of the reconciliation of antagonistic worlds and the reconciliation of antagonistic identities.[35]

Finding Heart: A Heart as Large as the World

Being able to reconcile two or more multiple worlds, it is fitting to say that the diasporized heart is a heart as large as the world. The experience of in-between-ness endows the diaspora people with a hermeneutical lens for seeing the world from the margin. The experience of in-both-ness gives them the lens for seeing the world in multiple and opposing sites. And the experience of being in-beyond endows the diaspora people with a perspective that transcends ideological fences of division for the interest of greater well-being. The diasporized heart is a heart de-centered and re-centered in the marginality that incorporates those that were traditionally perceived as irreconcilable worlds. Asian American heart is born out of this experience of the reconciliation of independent, oftentimes, opposing worlds. Being so, it is a heart that is as large as the world.

A dialogue in John Drinkwater's work *Lincoln: A Play* helps convey my point. A woman (Mrs. Blow) who was a zealot of the Northern cause asked President Abraham Lincoln if there was any good news regarding the Civil War. "Yes," said Lincoln, "they lost twenty-seven hundred men—we lost eight hundred." Mrs. Blow was ecstatic, saying, "How splendid!" Registering a deep dismay, Lincoln responded with a point, "Thirty-five hundred." But Mrs. Blow interrupted, "Oh, but you must not talk like that, Mr. President. There were only eight hundred that mattered." With sadness, Lincoln spoke to Mrs. Blow with measured emphasis, "The world is larger than your heart, madam."[36]

"The world is larger than your heart," says Lincoln to the woman in the dialogue. Obviously, her heart was small. The well-being of the other group was not in the embrace of her heart. On the other hand, a person who embodies the experience of in-between-ness, in-both-ness, and in-beyond-ness has developed a heart as large as the world. A heart as large as the world is a heart that knows that our lives, especially in a globalized world, are intertwined and interdependent. It is a heart that knows that it is not a contradiction to love one's country and still love global justice. And it is a heart that affirms that if others are not free, no one is free. Likewise, unless peace is for all, there is no peace at all.

A heart as large as the world is a heart that experiences the pain of the world, especially the pain of those who have suffered the most. It is a heart that embraces the pain of the other, even the forces that are antagonistic to one's interest, for it knows that the pain of one is the pain of all. We may live in different worlds and have different cultures, but at the most elemental level we connect with people in their joys and their sufferings.

It is disheartening to see people in the Middle East dancing on the streets after the terrorists accomplished their dastardly acts on September 11, 2001. It was difficult for me to imagine how a people can dance in celebration of that tragic event in which hundreds of people were buried under the rubble of the World Trade Center and a section of the Pentagon. Anger was my immediate reaction. But as I began to regain my senses, I was saddened at the human capacity to do such a horrendous act and to laugh at the tragedy that befalls others. Only those who have experienced acute disconnection from the human community can dance at the tragedy of others; only those who have lived daily in violence and death can laugh at the suffering and death of others.

Having our attention focused on the terrorists and those who danced on the streets may prevent us from seeing our connections to the violence. I want to point out that the violence of the terrorists and the laughter of their sympathizers are part of the whole cycle of violence in which the United States is not totally innocent, to say the least. This is not the place to recite the litany of terrorist acts that the U.S. has perpetrated all over the world. Much as it is difficult for us to hear, the act of the terrorists is a moral protest and a cry of desperation, even if it is morally indefensible. Knowing that terrorism is an expression of the cycle of violence at the global level and is an expression of a deep breach of human connection, we need to act in ways that break the cycle of violence and promote healthy relations among people of the world.

Let us not forget, however, that people from around the world were not indifferent to the cry of the victims of the September 11 tragedy. People of the Third Word have connected with the U.S. tragedy because they have known for so long what it means to live under the reign of terror and to lose homes and loved ones. Even in the Arab world, the September 11 tragedy was not perceived as just a U.S. tragedy. It was a global, human tragedy.

Having a heart as large as the world is a heavy burden and a challenge, but much more so when one is a citizen of a global power and at the same time occupying a marginal position within that society. This painful irony is exemplified in the all-Nisei 100th Infantry Battalion and the 442nd

Regimental Combat Team, which fought a war in the name of international freedom while their own families were placed in concentration camps by the U.S. government.[37] Indeed, they carried the double burden, but they decided to fight the war on two fronts.[38] They fought oppression within and the enemy without.

As "citizens of a country with the historic burdens of colonialism, slavery, and imperialism," asserts Anselm Kyongsuk Min, "[Asian Americans] need particular sensitization to this international dimension of U.S. power. They cannot simply disallow all political responsibility for what their political and economic representatives do overseas in their names."[39] As citizens of a global power, in spite of and/or because of their own marginalization, Asian Americans need the global sensibility of a heart as large as the world.

Since our world is not only the earth but also the whole cosmos, we need to think of the metaphor of a heart as large as the world as a heart as large as the cosmos. Our world is the cosmos, and we are related to it intrinsically. If the cosmos is our context, then we can say that we are citizens of the cosmos. Our citizenship is a planetary citizenship. More particularly, we are citizens of the planet Earth; we are "earthlings." We are not fitted to live elsewhere. We are not simply sojourners or tourists of this earth, though we often behave as such, but the earth is our home. We must stop treating this earth as a hotel in which we can just leave our mess after using its amenities. This is the only home we have, and let us stop entertaining the idea that we can put our eggs in another basket (e.g., the planet Mars).[40]

To say that we are earthlings does not mean, however, that we forget the particularities of our citizenship. I believe it is necessary to be reminded of this if, in our efforts to expand our citizenship to the wider cosmos, we are not to forget the unequal privileges we have received by virtue of our national citizenship. People who have suffered because of their national citizenship know that the rhetoric of planetary citizenship may serve to mask the power imbalance among nations and the privileges that citizens of affluent nations, no matter how ecologically sensitive they are, have enjoyed from the unequal relationship between countries.

Finding Heart: Finding Companions in the Construction of the America of Our Hearts

As the hub of one's being, the heart is connected to the various parts. It sustains and is sustained by connections. Heart is a metaphor for intimacy and connections. Intimacy and connections can only be carried out in reality through and with our companions. Thus, I speak of finding heart as finding companions along the way. If finding heart is finding identity, finding home, finding courage, and finding a heart as large as the world, finding heart is also finding companions in the construction of the America of our hearts.

The etymology of the term *companion* (*cum+panis*) carries meanings that shed light on what companionship is and how it may be nourished. Companions are those who share the life-giving and nourishing bread (*panis*).[41] Without the sharing of this bread, which we cannot do without, we cannot speak of companionship. But there is more to the literal bread that we share in order to exist. "As we journey through life," Dwight and Linda Vogel remind us, "breaking bread together serves as a metaphor for all the sharing we do: stories, pain, joy, sorrow, concerns, anticipation, actions, beliefs, differences, intentions, regrets. As we break bread together, we share our lives."[42]

The realization of the America of our hearts is not the task of a Lone Ranger or a Rambo. Saul Alinsky, in his characteristic eloquence, reminds us that "solo is dodo."[43] In this volume various Asian American writers have collaborated on a project that is close to our hearts. But we have included as our collaborators members of the European American race, especially those whose lives have been closely intertwined with the lives of Asian Americans for various reasons (Sharon Thornton and Randi Walker). Their participation in this volume is not in order to validate Asian American scholarship under white-dominated academia, but based on the understanding that the America of the Asian American hearts is the America that they share with others. Moreover, Thornton and Walker's participation is significant because they have taken to heart the challenges that Asian Americans are posing to the wider society.

Our focus on the Asian American diaspora people and their relationship to the dominant culture may make us oblivious to those people whose precarious plight cannot be disassociated from the presence and claims of diaspora people, by both the white settlers and newcomers from different shores. I am referring in particular to the "indigenous" people of America, or the Native Americans. I see the danger that the diaspora people, in their struggle to claim a space that they can call home, may not be different from the white dominant group vis-à-vis the Native Americans. Hence, I believe that diasporic discourse must take to heart the claims of Native Americans.

Likewise, Asian Americans must take seriously other companions along the way, such as other marginalized groups. The racial aspect of the American dilemma is more complex than black and white relations. In both of their chapters, Greer Anne Wenh-In Ng and Young Lee Hertig have made us aware of the tense and conflicting dynamics between racial minorities in the U.S. The heightening interracial conflict shows us that racial minorities must also learn how to live and work together among themselves.

Even as racial minorities engage with one another in a heart-to-heart dialogue, they must be vigilant of the white racist-capitalist society's genius to transfer the conflict to marginalized communities. The system thrives in pitting one oppressed group against another. We can cite as an example the phenomenon in South Central Los Angeles. Acting as "middle-agent minorities" or "immigrant entrepreneurs," Korean Americans were perceived by frustrated and depressed African Americans as representing the face of the dominant race in the U.S. In the racialized classism of the U.S., Korean Americans functioned as a "buffer zone" that protected the white establishment.[44]

In matters of theological collaboration, a book that I co-edited with Fernando Segovia, *A Dream Unfinished,* is a concrete step in the direction of greater companionship among racial minorities to realize the America of their hearts.[45] This project puts together the theological voices of Asian Americans, Hispanic Americans, and African Americans. I am aware that some collaborative projects have been published and that more are still to come. There is no doubt, however, that more substantive steps need to be undertaken.

Considering the global extent of the interlocking structures of domination and exploitation, companionship must be forged at the global level. Asian Americans must forge alliances with marginalized groups in other countries. Networking and coalition building must be done at the global level. And as the forces of closure are "glocal" in scope (globalized and localized),[46] so the expressions of the struggle must also be global in reach but particular enough to address differences. The local expressions must be respected as global linkages are established.

The America of Our Hearts Is Still in the Making

It is difficult to capture the America of our hearts' desire. To those who are expecting a grand utopian blueprint of an alternative tomorrow, we do not have any. Not only do we not have any, we purposely resist the temptation of offering a grand blueprint, which is the predilection of the dominant and the powerful. No contributor in this volume has offered a blueprint for the America of our hearts. If utopia means an ideal place where a new world is already realized, then we do not have that grand utopian blueprint. Rather, what pervades the pages of this volume are imaginings borne out of wounded but mending hearts. Instead of a blueprint, we have shared our pathos, longings, dreams, and visions with the wider public. We challenge the wider public to take seriously our claims and visions, for the America of our hearts is the America that we must learn to live and flourish in together.

We as contributors to this volume are aware that the forces of closure are very active in foiling the little light of hope that we have. But we have chosen to hope and have resolved not to give up the America of our hearts. Even as we know that the realization of the America of our hearts is not to arrive soon, we are not disheartened, because we have learned to find home in the journey and to find home in the struggle. Many of us will perish between "myth and morning," to use Elizabeth Janeway's phrase,[47] but we have chosen to believe that no effort for the sake of greater well-being is wasted and that no tears are forgotten, for they are embraced in the memory of the life-giving Spirit who never forgets, and they will find resurrection in the lives of the living.

It has been a long journey to the very end of this project. Yet I appropriate the words of an African American woman who, after participating in a Montgomery bus boycott, said, "My feets is tired but my soul feels good."[48] I wish, however, that this woman had found someone to massage her tired feet. My "soul feels good" for the realization of our collaborative book project. I know that this project would not have been realized without some faithful companions. It has been a great journey to this very end because of the nourishment of companions along the way. As I expressed in the opening of this concluding chapter, so I say in this closing paragraph: I close this collaborative project without in any way putting a closure to the conversation. And I close this work knowing full well that the America of our hearts is still in the making.

Notes

[1]Carlos Bulosan, *America Is in the Heart: A Personal History* (New York: Harcourt Brace, 1946; reprint, Seattle: University of Washington Press, 1973).

[2]Tildern Edwards, "Living the Day from the Heart," in *The Weavings Reader: Living with God in the World,* ed. John S. Mogabgab (Nashville: Upper Room Books, 1993), 55.

[3]Rita Nakashima Brock, *Journeys by Heart: A Christology of Erotic Power* (New York: Crossroad, 1988), xiv; Clark Williamson, *Way of Blessing, Way of Life: A Christian Theology* (St. Louis: Chalice Press, 1999), 253.

[4]Nakashima Brock, *Journeys by Heart,* xiv.

[5]Williamson, *Way of Blessing, Way of Life,* 252–53.

[6]José Comblin, *Retrieving the Human: A Christian Anthropology,* trans. Robert Barr (Maryknoll, N.Y.: Orbis Books, 1990), 217.

[7]Zillah Eisenstein, *Hatreds: Racialized and Sexualized Conflicts in the 21st Century* (New York: Routledge, 1996), 94.

[8]See Anthony Richmond, *Global Apartheid: Refugees, Racism, and the New World Order* (New York: Oxford University Press, 1994).

[9]See Lan Cao and Himilce Novas, *Everything You Need to Know About Asian American History* (New York: Plume, 1996), 10; Ronald Takaki, *Strangers from a Different Shore: A History of Asian Americans* (New York: Penguin Books, 1989), 31.

[10]Takaki, *Strangers from a Different Shore,* 22.

[11]Ibid., 132.

[12]Brandy Tuzon, "The War in Salinas," in *Filipinas* (October 1996): 66.

[13]Cao and Novas, *Everything You Need to Know About Asian American History,* 290.

[14]See Joseph Amato, *To Call It Home: The New Immigration of Southwestern Minnesota* (Marshall, Minn.: Crossings Press, 1996).

[15]Jeffrey Kah-Jin Kuan, "Diasporic Reading of a Diasporic Text: Identity Politics and Race Relations and the Book of Esther," in *Interpreting Beyond Borders,* ed. Fernando Segovia (Sheffield, England: Sheffield Academic Press, 2000), 162.

[16]See Segovia, *Interpreting Beyond Borders.*

[17]Rick Rocamora, "Unfinished Mission: The American Journey of Filipino World War II Veterans," in *Filipinas* (June 1998): 22–25.

[18]Takaki, *Strangers from a Different Shore*, 482.

[19]Edward Chang, "America's First Multiethnic 'Riots,'" in *The State of Asian America: Activism and Resistance in the 1990s,* ed. Karen Aguilar-San Juan (Boston: South End Press, 1994), 101.

[20]Jessica Hagedorn, "The Exile Within/The Question of Identity," in *The State of Asian America*, 178.

[21]Sonia Shah, "Roses, Rites, and Racism: An Interview with Sophea Mouth," in *The State of Asian America*, 122.

[22]Jung Young Lee, "A Life In-Between: A Korean-American Journey," in *Journeys at the Margin: Toward an Autobiographical Theology in American-Asian Perspective,* ed. Peter C. Phan and Jung Young Lee (Collegeville, Minn.: Liturgical Press, 1999), 23–39.

[23]Ibid., 39.

[24]Stephen Kim, "Seeking Home in North America: Colonialism in Asia; Confrontation in North America," in *People on the Way: Asian Americans Discovering Christ, Culture, and Community,* ed. David Ng (Valley Forge, Pa.: Judson Press, 1996), 2–3.

[25]Lee, "A Life In-Between: A Korean American Journey," in *Journeys at the Margin*, 31.

[26]Jung Young Lee, *Korean Preaching: An Interpretation* (Nashville: Abingdon Press, 1997), 118.

[27]Luis Rafael Sanchez, "The Airbus," *Village Voice* 39–41 (1984): 41, cited in Jung Ha Kim, "'But Who Do You Say that I Am?' (Matthew 16:15): A Churched Korean American Woman's Autobiographical Inquiry," in *Journeys at the Margin*, 104.

[28]See Jung Young Lee, *Marginality: The Key to Multicultural Theology* (Minneapolis: Fortress Press, 1995).

[29]Steven de Castro, "Identity in Action: A Filipino American's Perspective," in *The State of Asian America*, 317.

[30]Liddy Nacpil, cited by de Castro, in "Identity in Action," 317.

[31]Nelle Morton, *The Journey Is Home* (Boston: Beacon Press, 1985).

[32]Andrew Sung Park, "Church and Theology: My Theological Journey," in *Journeys at the Margin*, 172.

[33]Henri J. M. Nouwen, *Reaching Out: The Three Movements of the Spiritual Life* (New York: Doubleday, 1975), 147–48.

[34]Lee, *Marginality*, 63.

[35]James Nelson, *The Intimate Connection: Male Sexuality, Masculine Spirituality* (Philadelphia: Westminster Press, 1988), 111.

[36]John Drinkwater, *Abraham Lincoln: A Play* (Boston/New York: Houghton Mifflin, 1919), 57; see also Donald Messer, *Contemporary Images of Christian Ministry* (Nashville: Abingdon Press, 1999), 175.

[37]Nisei refers to Japanese of the second generation who were born in the U.S. They were granted U.S. citizenship in compliance with the Fourteenth Amendment. See Cao and Novas, *Everything You Need to Know About Asian American History*, 83.

[38]See Ronald Takaki, *Double Victory: A Multicultural History of America in World War II* (New York: Little, Brown, 2000).

[39]Anselm Kyongsuk Min, "From Autobiography to Fellowship of Others: Reflections on Doing Ethnic Theology Today," in *Journeys at the Margin*, 151.

[40]See Catherine Keller, "Eschatology, Ecology, and a Green Ecumenacy," in *Reconstructing Christian Theology*, ed. Rebecca Chopp and Mark Lewis Taylor (Minneapolis: Fortress Press, 1994), 326–45.

[41]Robert McAfee Brown, *Persuade Us to Rejoice: The Liberating Power of Fiction* (Louisville: Westminster/John Knox Press, 1992), 67.

[42]Dwight W. Vogel and Linda J. Vogel, *Sacramental Living: Falling Stars and Coloring Outside the Lines* (Nashville: Upper Room Books, 1999), 99.

[43]Cited in Larry Rasmussen, "Power Analysis: A Neglected Agenda in Christian Ethics," *The Annual of the Society of Christian Ethics* (1991): 12.

[44]Andrew Sung Park, *Racial Conflict and Healing: An Asian-American Theological Perspective* (Maryknoll, N.Y.: Orbis Books, 1996), 35–37. See Ivan Light and Edna Bonacich, *Immigrant Entrepreneurs: Koreans in Los Angeles* (Berkeley and Los Angeles: University of California Press, 1988), 17–18.

[45]Fernando Segovia, "Introduction: Minority Studies and Christian Studies," in *A Dream Unfinished: Theological Reflections on America from the Margins,* ed. Eleazar S. Fernandez and Fernando Segovia (Maryknoll, N.Y.: Orbis Books, 2001), 25.

[46]See Richmond, *Global Apartheid,* 227. "Glocalization," appropriating it from a Japanese marketing jargon, is an attempt to link macroscopic concerns and microscopic differences.

[47]Cited in Elizabeth Dodson Gray, *Patriarchy as a Conceptual Trap* (Wellesley, Mass.: Roundtable Press, 1982), 129.

[48]Cited in Karen Baker-Fletcher and Garth Kasimu Baker-Fletcher, *My Sister, My Brother: Womanist and Xodus God-Talk* (Maryknoll, N.Y.: Orbis Books, 1997), 147.